D0869142

THE RUFFED GROUSE DRUMMING.

Wisconsin Conservation Department.

DURWARD L. ALLEN

Our Wildlife
Legacy

REVISED EDITION

FUNK & WAGNALLS

NEW YORK

Funk & Wagnalls Paperback Edition, 1974

COPYRIGHT © MCMLXII AND MCMLIV BY
DURWARD L. ALLEN

Library of Congress catalog card Number 62–7980
COPYRIGHT UNDER THE ARTICLES OF THE COPYRIGHT CONVENTION
OF THE PAN AMERICAN REPUBLICS AND THE UNITED STATES
PRINTED IN THE UNITED STATES OF AMERICA

Published in Canada by
Fitzhenry & Whiteside Limited, Toronto

ISBN   0–308–10096–4

TO

William Carl Gower

This book is dedicated to the memory of a
good friend, hunting pardner, and one of
the nation's most promising wildlife biologists, who died of tularemia acquired in
line of duty on February 5, 1945, at the
age of thirty-three.

Acknowledgments

AS the saying goes, the opinions and attitudes expressed herein are entirely (though I hope not exclusively) my own. However, the help of others made it possible to write this book, and I have a particular debt to several colleagues in the Fish and Wildlife Service. Like many another project, the job was started and continued through the urging of Arnold L. Nelson, the most competent wildlife research director this science has produced. I have had the benefit of criticism on the entire manuscript, and aid over many a rough spot, by Fred H. Dale and Alastair MacBain. R. W. Eschmeyer, of the Sport Fishing Institute, gave me a similar painstaking and time-consuming review of the complete work and added his helpful advice where it was much needed. Particular sections of the manuscript were examined by other authorities who contributed valuable suggestions and facts and helped me avoid errors. For generous assistance of this kind I am obliged to Logan J. Bennett, William F. Carbine, Paul F. Hickie, Edwin R. Kalmbach, and Joseph P. Linduska of the Fish and Wildlife Service, Olaus J. Murie of the Wilderness Society, Lloyd W. Swift, Merle A. Gee, and Walter L. Dutton of the Forest Service, Victor H. Cahalane and Adolph Murie of the National Park Service, and Ben Glading, of the California Department of Fish and Game.

To my wife Dorothy and to Susie, Harley, and Steve, who carried on without me evenings and week-ends, I can only say I had no idea it would take five years.

D. L. A.

For Us the People

IF you and I are typical Americans, we have strong feelings about our inherited citizenship. Like the young mother with her first-born, we are most proud of things we couldn't help.

Our individual rights were earned by those who came before us, and we value them the more for it. They are defined by the Constitution, and we will defend them. But we also have *community* rights and responsibilities that are less well defined and less easy to defend. These are intimately tied up with the privilege of living in an America that we call The Beautiful and with our ideas of the pursuit of happiness.

The rich resources of this land have given us our national standing and character. But we have reached a point where an end to much of this common property is in sight. The question is whether we will use it wisely and in perpetuity, or whether we will use it up and be done with it. It is clear that national advantage lies in one course, although as individuals we sometimes might profit by the other.

Wildlife is one of those *renewable* resources that must be *managed* if we are to have continued benefits from it. The whole people have a common interest here. Many of them feel this intensely and they want to do the right thing. But specifically how can they serve that interest? In terms of public weal, what is sound and what is not?

On every side, wildlife problems are making news. The responsible citizen knows there are decisions to be reached and he is taking sides —frequently without adequate facts or a good background for judgment. He has needed, between two covers, an adequate boil-down of wildlife science properly related to the conservation (wise use) of other resources. That guidance function is the aim of this book. Our goal is a *sound conservation philosophy* from which an intelligent person can factor problems as they arise and reach his own logical decisions.

It is in this connection that conscientious leaders in many organizations are looking for professional counsel. Prominent, of course, are sportsmen's clubs and associations; hence game and fish are featured in these discussions. But this book is intended to serve all groups who have an interest in developing strong state and national wildlife programs. In such a connection, civic clubs, women's clubs, tourist associations, nature and wilderness societies, bird clubs, garden clubs, and many others are seeing their national function and their social responsibility. They want help and are getting too little of it. There has been another consideration in putting the story together: it is hoped that such a compilation of sources and arrangement of facts can be a time-saver for the teacher, whose job of training is a big one and whose hours of contact with the student frequently are all too limited.

This work is neither a professional job of debunking nor an indictment of anyone in particular. It is not another climb-upon-my-knee interpretation of deep science for the dumb public. In all humility, the field of wildlife management and land-use ecology is so new and so big that an author must be a bit foolhardy who wades in to concentrate and simplify. A better job can be done some years hence.

But we the people have much at stake. The enjoyment of wildlife and what goes with it are a part of our standard of living. We would like to keep it that way, and important assets of this kind are being lost. Few would deny that we must have knowledge and understanding, but the problem is taking on another dimension. Population pressures are catching up with us, and time may make the difference in many an issue.

One further statement is necessary: I have been employed by both state and federal agencies, but this treatment is not knowingly colored by any policy or program with which I have been connected. An impartial diagnosis is necessarily a cold-blooded one, and that has been the objective. My guiding thought has been that the patient—our wildlife resource—is ill; and it is important to all of us that the patient get well.

Durward L. Allen

Contents

ILLUSTRATIONS

The ruffed grouse—*Frontispiece*
  Photo by Wisconsin Conservation Service, Madison, Wisconsin

Following page 118
Texas prairie dog
  Photo by D. A. Spencer, U.S. Fish & Wildlife Service
Black bear in Yellowstone National Park
  Photo by U.S. National Park Service, Fish & Wildlife Service
Fox on the prowl
  Photo by the author
Coyote in southeastern Colorado
  Photo by E. P. Haddon, U.S. Fish & Wildlife Service
White Dall sheep, Mt. McKinley National Park, Alaska
  Photo by U.S. National Park Service
Valley of the Uncompahgre River, Colorado
  Photo by Jay Higgins, U.S. Forest Service

PART I

Numbers at work

CHAPTER 1

The Pilgrim's Progress

BEYOND the river and another range of Dakota hills the sun was an hour high. It was wiping a few lingering shadows from the deepest hollows when the great beasts appeared. They filed through a pass, took an old trail slantwise down the slope, and deployed onto the plain. The spring growth of half-cured grama was uncropped, and the animals fed northward, grunting like a herd of contented hogs. At one side, a white wolf trotted abreast of the leaders, sat on his haunches, and looked about idly.

Practiced eyes had seen the buffalo. A Minataree village spread across a distant knoll above the Missouri, and behind its surrounding picket line of tree trunks, dust was rising where men and horses moved among dome-shaped earthen lodges. Winter pemmican was gone, and hunger had brought alarm over the disfavor of an ever-whimsical Great Spirit.

Then word came from look-outs atop the lodges, and boys dashed wildly from the compound. They hauled in hunting ponies and jerked on the short halters, each with its noose snubbed tightly about the jaw.

With whip tied to wrist and armed with bow and arrow or iron-tipped lance, the near-naked braves straddled their lithe mounts and cantered out of the village toward the dark line on the prairie. Some distance out, the hundred-odd riders split, one line to right, the other to left. Within an hour they had completed a wide circle around the buffalo and were closing steadily toward them from behind the hills.

A bull raised his head and stopped chewing. Facing a slope to the west, he peered from beneath his dusty shag and snuffed the slight stir of air. Annoyed, he snorted, dug a horn into the turf, and pawed a shower of earth to the rear. As a horseman topped the rise forty rods away, he wheeled his lean ton of bulk and plunged toward the river. The herd went with him.

3

As they pounded away in a roll of dust, another line of ponies appeared in front. With yelps and howls the braves lashed their animals into a head-on charge. The stampede veered to left, lost momentum, and broke up in milling confusion. Bulls rumbled and bellowed, pawed the ground, and hooked one another. Sandy-red calves dashed about in search of their dams, and darker yearlings wove in and out looking for something to follow.

A heifer broke nimbly from the mêlée and raced away over the plain. But a pony cut in on her right and, stretching to his work, drew ahead. The brave who urged it on leaned forward, bow bent and arrow drawn to the head. The shaft flicked from the cord. Low down, above the brisket, the chalcedony point slashed through the heifer's vitals and the arrow slid on across the turf. The trained horse sprang aside and drew up, as the stricken animal stumbled to a halt and blew a spray of bright blood onto the grass. With a yell the Indian circled back into the dust cloud and confusion.

The encompassing line had closed, and arrows were thumping into the mass of bawling bison. A young chief rode up to the meanest bull in sight and buried his lance behind its shoulder. As he wrenched it free, fright-mad creatures hemmed him in and the frantic pony was pinned. Turning, the bull hooked a horn deep in the pony's chest and threw horse and rider onto the backs of the packed beasts. His mount went down, but the Indian, shaft in hand, leaped to safety and returned on foot to stab his weapon home, again and again.

In twenty minutes the torn sod was strewn with more than 200 carcasses. Not one animal escaped. The sweating horses stood head down and quivering, sides straining with exertion. A final groan came from the last dying buffalo as the braves gathered their weapons and counted their victories. Then they assembled for a smoke. A deputation carried the news to the old chief, and a throng of squaws and children, broken-down nags, and semi-loup dogs set out from the village to spend the day butchering out skins and meat. The "surround" of the Minatarees was a success.

INDIAN SUMMER

Eight hundred miles down the Missouri a tribe of Puncahs lived in some eighty lodges of dressed hides. Formerly the buffalo had come to them—bands of a few hundred in winter and spring, and vast herds during the August running season. Then the dark biomass might fill the valleys, and their roaring could be heard for miles across the hills. Unnumbered hooves cut broad ramps down river banks, and at times the stream was jammed with hordes that swam to east or west in the frantic struggle of the rut.

But white men had gathered to the river and buffalo had left the country. Now braves must penetrate far into the prairies to get meat and hides. There overwhelming numbers of Sioux from the north, Pawnees from farther west, and Osages and Kansas from the south intercepted hunting parties and cut them to pieces. The tribe was two-thirds women and its time was running out.

This was the prophecy of the great chief Shoo-de-ga-cha, who in 1832 sat with George Catlin overlooking the encampment and predicted the early end of his people. Their living was gone, and necessity soon would force them westward to dry another winter's meat. Alert enemies could be trusted to take full advantage of their weakness.

The troubles faced by this village were a beginning of what happened to the Plains Indians. Catlin estimated that some 300,000 of them had made their living from the bison herds between Mexico and Lake Winnipeg and from the Rocky Mountains to the great river. Small tribes like the Minatarees, Mandans, and Ricarees were able to live in their fortified towns on the Missouri and flourish amid enemies because the buffalo, except for painful intervals of scarcity, came within sight of their lodges. They had a standard of living, for the most part, that permitted long periods of idleness, with games and smoking a normal pastime for the braves.

From the buffalo they got the finest food on the continent. Hides of cows and calves furnished clothing and shelter, and the neck skin of a bull made an arrow-proof (and well-nigh bullet-proof) shield. Glue was boiled from hoofs and tendons, horns made spoons and ornaments, and sinews backed their short, powerful bows. Tribesmen dressed their hair with marrow-fat and warmed themselves by fires of sun-dried disks of dung.

From the bountiful earth the squaws raised a few vegetables and a limited crop of small-eared corn, but the Mandans habitually squandered their unripe maize harvest in an annual feast and depended on fall hunts and tons of dried buffalo meat for their winter keep.

Of the Sioux, on the central plains, Catlin said, "There is no tribe on the Continent, perhaps, of finer looking men. [The Snakes, it is said, had the comeliest women.] . . . and few tribes who are better and more comfortably clad, and supplied with the necessities of life. There are no parts of the great plains of America which are more abundantly stocked with buffaloes and wild horses, nor any people more bold in destroying the one for food, and appropriating the other to their use."

It was a good life for the strong, and those who lived were strong. For such an existence the Indian needed space, and he had that space because constant warfare kept his numbers down.

The turf of the great interior grassland was rooted in some of the most fertile soils on earth. The dark loam had formed in a climate featuring scant rainfall. Moisture stayed in the upper levels and returned to the air through evaporation, leaving nutrient minerals where they were in the humus-rich surface layers. There was little of the deep percolation and washing away of fertility that so characterized forest soils in higher-rainfall regions to the east.

On this vast pasture had developed the buffalo millions. They moved about, taking the annual growth of forage—tall grasses on the eastern prairies and shorter grasses on the dryer plains to the west. It was quality feed, and the herds failed to outgrow the supply only because of enormous natural losses. As a yearly occurrence, the beasts broke through rotten ice and drowned by thousands, the mass of carrion clogging the Missouri and other rivers for weeks in springtime. Bitter winters with superheavy snow left a hecatomb of rotting carcasses. The animals wandered stupidly into quicksand, and lost their calves in high-banked streams. They were subject to the constant culling of a huge and capable carnivore—the plains wolf.

Sometimes, the sod must have been destroyed in spots, especially by milling masses during the running season; and there we might expect a growth of weeds for a few years and an increase of the prairie dogs and ground squirrels that thrived on them. Such increases would be of interest, of course, to the lesser carnivores, the coyote, badger, kit fox, and black-footed ferret. But eventually the cycle would be complete and the manure that was trampled into runs and wallows would grow the tallest grass of all.

That the buffalo grazing had its effects was evident after the great herds were gone; for then some of the tall grasses of the forest-edge prairies moved rapidly westward, invading the region of the short grasses. But in general, the adjustment of buffalo and vegetation was a healthy one. The grass replaced itself to nurture new generations of animals and men—as the old, their mission accomplished, grew weak and disappeared under the ready ministration of the wolves.

The meat on which the Indian lived was a surpassingly rich and satisfying food. This was proverbial among the white invaders, and the vanguard of beaver trappers who looted the springheads of the Rockies for their annual take of "plews" quickly adopted the hunting and feeding habits of their red hosts and enemies. It was said that a man never tired of buffalo and could glut himself to ultimate capacity without ill effects. A dry heifer was first choice from a herd, or in any event a fat cow. "Poor bull" was the worst one could do, and often did; though the killing of males usually was a matter of diversion when powder and ball were to spare.

To seasoned travelers of the early West, the plains crossing was a time of personal conditioning and the chance to "make" dried meat against future need. The wild luxury of a buffalo feast, perhaps after weeks of shortage, was described by Howard Stansbury, who saw it first-hand on a War Department expedition to Great Salt Lake in 1849:

"Some idea may be formed of the great digestibility of this species of food, as well as of the enormous quantities devoured at a single meal, from the fact that the regular daily allowance or ration for one employee of the Fur Company's service is eight pounds, the whole of which is often consumed. It is true, however, that an old mountaineer seldom eats anything else. If he can get a cup of strong coffee, with plenty of sugar, and as much buffalo-meat as he can devour, he is perfectly happy and content, never feeling the want either of bread or vegetables."

It was significant that the mountain men who crossed the plains lived high and healthy on unlimited quantities of choice cuts, while expeditions of inept greenhorns were plagued with scurvy and other deficiency diseases and left many a shallow grave in their wake to be excavated by the frugal wolves.

In a novel DeVoto refers to as nine-tenths history, George Ruxton, a young Englishman, described the first encounter with buffalo near the Platte River in what is now Nebraska:

"There was merry-making in the camp that night, and the way they indulged their appetites—or, in their own language, 'throw'd' the meat 'cold'—would have made the heart of a dyspeptic leap for joy or burst with envy. Far into the 'still watches of the tranquil night' the fat-clad 'depouille' saw its fleshy mass grow small by degrees and beautifully less, before the trenchant blades of the hungry mountaineers; appetizing yards of well browned 'boudin' [small intestine] slipped glibly down their throats; rib after rib of tender hump was picked and flung to the wolves; and when human nature, with helpless gratitude, and confident that nothing of super-excellent comestibility remained, was lazily wiping the greasy knife that had done such good service—a skillful hunter was seen to chuckle to himself as he raked the deep ashes of the fire, and drew therefrom a pair of tongues so admirably baked, so soft, so sweet, and of such exquisite flavor, that a veil is considerately drawn over the effects their discussion produced in the mind of our greenhorn La Bonté and the raptures they excited in the bosom of that, as yet, most ignorant mountaineer."

W. A. Ferris passed through this same region when he crossed the Platte in 1830, headed northwest toward the Yellowstone. The impression the seemingly limitless herds of bison must have made on newcomers to the plains probably cannot be appreciated in spite of the fact that a few of them had the inspiration to make what record they could under difficult conditions. Ferris brings us a measure of his amazement in spite of the lapse of more than a century:

"Next day, Oh, there they were, thousands and thousands of them! Far as the eye could reach the prairie was literally covered, and not only covered but crowded with them . . . on the following day also, the number seemed if possible more countless than before, surpassing even the prairie-blackening accounts of those who had been here before us, and whose strange tales it had been our wont to believe the natural extravagance of a mere traveler's turn for romancing, but they must have been true, for such a scene as this our language wants words to describe, much less to exaggerate." *

When, upon occasion, such an endless amount of prime eating was placed at his disposal, the plains traveler, white or red, knew well enough the parts that best suited him. The Indian helped balance his

* Reprinted by permission from *Life in the Rocky Mountains*, by W. A. Ferris. Copyright 1940. Old West Publishing Company.

diet by making generous use of glandular and visceral tissues. He relished the tripe and intestine and even the "lights." He sprinkled liver with bile and ate it raw. When thirsty, he drank the green juices from the stomach. As DeVoto remarks, buffalo testicles were "the first Rocky Mountain oysters."

Stansbury's description of butchering indicates how "choicy" the hunter could afford to be in the midst of this prodigal effusion of Nature. Though it concerns the habits of the mountain men, the methods undoubtedly were adopted or adapted from Indian practice.

"Contrary to the custom among us, the skinning process commences by making an incision along the top of the backbone, and separating the hide downward, so as to get the more quickly at what are considered the choice parts of the animal. These are the 'bass,' a hump projecting from the back of the neck just before the shoulders, and which is generally removed with the skin attached: it is about the size of a man's head, and, when boiled, resembles marrow, being exceedingly tender, rich, and nutritious. Next comes the 'hump' and the hump ribs,' projections of the vertebrae just behind the shoulders, some of which are a foot in length. These are generally broken off by a mallet made of the lower joint of one of the forelegs, cut off for the purpose. After these come the 'fleece,' the portion of flesh covering the ribs; the 'depuis,' a broad, fat part extending from the shoulders to the tail; the 'belly fleece'; some of the ribs, called 'side ribs,' to distinguish them from the hump ribs; the thigh or marrow-bones, and the tongue. Generally the animal is opened and the tenderloin and tallow secured. All the rest, including the hams and shoulders—indeed, by far the greater portion of the animal—is left on the ground. When buffalo are plenty, the hump, bass, and tongue—very frequently only the latter—are taken, and occasionally a marrow-bone for a titbit."

This was the country and the claim that, already in the thirties, the Indian was losing. For only a few hundred years he had really made the most of it. The part-Arab horse that had escaped the Spaniards and gone wild on the plains was the cultural key that had given him full use of his environment, and thereby he prospered. The horse and bow provided a sufficiency of buffalo, but with them he could not destroy his resource, as the gun was to do later. Constant wars thinned his ranks and they weeded out the weak rather than (as nowadays) the strong. Biologically they did not harm him.

Contrary to storybook tale, the Indian was no conservationist, except by his limitations. He stampeded whole herds over cliffs or drove them into slaughter pens. Opportunity permitting, he fired the dry prairie grass to put the masses at his mercy. Catlin told of a Sioux foray in which 1,400 *tongues* were the sole booty, since the camp had abundant meat already.

Colonel R. I. Dodge, who lived and fought for thirty-four years (until 1882) among the plains tribes, said that during the spring and summer the Indians disturbed the buffalo as little as possible so as not to drive the herds from the vicinity of encampments. Hunting was usually by careful stalking; but even under such conditions, "Enough were killed to enable all to gorge themselves at will."

Probably few, if any, primitive peoples have been so plentifully supplied with an abundance of top-quality animal protein. From what Colonel Dodge recorded of their abilities in using it, they outdid even the mountain men:

"The Indian is an enormous feeder. But that corroborative evidence is so easily obtained, I should hesitate to give details of his wonderful capacity of stomach. In the course of a night of feasting, dancing, and story-telling, an average Indian will consume from ten to fifteen pounds of meat; and if he has an abundance of food and can make selection of the parts to be eaten, he will swallow, without indigestion or other inconvenience, not less than twenty pounds."

It was in autumn that the ready availability of huge numbers of buffalo counted most, for then winter stores were laid up in a series of large-scale community hunts. Runners were sent out to scout for favorable locations, near water and timber and with level ground for stretching hides. Then the band moved, and all hands turned out—braves did the killing and the squaws everything else.

Some idea of the enormous quantities of meat used is gained from the fact that in a camp of 400 Sioux lodges destroyed by General Sully on September 3, 1863 (i.e. before the advent of winter) there were "four or five hundred thousand pounds of dried buffalo meat."

The primitive association of soil and grass, buffalo and Indian, might have persisted indefinitely. Even when guns were acquired from the traders—purchased with beaver pelts, buffalo robes, and squaw rental—the herds might have stood the toll of purely frontier needs and commerce. But the opening of eastern and export markets for hides changed the entire picture. White men had no thought of cropping the buffalo. The herds were like a stand of trees—to be cut down and used. The Indians helped and got what they could while it lasted, in spite of the fact that many of them, like the old chief of the Poncas, saw what was coming.

LAST ACT

There is no doubting that the buffalo is our most spectacular example of a species that succumbed to the avarice of ignorant and wasteful men. In common with the forests, the bison herds seemed endless. But a tide of humanity drove westward, multiplying as it came. It was a characteristic biological force similar to those we habitually misjudge because of their small beginnings. If unchecked, they can take over the world while our backs are turned.

Liquidation of the buffalo took about fifty years. In its pristine range, and including recognized types such as the northern "wood bison" and western "mountain buffalo," the species extended from north of Great Slave Lake to a crescent of seasonally occupied country in Chihuahua and Coahuila in Mexico. Westward, they reached into arid valleys of northern Nevada and easternmost Oregon. They were plentiful east of the Mississippi and their grazing was a factor in keeping open the grasslands of Tennessee, Kentucky, Indiana and Ohio. There were a few along the Lake Erie shore of New York, and a salient of range extended to central Pennsylvania.

By 1800 the entire range had shrunk, and the well-traveled and occupied Mississippi Valley had become the eastern border of the bison country. The next twenty-five years saw the beginnings of real exploitation on the plains with a growing trade in hides, robes, and pemmican—principally to the profit of Indian hunters with abundant squaw labor.

Systematic hunting by white men became important in the second quarter-century and from 1850 on it grew with each passing year. The practical extermination of the vast herds in the sixties and seventies was made possible by the opening of the Union Pacific Railway in 1869, which split the northern from the southern range. The Kansas Pacific and the Atchison, Topeka, and Santa Fe further penetrated the depths of the buffalo bailiwick. To the plains they brought white hunters and rifles, DuPont powder and Galena lead, Green River knives, tobacco, and firewater. They carried tongues and hides, robes, and finally bones, to eastern markets.

In May, 1871, the main herd still was sufficiently intact so that Colonel Dodge drove for twenty-five miles through an immense aggregation of animals composed of "countless small herds" on a trip from Old Fort Zara to Fort Larned on the Arkansas River.

From Colonel Dodge's records, Hornaday estimated the buffalo actually seen on that day of travel at about half a million and the entire herd at around twelve million.

"No wonder," he said, "that the men of the West of those days, both white and red, thought it would be impossible to exterminate such a mighty multitude. The Indians of some tribes believed that the buffaloes issued from the earth continually, and that the supply was necessarily inexhaustible. And yet, in four short years the southern herd was almost totally annihilated."

He estimated that in the three years, 1872-74, nearly 3,700,000 buffalo were slaughtered from the southern range by whites and Indians. This herd occupied the country from southern Nebraska south through western Kansas and eastern Colorado into the Indian Territory (Oklahoma and Texas).

In well-organized outfits complete with wagons, cooks, skinners, and "hunters," exploiters of the buffalo took out from the railheads and lived for months in the open. The experienced hunter sneaked a herd on foot and hid himself in a commanding position within good range. With his heavy Sharps rifle and a plentiful supply of cartridges he was more than a match for the occasion, as he methodically picked off any animal that appeared about to bolt. The beasts stood around, stupidly sniffing at the fallen, and sometimes a hundred or more could be killed from such a "stand" without the shooter's moving from the spot. This was the ultimate mass-production development in buffalo killing.

J. A. Allen somewhat picturesquely described these hardy entrepreneurs: "They sleep generally in the open air, in winter as well as in summer, subjected to every inclemency of the weather. As may well be imagined, a buffalo-hunter, at the end of the season, is by no means prepossessing in his appearance, being, in addition to his filthy aspect, a paradise for hordes of nameless parasites. They are yet a rollicking set, and occasionally include men of intelligence, who formerly possessed an ordinary amount of refinement."

More and more "hunters" concentrated on the southern herd, building up to a crescendo of slaughter that finished the job in the winter of 1877-78. During December and January more than 100,000 hides were sent to market and by the end of the year the buffalo south of the railway were no longer worthy of commercial consideration. A few animals escaped and fled into southwest Kansas. In 1879, on the old Santa Fe Trail west of Dodge City, the last one was killed. The black millions of the southern plains existed only as fields of whitening bones and in the rich memories of a host of bloated coyotes.

Once the buffalo had numbered perhaps sixty million head. The northern herd now was reduced to around a million and a half. The outfits moved north, and the mopping-up did not take long. It began in earnest in 1880 with the building of the Northern Pacific west from Bismarck.

There were some complications to this operation since the government had treated with the Indians, promising that no white man would settle in this country and that neither Indians nor their game would be disturbed. However, with the efficiency characteristic of the times, legal barriers were circumvented, surveyors moved in and some were killed by the protesting Indians, General Custer and his men made their last stand, Sitting Bull won a battle but lost the war, his tribe was removed to a gameless reservation in South Dakota, the railway was built, hide-hunters swarmed over the plains, and the march of progress continued.

In 1882 the Northern Pacific shipped 200,000 hides. Two years later their records showed a total of just two cars containing 300 skins! The last real stand of the buffalo was in '83. Cree Indians and white hunters moved up the Cannon Ball River in North Dakota to engage the lone remaining herd of about 10,000 animals. They guarded potholes and built fires along river banks to keep the beasts from water. In about two months the herd was wiped out. Except for a few stragglers, these were the last of the buffalo.

RAW DEAL PROGRAM

In the history of the world, almost no resource that was plentiful and easily come by has been sensibly and conservatively employed for the benefit of mankind. Hornaday speculated, probably realistically, that the meat wasted during the great period of slaughter would have been sufficient for the needs of more than a million persons. Not a thousandth part of it was used.

There was little sympathy for anyone so visionary and impractical as to suggest that conversion of national assets into individual gain should in any way be impaired by concern for the future. Particularly would such foppish sentiment (today it's called "emotionalism") have been outside the ken of those ragged individualists who liquidated the buffalo.

The elimination of the bison would be more wholesome to reflect upon had it benefited more people for at least a little longer. But when initial prejudice against land that "wouldn't grow trees" was broken down and the agricultural possibilities of the mineral-rich grasslands finally were recognized, the rush of homesteaders was not to be contained. Regretfully, we must consider it to some extent an academic fact if the buffalo rotted under the stars. The final arbiter of his destiny was the fertility of his native range. He had to pass because of changed conditions.

And yet we know that the great herds would have been wiped out whether or not plow ever broke the prairie sod. The killing was calculated. It proceeded while Columbus Delano, Secretary of the Interior, turned his back, thereby creating tacit policy. By this means the Plains Indian was defeated behind the lines in a battle of logistics—his supplies were cut off.

In the words of E. Douglas Branch, "In Congress there were—as there always are—a few men who believed that the progress of Empire should be attended with a little decency." For several years efforts were made to enact legislation which would have provided for reasonable cropping, rather than destruction, of the buffalo.

In 1874 the Committee on Territories reported out a bill "to prevent the useless slaughter of buffaloes within the Territories of the United States." The first section made it unlawful for any person not an Indian to kill a female buffalo and the second prohibited the killing of more males than could be used for food or marketed.

The administrative branch of the Government had shown a keen awareness of the white man's responsibility for "civilizing" the benighted savage. The popular conception of this process involved ever-narrowing horizons for the Indian and the increased availability of western lands for the support of a higher culture. How the buffalo figured in this was not widely publicized but it did get into the congressional proceedings by virtue of the testimony of Representative Garfield of Ohio.

". . . I have heard it said, and said before the Committee on Appropriations, by a gentleman who is high in authority in the Government, the best thing which could happen for the betterment of our Indian question—the very best thing which could occur for the solution of the difficulties of that question—would be that the last remaining buffalo should perish, and he gave this as his reason for that statement; that so long as the Indian can hope to subsist by hunting buffalo, so long will he resist all efforts to put him forward in the work of civilization; that he would never cultivate the soil, never even become a pastoral owner or controller of flocks, never take a step toward civilization, until his savage means of support were cut off; and that his great support . . . out of which he secures the very meat he feeds on, is the herds of buffalo which roam the plains of the West. The Secretary of the Interior said that he would rejoice, so far as the Indian question was concerned, when the last buffalo was gone."

There were many in the Congress who questioned the morality of civilizing the Indian "by starving him to death." The argument that wildlife resources should be destroyed to bring this about was impugned as "a disgrace to anybody who makes it." But the weal of the westering settlers was ever in the minds of less idealistic members, and Representative Conger, of Michigan, expressed a kind of realism characteristic of those who find gainful employment in taking over the assets of unprogressive races. The bill under consideration would have permitted the Indian to go on living off the buffalo as of yore.

"Now, Mr. Speaker, my objection to this bill is this; that there is a privilege given to the wild, savage Indian that is not given to the poor civilized settler. My next objection is that the bill is utterly worthless in point of fact. There is no law which human hands can write, there is no law which a Congress can enact, that will stay the disappearance of these wild animals before civilization. They eat the grass. They trample upon the plains upon which our settlers desire to herd their cattle and their sheep. There is no mistake about that. They range over the very pastures where the settlers keep their herds of cattle and sheep to-day. They destroy that pasture. They are as uncivilized as the Indian."

To the credit of the Congress, a majority of the members were not impressed by this plea for the struggling (and voting) settlers. They decided that the buffalo was a national asset which should be utilized by less hasty and wasteful methods. They passed the bill and sent it to President Ulysses S. Grant for signature.

Whereupon it was pigeon-holed and nevermore saw the light of day.

From a few captive bands numbering less than 600 in 1889, enough stock was acquired by the federal government to establish our present museum-piece herds in national parks and game preserves. Thus the buffalo escaped extinction.

But as a wild species it disappeared from the great and "limitless" grasslands. The effect upon the Indian was according to plan. From a self-respecting (and -supporting) citizen of the wild, he was quickly reduced to impotence and utter dependence upon government dole. Dodge described the situation with the objectivity of an old hand at Indian killing, yet with a measure of feeling for the degraded red man:

"What was mere uncleanliness in the Indian's day of plenty, has degenerated into squalor. The Indian who only ten years ago contented himself with nothing but the very choicest portions of animal food, now, pinched by hunger, eats any and everything. Dogs, wolves, reptiles, half-decomposed horse-flesh, even carrion birds, all go to appease the gnawings of his famished stomach."

By the passing of the buffalo, the habitat of the plains red man was irrevocably altered and destroyed and a habitat for farmers and graziers was created. The deep loam of the prairies and the drouthy but fertile plains became the granary that a nation of tens of millions would require. These soils had supported relatively small numbers of men living under a crude hunting culture on a diet high in animal protein—a kind of exploitation regarded as inefficient among civilized men. At a "higher" cultural level the same land would sustain many more people on the cereals it could yield. It is the trend of the world as human populations grow.

The fate of the buffalo and the aboriginal American was neither fair nor pretty, but that's how it happened. Perhaps it is pointless to dwell upon what our ancestors did with the bounty of a virginal continent, except insofar as we can learn from it. But that is our interest, and the story teaches much of human behavior, politics, economics, and other considerations in latter-day issues.

Before we finish with the chapters to follow, we will see that this soil-grass-buffalo-Indian relationship is a simplified replica of what modern men face in living on the earth's resources. Each item in the system is dynamic and exists by compromise with the others. When any one fails to compromise, there is trouble for the whole. The buffalo was an essential link between Indian and soil; and when the herds were destroyed, the result was immediate. Winter blizzards howled across empty campsites where only a decade before they had drummed against the taut sides of lodges.

The life community of the plains contained the elements and forces to be found in other plant-animal communities both past and present. We will examine this biological network in some detail to determine what can be done with it and where we fit into it. Of the many courses of action, we will find that some are rank folly and others are proper and indispensable.

Sorting out such things has been a bit too tedious for us in the past, and we seem to be paying a price for the privilege of dodging issues. But problems are multiplying, and to all but the complete escapist a premium on understanding is evident. We will attempt to take the recent accumulation of facts and ideas, add them to the old, and arrange them in some sort of logical order. Realistically done, this should bring us out with a reasonable and orderly concept of how wildlife relates to those other resources that we call renewable and how all of it can be handled to our best advantage.

CHAPTER 2

They Grow in the Soil

MEN measure the yield of the earth in terms of bushels of corn, tons of hay, or bales of cotton. These are familiar quantities; they have meaning in expressing the difference between two fields or two farms. But to see the natural world with realism we will need many another unit by which to gauge the quality of land.

Colonel Dodge couldn't know that a buffalo is such a unit. As he stood awed at the profusion of life around him, he saw the herds but he didn't *perceive* them in terms of cause and effect. The vast numbers were there for a reason, and in chapters to follow we will see why it couldn't have been otherwise as long as there were *any* buffalo. Even a single animal did not grow from nothing, and whether there where ten thousand or a million of them in half of Kansas was as sure a test of the soil they trod as is the weight of grain spewed from the combines that crawl across the state today. But Colonel Dodge and others of his time understood such things only vaguely and by instinct, if at all. Nearly a century later we have a science called *ecology*, concerned with relationships, reasons why, and with seeing the order that certainly exists in the helter-skelter and happenstance that we once thought ruled the world of things that grow.

By now most people are acquainted with the well-worn saw that poor land makes poor people—both in numbers and quality. In time they will learn of such soil also that its deer and turkeys, its rabbits and quail, its coons and muskrats will be few, and frequently poor. In our present exploratory enterprise it will behoove us to get that well in mind. We are laying the foundation for a sound understanding of what is involved in growing wildlife crops for hunting, fishing, and—most of all—just enjoying. The story starts with the soil and, likely enough, comes back to it in the end.

18

THY ROCKS AND RILLS

Out where Missouri Ozarks are bordered by prairie is perhaps the most productive natural rabbit range in the country. It is a region of good land and mild winters. For many years farm boys in this area took cottontails in boxtraps and shipped them to eastern states for restocking. They caught more live rabbits than anyone had ever handled anywhere.

In 1941 an alert biologist took advantage of the situation and collected January weights on more than 175,000 of the animals. Then he lumped weights for various soil regions and compared averages. Rabbits in northeast Missouri ran a *significant third* heavier than those in the southwest part of the state. Why?

The difference evidently was soil fertility. Missouri, which has been called "the meeting ground of all of the important soil regions of the Mississippi Valley," is a particularly good place for work of this kind, and game specialists of the state are far ahead in such studies. Following the matter out, they collected rabbits and other animals from widely varying soil types. They found that the best individuals came from the most productive land; and the best were so much better than the poorest it can leave no doubt in anybody's mind.

Thus, the large leg bones of rabbits from fertile soils were up to 12 percent larger and had a breaking strength 37 percent greater than those of animals from poor land. They contained more calcium and more phosphorus.

The same sort of fertility relationship was found in raccoons. Here, too, the big robust animals were from the most productive agricultural counties. Weights then descended on a sliding scale to the counties of poorest soils and lowest productivity. Furthermore, fertile lands had *more* raccoons than the poor soils, but intensity of cultivation tended to reduce populations in the best farming areas.

It was found that even muskrats on streams draining good farmland were wearing pelts of better size and quality than 'rats on streams in poor land. Plotted against watershed fertility, the muskrat averages fell nicely into place—all except one. That exception was so striking they looked into the matter. What they found only helped to prove the rule. The entire upper portion of this stream was a commercial trout hatchery, and water that flowed from it was rich in nutrients from the abundant feed and fish wastes. Aquatic plants, minnows, etc. also seemed to be more plentiful and vigorous on this stream.

A statewide wild turkey inventory was taken in Missouri in 1941, and it appeared that, in this case too, soils were basically involved. The rather startling conclusion was reached that a single soil type, Clarksville stony loam, supports approximately 79 percent of the turkeys in the state. This soil, derived from limestone, occurs in rugged areas where the Ozark Plateau has been completely dissected by streams. Such areas are characterized by "balds," or open hillsides where the shallow soil does not support forest growth. Instead, vegetation consists of a scattering of shrubs, cedar patches, and post oak. The area of the balds is the state's best turkey range.

In the eastern Ozarks, land that looks almost the same but with soil derived from granite was found to support the poorest turkey populations in Missouri. Inherent fertility appeared to be the greatest difference between the two kinds of turkey range.

The specific ways in which mineral-rich soils benefit animals that live upon them are by no means well understood. A tangle of relationships needs to be unraveled, and even agricultural nutritionists, working with penned domestic animals under full control, are a long way from doing it. Nevertheless, one thing stands out clearly: Good soils yield the best crops, both in quantity and quality, of practically everything that lives upon them.

A Michigan game investigator found that on a tract of hilly farmland with plenty of cover and food the average cottontail rabbit occupied a winter range between five and ten acres in extent. Fall populations ran about fifty to the hundred acres and produced excellent hunting.

Forty miles away another biologist studied the rabbit by similar methods (trapping and tagging) on sterile sand plains supporting scrub oaks. There a wintering rabbit required roughly twice the amount of range, and fall populations were about a fifth of those found in the farming area. From spring to fall on the poor soil rabbits achieved little more than a doubling of their numbers, but on the more favorable range they increased nearly five times in the same period.

The work of nutritionists with penned animals leaves no doubt that proper food is the key to the ability of birds and mammals to breed and rear their young. In one set of experiments, it was found that egg production, fertility, and hatchability in captive bobwhite quail were affected by the calcium and phosphorus levels in the breeding diet of *their parents* a year before.

It is hardly to be doubted that soils exert their effects through good nutrition and that this comes about because vegetation is both abundant and rich in such things as protein and essential minerals. A captive rat colony at Yale University provided a good example of such factors at work over several years.

"In the rat colony . . . the animals have been inbred for many years without addition to the original stock. The manner of handling the animals has not changed. But since 1932 the stock diet has been changed by increasing the vitamin content and the protein content to allow a greater rate of growth. With the new diet, the average daily gain has increased enormously. The largest rats in this colony fully equal the largest rats yet produced by injections of pituitary growth hormone. Yet with this increased growth rate and increased size on the higher plane of nutrition, the percentage of fertile matings has increased from about 70 percent to over 90 . . ." This account was written in 1939.

If you read agricultural bulletins, you will find accounts of how domestic animals have recognized more palatable and presumably more nutritious plants grown on soil treated with lime and fertilizer. That wild animals have similar tastes may account for the unfortunate extent to which deer invade winter grains, hayfields, and orchards on back-country farms in the northern states.

Samples of soil taken from "salt licks" used by Rocky Mountain bighorns in northwest Wyoming showed no salt but much phosphorus. Forage plants of this area were low in phosphorus and animals evidently were resorting to the lick to correct a dearth of this important element. It was suggested that bone meal, phosphates, and ordinary salt be mixed with soil at these licks so that the animals could fulfil their needs by taking only a small amount. In the case of threatened species, like the bighorn, this might be something practical in the way of a "feeding program."

In 1941 the Ohio Division of Conservation planted several thousand Chinese chestnuts at the Turner Ridge Wildlife Area in Zaleski State

Forest. The site was inhospitable, and in five years the trees showed little growth and never bore any nuts.

Some of these were fertilized in 1946, and results could be seen within a year. Treated trees began to grow rapidly and the yellow leaf color turned to a dark, healthy green. The first nut crop was produced in 1947.

We could search out many another example to illustrate that all wildlife is rooted in the soil. The earth and its vegetation are the foundation for a pyramid of animal life. In the broad lower levels of this structure a multitude of creatures—most of them small—feed directly on plants, in which earth minerals and air gases have been united into digestible compounds by light power from the sun. Animals in levels higher up eat the ones below them, though all make use of some plant foods directly. And still higher in the pyramid, and still fewer in number, are the large and dominant animals—the ones that can, and do, eat the animals that eat the animals that eat the plants.

Information on soil-animal relationships is less exact than we would like. Many experiments are less precisely garrisoned with scientific checks and controls than could be wished for; but what there is probably gives us the outlines of earth-life economy. And it seems to be generally true that the hilly, rocky, sandy, or played-out lands are least productive of nearly all kinds of animals—in spite of the fact that we have assigned wildlife to such areas as a primary value. National forests, wilderness areas, and public hunting grounds fit this category; and it is proper and inevitable. Our highest-quality soils were long since preempted for intensive farming.

And here we have an important key to the wildlife abundance which used to set the old-timer to ruminating, misty-eyed, over the good old days. The huge game crops of a century ago were produced by some of the best soils on this continent. The prairie chicken in Missouri illustrates the situation well:

In that state all of the 28,000 square miles of prairie originally supported chickens. The total number may have been around a million, but in the fall of 1936 remaining birds were estimated at about 10,-000. Their present distribution with respect to land type is striking. There are none at all on the best soils, and very few on the next best.

An inventory showed that only medium to low-grade prairie soils now are producing chickens.

It is likely that modern farming and intensity of land use account for this. There is no doubt that the species once was plentiful on fertile soils, but these areas now are high in value and intensively used, with a maximum of acreage in corn. Lands where chickens still persist are lower in value, with less corn and larger acreages in hay and native grass. Agricultural operations seem to have eliminated this prairie grouse from most lands above "medium" in the fertility scale. The remaining birds live on the poorest soil. They are not high populations, but they are all we have.

These are some of the realities which attest that the good old days will not recur. Good lands are producing other things now, and wildlife only incidentally. But even yet we will find that their fertility tells, for game, fish, and many another useful creature.

HAPPY MEDIUM

In terms of fertility, land and water are one and the same, since it is water that makes available the nutrients in soil. In lakes and streams the relationship of dissolved minerals to aquatic life has become fairly well known.

The enrichment of fishpond waters with commercial fertilizers is now a widely used technique in the South. When some of the pioneer research was being done on this problem in Alabama it was found that unfertilized ponds could be expected to produce from 100 to 200 pounds of fish per acre per year. Similar fertilized ponds yielded up to 580 pounds of fish in one growing season.

In a controlled experiment two similar ponds were stocked with the same numbers and kinds of fish. One of these was fertilized, and the following November it yielded at the rate of 578 pounds of fish per acre. The other pond, which was left unfertilized, produced 134 pounds per acre in the same season. The added fertility meant an increase of 330 percent in the fish crop.

In Poland it is a common practice to drain commercial fishponds every four to six years. Landowners then cultivate and fertilize the soil of the bottom and sow some crop such as oats, rye, hemp, or peas, which can be left as green manure. This process greatly increases the growth of fish-food organisms and the yield of fish.

Long ago, Izaak Walton observed that he caught the biggest fish in streams that drained fertile valleys. Of course, the reason is that the quantity of mineral nutrients dissolved in natural waters is largely dependent upon the kind of soil through which that water percolates before it finds its way into lakes and streams. There it is headed for the sea, and when we take a crop of fish from it we are getting one more benefit from the fertility of the watershed. Infertile lands mean infertile water and a low turnover in aquatic life.

By way of example, it was found that fish production was low in New Brunswick lakes receiving drainage from soils underlain by such insoluble rocks as granite, quartzite, and slate. In five lakes the total weight per acre of all fish ranged from 17 to 36 pounds. Conditions were comparable on a sandy jackpine plain in Crawford County, Michigan. There, the relatively sterile water of How Lake supported 38 pounds of fish per acre. On better lands in Minnesota, the lakes have fish populations averaging about 150 pounds, but this is considerably less than the best. In central Illinois, the total weight of fish was determined for 22 isolated ponds and artificial lakes that were drained or poisoned. The standing population of fish averaged 600 pounds per acre. Floodplain lakes were found to support 400 to 500 pounds. Of course, these highly productive waters drain from some of the state's best farmlands and are correspondingly fertile. It should be remembered that the figures quoted include all species and sizes of fish, catchable and otherwise.

Variations in fertility also markedly affect life in marine waters. In the deep oceans adjoining the western coasts of North and South America there is a phenomenon known as *upwelling*, in which cold water, rich in nutrients, is brought to the surface by the action of off-shore winds. A heavy concentration of minerals in this water supports a prolific plant and animal growth which produces, in turn, an abundance of fish. Off the coast of Peru the water teems, seasonally, with anchovies, and it is estimated that some *million tons* of these small fish are consumed each year by hordes of cormorants, boobies, and pelicans which nest on islands along the coast. On these rainless islands, droppings of the sea birds pile up to an annual increment of about 150,000 tons. This "guano" is harvested, under a government monopoly, and used as fertilizer. Thus, by a wonderful and intricate biological mechanism, the fertility of the Humboldt Current is concentrated and removed from the ocean to be spread on the land to produce still other crops.

Upwelling waters along the Pacific coast of United States and Canada support a vast sardine fishery, and survival of young sardines in any given year is correlated directly with the extent to which nutrients are brought up from the depths. When upwelling is strong, the water is highly saline, food is plentiful, and a large generation of fish is produced. When the opposite condition prevails, survival of young sardines is reduced.

Actually, the difference between "fresh" and "salt" water is only one of degree, for it is the decomposition of rock into soluble compounds and the steady washing of these nutrients out of the soil that makes it possible for fish to grow in fresh-water lakes and streams. Through long ages, these waters have carried their burden of dissolved fertility to the sea, where they evaporate and thus build up the mineral concentration.

This means that early in geological history the seas were only slightly salty, and the first life on earth developed in such water. At certain times salinity of the oceans must have been much higher than now, for a large part of the earth's water was piled up in huge ice caps during periods of glaciation. When the glaciers melted, ocean levels came up and the mineral solution was diluted again. It would be interesting to know how productive of life the salt waters were in their times of concentration.

POLICY

In exploring methods by which wildlife crops can be most efficiently produced, it is appropriate that we start with the earth itself. The condition of the soil and its plant covering determines what any area will yield. Although this idea has been repeated to a point of monotony in recent years, it is not yet widely appreciated.

Have no doubt about it, the time has arrived when we must manage specifically for anything we want from the land. Every acre is being watched by someone with a single interest. Our renewable resources will be renewed only if we understand their requirements and plan it that way.

A fertile soil will not guarantee heavy game populations, but large game concentrations seldom develop on poor land. A naturally potent soil is one of the greatest assets we can have in setting out to improve conditions for nearly any species of wildlife. It follows also that anything done to conserve fertility and build up humus and mineral content usually will be a step toward a more abundant animal life—other things being equal.

Those other things are not equal when high agricultural value means laying bare the land from one road to another for production of cultivated crops. In such cases there may be practically no place at all for wildlife in the land-use economy. Lands intensively used for truck and other specialized produce frequently come under this category, and usually it is not feasible to try to do anything with wildlife under such conditions. On a unit basis, it is a crop too low in value to compete with products of the land that build houses and buy television sets.

We probably can learn from all this that our best investments in wildlife management will be on better lands in situations where we can grow our recreational crop as a by-product without interfering with the number-one industry. This applies to most farmland, and the things that can be done to have more quail, rabbits, and other creatures can in some cases also serve agricultural purposes for the farmer. To clarify this—a hedge is both wildlife cover and a windbreak. A living fence is a cheap way of confining cattle and it also is cover.

The United States Soil Conservation Service has a land-use capability chart on which they indicate possible uses for each of the eight classes of land they recognize. Wildlife is the one crop which, under some conditions, can be produced on all eight types, from best to poorest. This does not mean, of course, that it should replace things of greater value, but that it comes into situations where primary crops either cannot be grown or would not pay.

Conserving and building fertility are a first step in managing all renewable resources, including wildlife. For the most part our specialized type of management will be *built into other programs*. It is obvious that the wildlife man will have to know whereof he speaks in dealing with the farmer, forester, and grazier.

As one further step in considering fertility, we can do no business with anyone who is destroying it. Types of grazing, lumbering, farming, or other activities which deplete the soil or permit it to be washed away offer no possibility of better harvests for the sportsman. Anyone who is, at times, a hunter or fisherman would do well to realize this; it will clarify his interest in every issue.

CHAPTER 3

The One-Year Plan

PROTECTION Island was what the Oregon biologists were looking for. The staff of the wildlife research unit * at Corvallis was working with pheasants in the Willamette Valley and needed a small restricted unit of range where a sample bird population would be under full control.

Having no isolated area in their own state, they went north, half way across Washington, and found it—in the Straits of Juan de Fuca. It was 400 acres in extent and 2.6 miles from the mainland; that's farther than a pheasant will fly.

In the mid-thirties half of the island was farmed. The owner raised wheat, barley, and oats and there were pastures, woodlots, and sand dunes. An exceptional circumstance was that there were no ground predators, although it was on a migration route for hawks and owls, and there were resident crows. No pheasants had been on the island for many years.

In the spring of 1937, Arthur S. Einarsen landed on Protection Island with a crate containing eight ringneck pheasants. He liberated two cocks and six hens as an initial breeding stock. In the Willamette Valley there was a four-footed predator for every 200 acres. So, to simulate conditions there, two male house cats were turned out with the pheasants. Both being males, the cat population obviously was stable.

Islands make ideal outdoor laboratories. Protection Island was a small, test-tube environment with "walls" of water around it which kept the resident pheasants within definitely known limits and prevented other pheasants from moving in to complicate things. In the years that followed, field men combed the land regularly, counting birds and watching what happened.

* Research units are described on p. 286

28

Since the number of original breeders was known, it was easy to follow their annual increase. An inventory in the fall of 1941 showed *more than 1,500 pheasants* where five years before there had been eight. The build-up each year had averaged 277 percent!

This probably is a fair sample of the kind of increase that can be expected when even a few individuals of nearly any species are placed in conditions where a high survival of young is possible. The word *increase* is not particularly good here, for numbers tend to double and redouble. The biologist's term *irrupt* is more descriptive of what actually happens. It implies an almost explosive breeding force, and that's what we are dealing with.

This force is the means by which Nature overcomes tremendous losses of individuals in an annual turnover that is a prodigy of production and waste. Most sportsmen and many technicians do not fully appreciate the amplitude of this yearly fluctuation, and an occasional glimpse of high losses, without real understanding of the rebound that is due, can be misleading. It can cause undue alarm over a few dead animals; it can keep us from taking a full harvest of the available game surplus; and it can cause us to underestimate the possibilities in a small breeding stock established on the land. All are common errors.

The life expectancy of new-born small game or fur animals is considerably *less than a year,* and, as a reasonable average, a full-grown individual in hunting season stands less than *one chance in three* of being alive a year later. This fact is fundamental to a realistic concept of what is taking place in game populations. Newspapers and magazines constantly tell about those rare rabbits, squirrels, or pheasants that lived four or five years after being banded, and there is nearly always an implication that this is a sample of what regularly occurs.

To the population biologist this is an exasperating misrepresentation of fact. It is mass phenomena that count in managing birds, mammals, and fish, and we need to know what happens to the bulk of the annual crop. Small animals are like annual weeds. They spring forth in abundance, and then are wiped out before another growing season. Each year's increase is the source of most of that season's sport. A "decline" is nearly always a failure of the new generation to materialize in their usual numbers.

RINGNECKS CONTINUED

Another island, Pelee by name, is the southernmost point of land in Ontario. It is in Lake Erie, just out of sight of Point Pelee on a line with Ohio's Marblehead Peninsula. At the time when Chinese pheasants were being shipped to Oregon for the first really successful stocking on American soil, Pelee Island was a low-lying "skeleton" of limestone flats surrounded and separated by swamp.

In 1888 the Cleveland owners of the 10,000 acres put steam dredges to constructing twelve miles of canal. Since then the entire island has been drained and the landscape has assumed that characteristic look of top-grade Lake States pheasant range: Fields are flat and black, ditches are deep and wide, and spoilbanks are covered with giant ragweed and brush. Crops are lush and weeds are rank.

In 1927 not more than three dozen adult pheasants were brought to Pelee and turned out as breeders. The actual rate of increase is not known, but in five years the twenty-five square miles were so overrun with birds that landowners were complaining to the Provincial Government because of crop destruction. In trying to stem the wholesale overflow of pheasants, farmers searched out nests and broke the eggs.

In 1932 and 1933 hunting seasons of three days were held for island residents. They adopted a season limit of six birds, and the take had no visible effect on pheasant numbers. By 1934 it was evident that more birds would have to be shot, and non-resident licenses were sold for the first time. This hunt proved to be so profitable for the islanders that it was continued thereafter. Seven years after the initial stocking, they were taking an annual harvest of 10,000 birds, or *a pheasant per acre* from Pelee Island.

As we shall see, a superabundant breeding stock, such as must have existed on Pelee after the initial increase, does not produce in the same proportion as the beginning few, which seem to have a whole world to populate. The capacity for multiplication is there in every healthy bird, but controls become increasingly effective as numbers grow. In the case of island populations the build-up is contained in a limited area and we get a spectacular view of it, but the same reproductive potential is present in mainland populations.

Our ringneck pheasant is a hybrid of three or four races from Asia, and probably the best extensive range for it in the world is found in South Dakota. This gallinaceous health center was created by plowing the mineral-laden soils of the primitive buffalo pastures and the institution of grain farming, corn, and wheat being most important.

From the nineties to World War I, various private individuals made small backyard attempts to establish pheasants in South Dakota, but without success. In 1914 the state took the job over in earnest and during the next four years about 7,000 birds were liberated. Open seasons were held in limited areas in 1919.

During the next twenty-odd years, approximately 35,000 pheasants were trapped at concentration points where they had become plentiful and were moved into new range that had no breeding stock. Early in the program it became evident that this was to be pheasant country.

South Dakota has never had a game farm. Their establishment of the pheasant is an outstanding example of how such a job should be done. The fact that they got results quickly may have forestalled public pressure and foolish expedients that might otherwise have entered the picture and lingered on for many years.

We cannot doubt their success. In 1945 state biologists estimated the pre-hunting population at between thirty and forty million pheasants, but 1945 numbers probably were considerably less than those of the peak attained the year before.

DOWN UNDER AND ELSEWHERE

On Christmas day, 1859, the Black Ball clipper *Lightning* arrived in Hobson's Bay on the southeast bulge of Australia. She bore a consignment of twenty-four wild European rabbits destined for Thomas Austin of Barwon Park, near Geelong, Victoria.

Four days later the rabbits from across the sea were established in the promised land. Within six years Mr. Austin had killed 20,000 of them from his estate and estimated his breeding stock at 10,000. Unfortunately, this was just a beginning.

Within a few years it became evident that the rabbit in Australia was an outstanding biological blunder. There was alarm, then consternation, as the animals spread northward into grazing lands of New South Wales. In ten years they had invaded Queensland and occupied thousands of square miles. They leaped ahead like a prairie fire. Everywhere they scourged the vegetation. Five rabbits, they said, are equal to one sheep. In a series of wet years they would close in on the great desert areas, girdling woody growth and eating everything green. When the climatic pendulum swung back to dry, rabbits would disappear, leaving a blighted land smothered in shifting sand.

The people hunted, poisoned, trapped, dug out, ferreted, dogged, bountied, and killed rabbits in every possible manner. They erected thousands of miles of wire netting. They spent millions in public and private money. Domestic cats went wild, and European foxes were introduced. But the bunnies had a breeding potential that allowed for all such enemies. It made no difference.

More details are not necessary. Present purposes are served by pointing out what happened when a few rabbits were placed in a range where natural checks were minimized and a high percentage of the young survived. A population of animals is like a volume of gas, expanding in every direction as long as there is nothing to contain it. If the breeding process is maintained at an efficient level, killing adult animals is just "sweeping back the tide with a broom."

Theoretically, the best approach in "control" work is to fight fire with fire—to oppose the burgeoning population with a similar self-multiplying biological force. It was long recognized that the rabbits of Australia provided a classic situation for the introduction of a lethal disease.

Such a disease actually was found in "myxomatosis," a virus plague native to the Americas. Our own rabbits have a high resistance to it which is not shared by European rabbits. Myxomatosis was tried repeatedly in Australia, and in 1950 it went wild, killing rabbits like the scourge it was hoped to be. For a time it was the best rabbit control yet found. The disease is now well established, and wherever conditions become favorable, it will help the cause of rabbit reduction. But such are the checks and balances in wild communities that natural maladies have their own limitations, and myxomatosis has fallen far short of wiping out the rabbits (see notes, p. 347).

BAKER'S DOZEN

This record of a few successful introductions can teach us much about production possibilities in practically any common wild animal. It also indicates what an inhospitable place the world is for the creatures that furnish our fishing and hunting. We seldom find them overrunning the land, which they certainly would do if their numbers were not perpetually being worn away. Evidently an unremitting pressure exerted by the environment counterbalances the breeding force and frequently holds numbers at a lower level than we like.

There is no getting around it, Nature is a wastrel. She can produce lavishly, but she destroys in a like manner. One of the best examples of her caprice is the ignoble fate of *most* of the eggs laid by our best game birds.

If you told the average hunter that something was breaking up half of the pheasant, quail, or partridge nests in an area, the chances are he would view the situation with alarm or something more violent. Yet nearly any habitat in which half the eggs can hatch stands a good chance of being satisfactorily productive.

In one of the earliest comprehensive game-bird investigations, and a classic of its kind, Herbert L. Stoddard followed to completion the fate of 602 bobwhite quail nests. In this sample, 57 percent were unsuccessful. As a general average for the southeastern states, Stoddard estimated that from 60 to 80 percent of the nests failed to produce young. But, like other upland species, quail try again if their nest is broken up, and in the final analysis it was concluded that a majority of pairs finally manage to bring off a brood.

Similarly, in a three-year study covering 445 Iowa pheasant nests, nearly 77 percent were unsuccessful. This included nests which had only an egg or two when abandoned, and if these are eliminated from consideration, there still were failures amounting to 59 percent. Nevertheless, despite nesting losses of from 59 to 76 percent, it appeared that 70 to 80 out of every 100 hens eventually hatched a clutch of eggs—strong testimony to the effectiveness of persistence in overcoming high egg losses! In still another Iowa investigation 533 pheasant nests were studied. The percentage of *successful* nests for three consecutive years was only 39, 25, and 23, respectively. Here again, renesting was a compensating factor.

For present purposes there is no point in discussing what factors are responsible for these losses. Destructive agents (such as mowing machines and predators) vary in effect from one area to another, and in general it seems that if one thing doesn't get the nests, something else will. It should be kept in mind that nest failures of 50 to 60 percent do not necessarily mean that a species will not produce a good hunting season crop. On Pelee Island, in a year when a fantastically high pheasant population overran the land (1949) and when a harvest of more than a bird per acre was taken, nesting success was only 47 percent. This is of particular interest because such ground predators as skunks, raccoons, and foxes were absent, and even mowing was at a minimum.

MEASURED EQUITY

Repeatedly we will witness that for nearly any species a concentration of numbers means a deterioration of living conditions for the individual and a consequent reduction of fecundity. Conversely, a thinning of numbers improves the health, welfare, and productivity of survivors. Thrifty breeding stocks and maximum wildlife crops will nearly always be found in favorable environments that are not overstocked. The *ease* with which a pair of animals can protect and feed their young has a direct bearing on the success of the operation. But since we are dealing with a highly dynamic quantity, it's evident that the happy condition of understocking usually will be a temporary one.

An obvious limitation to numbers of all animals is the available food supply. How this may operate is well illustrated by the production of young in certain hawks and owls that feed principally on mice and other small mammals. When the numbers of rodents reach plague proportions, predatory birds actually produce more eggs per clutch and may nest twice in a season instead of once, as is usual. The size of the clutch decreases when food is scarce (as in a die-off of rodents) or adult birds may not breed at all.

Wild animals show their greatest productivity immediately after a few are introduced into top-quality range. This is the ultimate in understocking, and its result has been demonstrated repeatedly. The founding pheasants on Pelee must have brought through a major portion of their young for several years, and similar high production accounts for the outpouring of birds into unoccupied range in mainland areas.

Except for the initial build-up following introductions, it appears to be the regular thing for annual crops of our game birds to be reduced by half or even more before the eggs are hatched. After hatching, the wearing away of numbers continues, declining in rate as the birds grow larger.

It is a basic phenomenon that small animals have higher mortality rates (hence higher replacement rates also) than larger ones; and within a given species the risks to an individual are greatest when it is small, young, and relatively helpless.

To put it more vividly, perhaps, we can consider a young rabbit in the nest to be in the same prey category with the meadow mouse. As it begins to grow and run about, it has about the same enemies as a rat or chipmunk. By the time it is full grown it has reduced the number of threats to its existence and increased its life expectancy.

The terrific rate of production and loss among the smallest animals implies that their chief function in the living world is to turn herbage of the earth into a protein ration suitable for the nourishment of a horde of enemies.

It was this viewpoint that Seton expressed in remarking on food relationships of the carnivores: "When we shall have fully worked out the life-history of each of these species, I believe we shall learn that the whole of that vast, beautiful, important, and specialized production that we call the Carnivora rests on a broad simple basis of Muridae [mice] that in turn rests on the grass, that rests on the earth. We shall for each of these flesh-eaters write, 'it sometimes eats this and sometimes eats that, but by far the greatest bulk of its food is Mice.' " *

In a world where practically every creature must, sooner or later, have its existence justified, this natural function has been cited in favor of some of mankind's lesser and sometimes objectionable bedfellows. Robert Burns' "Wee sleekit cowrin' tim'rous beastie" had good reason for the panic in his breastie.

Of necessity, we are getting into the realm of population mechanics, which is a specialized subject and one basic to any understanding of wildlife management. Most large-scale errors in handling wild animal resources have stemmed from a failure to comprehend the forces at work in populations. Logic applying to an individual frequently has little relationship to the thrift and survival of a life com-

* Reprinted by permission from *Life Histories of Northern Animals*, by Ernest Thompson Seton. Copyright 1909. Charles Scribner's Sons.

munity. The average person gets only glimpses, here and there, of population doings, and he has little opportunity to add them up into anything approaching a pattern of behavior. Hence, assertions of the biologist, likewise disconnected, sound abstract and "theoretical." For the same reason, it is not surprising that issues having to do with human populations have made little public impression—especially since they seem to boil down to some rather glum prospects for humanity.

Here our point of emphasis is that numbers phenomena tend to be universal. They change only in detail as we shift from fish to fur to fowl. They apply similarly to humans, keeping in mind some particular conditions, and if it were possible to apply such knowledge, there is little doubt that mankind could be benefited thereby. In view of points discussed, and others yet to be considered, there may be profit in a brief look at our own population status.

As noted previously, it seems to be true that a high standard of living can exist only in an understocked habitat, be that habitat a deer yard or the State of California. As witness to what happens when people overstock their "ranges," we have only to look at the distressed areas of Latin America, Africa, and Asia, where populations have outgrown the resources available to support them. Birth rates are "explosive" and death rates tragic. Millions of people are born to an inheritance of poverty and hunger.

Compassion for such people is expressed in shipments of grain and medical aid. This helps to reduce deaths, which means that more people immediately survive and the problem of overcrowding is worse than ever. By an international pooling of resources, the living standard of a *reduced and stable* world population might, perhaps, be brought up to a satisfactory level. But in the population hot spots we are dealing at present with a problem that grows each time we do something to cure it. The only real and lasting benefit to overcrowded and impoverished (cause and effect) countries would have to come through a reduction of the rate at which people are being born, and that has not yet been satisfactorily accomplished.

A bright side of this is that when humans attain certain cultural conditions—one such condition is a high living standard—the birth rate goes down. There are countries (Ireland, France, Scandinavia) where the population is relatively stable at present; but there are others, like our own, where it is increasing rapidly. On a world basis, the numbers of the human race are growing by about 137,000 people per day (See note p. 348.).

In its ultimate development, our thinking in the field of conservation must be concerned with human populations. Resources can be measured only in terms of the number of people who are to use them. There has been a tendency to avoid open discussion of the population question, but growing difficulties are likely to change that. The subject is receiving scientific treatment by the sociologist and biologist, and the skills of both are needed. New books continue to appear and gain some attention, even though it seems to be a common idea that the destiny of man is not a proper field for professional inquiry.

THE ANNUAL TURNOVER

Probably because of their own liberal life expectancy, few people appreciate the drastic waxing and waning of animal numbers with the cycle of the seasons. This is evident in much of our writing on natural history. As the pioneers destroyed wildlife habitat, we are told, the poor wild creatures were herded together in ever-narrowing coverts, where their concentrations became easy prey for enemies and the avaricious market hunter.

That probably is the way long-lived humans would go down in defeat, but it isn't a realistic concept as applied to animals that are being largely killed off and produced anew every year. What actually happened was that as wildlife habitats were changed, they progressively produced smaller annual crops of the species being squeezed out and progressively more of those that were being benefited. Hence the tales of how one animal "drove out" another. In the Lake States the gray squirrel disappeared with the cutting of dense forests, but fox squirrels increased with the openings. The numbers of each reflected conditions on the land practically on a year-to-year basis.

We cannot manage, or even harvest, game and fish to best advantage until we have a realistic conception of the annual destruction and replacement of numbers. During the thirties we began to get reliable figures on such phenomena, and consistency now is widely evident.

Visualize a population of 100 valley quail, in November, around a waterhole in California's foothills. Out there the efforts of many competent field men have given them exceptionally complete information on their state bird. If these quail represented the average, 38 of them would be "old" and 62 would be birds of the year.

That is nothing to rush by; think it over. It means we can expect to lose 62 of these particular quail by a year from now, and that they will have been replaced by 62 young out of next spring's hatch. A quail that lives three years is an old-timer and make no mistake about it.

But November birds already have survived the worst trial period, as was evident in our look at nest losses. Turn the calendar around to May: Every 100 eggs in the nest during the breeding season will be represented by only 8.5 (we'll keep this fraction for a change) living breeders just twelve months from now. This is a population that is remaining stable from one year to another. With such losses a normal occurrence, is it any wonder numbers go up when restrictions are lifted?

Figures on midwest fox squirrels sound much like the quail statistics, even though the California bird averages 13 eggs to a clutch and a fox squirrel female produces three young at a birth—with an average for the distaff side of the population of 4 new-born squirrels per season. (Some females have two litters.)

We can consider these two creatures as starting with 13 and 4 young respectively, not bothering about a slight error due to infertile eggs. Yet they come out about the same in the fall. In the hunting kill in a normal year roughly two thirds of the squirrels will be sub-adult animals and the other third will be what is left of last winter's breeding stock. Before shooting starts we can figure that Nature has marked approximately *66 out of every 100* individuals in the population for elimination before another year is gone.

Such a comparison indicates that the fox squirrel maintains its numbers with a much narrower survival margin than the quail and hence that it must take better care of its young and bring through a higher percentage to fall. That is exactly the case.

A two-thirds turnover of grown animals looks high, but in some species it is far higher than this. If we went into the situation for such small creatures as mice, figures would be almost fantastic, but the points of importance can be well illustrated without going beyond those species that give us our recreational wildlife crops.

In years before the pheasant "depression" of the mid-forties, a heavily hunted area in southern Michigan showed an approximate age ratio in the fall kill of 1 old cock to 10 young. In a sample of 766 cocks examined on road blockades in 1940 (representing a large area of southeastern Michigan) the ratio was 1 to 10.4. On 8,000 acres representing some of Michigan's best pheasant range, a unit subjected to exceptionally heavy hunting, the average ratio for three years was 1 old cock to 18 young of the year. On this area the rooster pheasant that lived to breed just once had to have a special understanding with Lady Luck.

Of course, these figures are on male birds where only males are hunted, but from a Wisconsin refuge we can get an idea of the turnover in both sexes on a tract where shooting did not enter in. Here it was found that from hatching time to winter there was a mortality of about 84 percent of young pheasants; and from one winter to the next there was a loss of 70 percent of the individuals. Cocks were not known to live more than 3 years, and a given generation of hens was all gone in 4½ years. If you started with a winter population of 100 pheasants, the number of survivors in four succeeding years would be:

$$100 - 30 - 9 - 1.8 - 0$$

A Russian who worked on age composition in the population of a European squirrel computed a survival series that resembles the one for Wisconsin pheasants. Starting with 100 young animals, the expected annual reduction would be:

$$100 - 10 \text{ to } 15 - 3 \text{ to } 5 - 1 \text{ to } 2 - 0 \text{ to } 1$$

Mortality among young fish, of course, is very high and direct comparisons with birds or mammals are difficult. However, a study on Hunt Creek, a trout stream in Montmorency County, Michigan, indicated the approximate survival to be expected among brook trout young of the year that have lived to September. Starting with 100 fish the first year, the population would decline about as follows in that particular water:

$$100 - 66 - 42 - 6$$

In Hunt Creek the six fish at the end of the series had reached

legal size of seven inches or more, and it took 100 September fingerlings three years before to produce them.

In discussing the average survival of wild trout, Cooper said, ". . .
about three trout survive their first year of life for every 100 spawned.
. . . After their first year, survival is much better, but still about 75 percent are lost to fishing and other causes during their second year and
each year following. It is evident that a natural year class of trout is
very quickly depleted, and it is only the rare fish, one in 100,000 or so,
that lives to be 5 years old. . . ."

Even for such large (and slower breeding) animals as deer most
people undoubtedly far underestimate the turnover rate, and this has
been important in giving us unrealistic cropping policies. Figures
compiled at Massachusetts checking stations indicate that a generation
of 1½-year-old deer would show a year-to-year decline as follows:

Age	Number checked
1½	535
2½	387
3½	247
4½	102
5½	55
6½	26
7½	17
8½-9½	10
10½ & older	6

Fawns could not be used as a starter in this series because it was
obvious that hunters were not bringing a representative sample of
fawns to the checking station. Otherwise, the progressive decline
probably represents the history of a generation of deer that had
reached the age of 1½ years.

It is suggestive that at a station in Michigan, where more than
1,500 fox squirrels were ear-tagged by biologists over a six-year period,
only 2 animals were known to have lived more than 5 years. Of
1,400 cottontails similarly marked, only 2 were accounted for after
4 years. It's plain enough that wild-living animals seldom die of old
age.

The first game-bird age ratios were taken in the late thirties, but
since then a sampling of the fall kill for ages has become a stand-

ard technique for judging the success of breeding seasons. Nearly all these ratios reflect the annual turnover of the population in terms of the mortality of adults and their replacement with young. Among northern quail the percentage of young birds is consistently around 80 to 83 percent. If 8 out of 10 birds in fall coveys are young of the year, then obviously 8 out of 10 must die in the next twelve months unless the population increases. And when increases do occur, they are likely to represent an increase in survival of the season's young rather than a hold-over of adults.

The sampling of age ratios has a practical application in management, since it usually indicates the success of the breeding season, and this information can be used in future correlations and forecasting. In Finland, where the population of squirrels reaches a peak about every five years, the animals are considered to be prosperous when the annual turnover is 65 to 70 percent. This is the time for a heavy harvest. An increasing accumulation of such information indicates a surprising similarity in yearly losses among many animals that fall into the general class of small game.

Ruffed grouse can be aged by wings and tail feathers, and Massachusetts specimens turned in by sportsmen in 1947 indicated that 63 percent of the kill were juvenile birds. Michigan got similar information by separate weeks for the three-week hunting season. In 1945 percentages of birds of the year were 59, 56, and 50. The following year breeding was more successful and these percentages were 82, 81, and 75. Both years indicate that young grouse tend to be taken more easily early in the season.

That the turnover in waterfowl is comparable to these records for upland game is indicated by Cottam's statement that "on the basis of about 125,000 banding returns from wild ducks, we are compelled to conclude that the life span of fully 70 percent of these birds, which reach the flying stage, is considerably less than one year."

Do we need more evidence that there is a pattern in Nature that we can learn to recognize for individual species, and which will be useful in controlling those factors which have most to do with the annual boiling down to either large or small numbers?

What happens to an individual animal may be one of a wide choice of fates; but what happens in the population is subject to statistical averages and can be predicted, when we know enough about it. For a given set of conditions on the land there is a norm for the mechanics of death and replacement. A departure from that norm may be the clue to disaster and what caused it.

INCREMENT

If no mortality occurred, a quail population would increase by about 700 percent from spring to fall, since a pair will average 14 young. Naturally, they fall considerably short of this. For Missouri it has been calculated that an average post-hunting covey of 16 birds will be reduced to 5 by the spring breeding season and that this covey remnant of 5 will increase to 23 by fall. Hence 100 wild breeder quail in the spring would be expected to increase to a fall population of 460. These figures may seem inconsistent with age ratios cited, but they are not because some adults die between spring and fall. In Missouri the difference between 16 and 23 is the hunting crop.

Quail do not by any means achieve 460 percent in all areas. The extent to which a given habitat permits an average breeding stock to multiply its numbers from spring to fall is one measure of range quality. Two Boone County, Missouri, study areas, each of more than 2,000 acres, had spring-to-fall increases of 345 and 370 percent, respectively, in 1946.

Rabbits, too, follow the same general pattern of production. On a 150-acre tract at Ames, Iowa, in 1942, the spring breeding stock of cottontails was 28 and the fall population was 74. Allowing for some loss of adults, each pair achieved a production of about four grown young in the fall. Annual crops were about the same on this tract for the six years of the study. The area was not hunted and evidently was carrying its maximum population.

In New York, April populations of pheasants tend to be about the same from one year to another. Studies have shown that the September peak of numbers is about two and one-half times the April population. By December (after hunting) the birds will still be twice as numerous as in April—after which the population is reduced by half before another spring. In referring to the annual winter decline, Benson and Robeson remarked significantly, "Strange as it may seem, this 50 percent reduction takes place whether the Winter is harsh or mild, and whether predator populations are up or down."

Rates of increase tend to decline as progressively larger species are considered. Thus, Michigan raccoon populations increase about 1.5 times from spring to fall. Deer may renew their numbers by 35 to 45 percent on the average, while the annual increment for Yellowstone elk is about 21 percent.

These slower rates are geared to relatively greater capacity for individual survival, but practically all kinds of animals are capable of spectacular increase through doubling and redoubling their numbers when conditions become favorable.

An examination of the rates at which animals multiply might leave the impression that, whatever else this world lacks, there should be game to satisfy our wildest desires. If so, the idea is at some variance with the economy of scarcity so familiar to most sportsmen. The sad truth is that we are falling ridiculously short of possibilities.

The natural productivity of living things is almost beyond belief— when certain key conditions are in proper adjustment. It appears that our logical job in wildlife management is to determine what those conditions are for each species in each type of range and then learn to control them. In fact this probably is the only way, as applied to game and fish, to get what we want on the scale we must have.

There are two points of particular emphasis in this chapter: Our populations of small animals operate under a one-year plan of decimation and replacement; and Nature habitually maintains a wide margin of overproduction. She kills off a huge surplus of animals whether we take our harvest or not.

In managing our wildlife crops there will be frequent need to reflect on these realities.

CHAPTER 4

So Many and No More

EVERYONE who hunts and fishes has observed that some areas are better than others for his favorite sports. A certain tract of farmland gives him his best luck on pheasants, and an entirely different set of conditions is good for top-grade grouse hunting. By experience he knows that he can catch trout consistently on a particular stretch of a given stream and that one shore of a certain lake yields big bass more often than other waters of his acquaintance.

This is to say that for any kind of animal you can find a gradation in ranges from low to high productivity. The sportsman recognizes this, but ordinarily its significance does not greatly impress him.

To the wildlife scientist the range-quality phenomenon is a book of revelation. It unlocks a vast realm of possibilities; for if he can make good range out of poor range—then he has done it! He has increased the crop by manipulating those factors which, for a given species, permit its tremendous inborn breeding productivity to be expressed. In its simplest terms, that is the objective and method of modern wildlife management.

How are we to measure range quality? In many cases we can't look at it and be sure, because all the things that animals need are not sufficiently well known. Within limits a trained observer can make a fair-or-better estimate of what is likely to be a productive area for species he has worked with, but the final proof is *what it actually is supporting.*

The biologist's term for this is "carrying capacity." If a given land unit will support a quail per acre in the fall, its carrying capacity for that species is high. The same area may have a low carrying capacity for wild turkeys.

The most important thing about this ability of land or water (or combination thereof) to support a given kind of animal is that it has

44

strict and measurable limits. If a farm has a spring rabbit population of about two dozen animals year after year, it is likely that the physical features of that farm in terms of cover, food, etc. do not provide winter accommodations for more bunnies.

Nothing we do to the rabbits themselves is likely to change that for very long. We can wipe them out in a given fall (it isn't easy in favorable range), but a few breeders will move onto the tract from nearby and repopulate it in a single season—or two at the most. Or we can trap rabbits somewhere else and "stuff" our land unit with more animals than could survive there naturally, but nature goes to work on the surplus and by hunting season we have about the usual number again. There is some time-lag in these adjustments, but they are rapid enough to discourage such "direct" methods whenever anyone bothers to find out what the real results are. Of course, it's common enough for results to be assumed.

The biologist sees repeatedly what can be accomplished by changing the conditions under which an animal population lives; and conversely, he observes even more frequently that population levels are not affected for any appreciable period by any other approach to the problem. So impressed is he with these unfailing truths that they enter into his calculations almost as a matter of instinct. It is his basic assumption that in a given area in a given year there will be a well-defined limit beyond which the numbers of a species cannot go. Of course, the environment may change from year to year, and this may change population levels from the average, which occurrence only emphasizes the validity of the carrying-capacity idea.

A simple example of this is the relationship of rainfall to the grazing capacity of western ranges. Temporarily, drought may come to nearly any area and raise hob with its productivity of grass and livestock. Yet grazing specialists find a useful correlation between *average* annual precipitation and the number of cattle which various ranges can support without being run down. Where precipitation is between 5 and 10 inches, it takes from 60 to 200 acres to carry a cow for one year. In areas with from 10 to 15 inches of precipitation, a cow can be supported on from 35 to 80 acres. And so it goes: where rainfall is over 30 inches, only 3 to 12 acres are required to feed an animal unit for 12 months. All of these figures are for ranges in good condition, i.e. not overgrazed and depleted in years past.

If we knew enough about wildlife, we could make up a table of carrying capacities that would show a similar correlation between numbers of animals and quantitative measurements of various things in the environment. Of course, most such tables would be complex, and no one knows nearly enough at present to do more than a crude job of constructing them. For now it will be sufficient if people concerned with the production of birds, mammals, and fish will get the carrying-capacity idea well in mind and use it in their thinking. More than any other one principle, this will bring about a meeting of minds between the sportsman and the specialists who are working for him.

LIMITING FACTORS

There are two ways of looking at the manipulation of wildlife habitats: One is that we are endeavoring to provide conditions which permit breeding potential to be expressed. The other is that we are trying to eliminate those conditions in the environment that prevent such expression. If you consider it from the latter viewpoint, you are dealing in "limiting factors." It's all one and the same thing, but this approach is particularly helpful in visualizing the seasonal bottlenecks through which an animal population goes every year.

Let's set up a little problem on area X. To support a fall population of 50 rabbits it must have 100 units of winter cover, no more than 100 units of spring rainfall, no less than 100 units of woodchuck dens, no more than 100 units of cats and foxes, and not less than 100 units of the best rabbit foods. Our term "unit" covers nothing specific here; it is a theoretical quantity. We will say that this year the area fulfills all qualifications and the fall population is 50 rabbits.

For experimental purposes next year we will reduce winter cover to 80 units leaving all the other items as they are. Immediately winter cover becomes the bottleneck—the limiting factor—that reduces the rabbits to, say, 40. Leaving winter cover at 80 units, another year we will experimentally reduce food to 60 units. Now food becomes the key item, and it cuts down the population still lower, perhaps to 30. With food remaining at an index of 60 units, let's restore cover to 100 and see what happens.

It doesn't work. There still is food enough for only 30 rabbits and that's all we have. Let's up cats and foxes to an index of 110 and restore food to 100. Food is no longer the limiting factor and predation pressure has taken its place, allowing us 45 rabbits.

Evidently that's the way various factors operate in turn to restrict the expansion of a population. Of course, two factors brought to bear at once may have mutually inhibiting or compensating effects and the final result will be different than if either was working alone. As pointed out above, when the life requirements of an animal are in plentiful supply, a given environmental pinch may not be effective until numbers have reached a certain level. Fifty rabbits might be almost completely secure from fox predation in the cover pattern of a certain section of land, but if rabbits increased to 200 it might be possible for foxes to take 20 percent of the population. In this case, although predation appears to be the factor limiting the rabbit population, it does so within limits imposed by cover.

Weather extremes may have a similar relationship to the type and pattern of vegetation. Typical southwest Virginia grazing country is about half pasture, and the other half is equally divided between woodland and cropfields (corn-wheat-clover). It can be expected to carry a fall population of about 10 quail to the hundred acres. A five-year study showed winter losses averaging approximately 55 percent. This is poor range, with a marked shortage of winter cover.

Under these conditions carrying capacity varied from one winter to another in terms of weather. Losses of quail were directly related to the number of days during a season when the ground was covered with snow. It is to be expected that, as a favorable cover pattern is built up, the effects of weather will become less and less evident and winter may cease to be the season that limits numbers.

In south Texas, weather has a different effect on carrying capacity for the bobwhite and scaled quails. In spring the birds pair off, but few will nest unless there is rain to green-up the country. When drouth comes, quail are deprived of green foods and necessary amounts of vitamin A. They fail to breed, lose weight, and decline in numbers. Four times in 20 years, Valgene W. Lehmann, King Ranch biologist, saw south Texas overrun with quail, each time after two years of high rainfall. The birds practically disappeared in 1950-51, when a severe drouth was followed by a winter with freezing weather.

As these examples indicate, carrying capacity is a seasonal characteristic. It is the favorable conditions of summer that permit animals to breed and increase at that time. When something happens to reduce spring or summer below par, fall numbers decline. The same situation is described by Fearnow in pointing out that certain eastern trout streams "provide satisfactory conditions for trout during ten months of every year, but two months of low water and high temperatures plus recurring floods, create a bottleneck that restricts or destroys their usefulness."

Think about this and you'll see that one season out of the year *always* will be relatively less favorable than the others. It may be consistently so or it may be only "next worst" occasionally when things go bad at a different time of year.

For any particular species the squeeze period may vary also with different parts of the country: In the North, hard winters probably are the most important limitation to quail. Breeding season weather might be of first importance to pheasants. Move south and factors other than winter storms take first place for quail. Pheasants are eliminated altogether for reasons as yet only partially explained.

In primitive times, gray squirrels that inhabited northern lake states and Canada were nearly all of the black phase. Southward, the early hunters began to get grays, until in southern Illinois, Indiana, and Ohio nearly all of these squirrels were of the gray phase. Don't ask why. It was all one species, but northern forests could support more blacks than the southern ones and the latter were better for grays.

It is evident that the habits and characteristics of a species are directly related to habitat carrying capacity. Mobility is particularly important in this respect. It is possible that a cottontail might find all of its life requirements within an acre of land. A bobwhite in good range will need only a few acres. But in the rugged benches and ridges of the semi-arid Southwest, scaled quail ("cottontops") are believed to have a daily range averaging about three miles.

We will find later that in improving habitats we are much concerned with bringing the essentials for survival into closest possible association. This reduces the area necessary to support an individual or group and thereby increases carrying capacity.

SOCIAL WHIRL

A logical question might arise here: Just what happens when limiting factors have been reduced, one by one, until a species has practically achieved a Utopian "freedom from fear." Some of the examples of overpopulated islands cited in the last chapter give a clue to this. Social intolerances within the species itself are likely to become the limitation. In fact they may be important in ordinary population densities.

Have you ever driven through pheasant country in spring and seen two cock birds fighting in a hillside pasture? The chances are good that those birds have clashed on an imaginary line separating the "territory" of one male bird from another.

Most species of birds and many mammals are "territorial." This is a habit pattern that may be an important limitation to the number of individuals an area will support. The most common and recognizable type of territoriality is that of birds on their nesting grounds. Typically a male establishes exclusive rights to an area of a size and nature peculiar to his species and proceeds to defend this claim against trespass by all other males. He will sing and display to attract a mate, and ordinarily the female will nest and young will be reared within the defended territory.

The territory of a cock pheasant is called his "crowing area," for good reasons, and woe betide the wandering male who enters the claim of an established early comer. Probably most hens nest in the territory of the cock in charge and the management frowns on their being cordial with intruders. It is obvious that these birds will tolerate only so much crowding during the nesting season, as far as actual territories are concerned, although individual males may rise manfully to the occasion and expand the family circle to include 8 or 10 hens when the market is favorable.

A few years after pheasants were introduced to Protection Island (p. 29) they had reached an almost unheard-of abundance and cocks actually exceeded the hens in number. Winter losses were light and predation averaged less than 9 percent of the total population in a year. The birds were healthy and egg fertility was more than 92 percent. Adult pheasants were nearly immune to many of the ordinary causes of mortality.

Under these conditions a high loss of eggs and chicks developed. Normal social (territorial) relationships were badly disarranged. Nesting hens were molested by the excessive numbers of cocks, many nests were abandoned, and dropped eggs and community nests were common.

It is probable that a social intolerance of crowding explains the fact that in seven years of study on Minnesota ruffed grouse, breeding numbers never exceeded a bird per four acres. This in spite of the fact that October populations varied markedly for individual years. Ralph T. King, who carried on this intensive piece of research, took October and April inventories which gave figures for the annual fall maximum and the breeding population that followed. On a non-hunted, 1800-acre tract of good range he found the following numbers in birds per hundred acres:

Year	October	April
1931	29	
1932	41.6	24.6
1933	55.2	25.2
1934		25.1

Regardless of how many birds entered the winter on this area, there was one per four acres as a spring breeding stock. This is obviously another expression of carrying capacity, and King accepts it as the maximum that ruffed grouse can be expected to attain in that region. Although there was no precise evidence as to just how the population was shaken down to this level, the most likely explanation was "intolerance of greater crowding or the exercise of individual territorial rights."

On British grouse moors it has long been recognized that old male birds are most aggressive and establish larger territories than young cocks. Hence the deliberate reduction of old cocks in favor of young ones has been a part of management on such areas.

Population pressures seem to exist almost universally among wild animals, and this guarantees the rapid spread of a species to all accessible range. This is evident in the rapidity with which new animals move into tracts where a species has been shot-out or otherwise reduced below the level of adjacent areas. A population seems to "percolate" through a region like water through a sandy soil, seeking its level with relation to barriers (limiting factors) and the "absorptive" quality (carrying capacity) of individual habitats.

This implies that the pressure within a population probably is occasioned by animals that are poorly situated, and in some cases perhaps even wandering, for want of a place to settle down. Such pressure is built up through annual overproduction in the breeding period, and there is some lag in the whittling-down of numbers to carrying capacity. That, of course, is the level where most individuals would be comparatively secure. The reduction probably is seldom complete or security absolute; but since poorly situated individuals run about the same chances every year, survival tends to be uniform from year to year for a particular habitat.

Biologists have long known that their researches on mass phenomena are most effectively rewarded when they can study populations of small animals, in which large numbers can be dealt with and changes are of short duration. Just such a situation can be cited in a study of birds as a control agent of spruce budworms in a Maine forest. Many of the points we have made show up graphically in this one experiment.

For two years in June and July, breeding songbirds were censused and then an attempt made to shoot them entirely out of a 40-acre area. Budworms were being counted to learn the result of bird reduction. How the bird population reacted to the killing-off has significant implications.

In the first place, it was found practically impossible to reduce birds much below 80 percent of their original numbers. New individuals steadily moved into the vacated habitat. As a result of the shooting, no young birds were reared on the tract in 1949, yet in 1950 approximately equal numbers of essentially the same (migratory) species were found there, and male birds even established themselves in the *same territories* as their deceased predecessors of the year before.

It seems to mean that there were population pressures in all these species which caused any unoccupied living space to be filled-in quickly. It indicates also that this unit of range possessed features, recognizable to birds, which permitted it to support consistent numbers of particular species and which caused a population, eliminated one year, to be nearly duplicated the next.

There is order and there are measured quantities in the woods—which presage that in the fullness of time ecology (the study of relationships) may become a more exact science.

FAVORED FEW

Carrying capacity may have its most important effect by influencing productivity of breeding stocks of various sizes. In a given area, as the number of breeders increases, the production and survival of their offspring is proportionately reduced—a relationship sometimes referred to as "inversity." This is not true as long as a population is far below "normal" stocking, but after a reasonable build-up it seems to hold.

A good example of this was recorded in Iowa after the hard winter of 1936-37 had killed a large part of the quail population. On a study area of several thousand acres, breeding stock in the spring of 1937 was only about one bird per 86 acres. The spring was favorable and each pair of birds nested under practically non-competitive conditions. By fall the population had increased by a whopping 457 percent.

In the spring of 1938 the surviving breeding stock was up to about one bird per 16 acres, but in spite of favorable weather conditions again, the season's increase dropped off to 183 percent.

Once more a mild winter permitted a large number of breeders to come through, and by May 1939 there was a quail for every 6 acres—which is a heavy breeding population. Under these conditions, the birds were able to achieve only an 84 percent build-up by fall.

It appears that as successively larger breeding stocks produced more young, limitations of the environment were asserted and reduced the proportion that could survive.

This same sort of thing appears to occur in pheasants, as indicated by an Iowa study in progress at the same time as the above quail work. On a tract of several thousand acres there was a sex ratio of 3 hens to 1 cock and a population of 25 birds per section in the spring of 1936. By fall, numbers had increased to about 100 pheasants per section. The following spring there were 60 breeders per section with a sex ratio of 2 to 1, but fall populations still were from 100 to 125 birds to the section of land. In the breeding season of 1937 another increase took place, with 70 birds and a sex ratio of 1 to 1. Fall production was the same as the year before.

Neither changes in the numbers of breeders nor changes in the ratio of cocks to hens did much to alter the fall maximum that this population could reach. It appears that during those years the land could carry 100 to 125 pheasants on 640 acres as an annual peak and that there were more breeders than necessary both in 1936 and 1937.

The operation of the carrying-capacity limitation is clear in a table given by Overton representing the reproduction of quail on the Virginia Polytechnic Institute farms at Blacksburg. For 4 years, the number of breeders and resulting fall populations were as follows:

Year	Birds per 100 acres		Percent of increase
	Spring	Fall	
1937	4.3	12.7	195
1947	3.0	10.7	257
1948	2.2	10.7	394
1949	5.1	11.4	120

Although in 1937 and 1949 the number of breeders was much greater than in 1948, fall populations were only slightly larger. Any one of these breeding stocks was capable of producing more young than could be supported by this habitat, and fall numbers were reduced to about the same point every year regardless of the size of the surplus. This meant that the percent of increase was greatest for the smallest number of breeders and least for the biggest breeding stock.

All of which brings up an interesting question: Could we, for our own amazement, deliberately shoot down a spring breeding stock and witness a "compensatory" increase in productivity as Nature tried to restore numbers to the carrying-capacity level? They tried it during the long-continued studies of ruffed grouse in New York, and the answer is, it works.

On 777 acres, the birds remaining after fall shooting were hunted persistently during the winter and reduced to a low level. One complication to the test was that more breeding stock filtered into the shot-out habitat in the spring. But in what can be called a "moderately sparse" breeding stock, the percentage of annual increase was con-

sistently higher than in a check area where there was no artificial re
duction of breeders. For three years the percentages of increase were:

	Normal breeding stock	*Reduced breeding stock*
1935	19%	100%
1936	84%	116%
1937	130%	161%

This study was made at a time when grouse were beginning to recover from the cyclic reduction—hence the progressive increase in annual production on both areas.

Frank C. Edminster, who reported on this work, concluded that
". . . definite substance supports the contention that as populations
approach the range carrying capacity, their productivity declines."

Reducing a population has the same effect as creating a larger
range for the survivors. In either case expansion immediately follows.
This has given rise to the apt expression that "Nature abhors a vac-
uum." It's a good thought and a truth for which we can be thankful.

LIFE QUANTITIES IN WATER

The fish specialist has some important advantages over the man
who works with birds and mammals. At least in some cases he deals
with environments having well-defined limits, and he knows that the
life they contain will not wander away or cross certain boundaries.

The carrying capacity of water areas frequently can be measured
accurately. For the most part the *amount* of life a pond, lake or stream
can support depends upon dissolved nutrients (call it fertility or food
supply). The *rate* at which those nutrients are converted from one
form of life to another (i.e. fish production) depends upon temperatures and the amount of sunlight that penetrates the water. There is
a "life reaction" in the water that speeds up as you increase the temperature of the system and slows down as you cool it off. Since sunlight governs the total energy budget for the year, in waters of equal
fertility the annual fish crop increases with the length of the growing
season. An Illinois biologist calculated fish yields in terms of percentage of carrying capacity for seven localities from Vilas County, Wisconsin, to New Orleans. The variation progressed from 21 percent in
the north to 118 percent in the south.

Just to visualize the food situation in simple form, put a 10-inch bass in an aquarium, standardize the temperature at 70° F., and start weighing out his food. You will find that this bass will maintain weight if fed three fourths of one percent of his weight in minnows every day. If you want him to show maximum gain, it will be necessary to feed about 3.5 to 4 percent of his weight in minnows daily. More than this will largely go to waste at 70°, but he can use more and grow faster if you increase the temperature (that's the reason for the out-size Florida bass). If minnows are fed to this bass at optimum rate, it takes 2.5 pounds of them to add a pound to our experimental fish. If you take all food away, the bass uses its own tissues to operate its body machinery and loses a half of one percent of its weight per day.

You are not likely to carry out this experiment; but you won't need to since it was done, reliably, by D. H. Thompson at the Illinois Natural History Survey. It illustrates the fact that life is measured out *in pounds* in the water and that production depends upon the input of food and the rate at which it is utilized.

In natural waters the energy of the sun powers a reaction in plants (mostly the microscopic algae that make water green) to convert dissolved minerals and carbon dioxide into more plants. These are consumed by small animals which are eaten by bigger animals which go to feed such practical animals as bass.

If you cut off sunlight, the whole business stops. In fact, prolonged periods without sunlight will reverse the process. This comes about in winters when snow covers the ice of northern lakes. Then plants die and decompose. They stop giving off oxygen, the processes of decay use up oxygen, and fish die. That's the source of our well-known "winter kill." Lakes that are deep and have a big volume of water and less organic matter will come through much better than shallow lakes where oxygen is depleted quickly.

Modern fishpond management is approaching the status of an exact science because it has been possible to measure carrying capacity accurately and control it precisely.

In the course of the work in Alabama by Swingle and Smith it was found that in one growing season unfertilized ponds of this particular area yielded approximately 100 pounds of bluegills per acre regardless of how many fry were stocked in spring. For example, two similar ponds were stocked in May—one with 26,000 fry (per acre) weighing 2 pounds 5 ounces, and the other with 13,000 larger fish weighing 180 pounds. The following November the ponds were drained and fish weighed. The first pond contained 105 pounds of fish per acre: a gain of 103 pounds. The second pond yielded 92 pounds per acre: a *loss* of 88 pounds.

A single pond of 1.8 acres, two years in a row, gave the following results: In February 1935 it was stocked with 4,485 young fish of several species weighing approximately 41 pounds. That fall the yield was 293 pounds. The following year only 236 fish weighing 24 pounds were stocked, but the November take was 296 pounds—practically the same as the year before. In fishponds carrying capacity can be determined with certainty. Proper fertilization, of course, immediately increases it and results in a greater yield of fish.

A fact we need to appreciate fully is that carrying capacity adjustments take place practically from year to year both in the case of dry-land species and for life in the water. For example, Lake Senachwine in Illinois has an area of about 6,000 acres when the water is up, and it has a standing population of bass, crappies, bluegills, and similar species totalling 50 to 55 pounds per acre. Drouth may shrink this lake to 3,000 acres in a single year, but the fish population shrinks with the water area and is maintained at the same per-acre poundage, expanding again when the level goes up. In impounded waters this "draw-down" technique is being increasingly used as a cure for overpopulation and stunting—one of the most common reasons for poor fishing. Reducing the water area cuts down the numbers of fish, and reflooding promotes an immediate and rapid growth in the survivors.

In Michigan the growth rate of fish was studied in four lakes after a winter with prolonged snow had brought heavy mortality under the ice. During the year following the die-off, nearly all species in the thinned-out populations of the four lakes showed a marked increase in growth rate. The more rapid growth of individuals tended to compensate for reduction in number and hastened the return of the standing poundage of fish to what the particular water could support. In this case what looked like calamity undoubtedly helped make a generation of big fish available to fishermen. The increase in growth rate was perceptible for only one season. After that, other generations of young fish undoubtedly entered the food-competition picture and growth rates declined to normal.

The strictly limited carrying capacity of bodies of water in terms of pounds of fish per acre implies endless possibilities for shifting that poundage from one species to another. Lake Senachwine showed recurring adjustments of this kind. There were years when 90 percent of game fish in the lake were black crappies, and in other years the white crappie and bluegill would be predominant—but the weight of fish remained about the same.

In his discussion of Illinois lakes, Thompson makes a point that should be understood by everyone interested in growing a crop of fish. He notes that it takes about five pounds of food (in the wild) to make one pound of fish and that it is desirable to convert water fertility by the most direct route possible into fish we want to catch: "From this standpoint it is bad practice to introduce forage species for the sole purpose of feeding game fish. It is much better to use a fish with a high reproductive rate and a long spawning season, such as the bluegill, which will furnish good fishing when it grows too large for game fish to swallow." Many a stocking project undoubtedly has worked directly against the interests of the sportsman.

Implications of the carrying capacity principle lead naturally to the proposition that we have large quantities of carp, buffalo, dogfish, gar and other rough fish in many waters, and that these species are *taking the place* of substantial populations of more desirable game fish. For the sportsman it would obviously be much better to have rough fish replaced by bass, walleyes, pike, and bluegills.*

That is a common situation, and rough fish tend to get the upper hand by increasing turbidity (which reduces sunlight and hence vegetation) and by virtue of their higher reproductive rates. The latter characteristic also makes it well-nigh impossible to get rid of them by such means as trapping and seining. A 25-pound female carp from Iowa's Lake Okoboji was found to contain 6 pounds of eggs—a total of more than 1,700,000!

The carp has another advantage in competing with game fish. This Asian (*not* German) species is a bottom feeder and takes small animal life and plant debris directly. That is, it eliminates all those steps

* As we will see, however, carrying capacities are comparable, pound for pound, only in the case of fish with similar food habits.

in the "food chain" that nutrients must go through before they can be converted into carnivorous fish like bass. Hence, available food materials that would be tied up in intermediate stages in a bass lake *go directly into carp* in a carp pond. This eliminates a large poundage of small creatures and increases the carrying capacity for carp far beyond what it would be for game fish.

Mixed fish populations in nine Illinois lakes averaged 600 pounds per acre, of which game fish made up about 10 percent. But in lakes with only game fish (including sunfish, etc.) these species aggregated from 200 to 300 pounds per acre. And in lakes populated exclusively by such fish as carp and buffalo, carrying capacity was around 1,000 pounds per acre.

THE FORAGE USERS

The foregoing discussion of carrying capacity has dealt with situations in which the numbers of animals are directly and definitely limited from year to year by conditions on land or in water. In general the situation is somewhat different for large, hoofed animals which feed directly on vegetation. Obviously, unless limited by something, any population of herbage-eating animals could multiply to a point of completely destroying the plants upon which it lives. Under primitive conditions natural enemies of such species undoubtedly kept their numbers within bounds and prevented this, since any concentration of individuals immediately became particularly vulnerable to predation.

Carrying capacity of big-game range, which frequently is limited by the amount of winter forage present, can be measured in much the same way it is calculated for domestic stock. And, also like domestic grazing animals, various species exist in competition with one another when they use the same food supply.

For example, the northern Yellowstone range is being used by five species of big game. As a rough comparison of forage requirements, one buffalo is about equal to two elk, and one elk is the equivalent of two deer, or two antelope, or two bighorn sheep.

In 1949 there were approximately 9,500 elk, 400 antelope, 400 bison (buffalo), 500 deer, and 200 bighorns using this range, which adds up to roughly 10,850 elk-units of big game. For the different species the elk units were as follows: elk—9,500, bison—800, deer—

250, antelope—200, bighorns—100. By such a yardstick it is evident that the elk of this area are using a large share of annual forage growth, and that the position of mountain sheep is particularly unfavorable. The between-species management problem was expressed by Walter H. Kittams of the Park Service at the Absaroka Conservation Committee meeting in the spring of 1949:

"These figures clearly show how the elk exceeds all others in competitive forage requirements. We do feel that these other animals are an essential part of the fauna of Yellowstone and that the northern range should be maintained so that all of the species have the opportunity for a natural existence. The bighorns have declined. There are numerous factors involved, it seems, in actual control of herd size; but a great deal of it appears traceable to range. And it is a known fact that bighorns cannot compete successfully with elk—the elk are much more versatile. Bighorns seem rather finicky about the particular species of plants that they will eat. One can go down on Coal Mine Flat and often see elk and bighorns close together in critical areas. Bighorns are not animals to get out in deep snow—they remain on the steeper, exposed slopes. This relationship, where we have only one bighorn unit to 95 elk, shows how hopelessly he is outnumbered."

This situation has been brought about by the elimination of important natural enemies and the failure, in establishing the park, to include adequate year-around range for big-game herds. At the time of Lewis and Clark it was to some extent true that the wolf and cougar allowed the grass to grow. We will examine this situation further in a later chapter.

CARRYING CAPACITY

The carrying-capacity principle is a reiteration of the well-known adage that you can't get something for nothing. It asserts that two rabbits do not occupy the same space at the same time. Any animal—man, mouse, or amoeba—needs a certain amount of a given quality of range to exist in health and beget its kind. A given set of conditions produces not only certain species, but also given *numbers* of individuals. Populations seek their levels, and adjustments take place rapidly, provided only that there are a few breeders capable of reproducing themselves.

We have laid some emphasis on the fact that under similar conditions small breeding stocks show a greater rate of increase than large ones. A few breeders have leeway to expand up to a point where the environment is fully stocked. A large number of breeders produce far more young than can possibly survive and these are cut down to fit the habitat. A sudden improvement in range means that the wearing away of numbers for that year will not be so drastic, and the result will be a higher population.

In his work on the grouse, King found that the new generation of young were reduced by 75 percent (starting with eggs) by October and the adults by 10 percent in the same period. He pointed out that if some means could be found to increase survival of young by just *one bird per brood,* this would result in a boost of the hunting-season population by 57 percent!

It is such possibilities as this that pose the great challenge to the wildlife manager. He sees these great tools at his disposal, and he sees the almost hopeless futility of any other approach; since every year Nature is doing an imposing job of *mass overstocking* that comes to nothing in the face of that aggregation of limitations that we call carrying capacity.

Now that we have taken this power-packed mechanism apart to see how it works, we are ready to look into practical ways of using it to obtain our object of bigger wildlife crops.

CHAPTER 5

The Management Strategy

To many a sportsman the term "range improvement" is becoming somewhat irksome. It may well seem that everything he suggests to professional wildlife men is brushed aside with the answer that the real solution is to develop better conditions on the land. This is especially true where progress has been best and management has been most scientific.

One of the reasons why habitat development may be difficult to visualize is that we seldom get exactly the same story twice. And that, in turn, derives from the fact that any one job of improvement depends upon a list of conditions that can vary in many different ways. We are not suspicious of mathematics because different problems usually have different answers. We know that there are definable rules by which anyone who wants to work on it can learn to get the proper result.

Actually, such rules are developing in wildlife management. They lack perfection, but the method is here to stay, and even in the rough the principles make sense and give results. To anyone who takes the trouble to get them in hand, the talk of game and fish biologists will no longer be an abstract mumbo-jumbo. A sportsman should be prepared to criticize people who work for him, but his criticism should not be of specific measures unless he understands the pros and cons of the logic behind them. Any judgment of a scientist should be upon how well he applies the scientific method. Since science is exact knowledge, results themselves will tell in the end.

The two foregoing chapters aimed to demonstrate that animal populations have an innate tendency to expand and that environments contain this force at high or low levels depending on whether they are favorable or unfavorable. This mechanism has evident possibilities as a means of increasing or decreasing animal numbers, and for that reason it is the obvious approach for the wildlife manager. A full appreciation of these basic relationships was in the background when, as early as 1929, Leopold made this statement in a report of the Committee on American Wild Life Policy: "If there is any breeding stock at all, the *one and only thing we can do to raise a crop of game is to make the environment more favorable.* This is a mathematical axiom, and holds true for all classes of game at all times and places. It is the fundamental truth which the conservation movement must learn if it is to attain its objective."

Obviously, this proposition is something to be examined carefully.

WILL IT WORK?

In discussions of habitat improvement the question frequently is heard: "Will it really work? Where can I find a clear-cut example of the effects of environmental change?"

The answer is that it always has worked and examples are all about us. The most convincing evidence of the effectiveness of the method is historical in character and occurs on a vast scale. For some reason, these widespread changes do not seem to be so satisfactory for some people as limited, deliberate demonstrations on a few thousand acres. So, in this and the next chapter we will sample both kinds of information.

A climatologist or plant ecologist would look at a rainfall map of the United States and deduce immediately that precipitation in the eastern third of the country should permit the land to support forest vegetation. And that is what the first settlers found there, although the prairies fingered eastward into southern Michigan and northern Ohio, into large park-like openings in Kentucky and Tennessee, and across the "Black Belt" of Alabama.

In northeastern United States, the last glacial recession took place from about 17,000 to 7,000 years ago. Following which, climatic fluctuations continued, and during dry phases the grasslands of the prairie region were extended eastward. In times of higher rainfall, forests closed the easternmost openings and encroached westward toward the plains.

East of the Mississippi, fires of natural or Indian origin and browsing by buffalo and other hoofed animals helped hold back woody vegetation from land that climatically could have supported it. But when Indian and buffalo finally were eliminated, and the Kentucky-

Tennessee country became less "dark and bloody," trees moved rapidly into the western openings. Woodlands sprang up where plows could not turn the land and make clearings permanent. This also occurred to south and north, but agriculture and open fields spread wherever soil was suitable and in some places where it was not. Originally, about half of continental United States had been covered with forest—slightly more than a billion acres. The forest area now is roughly 624 million acres, of which only about 45 million acres can be said to approach the primitive condition.

In large part, hardwoods were destroyed to clear land; in the North, big business lumbering took the great pineries progressively from watersheds of the Kennebec and Androscoggin in Maine west to prairie fringes of Northern Minnesota.

This was mass habitat change; and many birds and mammals built up, died out, or flowed hither and yon in the wake of it. Particularly affected were those species we now speak of as "farm game." They require brush, trees, and openings, and once they lived on the forest edges.

Frank Forester, a knowing observer of the early 19th century, was quick to perceive what was happening. Many birds and mammals were declining, but this was not the whole story:

"Other species of game, so far from flying cultivation, or abhorring the vicinity of civilized man, are literally not to be found except where the works of the ox and the man are conspicuous; never being seen at all in the wilderness proper, and giving cause for some speculation as to their whereabouts, their haunts, their habits, if not their existence on the continent, previous to the arrival of civilized man, from realms nearer [sic] to the sun.

"Neither the Woodcock nor the Quail . . . are ever found in the depths of the untamed forest, aloof from human habitations; although both genera frequent, nay require, woodland . . . for their habitation. Moreover, in places where they are entirely unknown to the first settlers, where they do not in fact exist at all, they speedily become abundant, so soon as the axe levels the umbrageous forest, and the admitted sunbeams awaken or mature the germs of that animal or vegetable life, on which the birds subsist."

In low grassy glades and marsh edges the woodcock had seasonally made its home; the transition zone between prairie and woodland was the primitive range of cottontail, fox squirrel, and quail. But the "umbrageous" forest had so dominated the region to the east that all such species were few and inconspicuous. As clearings were made, they extended their holdings, and they reached high densities because cover and food were plentiful. We should keep in mind also that the soils which bore the outsize game crops of yesteryear were at their all-time best. Changes since have been largely for the worse.

While we are at it, there may be profit in pointing out that conversion of the wilderness to agriculture built a habitat in which a later generation of hunters would find it possible to introduce the pheasant successfully. It is unlikely that pheasants could have survived anywhere in the country prior to the advent of grain farming. As late as 1916, in spite of repeated stocking, only a scattering of the China birds were to be found in California's Sacramento Valley. But, with the introduction of rice raising at that time, they built up to such densities that the valley is now one of the most productive pheasant areas in the nation. Obviously, rice and what went with it (e.g. alfalfa) constituted successful habitat management.

Eventually, the farm-game species that had spread over thousands of square miles of newly created range encountered another trend—clean farming. The habitual free ranging of cattle and hogs in forest areas continued as the grazing of woodlots. By sheer momentum, the steel-bitted American ax, finest implement of its kind, kept swinging with hair-line precision—on light soils, steep slopes, stream banks, and many another site that should have retained its protecting mantle of woody growth.

The clean-farming urge was a psychological *coup de grace*, a final kick in the pants, that the farmer gave the forest which once had hemmed him in. It was explained in other ways, of course, but the truth was that Americans in the eastern forest area developed a bare-soil complex. Brush was unsightly and the only good tree was a sawlog. By the strength of his arms the pioneer started the job, and in his capacity to beget more of the breed he finished it. The impulse to "clear the land" developed an impetus that keeps it going to this day. In addition, apart from this clean-farm folkway, agricultural developments have been largely toward greater intensity.

For the turkey, ruffed grouse, and gray squirrel the clearing of the hardwoods and settlement of the land were management in reverse. They dwindled and disappeared, and with them went other forest species such as the deer, bear, bobcat, gray fox, panther, and wolf. Limited cutting would have favored all of them; but they could not live where the landscape became dominantly farms, cut up by roads, and where even swamps and marshes were drained and pastured.

Early lumbering operations, carried out on areas that were to have a forest destiny, brought about great and evident shifts in wildlife populations. As the logger moved on, the slash he left became the tinder for fires that devastated huge areas of the North. Repeated burning left plains of sod and bracken dotted with the blackened stumps of pines from which no living seed survived. From the prairies of Wisconsin and Minnesota, the prairie chicken and sharptail spread north and east into a new habitat.

By the late thirties these birds were being hunted in openings the length of Michigan's Upper Peninsula, but more changes were under way. Years of drought permitted the aspens to take over dried-out marshes. Good fire protection allowed "popples" and birch, fire cherry and sweetfern to march out across the openings. Where this took place, the prairie chicken declined. For a time sharptails would increase with the brush, but as the forest margin closed in, they too disappeared.

There was another factor: The openings were easy to furrow and cheap to plant with pines. Many a productive grouse range was obliterated in reforestation work by the CCC and other agencies during the depression period.

Most foresters now recognize the game yield as a co-product with sawlogs and plan their operations accordingly. In northern Michigan people saw that openings must be saved if chicken hunting was to remain a sport for them. It also became evident that controlled fire was one of the few economic ways to keep land clear, but there was much to be learned about it.

Deer showed the most spectacular increase of all as brush-stage forests developed. They had been nearly absent from extensive stretches of mature timber. What was a common condition across the North was understood and ably described by a taxidermist in northern Minnesota:

"The Ponsford region, abounding as it does in lakes, prairie land

and heavy timber, has always been a veritable paradise for wild game. However, the white-tailed deer, the favorite sport of the huntsman today, did not inhabit the regions in early days as the old-time Indians affirm, but lived more in the southern part of the state. With the advance of white civilization, the deer steadily moved north. In fact, our big thick timber with its lack of underbrush to serve as food supply and protection, would not have been a congenial habitat for the deer."

Cut-over timber land has shown this upsurge of deer in nearly every section of the country. Details will be left to a later chapter, but here we need to recognize that large-scale modification of habitat brought about these wildlife changes. We have spoken of them as "historic," but some still are going on. The woodchuck had lived on the edges of rocky forest openings in the Northeast, and it multiplied with the hayfields. Only since 1900 it has spread southward from Pennsylvania into Maryland's eastern shore. In the same period the opossum has moved north and occupied southern Michigan—it seems to prosper there, in spite of the fact that, almost invariably, the tip of the tail and outer half of the ears of a young animal freeze back and slough off in its first winter.

A look at the past bears witness that both the betterment and deterioration of ranges is immediately effective in changing the numbers of wild animals. The result is plainly visible when such alterations are widespread. On a small scale they are obscure and difficult to measure, and that is why we have so few planned demonstrations. Nevertheless, experimental evidence also is accumulating. Action management programs will involve methods tailored to fit specific situations. But to approach this intelligently calls for understanding of some fundamentals that we already have touched upon without full recognition.

PLANTS THAT SUCCEED

Almost anywhere a piece of soil is laid bare and then left alone, there will be an orderly sequence of plant communities that, with the passage of years, will invade it and be replaced. For most parts of the country this *succession* of vegetation types is to some extent understood and predictable. The last stage of development, or "climax," in a region is capable of renewing itself indefinitely. In theory, it should be able to hold on until the climate undergoes a change; then a different climax might appear.

Plant succession is an almost universal phenomenon that comes into nearly any plan for managing wildlife on the land. It means that practically anything we plant is going to be invaded and displaced by something else and that some sort of "maintenance" will be necessary if, for instance, an herb or shrub stage is what we want in a region of forest climax.

To take an example, if we laid bare the soil of a fairly level till plain in glaciated southern Michigan, we might expect the succession of plant communities to be about as follows:

The first year, seeds that might have been dormant in the soil for years would germinate and the bare earth would be covered quickly with such annual weeds as ragweed, lamb's quarters, redroot, tumbleweed, panic grass, and yellow and green foxtail. Incidentally, this initial stage may produce two or three hundred pounds of seed per acre and most of it is excellent food for many birds and mammals.

The second year some of the annuals would appear again, but with succeeding growing seasons they would die out and be replaced with perennial weeds such as goldenrod, aster, fleabane, bergamot, St. John's wort, and various sod grasses. These in turn would be invaded and give way before dewberry, blackberry, raspberry, and nightshade. Then, among the briars, a more permanent vegetation, the shrub and small-tree stage, would begin to appear and thicken with each passing year. Prominent species very likely would be sassafras, elder, cherry, grape, and hazelnut. As these matured, seedlings of elm, soft maple, ash, hornbeam, oak, and hickory would become evident and gradually shade out the shrub community.

If the site and soil were well drained, especially a bit on the dry side, the chances are good that it would come to support a woodland dominated by several species of oak and hickory. Flowering dogwood and shadbush probably would be prominent in the understory. This forest type might be preserved for hundreds, or even thousands, of years by conditions of soil or slope that were too dry for what is generally recognized as the true climax. Since in this area there is another stage, the oak-hickory type would be considered a "subclimax."

Starting with the open water of a lake, another successional series would appear as the lake was filled in by silt and plant material. Then the site would go through sedge-marsh and bog-shrub stages until it was taken over by a lowland forest dominated by such trees as red maple, elm, black ash, and swamp white oak. This also would be a subclimax dependent on conditions that were *too wet* for the climax.

But the oak-hickory woodland would gradually become more moist due to the accumulation of humus in the soil, and lowland woods would be built up and dried out from the same process. When both attained a suitable moisture condition—an intermediate situation toward which all sites tend to develop in the course of centuries—they would be invaded by beech and hard maple, which would characterize the climax forest. In such a woodland we would be likely to find also basswood, white ash, red and white oak, cherry, shagbark hickory, and tulip tree (in southernmost Michigan). The dominants in this association can reproduce in their own shade and thus the type is perpetuated.

This is a telescoped view of plant succession in one area. Elsewhere the stages and final climax would be different. Vegetation types are everywhere mixed by variations of water supply and drainage. Woodlands follow well-watered bottoms out across the prairies, but in the upland woody plants cannot compete and are robbed of water by the grasses, which become dominant. On dry plains, when adapted grasses are destroyed by too-heavy grazing, certain shrubs may spread and take over large areas. Sagebrush and mesquite now dominate horizons where they were nearly or wholly absent a century ago.

Fire in the wrong place has long been recognized as one of the great enemies of mankind. The destructiveness of a crown fire in the pines has been demonstrated repeatedly in many sections of the country. Yet it has been observable in some areas that hardwoods sprouted vigorously following a burn (most conifers do not, but must seed in again), and game populations built up to greater densities. Fire set the succession back to early stages, and certain animals were a part of these stages. The study of burning as a wildlife management tool was an obvious development.

This idea was not entirely new. On the moors of Scotland it had long been recognized that heather, in which the red grouse thrives, is a second stage in the succession—it follows an initial growth of grass, bracken, or moss. Game keepers learned to maintain the heather by careful burning.

In southern states of this country, burning had been the means, since primitive times, of establishing pine woodlands on the land. On many soils pines were the first trees to occupy land laid bare by cultivation or burning. A slow ground fire, properly controlled, exposed spots of bare soil to seeding and did negligible damage to older trees. It prevented the development of dense tangles of brush and briars, stimulated the growth of legumes, and left good quail range in its wake. Herbert L. Stoddard studied and refined the technique of burning and was using it in operational quail management in the twenties.

With help by the Conservation Department, certain northern Michigan hunting clubs were improving deer ranges by burning in the late thirties. In 1940, with the problem of controlling successions for grouse and deer before him, Ben C. Jenkins began a three-year study of the history and plant cover of the state's northern burns. He reached several significant conclusions: To maintain desirable openings, such areas should be burned over every five to ten years, either in late fall or early spring. Light burns in woody cover increased not only sprout growth but (probably through the quick availability of plant-ash fertilizer and reduction of acidity) legumes and the fruit crops of shrubs. Fires also eliminated debris that made logged areas almost inaccessible to hunters and they served to open up the second-growth of hardwoods that otherwise formed undesirable solid stands. The burning of oaks was not recommended, since it takes fifteen to twenty years for them to reach mast-bearing age.

Burning and block cutting will be much involved in controlling plant successions in forest-game lands. Fire will not be useful everywhere, of course; you can burn a northern Michigan sand plain, but on a Pennsylvania mountain fire would be difficult to control. Whatever the means of attaining the condition,* it is evident that early successional stages support the greatest amount and variety of wildlife, and a perpetual program of maintenance will be necessary to preserve

* The Pennsylvania Game Commission has employed bulldozers to create openings and early successions in grown-up forest areas. They find that no method will work where over-numerous deer wipe out sprout growth as fast as it appears.

the age pattern of vegetation that will mean satisfactory game yields. Like all wildlife management that is carried out on a scale great enough to be important, these operations must be incorporated in every possible way into a primary use of the land—in this case forestry.

On natural grasslands it is readily observable that certain rodents and rabbits are creatures of early successions. These are weed stages, and the animals that go with them have been referred to realistically as "animal weeds." What happened to a prairie-dog colony on the Wichita Mountains Wildlife Refuge is an excellent example of plant-animal succession. It also illustrates how "biological control" of a range rodent was accomplished by conservative land use.

Land now in the refuge was taken over by the Biological Survey from the Forest Service in 1935, and two years later grazing permits were terminated. The heavily-grazed range was permitted to recover under relatively light use by refuge herds of bison, longhorns, and various game animals.

When the refuge was established there were several active prairie-dog colonies. One of these, the Grace Mountain town, was designated to be preserved in its natural condition without any "control." Colonies near the edge of the area were eradicated, and others were partially poisoned at intervals.

In 1946 it was discovered that vegetation on the relatively undisturbed land around the Grace Mountain town had returned to practically its original tall-grass prairie condition. It also was found that the prairie dogs had failed to thrive and were rapidly vanishing from the scene—something that actually happened a year later.

A mile distant from this town, bison had concentrated on a bench occupied by the Baker's Peak prairie-dog colony. This town was partially poisoned with "1080" in 1946, but the remaining animals continued to thrive, as did other similarly treated colonies that were in areas heavily used by big game. It was plain enough that plant succession had destroyed the Grace Mountain town.

As they gained experience, biologists have learned that the march of plant-animal communities across a given site is something they must understand and be able to predict. It is involved in managing wildlife in every type of land and many kinds of water. The nature of inland and coastal marshes can be changed radically by slight alterations in water level. New, and often inferior, vegetation types frequently take over large marshes a season or two after they, or other nearby lands, are ditched for mosquito control or to improve grazing. If the planner of such operations knows plant succession and the habitat relationships of muskrats, waterfowl, and other involved species, he frequently can protect wildlife values or at least salvage a part of what might be lost. The results of ignorance in this field are all about us.

DESIGNS ON THE LAND

Habitat improvement consists in bringing into useful association those conditions needed by a species for reproduction and survival.

In the case of a migratory bird like the blue-winged teal, the essentials in its existence might be scattered well over the continent. For a pair of these ducks a prairie slough with a fringe of marsh, somewhere in Alberta or Saskatchewan, might be exactly right for rearing the annual brood. On the migration south there should be stop-over waters and marshes down through the central prairie region or the Mississippi Valley. These way stations would need to afford reasonable protection from weather and enemies and a sufficient supply of favored foods, especially the pondweeds, sedges, and smartweeds, and such animal life as insects and molluscs. The wintering area of this pair and their brood might be the Laguna Coyuca, in the State of Guerrero, far south on the Pacific coast of Mexico, where Logan J. Bennett found 3,000 of them feeding and resting in the shallows on December 29, 1936.

Some mammals like the caribou and fur seal, some fish like the salmon and albacore, and some birds like the blue-winged teal and woodcock have not been able to find all their life necessities in a locality small enough to be within the daily range of one individual. So they have developed the migratory habit and, with the changing seasons, move about to find the things they need.

Most of our creatures are not so mobile, and their ability to get along in an area depends upon the association of living accommodations. In the environment of an animal the presence or absence of some vital necessity is of obvious importance. However, all physical essentials may be present and production still can be low. It may be the *pattern* that is wrong. Aldo Leopold likened an animal habitat to a city, and his discussion of its carrying capacity has become one of the classic allegories of wildlife science:

"A city includes all of the environmental 'types' which human animals require for thrift and welfare. If, however, all the kitchens were situated within one quarter of a given city, all the bedrooms in another quarter, all the restaurants and dining-rooms in a third, and all the parks and golf courses in the last quarter, the human population which it would be capable of supporting would be considerably reduced. The extent of the reduction would vary inversely to the mobility of the inhabitants. In fact, it is only the recent artificial extension of the human cruising radius by means of mechanical transportation that would allow such a city to be inhabited at all." *

The wildlife technician is concerned constantly with the arrangement of things. With no change in the total acreage of various cover types, he may be able to shuffle them around and double or triple the number of animals a given area will support.

Favorable situations are easily identifiable in the case of a species like the bobwhite. It is common for a landowner to point to a corner where woodland, brush, and cropfield come together and assert that "A covey has been there every fall for seven years." What he means is that this unit of range *produces* a (different) covey every fall. If he had ten such units he would have ten coveys. Take the one covey site, separate its components and move them to opposite corners of the farm, and he would have no quail.

This idea of bringing different vegetation types into close association has become an important principle to the wildlife biologist. He calls it "interspersion," and the borderline that is so favorable to game is referred to generally as "edge." But whether labeled or not, the idea can be seen in almost any management plan—as, for example, the specifications written by Wheeler for the wild turkey in Alabama:

"Optimum turkey range may be described briefly as: a well-watered, forested area that is composed of a variety of timber types of which approximately 50 percent is hardwood, one-half of which is mature oak, and that is broken by well-distributed forest clearings that support rank growths of native grasses, legumes and plants that produce succulent fruits."

On the edge of the thicket a rabbit has cover and food within easy

* Reprinted by permission from *Game Management*, by Aldo Leopold. Copyright 1933. Charles Scribner's Sons.

reach at the same time. On the edge of the field a pheasant can dust in reasonable security—with the brushy fenceline at hand for a safe retreat. On the edge of a clearing the grouse plucks clover and strawberries and dives into the forest when alarmed. On the edge of a drop-off the black bass scouts weed beds on one side and has cool depths handy on the other.

In general it is possible to increase interspersion and the total amount of edge by breaking up large blocks of any one kind of cover and mixing different types together in *small units and irregular shapes*. How practical it is to do this depends upon the primary use of the land. You can't lay out a farm just for quail nor a forest just for turkeys or grouse. But there are places in both farm and forest land where additional consideration can be given to game, fish, and fur values without impairing crop or timber production.

As we have seen, long-range planning, in terms of the natural development of life communities, is one of the realistic and efficient ways to bring land into condition for maximum production of wildlife crops. The animal component in this system is not to be neglected, since many species have important effects on their environment and on other animals.

On a section of the Wasatch National Forest in northeastern Utah, a study showed that beavers had more than doubled the acreage of water suitable for cutthroat trout. On 620 miles of stream beavers impounded 358.5 acres of water that provided deep, shaded pools, favorable food conditions, and rearing places for young fish. The 1,143 ponds also helped stabilize stream flow. The beaver were managing trout.

As examples involving the interspersion idea, it is common for marshes of uniform depth to be occupied by solid stands of a single kind of vegetation. Muskrats may eat out the cattails and create pools where aquatic plants useful to waterfowl may grow. Along the Gulf Coast, alligator holes sometimes provide the only breaks in thousands of acres of (for example) sawgrass. Obviously, regulating the numbers of muskrats or 'gators will have its place in developing favorable duck habitat.

By far-sighted methods and a utilization of natural processes we can approach the range-improvement problem on a scale that should make a showing in terms of public benefits. How great the challenge is can be seen easily in a trip across nearly any state—or the entire country. The acreage of land upon which any intelligent wildlife management has been practiced is so small as to be almost inconsequential for most species. "Too many states," said Gabrielson, "are like small boys going swimming for the first time, dabbling their toes in the water rather than really getting into the job."

However, there is one aspect of this situation that can be encouraging: What productive capacity our lands now have for game and what yield of fish our waters still possess came about almost entirely by chance. In fact, we have done the wrong thing so consistently it's a tribute to Nature that our affairs are not in worse shape than they are. This being the case, an intelligently planned reconstruction should do great things. That is no illusion; but we have made such a small start that few people even know where the possibilities lie.

WATER AND EARTH

When a stream is in its natural state, fed by a stabilized watershed, and supporting the kind and quantity of life that is adapted to it—there will be little need for improvement.

In the 1870's my grandfather could sometimes be found, on bright Sunday mornings, standing barefoot on a rock at the edge of a riffle in the Wabash River. He watched the black bass that maneuvered in the clear water among waving strands of wild celery, and with a bow and arrow he sometimes shot half a bushel of them before church was out.

Stream improvement in large degree is restoration. For many decades, the Wabash has been brown with colloidal clay from Indiana farmlands. Sunlight is excluded and few green plants can grow in the turbid water. Bass have suffered—the fish population runs strongly to carp and catfish.

Certain rivers, like the Missouri, Rio Grande, and Colorado, always have been silt-laden and probably always will be. But those that drained forested lands were clear for most of the year. In such regions the color of our streams is a measure of land-use practices. When the Wabash still was clear and full of water plants, my grandfather helped lay a corduroy road north out of the valley across the uncertain footing of a swamp. Today a paved highway lies over the rotting remains of those buried timbers and there are cropfields on either side. The soil of many of the fields is nearly the color of the underlying clay. Once it was black and fertile, but a thick surface layer long ago went down the river to be spread by flood waters over Mississippi bottoms or added to the delta below Lake Pontchartrain. The fields still are productive and they can be made more-so rapidly by modern practices. But it costs money, and a more provident farming system would have put that topsoil to better use.

Highway engineers have long considered it their privilege to gouge deep gashes across the land and then turn their backs on the raw, steep grades. With every rain the gullies grow, and tons of silt are piled into lakes, ponds, and waterways. It is normal for lakes, over long time periods, to be filled by erosion and the deposition of plant materials. But crude land use has accelerated the process, and many a citizen has seen a fine recreational lake become worthless within the span of thirty years.

We seem to be learning, but slowly. Recently I flew over an area of Wisconsin where the pattern of contour agriculture was solidly blocked in. It personified stability and permanence. It was a picture of man living at peace with the earth. Elsewhere the beginnings, or better, can be seen, often in proportion as agencies have worked together for the common good or indulged in jurisdictional wrangles. The sodding or seeding of banks and berms is now commonly included as part of the cost of highway, bridge, and other construction projects. Grades are held within the angle of repose (at least, this is intended) and mobile blowers cover them with a protecting mulch of straw. If the next rains are *gentle,* the seeding makes good.

This is the management of lakes and streams. It begins on the height of land, and the great bulk of the work will have been done before ever we reach open water. Only in a measure will the ideal ever be attained. But what we should strive for is a year-'round supply of water that flows slowly and *comes clean* from the land. A humus-charged, absorbent soil that will store rain as it falls is the first requisite to healthy streams. Runoff is filtered through mats of vegetation that retard flow and prevent silt from being carried. The electrochemical effect of rotting plant material precipitates colloidal clays. By the percolation of water through soil and rock it is added to the water table and maintains springs that hold stream levels up and temperatures down in hot, dry weather.

This too is flood control. The Mississippi system has flooded since glacial times. But the high and frequent crests of the last half century are partly man-made. The loss of soil that is so striking to one who crosses the prairies has occurred since the grass was plowed under, and it signifies one thing—water in a hurry.

Engineering structures will play a part in irrigation, transportation systems, and flood control. But they are futile without land stability. Geological erosion is normal for many arid lands in the west; but overgrazing, in particular, is cutting down the useful life of such impoundments as Elephant Butte reservoir on the Rio Grande (much of the time it reminds one strongly of a huge empty bathtub) and Lake Meade behind Hoover Dam on the Colorado. Based on a survey of the Soil Conservation Service it was estimated "that as a result of silting alone 21 percent of the Nation's water-supply reservoirs will have a useful life of less than 50 years, another 25 percent will last 50 to 100 years, whereas only 54 percent will provide enough storage to suffice for present requirements (not the estimated future needs) 100 years hence."

"On the basis of these and a few other economic studies, it seems apparent that the average annual damage to all reservoirs in the United States is not less than $10,000,000. Damage may be several times this amount . . ."

This is one of the ways in which the American citizen is paying for destructive land-use practices. A still greater payment is in the loss of streams and lakes for recreation. Here industrial and domestic pollution comes prominently into the picture. The acid effluent of mines, oil from ships, and oxygen-depleting sewage and factory wastes have converted many eastern streams into fuming sumps. Where oyster beds have not been buried in the silt of harbors, they may be contaminated and unsafe for use.

Clearing up rampant ills of the land and recovering our drainageways from deliberate expropriation as sewers is the biggest job in "stream improvement" and the biggest job in fish and wildlife management. Compared with this major undertaking, whatever else we may do is of minor consequence.

The need for a land-use approach to water management is now widely appreciated by fishery biologists. Fearnow's outline of the essentials in eastern trout stream improvement typifies the thinking of most wildlife specialists. "Trout fishing," he said, "is, in large measure, a by-product of good woodland management."

To him who wants something short, spectacular, and simple we must bring disillusionment. You bake the cake before you apply the frosting. These major considerations are the *strategy* of wildlife management; and that must be sound and right before our *tactics* ever can mean what they should. There is much to be done in the realm of tactics, and the wildlife manager is largely concerned with the techniques they involve. But strategy must be plotted at high places in federal and state governments.

There the way is rough and slow. Progress is perennially impeded by political expedience and the ever-full pork barrel, vested interests with their well-heeled lobbies, the empire building of bureaus, and plain, old-fashioned, ecological ignorance.

In common with liberty, democracy has many crimes committed in its name, but it also produces great leaders and great ideals and leaves the way open to those who want to learn what is right and work for it. We want nothing different—only a better democracy.

CHAPTER 6

Shuffling Things

ANYONE who needs to see habitat improvement demonstrated, according to plan and on a small scale, probably can find a way to perform this experiment:

Let him take a spot of waterlogged soil, however small, and with a low dike or by other means flood it to a depth of two to three feet. He will see a whole new complement of living things move in to make use of his handiwork. Depending upon where he is, some of the more interesting possibilities are ducks, coots, rails, gallinules, herons, bitterns, shore birds, muskrats, mink, raccoons, and many upland animals that will make use of the fringes. With the growth of cattails or bulrushes, redwings and marsh wrens will certify beyond all doubt, that their habitat has been improved.

Actually, no one need go to the expense of a personal experiment. Flooding projects are an important feature of nearly every state's wildlife restoration program. The simple expedient of placing nest boxes on poles in shallow water is restoring nesting wood ducks to natural and man-made water areas where there were none before. Some states furnish boxes free to sportsmen who will erect them according to specifications.

These operations, on the site to be affected, are what we have called "tactical" management. In the resource conservation battle we are concerned now with the horizon of the infantry. We will examine some significant examples of more-wildlife operations at land level.

WORKING WATER

In the last chapter we stressed the fact that stream improvement is largely a matter of keeping soil where it belongs. But that does not eliminate the possibility of using stream-bed techniques in the proper places. To some extent this has been a field of disillusionment, mainly because many unguided or misguided projects carried out in the public-works era of the thirties did not have the effect of providing boom-time fishing on any creek that happened to be near a CCC camp.

It should be evident, in the light of what we have observed in other wildlife habitats, that the plan for any stream must be custom-tailored in terms of that stream's deficiencies. This is a job for an expert, and the experts are learning how.

Michigan's Hunt Creek Fisheries Experiment Station was established in 1939 to make year-'round studies of just such problems. To begin with, they took a five-mile section of Hunt Creek, with its feeder streams, and made a three-year study of it—food production, fish population, and fish yields. Then all applicable methods were used to do a job that looked, to the naked eye, like improvement.

"After another three-year period had elapsed, it was demonstrated that the legal-size trout population of the improved section had increased in numbers by about 130 per cent, despite an ever-increasing fishing pressure." There is no doubt that in some places stream-bed structures will produce more trout if the work is properly done.

The ills which improvement work seeks to cure are mainly by-products of land and forest abuse on the watersheds of once-good streams. Siltation has broadened and shallowed many a northern river, whereas trout need deep holes, plant beds, and riffles. To keep it cool (except at high altitudes), trout water should have plenty of shade, but stream-bank logging and grazing have let the sun into long stretches. Fish also need the cover of bank brush, stumps, snags, and dead-heads; and for many years salvage operations have snaked old pine logs out of the beds of northern rivers and sent them to the mill.

Cessation of unfavorable watershed practices eventually would allow drainageways to recover their primitive condition, and that will be the crux of management policy; but in some cases recovery can be speeded and the end product made even better than "what comes naturally."

Stream improvement structures are mainly barriers such as dams, digging logs, rock or log deflectors, and bank covers. The impediments and deflectors cause the water to dig holes, wash out spawning and feeding riffles, pile silt into bars, and create mucky areas and plant beds.

Much of the objective is to increase food production. Counts of fish-food organisms on six Michigan trout streams showed that sand produced the least food and if this is given a rating of 1, then other bottom types would have ratings as follows: marl, 6; fine gravel, 9; gravel and silt, 14; rubble, 29; mucky areas, 35; muck, sand, and plants, 67; moss on gravel and rubble, 140; and certain kinds of water plants, from 159 to 452. Obviously, a stream with long stretches of shallow, sandy bottom would be a poor place for trout.

The character of streams is changed through the simple mechanics of letting water do the work. In discussing this kind of program in the Intermountain Forest Region, R. J. Costley, of the Forest Service, pointed out that "If the velocity of a stream is doubled, the digging power . . . is increased four times and the carrying power sixty-four times. It is the controlling and directing of this power that is effective in so altering . . . conditions as to modify limiting factors and thus 'step up' the carrying capacity of the stream."

Obviously, ice and flood conditions complicate the improvement problem and necessitate extensive experimentation to determine what type of structure will do the job best, last the longest, and cost the least. In Michigan, O. H. Clark built deflectors of cubical concrete blocks, two feet on a side, each with a large iron ring in one face to make handling possible. As might be expected, the blocks are wearing well. In his work with structures, Clark also got at some basic features of stream management. He increased the *length* of the stream and available fishing water by building diversion dams and forcing water through long-abandoned oxbows and bayous. On the Little Manistee River, silt and muck were flushed out of a new section 1,700 feet in length within two days after the dam was closed. Other work with low-head dams near the headwaters of streams spreads the flow out over pervious soils and replenishes ground waters that emerge as a stabilized yield of cool spring water farther down.

Stream improvement has been studied in nearly every section of the country where trout are important. It is according to expectation that the same methods cannot be used everywhere. Mountain streams of the West have steeper grades and wider seasonal fluctuations than those in forest areas of the East. This makes dams especially useful in the creation of pools and greatly reduces the possibilities of using deflectors.

One of the most systematic tests of the effects of stream improvement was carried out by C. M. Tarzwell and M. A. Gee, of the Forest Service, on the Tonto National Forest in Arizona. Horton Creek and Upper Tonto Creek were found to be closely comparable in length (3.5 miles as against 3.8 miles) and other conditions. The two streams join at an altitude of 5,850 feet. Horton Creek was improved during 1933-35 by means of a CCC project, and Tonto Creek remained in its natural condition.

A complete creel census in 1936 and 1937 showed that in the two seasons Horton Creek (improved) yielded 54.2 and 59 pounds of trout per acre as against 45.6 and 42.4 pounds per acre for Tonto Creek. The difference in production was considered to be due to the improvement program, and the better conditions in Horton Creek also were reflected in higher productivity of trout foods. On an acreage basis, the improved stream was supporting 84 pounds more of food organisms than the unimproved creek.

This is a quick and somewhat inadequate look at the habitat improvement that fisheries biologists are applying to trout streams. At present we can attempt no appraisal of the economics of such methods. What it costs to produce a pound of trout, pro-rating the improvements over X-number of years, will vary greatly and depend on what was there in the beginning and how intensively the fish crop is to be utilized. For now we can observe only that, within limits, such methods work and that they undoubtedly will be refined as time goes on.

FORMULA FOR QUAIL

In dealing with shortages, the wildlife specialist is perpetually on the lookout for pieces that may be missing in the environmental puzzle. When a dearth of game or fish is due to only one important minus-item, you have the simplest of all problems in diagnosis. After you know what is wrong, the rest may be easy and practical—or not, as the case may be.

One of our most spectacular examples of habitat improvement originated from the fact that water is an important limitation to quail in arid lands of the West. After California investigators had spied on the family life of the valley quail sufficiently to have a passably good quail's-eye view of the range, they began to see that drinking water *every day* was a necessity in bringing young birds through the summer-long drought and into the season when they could be hunted. Once they knew what was needed, the way was clear to finding a practical means of providing it.

The result has been one of the strangest gadgets that is likely to serve the sportsman—"Glading's gallinaceous guzzler." Named after Ben Glading, a key man in developing it, the guzzler has become the difference between quail and no quail in large areas of dry foothills and desert brushlands. In addition to the valley quail, the Gambel and mountain quail also profit from it.

The theory behind the guzzler grew out of the willingness of these western birds to *go down* for their water. It was found that they would run twenty feet or more down an old mine shaft or six feet into a ground-squirrel burrow if there was water at the bottom. The country they live in may have eight or ten inches of rainfall, but it all comes in the October-to-April period. Now, if this rain could be collected and stored underground where evaporation would be cut down and larger animals couldn't get at it—you can see how the idea developed.

The first crude guzzler was put together of concrete slabs. It had a wooden top and a narrow ramp along one side that led underground to the water. It didn't work well because the birds had to queue up to get a drink. It kept them waiting around and exposed them to enemies. The men who built and tried "the thing" attested that the birds were passing out tickets!

So a new model was designed and given its shake-down tests. It worked so well that in 1946 the Bureau of Game Conservation reported that, "In the arid parts of California, phenomenal results have been obtained from development of watering places for quail and other small game . . . coveys of up to 200 birds have resulted from the placement of watering devices in formerly dry and birdless areas."

Large-scale work began in 1948 with a budget of nearly $100,000 under the state's Federal Aid program. The first production-model guzzler had its own little watershed in the form of a concrete apron. The size of this was nicely calculated in relation to local rainfall. The apron funneled into a broad ramp that led down to water under baffle slabs that reduced the surface exposed to evaporation. The guzzlers hold about 650 gallons. They fill every winter and the water supply lasts through the entire dry season. Except for the apron and opening, they are entirely underground.

The California commission places water developments on private ranches by agreement with the owners. Sites are fenced against stock, and brushpiles or other cover established around them. New refinements and simpler building methods have materially reduced costs. The latest guzzler is built of plastic and glass fiber and can be handled by one man. It is easier to install than the original concrete model.

As of 1958, California technicians had installed more than 2,600 of the watering devices and thereby improved roughly that many square miles of quail range. The work was making several hundred thousand more quail per year available to hunters. That's how one "limiting factor" was dealt with.

EVENTS AT ASHLAND

Management is most easily demonstrable where we can deal with a single, major, environmental need. Some situations will permit this approach and most commonly when one species is being dealt with.

However, most wildlife problems are not this easy—or rather they are still more difficult. Habitat improvement usually will affect several important birds and mammals and many of secondary interest. It will be brought about by modifying, or adding to, the things that are being done by some businessman who is working with land crops.

One of the outstanding examples of this kind of program was carried out in Missouri. It was a research job of the Conservation Commission and the wildlife research unit at Columbia. It began in 1942 and was aimed particularly at the bobwhite quail, although the effects on rabbits also were evident.

Two areas of rolling farmland were used; the West Ashland tract of 2,070 acres, and the New Salem area of 2,260 acres. The first three years of the experiment do not concern us now, although we will need them later. It is sufficient to say that for three seasons game technicians stocked the West Ashland unit with additional breeder quail from the game farm but were unsuccessful in producing thereby a larger crop for the hunter.

The second phase of the experiment began in the spring of 1945. They kept the New Salem area as it was for use as a "control." At West Ashland they went into high gear in the promotion of modern farming practices. The operations recommended to farmers were those currently recognized as good land management by agencies concerned. To get such methods into use in short order the Western Cartridge Company provided a subsidy that doubled the "benefit" payments already available from the government. In addition to the Missouri Wildlife Research Unit, the Extension Service, Soil Conservation Service, and Production and Marketing Administration had a part in the program.

They made soil maps and farm plans. They established contour farming, improved pastures, and made generous use of lime, fertilizer, and green manure. In fencerows, waste areas, and wildlife borders they planted sericea lespedeza, sweet clover, multiflora rose, and other shrubs and trees. The development went ahead steadily for three years.

In the fall of 1945 the tract had 13 coveys of quail. During the next four years these increased to 17 coveys in 1946, 18 in 1947, 31 in 1948, and 44 in 1949, when the experiment ended. As of 1945, the fall population was 9.3 birds per hundred acres, and there were 29 per hundred acres in 1949.

With increases of this consistency and magnitude, we can hardly doubt that this project demonstrated the validity of a common contention among wildlife biologists: that good agricultural practices plus reasonable consideration for wildlife are the most important part of a management plan for birds and mammals. Care of the soil, building of fertility, and some appreciation of what we may call "rural landscaping," will surround nearly any homestead with living things that add value and interest for most people.

We noted in the second chapter of this book that fertile, hence agricultural, soils have the greatest productive potential for wild animals the same as for other crops. Such lands surround most of our sizable urban centers where the demand for hunting is greatest. It seems evident that the nation's farms offer the best possibilities for growing wildlife crops that will be intensively used by two categories of the human population: (1) a minority who hunt with guns, and (2) a large majority of all ages and sexes who just enjoy a world that is green and peopled with creatures that sing, fly, run, and leave tracks.

Small though it is, there is now a directed effort toward the development of specific wildlife management measures that will fit into a

farmer's business. In some cases they also offer him agricultural benefits. Several of these measures were used at West Ashland. Few of
them have been proved quantitatively and individually and most will
be improved upon. But theoretically they are sound, and they seem to
offer the best hope now in sight for more of some of the things we
want.

Living fences of multiflora rose have particular promise as a means
of achieving low-cost fencing and wildlife cover in one operation.
They probably will have greatest usefulness on the prairies where
cover is at a minimum. Rose fences on property lines are ideal trespass
control. Contour hedges are sightly and have practical value as boundary markers in large strip-cropped fields. Field borders of various
shrubs—especially bicolor lespedeza in the Southeast—make wildlife
food and cover on otherwise unproductive strips along woodland
edges. Brushpiles in the woodlot make immediate cover for rabbits
and other animals, and placed around gullies or other "odd areas"
about the farm they are the means of establishing new thickets of
native vines and shrubs. Birds perch on the brush and their droppings
are laden with viable seed. In the woodlot wildlife can be favored by
preserving den trees and girdling hollow "wolf trees" which need
culling out for the benefit of future timber crops. Mast trees such as
walnut, oak, and hickory can be planted or allowed to grow in fencerows or on woodlot edges. There they develop large crowns and produce large nut crops.

Such methods will vary from one part of the country to another.
Regionally the kinds of shrubs used will be changed or new wrinkles
developed to serve a specific need.

A measure that deserves particular mention is the farm fishpond as
it is now used in southeastern states. Such a pond usually is built in
an old gully or on a side hill where it receives the runoff from a few
acres of well-protected watershed. It is stocked with specified numbers
of bass and bluegill fingerlings, which are obtained from state or
federal hatcheries. The program is being pushed rapidly, with federal
help, in state soil conservation districts.

There is insufficient space here to treat the details of these management techniques; but it may be just as well, for many are only in the
formative stages.

FAUNA ON RELIEF

It will have occurred to many readers that there is a category of measures commonly accepted as a part of wildlife management which we have not touched upon. The wildlife biologist calls them "artificial," since they make no effort to utilize natural capacities. They are techniques aimed, not at populations, but at individual animals. In contrast to the wholesale potentialities in semipermanent habitat work, they are management at the "retail" level.

Probably the best example is artificial feeding. Occasionally a hard winter will hit the northern states and a move will get under way for a large-scale program to feed the pheasants. Usually one man or a group (with connections) will get the notion and sell enough people to create real pressure.

The trouble with such methods, even when applied to deer, quail, or other species that actually may be starving, is that the job is too big to be approached in this way. Almost any state could spread its entire game-management budget over the land in the form of feed, but by the time this could be carried out a crisis would have done its damage and passed on. Even if, by expensive preparations, we were set to meet the emergency, the range and numbers of almost any important public game resource are so large that the effort would be lost in thousands of square miles of bleak winter scenery.

It is true that a farmer, with his eye on a covey or two, might handle the situation and bring through a few birds that were important to him. Intensively and on a small scale, *where cost is no object,* private management can be successful in the use of methods requiring the continued application of labor and materials. Game farming for the production of hand-reared targets is in the same class. But for our numerous and increasing public the task is huge beyond all practical limits. Our methods will need to be directed toward wildlife habitats that are "self-operating" and do not require annual expenditures.

Considered generally, artificial measures are leaky-bucket techniques. We keep pouring and pouring and trying our best to fill the bucket, but as long as there are holes in the bottom (habitat) the untiring attrition of natural pressures (no less than the law of gravity) will prevail in the end and bring us back to the starting point. Although we have discussed them here, such expedients are not true habitat improvement; when carried out with public money, they are faunistic boondoggling, chiefly significant in delaying the more permanent achievement on which a program for all the people depends.

It seems likely that three fourths of the management job through which citizens at large can be served will need to be brought about by a mind-over-matter approach. There will be no real success without enlightened staff work, long-term strategic planning for coordinated and conservative use of resources, through which wildlife is given consideration and employment in major industries on the land. Probably the other 25 percent can then be done with wildlife funds in local habitats and in terms of local values and interests.

To face it, we have no complete and satisfactory mechanism for accomplishing either the large or the lesser task. But it probably represents some progress to know where the problem lies and on what scale it will have to be handled.

CHAPTER 7

Boom and Bust

IF the management significance of the foregoing chapters were to be boiled down to a single idea, it probably would be this: The way to have wildlife in abundance is to provide its life necessities on the land and in the water. That will be our conclusion when we are through with this book, and it will be the maxim of wildlife technologists a century hence when they know a great deal more than now.

However, it would be a half-truth to leave the matter there. A hunter who enjoys good grouse shooting this fall and comes back to the scene of his success a year hence to find nothing—"Well," he is likely to say, "what about it?" There may be no apparent change in the place at all.

As if the ordinary difficulties of management were not enough, there are causes for wildlife scarcities that go beyond such things as cover, food, overshooting, etc. Unless they realize this and are prepared for it, the hunter and technician are going to be disillusioned and lose faith in the very things that are working for them.

We have examined the waxing and waning of animal numbers with the seasons and in a few cases we have seen the mechanism at work. A striking consistency in production is evident where habitats are, for a time, free from extreme variability in important conditions.

But it is well known that such variability does occur. Weather is proverbially undependable, and it affects animal populations in a multitude of ways. Also, there are long-term population changes, some of which appear to be regular and predictable as gross trends over large regions. Whether these "cycles" are real or only apparent is a perplexing subject that has furrowed many a scientific brow. We cannot go far with it here; but there are cause-and-effect situations which nearly anyone can learn to identify with reasonable accuracy. If you can anticipate, or even recognize, an occurrence and realize that it has happened many times in the past, you are less likely to think the world is falling apart and be stampeded into some wild and wasteful scheme when it does come about.

THE MAST FEEDERS

In the fall of 1834, Bartholomew County in south-central Indiana was the scene of a squirrel hunt not unique in its day, but the like of which will not be seen again.

The floor of cool forests in the rich flat-lands was deep with the mast of beech, white oak, and shagbark hickory that crunched into the cushiony duff at every step. Ridges were strewn with the bounty of chestnut oaks, and everywhere timber was a-rustle with swarms of fattening gray squirrels.

More than a century of development had brought the Kentucky rifle (née Pennsylvania) to a high state of perfection, and barking a squirrel at 60 yards was largely a matter of the clear eye and steady hand.

The good men and true of Sand Creek Township considered themselves the elite of the squirrel-hunting world and did not hesitate to advertise it. The riflemen of Wayne Township denied this presumption and challenged them to a contest. The two townships agreed that each would select 50 hunters who would shoot squirrels for three days, at the end of which a grand barbecue would be held, with the losing side footing the bill.

The full details of this shooting fest are not available, but enough was recorded to give some idea of the abundance of the gray squirrel in some of its best native range. The winner of the hunt presented *900 squirrels* at the end of the three days and the runner-up had 783!

Such abundance was not just a local occurrence. Squirrels took heavy toll of cornfields in forest openings, and in 1749 the colony of Pennsylvania paid bounties on 640,000 of them. There was a time in Ohio when county taxes were payable in squirrel scalps, and an early record mentions a gunner who killed 160 in a day—at a time when they were not especially plentiful.

Among frontier hunters the gray squirrel was known as the migratory squirrel, and with good reason. Periodically its numbers built up to a density that became intolerable to the species itself. Probably it is safe to say that the climax in this increase always occurred during a year when mast production was heavy. September and October are the season when young animals are on the move to find comfortable sites for future living, but that is different from the pervasive restlessness that seized entire populations. They would begin to travel, evidently in one direction, not stopping for lakes, streams, or anything else.

During such a movement the residents of Saginaw, Michigan, would awake, mornings, to find bedraggled black squirrels (the commonest color phase in the North) perched on every piling in the river. In a southward migration near Racine, Wisconsin, the animals were passing for two weeks, and it was a month before all had disappeared.

After a migration the woods would seem deserted of squirrels, but it did not take long for their numbers to become conspicuous again. The best evidence indicates that northern gray squirrels could be expected to migrate about every five years.

They were going nowhere, and they got nowhere. On these marches mortality was heavy from all causes, and the numbers were worn down and dissipated. Over large areas gray squirrels disappeared when dense forests were cut, but here and there the animals have again become sufficiently prosperous so that a reversion to the old migratory habit has been observed.

The migrations, it seems, were a device for clearing the land of a too-numerous population and converting a million animals back into the humus of the earth. A part of the time, at least, the gray squirrel is sufficiently immune to the effects of external controls (disease, predators, etc.) so that in the course of the ages it has developed a *sociological* means of getting rid of excess numbers.

In contrast, the fox squirrel is not habitually migratory. Probably because it inhabited forest *edges* rather than extensive continuous stands of woodland, it did not build up, in depth, to mass hordes like the gray squirrel. Nevertheless it did, and does, become highly abundant periodically, and studies in the Midwest have shown what happens:

There comes a spring when a late frost, or some other climatic condition, nips the mast crop before it gets started. A food scarcity develops, and young animals are brought into competition with the abundant adults for what acorns and other nuts are still buried in the ground. Ordinarily, from early summer on they would find the oaks and hickories weighted with green mast to be had for the cutting, but now this basic supply is missing. As mentioned previously, a healthy fall population of fox squirrels should contain about two-thirds young of the year. But when numbers are high and food short the mortality of young is far greater than usual. By autumn they may compose only a quarter of the population.

The real crisis comes when a poor mast year is followed by an old howler of a winter. Ordinarily the squirrels would be well layered with belly fat, and in periods of deep snow, ice, and blizzards they would roll up in the nest and snooze it out. This winter they are thin and must have food regardless of weather. It is hard to find and hard to dig up. A diet of buds will not sustain them for long. The scabies mite (mange) is ever-present and on weakened animals it takes over. Part or all of the hair falls out and open lesions develop in the skin. Undernourishment appears also to induce a deficiency of blood sugar that gives rise to fatal seizures of shock when the animal is excited or over-exerts. Many squirrels become so weak they no longer can climb. They starve, freeze, and are easily taken by predators.

But the end is not yet. Fox squirrels usually breed in midwinter, and in this year of sorrows bare survival is the best they can do. Only those animals come through that are in the most favorable locations. The new crop of young may be drastically reduced or entirely missing in the spring that follows.

Although this situation was first observed in Michigan, it probably is a frequent occurrence in northern squirrel ranges, and something similar has been recorded in Europe. Squirrels are the foremost game animals in Finland, and extensive field research shows that they fluctuate radically in numbers about every five years, usually with ten years between major peaks. In a large area where they were studied, the animals died off within a couple of months in the fall of 1943. It was estimated that the drop in numbers was such that there was one animal where there had been 450 before.

Food failures have been a cause of squirrel declines in that region also, but probably of greater importance are the epizoötics * that go through the population when numbers are at their maximum. Coccidiosis has been of particular importance. Shortages of fir cones, a

* The same as an epidemic among humans.

primary food supply, appear to help induce diseases in the same manner as in Michigan.

It is a recurring picture of numbers building up to a point of instability, the downfall being brought about by one cause or another, or by a combination of causes. A dense population of animals is a precarious structure. It becomes weaker as it builds, and what triggers the collapse is, perhaps, not too important. It is highly important, however, for the sportsman to realize that a reduction from abundance is almost always inevitable.

BR'ER RABBIT UNBOUND

For most purposes, one head of small game per acre is generally accepted as about the maximum population it is reasonable to expect as a result of good management. In fact, for a given species, one animal per acre as an annually recurring maximum would make nearly any area known for its hunting.

Although this applies to rabbits as much as to quail or other species, it is true that under exceptionally favorable conditions rabbits and hares may reach levels of abundance they are unable to maintain for long. A good example of this is what happened to the cottontail on 3,600-acre Fisher's Island (New York), which lies two miles off-shore from New London, Connecticut.

The island had excellent cover, and about 1925 several dozen rabbits were introduced. House cats were the only mammalian predators present. By 1938 the cottontails were so plentiful they were doing serious damage to shrubbery around lawns and golf courses. That winter a bounty of 20 cents per pair of ears resulted in a kill of more than 3,000 rabbits!

The bounty was removed, but another kill of 1,200 was taken the following winter. There was no evident decrease in the rabbits, and in the fall of 1940 the population was estimated by New York game biologists to be approximately 10 per acre. At that time the animals appeared to be in good condition.

During the next two years there were numerous rabbits found dead, and living animals were heavily parasitized with ticks. Another field investigation in the spring of 1943 showed that the population had declined to about one rabbit per four acres, and the animals were dying off. Remains of 119 of them were picked up, and 33 were fresh enough for examination. The dead rabbits had been carrying an average of 65 adult ticks plus an undetermined number of tick nymphs. All of them showed evidence of anemia, and many infections had resulted from the tick bites.

These ticks (of two species) had been present from the start, and under ordinary conditions they would not especially bother the host. But when rabbits became overconcentrated, conditions evidently developed which enabled the external parasites to take over and bring about a drastic reduction of the population. It was similar to the way the scabies mites got the upper hand of the Michigan fox squirrels during a winter of starvation.

These are good examples of how *density-dependent* factors operate. The more animals there are the more rapidly a disease (including such parasites as ticks and mites) can spread and the more certainty there is of a quick reduction of the population. In a year when snowshoe hares in Minnesota increased from 275 per square mile to 420 per square mile, the tick infestation rose from 2,400 to 4,900 per animal. Thus, roughly a 50 percent increase in rabbits seemed to have made possible a 100 percent increase in ticks. With ticks multiplying at twice the rate of the rabbits it is apparent that this could not go on for very long.

It has been recognized since early in the present century that about every ten years there is a spectacular boom and bust of snowshoe hare populations along the northern fringe of the United States and in Canada. The regularity of this phenomenon first became apparent in the fur returns of the Hudson's Bay Company. Skins of this northern hare have been an article of commerce with export records available since 1821.

Records of the Hudson's Bay Company have been studied repeatedly, and especially in connection with a thoroughgoing investigation of the hare cycle by Duncan A. MacLulich, then of the University of Toronto. Deriving his information from all available sources, including intensive field work, MacLulich reached some significant conclusions:

In past and current records he identified peak years for snowshoe populations in 1856, 1864, 1875, 1886, 1895, 1914, 1924, and 1934. Hare numbers in Ontario were found to vary from one per square mile at the low of the cycle to more than a thousand at the maximum. The greatest density observed was 3,400 per square mile!

From the evidence available, a theoretical ten-year sequence of year-end populations on a square mile of hare range was determined to be as follows:

$$4 - 12 - 36 - 108 - 324 - 1,396 - 4,188 - 288 - 18 - 2$$

This series shows the steady build-up to a maximum when the breeding stock reproduced in the eighth year. In the summer of that year (typically) an abrupt die-off is represented as occurring.

The decline that MacLulich observed began in 1932 in a small area of southern Ontario and progressed to the central and northern parts of the province in 1933, 1934, and 1935. A summary of reports and observations from widespread areas indicated that sick and ailing hares were common, and infections of various kinds and heavy parasitism frequently attended the dying-off. These conditions varied from one area to another, however, and no specific disease agent could be designated as particularly important. It appeared that local decimation was not always brought about by the same factor but that some lethal agent became effective when the population reached a point of topheavy abundance. "The length of the cycle is about the same each time because it depends chiefly on the time the population takes to grow from scarcity to abundance . . . and secondly on the time required for the . . . reaction."

Here, according to MacLulich's interpretation, the density factor was not only involved, but it developed with a constancy that imparted a relatively precise timing to the "bust" of populations at intervals of about a decade.

In Minnesota, during the mid-thirties, the snowshoe hare population underwent a reduction that appears to have been related to the widespread decline in Ontario. In the Lake Alexander area, R. G. Green and his associates carried on an intensive study of populations and pathology from 1931 to 1938. What they found seems to agree fairly well with the general picture of the cycle as given by Mac-Lulich.

Earlier observations indicated a build-up in hare numbers from 1928 on and this continued to 1933, at which time the maximum density of nearly 500 to the square mile was attained. In the two years following, there were local reductions and in 1935 there began a sharp drop in numbers that extended through 1938. The low point at that time was represented by populations about 10 percent as large as the maximum.

The Minnesota work was unique and particularly significant in that it revealed the presence of "shock disease" in the declining population and showed that in this case, at least, the condition largely affected young of the year rather than adults or the entire population. This type of shock was found to be caused by a deficiency of blood sugar similar to what was identified later among Michigan fox squirrels. Hares taken in box traps, handled, or just held in pens, went into convulsions followed by a coma and death.

Whether shock disease might have been involved in the reports of "dopey" rabbits received by MacLulich in Ontario is conjectural. Why it appeared with high population density and its subsequent abatement were obscure at that time. More light has since been thrown upon it, and it is now coming to be looked upon as one of the most characteristic of density-dependent diseases.

William Rowan, for long an investigator of the cycle in Alberta, gave a graphic account of the snowshoe-hare crisis in the early forties:

"In 1942 rabbits had attained a peak. They were so numerous that even within the city limits of sprawling Edmonton . . . rabbits could periodically be seen scuttling out of the way of cars right in town or chased by dogs across vacant lots.

". . . Bill Schmidt of Fawcett, Alberta, exterminated his cat on account of the surfeit of rabbits. The cat had produced a litter of kittens in the horse barn and apparently decided to rear them on rabbits. She would bring in anything up to 20 per day and deposit them all over the floor for men and horses to slither on till the situation became intolerable. When a cat can kill up to 20 rabbits daily the supply may certainly be deemed unlimited!

"In 1942 nearly six million rabbit skins were shipped to felt and hat manufacturers of the United States from Alberta's northland, a kill that was barely enough to scratch the surface of the hare population. Yet, such is the nature of the crash, that in the year that followed (1943), contracts had to be cancelled and shipments discontinued for lack of rabbits."

The snowshoe hare does not starve or migrate; disease seems to be the regular mechanism for relieving the insupportable density that it attains. In effect, it depletes the food supply and crowds its habitat to a point where the result is an outdoor slum, and pestilence of one kind or another does the deed. Physical ailments seem to spread into less favorable range where numbers are low, since the wiping out is not restricted to heavily populated areas.

During a peak of numbers, when hares are swarming through the thickets, they practically eliminate reproduction of forest trees in large areas. Later, in the low of the cycle, new generations of trees spring up, thus producing a forest of definite age classes in which can be read the history of rabbit fluctuations for decades long past.

Radical variations from abundance to scarcity are especially characteristic of certain northern animals and they are by no means limited to this continent. Extensive studies in the Soviet Union have shown the almost universal occurrence of fairly regular population rhythms in birds and mammals of economic importance. "For instance there is a good 'yield' of white hares in the European north of the U.S.S.R. at intervals of 8-11 years (usually 9), and in the central zone of the country at intervals of 4-9 (usually 7)."

It may mean something, as suggested by Leopold, that some of our most typically cyclic species (including the western jackrabbits) feed upon plentiful low-grade foods such as weeds, buds, and bark. Plenty of food probably is a key item in permitting them to increase to a point of lethal overpopulation.

The ideal of perpetual abundance is something we like to anticipate, but it is largely an illusion. It will be healthy realism to remember that too many animals of one kind in a limited area pollute their own environment or in other ways make it less favorable, and the result is certain. We must accept the fact that we can not have maximum numbers indefinitely.

FLESH-FEEDERS OF THE NORTH

While the snowshoe hare is fresh in our minds, we should mention that it forms the principal food supply for the northern lynx, and the fur records on this animal also show a ten-year cycle of ups and downs that correlates closely with that of the hare.

Although the investigator may look long, he probably will fail to find an example of a predator species that alone "controls" the numbers of a widely distributed prey species, yet here seems to be a clear case of such a prey animal bringing about periodic and drastic reductions in its principal enemy.

Concerning the close relationship between lynx and hare, Seton observed that: "Of all the Northern creatures, none are more dependent on the Rabbits than is the Canada Lynx. It lives on Rabbits, follows the Rabbits, thinks Rabbits, tastes like Rabbits, increases with them, and on their failure dies of starvation in the unrabbited woods."

In the northern portion of the Quebec Peninsula a relationship reminiscent of the hare and lynx is found between mouse-like rodents and foxes. In Ungava the species involved are chiefly the lemming and arctic fox; farther east, in Labrador, the principals are preponderantly the vole and "colored" fox. There is much overlap of range, and several other rodents enter the picture also. The colored fox includes the three phases, red, cross, and silver.

In Labrador, the take of colored foxes during a 92-year period showed a striking oscillation in periods varying from 2 to 6 years. The average length of the 23 cycles was 4 years, and 13 of the 23 were exactly of that duration. The white foxes of Ungava have a similar round of abundance and scarcity and in both cases the underlying cause is seen in a radical build-up and die-off, about every 4 years, of the rodents which form the food mainstay of the fox.

These rodents also are the principal food item of the snowy owl, which evidently builds in number during times of abundance and then is caught short when the voles and lemmings disappear.

But the owl, being a mobile species, drifts southward, usually about hunting season, and invades northeastern United States. It is then that every outdoor page carries photographs and speculation about the white visitors from the North and every taxidermy shop does a rush business in owl "trophies." Actually, the birds have little fear of man and it is likely that few of them last out the winter. The influx of owls, at about four-year intervals, reflects the rodent cycle of the barrens.

Practically all cycles show regional variations—the peak may be reached here this year and farther on next year; yet a rough coincidence usually can be observed. Elton has pointed out that the cycle in mouse-like rodents (and, as we have seen, in other species such as the hares) is a circumpolar phenomenon. "A similar violent fluctuation, keyed to lemmings, with different species of lemmings, but practically the same species of owls and foxes, is found in Lapland, Novaya Zemlya, Arctic Siberia, Kamchatka, Alaska, the Western Arctic and the Arctic Archipelago of Canada, and in North and East Greenland."

It seems to be true that, as one proceeds southward from the Arctic, with its stark, violent, and relatively simple relationships, into warmer regions, the tendency toward regularity in population changes is lost in a welter of cross-purpose factors and extreme variability in local conditions.

When the food situation deteriorates for an abundant arctic fox population, it appears that short-range emigration and the onset of disease are more characteristic developments than outright starvation. The carnivores seem to be particularly susceptible to diseases, such as rabies and distemper, that affect the central nervous system. Epizootics of this kind among foxes, wolves, and sled dogs are well known in the North and they occur commonly in other regions when a species becomes too plentiful.

Cowan reported a rabies-like disease as being responsible for a widespread die-off of foxes on the Mackenzie Delta in the winter of 1944-45. Red foxes (heretofore referred to as "colored") had been plentiful over the western Arctic region in the early forties and in the winter of reduction there were reports of ailing and "crazy" foxes that ran in an aimless fashion, blundering through thickets or making perfunctory attacks on trappers. Dead foxes were encountered frequently. That winter rabies was identified from an arctic fox, a wolf, and a sled dog in Northwest Territory. There were other reports of peculiar behavior on the part of wolves that entered camp and fought with dogs—which afterward sickened and died.

The increase of foxes in the forties included most of the United States and Canada. Rabies outbreaks were widespread and particularly serious in New York and Pennsylvania. Biologists freely predicted that the fox could not maintain this high density, and during the fifties reports of disease and regional die-offs were frequent. However, recovery was rapid in most cases, and Reynard held out well against any general disaster until 1956. At that time an "Arctic" form of rabies was spreading into Ontario and it practically wiped out the abounding foxes during the next two years. As would be expected, a few durable animals survived, and by 1960 trappers were noting local increases. Why the disease did not cross the waters into Michigan is a good question.

Mange was widely evident amid the general over-abundance of foxes. Lean, unthrifty, and mangy animals are evident to trappers and hunters; when many foxes are in this condition it is commonly a first index that an unhealthy population status has been reached.

Something similar happened to skunks in the Midwest, and possibly the East, from about 1938 to 1941. From a low point around 1933, the species had steadily gained in numbers and was abundant in many areas previous to 1939.

Reports from fur buyers indicated that in the late thirties skunks were declining in northern Ohio and Indiana. In the winter of 1939-40 the trend appeared unmistakably in Illinois and trappers in the southern counties of Michigan were reporting sick and dying skunks.

It so happened that skunks were being intensively studied that winter at a state wildlife experiment station near Lansing. When a disease hit the animals, it was ascertained immediately. There was abnormal fighting among skunks, and the animals wandered about in daylight acting "crazy" and irresponsible. Many died in winter dens and elsewhere.

The disease was diagnosed as a virus infection of the brain—in short, "encephalitis." Accounts of trappers indicated that this condition was widespread. In Michigan the slump lasted at least through 1942, after which it appeared that skunks again were slowly increasing.

With plenty of food, it seems, the carnivores are able to build their numbers to a point that is both uneconomic for man and unhealthy for the species concerned. Sometimes, with no evident change in food conditions, the flesh-eaters are laid low by maladies that seem always to be featured in their periods of ill fortune—rabies, distemper, encephalitis, and mange.

At other times the portent of hard times comes with a scarcity of food, which may operate directly or prepare the population for an epizootic of characteristic disease. Probably this is an oversimplification, but it provides us with a reliable working hypothesis of what to expect when Br'er Fox appears, as Herr Hitler once did, about to sweep all before him.

CYCLING GROUSE

Ordinarily we think of the sharptail as a prairie grouse—or a prairie-edge grouse—and rightly so, since it did and does characterize the brushy fringes of northern grasslands. However, there is a less well-known race of this hale and rugged gamebird that inhabits openings, thickets, and birch-clad slopes of the forested region from central Alaska across northern Canada to the eastern watershed of James Bay.

Like many birds and mammals, the prairie sharptail is cyclic in about ten-year periods, but fluctuations of the far-north bird have not been sufficiently well recorded for the pattern to be clear. It is known, however, that this race was building in numbers in the late twenties and in 1932 reached a peak higher than anything previously observed.

The way northern sharptails reacted to superabundance recalls mass migrations of the gray squirrel. In mid-October, 1932, flocks great and small began moving southward from the region around Hudson Bay and the Quebec side of James Bay. There was a spectacular full-scale exodus for about three weeks, after which the movement in the north gradually declined.

By the end of October sharptails had appeared 200 to 300 miles south, far beyond their normal wintering range, on a broad front from the Tamiskaming District east into Quebec. The flight continued through November but was losing its original headlong impetus. Flocks arrived at North Bay, Ontario, in December and reached a western limit on the shores of Lake Superior north of Sault Ste. Marie. By that time the flow had spent itself and the birds wandered about waiting for fate to overtake them. The emigrants were marked surplus, and some unseen Pied Piper had led them southward out of the too-fecund land that had spawned them.

This classic "grand lam" of the sharptails appears to exemplify what may happen in a variety of species under proper conditions and at times of great abundance.

Few people would conceive of the quail as being much of a traveler, yet in times past "crazy flights" of the bobwhite were well known in the Mississippi Valley. A. W. Schorger * has cited records to show that following the middle of the last century quail had a period of unmatched prosperity in Wisconsin and it was not uncommon when numbers were at their fall maximum to have towns and villages invaded by flocks or mass flights of the birds.

Whatever the mechanism or the stimulus that sets off such emigrations of animals, it usually appears in some way to be tied in with overpopulation. Relief from abundance by this means may represent an alternative to disease. It is possible that the pressure of numbers sometimes gets intolerable and mass movements occur before the expected epizoötic can get going.

Whatever the specific factors involved, these movements are not the method by which numbers usually are controlled in the gamebirds. Grouse, especially, are typically cyclic in all of the northern hemisphere.

Our own ruffed grouse probably has no peer as a shooting bird, but the supply is well known for being here today and gone tomorrow. In the twenties and thirties "crash" declines of ruffed grouse caused consternation in a number of northern states. At that time the approach to any wildlife question was habitually speculative, and people thought the grouse, like Clementine, was lost and gone forever. Manful efforts were made to rear the forest drummer in captivity but, fortunately, they were not outstandingly successful and the conservation movement was spared the deception of large-scale propagation programs to "bring back" *Bonasa umbellus*.

The grouse brought itself back, as it has every decade as far back into the past as passable records go. The precipitate decline of the early forties was predicted in advance by many a biologist in the northern states and Canada, so for wide-awake sportsmen there was less than the usual dismay.

The reliability of the grouse supply can be judged from Grange's statement that the period of high population is three years or longer and the low is five years or longer. Thus top-grade hunting can be

---

* Every state should have such a wildlife historian. From a multitude of obscure sources and with infinite and scholarly patience, Dr. Schorger has pieced together the past history of some of Wisconsin's most important wildlife species and recorded it in the Transactions of the Wisconsin Academy of Science. A similar job is being done in Missouri by Daniel McKinley.

expected in perhaps three or four out of every ten years. Grange cited his own recent data and records in the literature which together covered a period from 1857 through 1947 for Manitoba and Wisconsin.

Although these records apply specifically to prairie chickens and sharptails, they can be taken provisionally to indicate what has happened not only to the ruffed grouse but also to various other birds and mammals. Grange lists eleven species as the minimum number participating in the Lake States. Here is his comment on the above series of records:

"Assuming that the Wisconsin-Manitoba cycles operate on the same time-table (as the evidence shows in two instances) we thus find that for a period of 90 years and for ten consecutive lows, the grouse cycle has occurred on a regular 10 year amplitude. In eight of the ten cases the periodicity indicated was exactly 10 years and in the other two instances the variation was only 1 year. The presumption, therefore, is that the periodicity has been regularly ten years for the lows."

Detailed study of the grouse cycle reveals a multitude of complicating variations. It is difficult to determine exactly which year is *the* low for a given locality, since several years are low and our criteria for estimating numbers are crude. Several investigators have shown the spotty nature of the depression, with lags for local areas within a state and also more generally for regions. Variability between species also appears—the Wisconsin prairie chicken seems to die off somewhat ahead of the ruffed grouse, and the muskrat has peaks several years before the lynx.

One of the most clear-cut studies of ruffed grouse in a period of decline was made by C. H. D. Clarke in the early thirties. Intensive field work at representative stations in Ontario was supplemented by questionnaires distributed to other provinces of Canada.

These investigations showed the distribution pattern of the cycle and indicated that in this case it started in the east and progressed westward. The first manifestation of a decline appeared to be a reported slump in the numbers of Newfoundland ptarmigan in 1928-29. In 1930-31 reports indicated a die-off of ruffed grouse in Nova Scotia. A year later, at Bigger Lake, Ontario, Clarke observed a failure of the crop of young birds and there were well-distributed reports of similar occurrences elsewhere. By 1933 it was evident that a widespread reduction of grouse was in progress.

"Thus during the summer of 1933 the dying-off of young birds extended from the Atlantic coast into central and northern Ontario in patches, and from the north-west of Alberta and British Columbia into central British Columbia and a few parts of Alberta."

In 1934, Clarke studied grouse reproduction at Brule Lake, Ontario, and witnessed a progressive loss of young that aggregated 80 percent by September. On this basis he constructed a table comparing seasonal numbers in a year of normal increase on the upswing of the cycle with a dying-off year. The figures used are an expression of reproduction in the territories occupied by 10 breeding pairs:

	Normal	Year of dying-off
Adults in spring	20	20
Adults plus young at hatching	108	108
Adults plus young in fall	72	46
Adults in spring	30	15

This comparison indicates an increase of 50 percent in the spring population as a result of "normal" breeding (on the upswing of the cycle) as against a reduction of 25 percent in the year of decline. A second year of reduction would leave only 11 birds, and this evidently is what occurs in the downgrade of the cycle.

The pattern of losses found at Brule Lake was evident at other field stations and could be identified in the communications of widely scattered observers in 1933. As for what followed, ". . . the questionnaires covering the 1934 season [showed] that in the whole of Canada the areas which passed through 1934 without having had a decline in numbers were exceptional."

In his intensive field studies Clarke found the summer mortality of young grouse to be associated with a high incidence of infection by a blood parasite (*Leucocytozoön*) that produces a disease resembling human malaria. A different species of this parasite is known to be carried by a black fly, and any fisherman knows how plentiful these insects are in the North.

That is about as far as present information goes. Various species of *Leucocytozoön* are widely prevalent among birds and are suspect as important decimating agents. The need for intensive and continued research is plain enough, but no agency has yet been sufficiently concerned (or sufficiently well informed?) to sponsor such a job.

As an aid to field surveys sportsmen sometimes are asked to save the wings and tails of grouse killed in the hunting season and send these to state technicians. The idea is to get an age ratio that will indicate breeding success. In Michigan the year 1942 represented a population peak and numbers fell off sharply from 1943 to 1945. A sampling of the 1945 kill showed an age ratio of 55 percent young and 45 percent adults. This does not indicate a particularly successful breeding season. In 1946 grouse populations began to recover, hunter success improved, and young birds in the kill increased to 75 percent. Such a ratio indicates prosperity, although the proportion of juveniles goes even higher in a year of bumper production.

No implication is intended here that *Leucocytozoön,* or any other known factor, is *the* active agent in grouse cycles. The evidence is convincing, though not conclusive, that this disease was involved in the decline studied by Clarke. The parasite is characteristically virulent in young birds, and loss of the new generation seems to be a consistent feature of the reduction. However, there seem to be variations in the cycle mechanism from one region to another and from one decade to another.

Particularly in the case of game birds, there have been declines which appeared to be associated with climatic extremes, and especially a deterioration of conditions during the spring breeding season (See note p. 354). This factor was reported as responsible for the 1943 reduction of sharptails and Hungarian partridges in Western Canada and probably was involved in the almost continent-wide pheasant "depression" in the forties.

All of which serves to complicate the cycle problem still further. In commenting on their study of the 206-year lynx cycle record in the Canadian Arctic, Elton and Nicholson made this significant statement: "We have at present no clue at all to the nature of the factor controlling the enormous wild-life rhythm in the northern forests, except that it seems almost certain that climatic fluctuations must play a controlling part."

FISH STORIES

Most of the types of fluctuations that occur among mammals and birds can be identified also in fish populations, and some that are new and different appear as a result of conditions under which aquatic life is renewed. A brief sampling will illustrate this, and no more than that is practical here.

In 1912, the planting of a shipment of smelt eggs in Crystal Lake, Benzie County, Michigan, inaugurated one of the most intriguing fish stories in Great Lakes history. Other plantings probably failed, but this one, after a slow start, made good with a vengeance.

It was six years before the first fish appeared. In 1918 they made a spawning run up Cold Creek from Crystal Lake. In 1923 they were found on the east shore of Lake Michigan, and a year later they had crossed to Big Bay de Noc. In 1928 nets were taking them in the Wisconsin waters of Green Bay. Steadily new horizons were invaded in the big lakes, and a few smelt even got through to Erie; but the mass abundance remained centered in Lake Michigan.

For years the smelt was looked upon by fishermen as a nuisance, and trepidation was felt for the possible effects of its burgeoning numbers on native fish. Then in 1931 Wisconsin commercial netters took, and sold, 86,000 pounds of smelt. The demand was good and the supply prodigious. Top production was reached in 1941 with a total catch for the market in Lake Michigan of more than 4¾ million pounds.

In the meantime April spawning runs up northern streams had drawn off-season tourists by the thousand. Smelt festivals became an annual vacation event. Torchlight crowds waded hip-deep in wriggling rivers of slender, green-and-silver fish. They dipped them out by the ton. The take by "sport" fishermen in the two states was more than double the commercial catch. Rolled in flour, browned crisp in deep fat, and eaten bones and all, the 7- to 9-inch, delectable, 5-cents-a-pound smelt took its rightful place on the table of the gourmet and as king of the fish fries.

It got better and better, an industry was established, and in the public eye the smelt came to symbolize inexhaustible manna. Nature, they thought, wore a waxen smile. Not so the biologist. The more the smelt prospered, the more sour-puss certain he became that it couldn't last. The little fish that went to market were riding for a fall.

In 1942 it came. Somewhere in central Lake Huron, the smelt began to die. On October 3, at Black River, a Michigan conservation officer saw them washing ashore.

The blight ran through the lakes like the flash of a powder train. Smelt died in Saginaw Bay, Georgian Bay, and the North Channel. The contagion spread through the Straits of Mackinac into Lake Michigan. By the end of November it had reached Point Aux Barques, and in February the smelt were dying in Green Bay, the center of the fishery.

It took just 4½ months for some sort of epizoötic (it hasn't been spotted to this day) to wipe out perhaps 90 percent of the smelt. In 1944 a meagre 4,500 pounds were marketed. After that they began to increase again. By 1950 near-record catches were being taken.

The die-off of smelt came a year before conditions deteriorated for small game and it may be a case simply of a species that got too plentiful. On the other hand, what has occurred will occur again, and it may be that the smelt will come and go with regularity. This happens to other species of fish, and the causes are diverse.

A bottomland lake in the Illinois River Valley has exhibited cycles of four to five years in the size and abundance of black crappies, even though the poundage remained the same from year to year. At one end of the cycle the fish would be ten times as abundant, but they would be only one-tenth as large.

The reason for the fluctuation was cannibalism, and here is the way it worked: At a time when the population consisted of a few old fish, these breeders produced a large crop of young, many of which survived. In the years that followed, this generation grew and spawned, but its food requirements were so great it devoured both its own young and those of other species. No new generation of crappies could be established and the dominant brood, like the little recruit, just grew and grew. Finally the old fish reached the end of their time and died off, leaving another numerous generation of young to repeat the process.

"In this way the crappie not only produces a cycle in its own kind but imposes it on many other non-cannibalistic fish. This has a striking effect on both hook-and-line and commercial fishing. During part of the cycle . . . as many as 99 percent of the black crappies are of catchable size. This is followed by a period when there were as few as one or two percent of large fish."

Atlantic salmon in the Maritime region of Canada furnish another good example of cyclic behavior. Annual yields of these fish were studied by Huntsman from 1870 to 1930 (See note p. 355).

Of greatest interest here is the fact that figures for four regions from the Gaspé Peninsula to the Bay of Fundy were examined separately and the existence of a general 9- to 10-year cycle clearly established. In the case of St. John's River fish it was possible to determine the average period as 9.6 years. And this fluctuation of salmon *showed depressions coinciding with cyclic lows of the snowshoe rabbit in the North.* The rhythm was of unknown origin and in it salmon seemed to be responding to the same influence that conditions the waxing and waning of many other creatures.

PULSE OF NUMBERS

Another comprehensive putting-together of the evidence on cycles was carried out by Lauri Siivonen, Director of the Game-Research Institute, Helsinki, Finland.

Dr. Siivonen's basic material was the long-term and detailed records on black game and capercaillie in Finland, and he made use of the published records on all species from North America and Europe. After extensive statistical studies, he concluded that the short cycle of 3 to 4 years that had long been recognized in some far-northern species was a universal basic rhythm for cyclic birds and mammals. He found its average length to be 3⅓ years.

This analysis indicated that the 10-year fluctuation in grouse, hares, and certain carnivorous animals is an exceptionally high peak of the 3⅓-year period. It becomes most marked when the short cycle is lengthened by a year or two.

It was suggested also that major deviations from the norm were likely to appear "in connection with a period of general, great, climatic disturbances . . ."

There are still other findings to be added to the file of cycle information. In discussing animal numbers we have given proper weight and emphasis to the matter of density. Although it probably is not the entire explanation, it undoubtedly is a key condition in cycle mechanics. Investigations in the realm of physiology have helped to clarify understanding of what is commonly called "shock" or, more generally, stress.

It is known to most people that there is an automatic body reaction to conditions such as anger, fear, pain, etc. Crudely stated, this involves secretions of certain ductless glands—in particular, portions of the pituitary and adrenals.

Wild animals have similar reactions that undoubtedly have survival value in stimulating the individual in the presence of danger or discomfort. It has been found, however, that when living conditions deteriorate and an animal is under constant physical harassment, its reaction mechanism becomes exhausted and shock symptoms develop.

J. J. Christian assembled information on this subject and concluded that shock was most likely to appear during the severe weather of winter following a fall population peak. At such times the number of animals in a given area undoubtedly is far beyond normal carrying capacity and a condition of acute biological squalor develops. Concentrated wintering populations would be subjected to a variety of unfavorable influences: "(1) food scarcity, (2) lack of proper cover, (3) increased muscular exertion resulting from longer food forage trips, (4) fights with other individuals . . . (5) increased exposure to cold from longer forage trips and inadequate cover, (6) fighting resulting from territorial encroachment . . . (7) utilization of inadequate foods, (8) increased exposure to predators due to lack of cover as well as migration of predators into areas of abundant food supply in the form of a peak population, and (9) nutritional deficiencies."

These are the environmental burdens that were involved in the winter of hard times described for Michigan fox squirrels. They bring on a chain of physical abnormalities that includes blood-sugar deficiency, adrenal enlargement, reduction of sugar storage in the liver, liver degeneration, diminished fat, and changes in blood chemistry.

Shock undoubtedly is the most characteristic density-dependent factor yet discovered. Christian suggested that it might be a primary cause of cyclic declines in mammals—directly or in predisposing a population to other ailments. In this case the length of a cycle would depend on the reproductive rate and the time required for a population to build back up again.

Superficially it would appear that the multiplying tensions which develop in animal concentrations have some parallel in what seems to be happening to people exposed to the complex existence of large cities. We hear much speculation about how the rapidly mounting stresses of modern living are reacting on the mental and physical health of the individual. Nervous disorders, ulcers, psychosomatic diseases appear to be on the increase—unless we are misled by the fact that they are just getting recognition. The fact that many wild animals develop the shock syndrome when there are too many of them, and frequently are killed off wholesale, might indicate that such creatures are socially less calloused than man. Nevertheless, although humans have ways of softening the impacts of their enviroment, the evidence suggests that this ability is far from perfect and that we, too, have reactions akin to the physical break-down that overtook the squirrels and snowshoe hares.

Undoubtedly the improved understanding of population stress is another important piece in the puzzle, but the picture is not yet clear. Sometimes a collapse of numbers come independent of any known cyclic trend. But when the ten-year peak has been reached and the slump is due, populations great and small are toppling. At such times susceptibility to unfavorable influences becomes striking.

If we are dealing entirely with a density phenomenon, then it should theoretically be possible, by heavy shooting, to prevent grouse or other game species from building up to the lethal peak. This is something that could best be tried on an island, and thus far it has not been done. Certainly, something would be learned from such an experiment.

But if population declines were induced entirely by crowding and habitat deterioration, that would not explain why such dissimilar creatures as the grouse and hare cycle together and how so many other pulsations, on at least a continental scale, could be so nearly in phase. Something appears to be lending an approximate coincidence to widely diverse events.

Many investigators have looked for some basic cosmic rhythm that could account for this. Sunspots were under suspicion, but the cycle in question was found to be slightly longer than the biological fluctuation. Variations in atmospheric ozone (tri-atomic oxygen) also have been considered a possibility. Nothing satisfactory has been found, but the search undoubtedly will go on.

It cannot be doubted that the earth is much affected by many kinds of radiation from the sun and outer reaches of the universe. Maxwell O. Johnson, working in Hawaii, pointed out that the major and minor planets have important electromagnetic influences on the sun and that these are most potent at times when two of the planets are in the same heliocentric longitude (i.e. lined up with the sun). Such formations recur at regular intervals, and the time elapsing between two similar ones is referred to as the synodic period for the two planets in question.

Johnson found that there were cycles in rainfall corresponding to the combined effects of synodic periods of the planets. It is especially thought provoking (in the light of Siivonen's findings) that in Pacific precipitation records he identified a 3.32-year cycle "superimposed on a 10-year cycle, or six cycles in a 20-year periodicity." In records of mean annual temperature from New Haven, Connecticut, he found that the "most probable . . . periodicity was a 20-year one with six shorter cycles . . ." * (See note p. 356).

This is not to imply any explanation of the apparently regular coming and going of animal numbers, but to point out that such a phenomenon would by no means be unique. The natural world is geared to an assortment of repetitive events—night and day, summer and winter, high and low tides. They are dependable and can be foretold, but conditions accompanying them are not always the same because of variables on earth and mutually interfering cosmic influences that may appear irregular, but which may be part of a long-term symmetry of motion.

There is hardly any doubting that in the first half of this century, and probably before, we have had some entirely real periodisms of about ten years covering a variety of wildlife species and occurring in a spotty but convincing pattern over large regions. Conceivably, recent regularity could be coincidence. Whether or not it is maintained will be the real proof one way or another. All will agree that this should be a field for continued inquiry. The crux of the matter is the extent to which population fluctuations can be predicted. When we know that, we may or may not have the making of an action pro-

* Reprinted by permission from *Cycles in Weather and Solar Activity,* by Maxwell O. Johnson. Copyright 1950. Paradise of the Pacific Press, Honolulu.

gram that will level off the boom and bust and give more consistent production.

In the meantime we can expect that certain species in certain regions will decline at intervals despite anything that can be done at present. Expenditures for such expedients as stocking or predator control will have no bearing on the recovery. In addition, it is being recognized that there is little point in closing the season when grouse are down. At such times hunting effort declines with the birds, and the Nimrod who fares afield with his dog has little to show for it.

It should be emphasized also that we still are doing business in terms of good and poor range. A favorable area is one where a game animal, *a part of the time,* reaches a density that results in good shooting. It may support a low population temporarily. But in unfavorable range the spread in numbers is from low to lower, and hunting will be poor at its best.

There is no reason for doubting that the improvement of habitats is worthwhile, even for species whose numbers are governed in part by things beyond control. We can vastly increase average production by remedying all the deficiencies within our power to handle.

When climate, disease, or the ten-year disaster work against us, we can nod knowingly—and save our money.

PART II

Paths and by-paths

CHAPTER 8

The Harvest

WHEN Meshach Browning settled in Garrett County, Maryland, in 1801 he had only three neighbors, the nearest two miles away. He shot deer and turkeys, almost at will, in his dooryard. Each fall Browning took his dogs to nearby areas where chestnut, beech, and oak mast was plentiful and with little difficulty (except for packing them home on horses) killed 15 to 20 bears and as many or more deer which were salted down to support his expanding family.

For 44 years he hunted this region, and he saw the game dwindle from abundance to a point where, in 1835, despite skill and experience, his energy no longer was adequate to the task of finding and killing a deer.

During the first half of this period the game-producing range was relatively undisturbed. The yield potential of the mast-bearing forest was prodigious. Deer entered winter in prime condition. Bears were so fat they sought out mud wallows to keep cool prior to hibernation time. From the back of one of these animals Browning cut six inches of fat in preparing it for the brine.

The game supply was largely unaffected by food demands of the scattered population and even by the shipment of sleigh-loads of venison saddles and bear meat to Baltimore markets. It also supported a numerous population of wolves and panthers.

Local people saw large numbers of animals killed. No doubt here, as elsewhere, they associated this killing with the decline. Yet Browning saw, and described, something of much more importance.

Cutting, burning, and hog raising reduced the mast crop, and fields were cleared in the bottoms. Tall grass in the "glades" where deer and turkeys had fed was pastured flat by herds of cattle. The back country was opened up, and there were no longer large, undisturbed areas where deer could yard and bears might den up for winter. The face of the land changed and productive game range disappeared.

As civilization seeped into the hinterlands, game concentrations were broken up wherever they occurred on fertile soils. (They seldom were found anywhere else.) The gun took its toll in passing, and as much as opportunity permitted; but farm crops and livestock were what worked the land over to a new destiny.

During the settlement period a man's prowess as a hunter was judged by the amount of meat he could pile up. A buckboard loaded with prairie grouse, ducks, and curlews was witness to skill and sporting blood. The standard hunting photograph of the nineties and later featured keen-eyed Nimrods posed symmetrically before a back-drop of strung-up game with a selection of local predators thrown in by way of hors d'oeuvres.

In the public eye this is now recognized as the game-hog era, although it will be graceful to acknowledge that but for a later birth you or I might well have been second from the left in those pictures.

In the first chapter we witnessed the destruction of the buffalo. It was the greatest game resource we ever will have and the gun wiped it out in profligate waste. Realistically, we should not call this "hunting," and hunters, in the modern sense, should not share the burden for what was, in the main, commercial exploitation.

Nevertheless, the hide hunting, and irresponsible shooting by a few "sportsmen," left a deep impression on the public mind. They helped establish the gun as an instrument of destruction and fostered a widespread assumption that *all* shooting is a step toward extermination of our native fauna.

Of course, this suspicion of the gun as a destructive agent is valid up to a certain point. But beyond that point it is a prejudice that impairs the adequate harvest of surplus game.

There are times when a little shooting is too much, and in other cases a generous harvest is a must. The sportsman will lose heavily unless he can discriminate.

THOSE REMAINING FEW

In considering the position and function of the gun, something can be learned from the past and present of the grizzly. Due to indiscriminate killing, poisoning, and giving it the "outlaw" treatment

as a predator, this top-flight game species is even now heading for
the red side of the ledger. Grizzlies have been cleared from the greater
part of their former range. Annual inventories of the Fish and Wildlife Service indicate that there are slightly over a thousand of them
left in six states. Three states report less than ten each.

In Montana this animal was considered to be worth a study, and
the work began in 1941 under Federal Aid. In 1947, in his report
on the work, Robert F. Cooney stated: "It is evident that the grizzly
bear has reached a critical stage. Care must be exerted in carrying
out management plans for further protection and maintenance of this
rare game species, in desirable back country areas."

Grizzlies are slow breeders, and it was found that the hunting kill
was an important factor in holding numbers at a low level. Spring
shooting was especially effective. It was an off-season for guides and
packers, and bears were easy targets after they emerged from hibernation and were feeding in snowslide areas and open meadows.

As a result of this timely work, the Montana Fish and Game Commission eliminated the spring open season and confined hunting, for
most areas, to a month in the fall. The state now has the bulk of the
nation's grizzlies—about 600 animals. They probably are reasonably
safe in these tracts of rugged wilderness. This is by default, of course
—it is poor country for raising sheep.

Although the gun can be a menace to the continued existence of
the grizzly, the present low ebb of this species is a result of "control"
more than hunting. Much of this control obviously was necessary,
since the animal once was widely distributed in regions whose primary
long-term value is in livestock production. Montana has decided where
the grizzly can be preserved and how to do it.

Hunting can finish off nearly any game animal whose range has
been so restricted that it is confined to small areas. This is almost always the case where a species has dwindled to the danger point.
Good examples are the trumpeter swan, which is being preserved primarily on the Red Rock Lakes refuge in Montana, and the sandhill
crane, which still manages to find a few suitable nesting sites in
widely scattered marshes.

The diminutive Key deer, found on Big Pine and several other
Florida keys, is another species in jeopardy. In 1950 only about 32 of
these pint-sized whitetails survived under harassment by poachers and

wild dogs. Public interest was aroused and a national wildlife refuge created. Congress authorized land acquisition in 1957, and several parcels were purchased by private contributions. By 1960 the deer were up to 200 and their outlook was much improved.

When any game animal becomes so limited in distribution and number that the remnant population can no longer produce a harvestable surplus large enough to be of importance as a public hunting resource, *then shoooting of that species should end.* As sportsmen we should insist on the principle that such a population remnant becomes a *national* charge—and not the property of a few local residents whose privilege it is to write "finis" to the story of another member of our dwindling fauna.—Which brings us to a major problem.

STORM BIRDS

There is something unique and stimulating in the hunting of waterfowl, and it has long been a feature attraction for American sportsmen. No other experience is quite like that of crouching in the blind on a dull November day with a raw norther whipping tentative gusts of snow out of lowering clouds. When birds appear, they may be any or several kinds from a selection of twenty or more species. They may come in or they may not. But when they do, the shooting (and the eating) is like nothing else. Duck hunting hath charms to soothe the civilized breast.

Perpetuating this sport has become one of our foremost conservation problems. Migratory waterfowl are one type of game that was most plentiful when the continent was in its primitive condition, and aside from short-term ups and downs the resource has been in steady decline for more than half a century.

The downgrade of waterfowl has been a function of dwindling habitat. Most of these birds are produced annually in potholes, lakes, and marshes in the great interior prairies of northern United States and Canada. Each fall, breeders and their progeny are moved southward by storms that presage freezing weather. They filter down well-watered lanes of travel to ice-free wintering grounds on the Atlantic shore, southern swamps, the Gulf coast, tule-bordered water areas of the West, and lakes and marshes of Mexico. In spring there is a reverse movement, by the same or different routes of flight.

Ducks and geese cannot live without water, and widespread drain-

In primitive times it was probably local destruction of the grasses by buffalo that kept the prairie dog in business. This plump specimen is thriving on early weed stages in the Texas grasslands. (Fish & Wildlife Service.)

Glading's "gallinaceous guzzler," an underground watering device, has done wonders in producing more California quail. (California Department of Fish & Game.) Below, a study in protective coloration: a male bobwhite on the alert, Crab Orchard Refuge, Herrin, Illinois. (Fish & Wildlife Service.)

Top, left. A deeply eroded gully on a Wisconsin farm before the growth of protective vegetation. Below, the same gully, with newly planted willows and black locusts provides good cover for useful wildlife. (Soil Conservation Service.)

Bobcats have their place in the natural scheme of things. This one became the mascot of CCC boys in Chelan National Forest, Washington. (Forest Service.)

age of wetlands has been the most important single factor in reducing the vast flocks that once clouded the sky above our waterways. In 1956 the Fish and Wildlife Service completed the first reasonably accurate national survey of wetlands. It indicated that the original extent of such areas was about 127 million acres, and a minimum of 45 million acres of "primitive marshes, swamps, and seasonally flooded bottomlands are now devoted to crops, pasture, and other dry-land uses."

On northern breeding grounds, potholes and marshes have been drained in favor of grain farming and grazing. Such areas also disappear steadily through the natural deposition of vegetation and by siltation from the erosion of agricultural lands. Thus the duck crop has diminished at its source.

Water and feeding areas also have disappeared from the flight lanes. This has concentrated birds on remaining waters and exposed them increasingly to hunting, which has grown steadily heavier. The same process has diminished wintering grounds and reduced food supplies which are needed for the sojourn in the South.

Drought years of the thirties worked havoc with our waterfowl, reducing both breeding areas and birds to an unprecedented low. Inventory methods lack much of the desired accuracy, but there may have been less than 30 million ducks and geese of all kinds on the flyways in 1935. With more rainfall, water came back, and marsh-restoration projects were carried out with the help of public labor programs. By 1943 the birds were estimated at 140 million. Then more dry weather on the plains and another decline.

Since ducks are interstate travelers, they are subject to federal regulation. It has become the annual duty of the Fish and Wildlife Service to institute rules on methods of hunting, bag limits, and open seasons. In doing this there have been two objectives:

1. To preserve the resource.
2. To distribute the allowable kill as equitably as possible.

It is almost inherent in the situation that in the presence of a diminished supply of waterfowl completely satisfactory regulations could not be formulated short of divine guidance and the cooperation of every hunter. Presumably neither of these factors has been operative.

Commercial and private duck clubs have made heavy investments, and waterfowl hunting has provided the livelihood of guides, boat liverymen, and caretakers. Large sales of guns and ammunition are involved. The closing of a season or even the drastic curtailment of hunting is not to be undertaken lightly, as responsible administrators have learned.

Obviously, we should do all within our power to send back north enough ducks to stock the available breeding range. But no one of us can be a good judge of what regulations will accomplish this. From my blind the scenery may be wonderful, and from yours it may appear that the ax is about to fall.

After the end of the war in 1945, waterfowl hunters built up rapidly. The annual sale of federal "duck stamps" reached a peak of 2,-369,940 in 1955-56, after which demand dropped off—by three-quarters of a million in two years. In view of the need for more money in the waterfowl program, Congress raised the price of a stamp from one to two dollars in 1949 and to three dollars in 1959. On July 1, 1960, the lawmakers ear-marked all returns from duck stamp sales for land acquisition, thus recognizing the urgency of preserving our remaining wet areas for waterfowl—and likewise implying that they would appropriate other funds for such functions as land development, law enforcement, and research.

These moves can be critically important to the preservation of waterfowl hunting and (even more important) waterfowl "seeing." We can do some things to improve and increase habitat and other things to reduce the destruction of existing habitats. But despite all such efforts, our shooting certainly must be rationed, and it will have to be done by one government agency. More research is badly needed to determine the potential and actual productivity of little-explored regions of the North. But for now a vast network of observers—state, provincial, federal and private—annually gather the best records possible, which are compiled and interpreted with increasing efficiency. The resulting regulations are a conscientious effort to do the best possible job for the resource and for the greatest number of people.

Your duck season and my duck season may be disconcertingly short. But a given bird is exposed to *somebody's* open season almost from the time he leaves the breeding ground until he arrives on a wintering area. Even when numbers are drastically reduced by a dry year, ducks and geese are vulnerable because of the manner in which they funnel through concentration areas on the way south. This is a big difference between migratory waterfowl and resident upland game.

Although productive habitats have been greatly reduced, we can have good waterfowl years when climatic conditions favor. But poor years are going to be much more frequent than in the old days. Much is yet to be learned of the dynamics of waterfowl numbers. But to some populations, in some seasons, the gun may well be a limitation, and it's the only one we can control *on an annual basis*. Our policy should be to cooperate in this as necessary, to take measures for protection of the water areas we have, and to build new ones as rapidly as funds and technology permit.

THE DIVIDEND

Thinking conservationists of the past 40 years have become increasingly disturbed at the continuing trend of two approaching curves: a declining curve representing the narrowing down of some types of game range, and a rising one indicating the accumulation of new recruits by the army of sportsmen. Somewhere, they logically opined, the twain shall meet, and that will be the fade-out by important members of our sporting fauna.

There is no disclaiming this steady increase of "wildlife problems" as the human population grows and water and land areas, great and small, are "developed" for the production (magic word) of crops that are needed and other crops that add to national surpluses bought by the taxpayer for storage and eventual waste. As we have seen, a population (including the human one) is a dynamic thing that goes on expanding as long as there is a place to expand to and anything to support it. Presumably, we may hope, even an expanding economy will at length refuse further distention, and if the seams hold we will have a condition approximating stability. This implies a relatively static population that uses resources only about as fast as they are renewed or substitutes can be devised.

This will be an era in which wildlife quantities will be carefully measured and each species will have its own particular kind of planned economy. Our fumbling management programs of the present aim in that general direction.

The sinister aspects of what appears to be an approaching crisis have prompted writers, administrators, and technicians to be designedly conservative in dealing with the game harvest.

This has been a good and prudent policy, since all too often there has been a total lack of precise knowledge of the effects of shooting. However, we now can approach the matter with somewhat better equipment. We have measured some populations and some hunting kills. There is much more to be done, but meanwhile there are facts waiting to be used.

A large part of management will be to know the size of the crop we are producing and to use that crop with efficiency. A truth that is widely unappreciated is that game crops do not "store up" from year to year. Like apples, they must be picked when ready, and waste will result if our wildlife investments are not followed up by realistic harvests.

The conservatism that has been preached at the public has struck home, and now we have the curious twist of events whereby technical men frequently are urging liberalization of restrictions against stubborn, and sometimes violent, popular resistance. Understandably, the sportsman can hardly believe his ears, because the story he now hears is so different from the one told him only a few years ago.

Two ideas, in particular, are relatively new and essential to an understanding of how shooting fits the annual cycle of animal populations. One is that the relative size of the permissible harvest can and does vary with the quality of the range. The other is what we can call *compensation*. Briefly, it means if one thing doesn't get them, something else will. It accounts for the poor storage qualities evident in an unharvested game crop. Both of these ideas will appear in the following discussions of individual species.

THE ELUSIVE COCK

The literature on pheasant stocking is replete with references to areas "where cocks have been shot out" or where the birds "have been reduced by overhunting."

In the late thirties, Michigan biologists were becoming a bit curious about this evidently common phenomenon, since there had never been an area in that state where a spring scarcity of cocks could be demonstrated. Accordingly, when they established a new experiment station in the farmlands east of Lansing in 1939, they decided that a realistic test of hunting effects would be a part of the program.

For hunting purposes, about 2,000 acres of state and private land were opened to the public each fall at the Rose Lake Wildlife Experiment Station. It was farmland of moderate fertility, representing the hilly, glacial-moraine type that is common in the state. Likewise it was pheasant range of only medium productivity.

First as a matter of trial, and then as a matter of policy, hunting was not limited, although it was spread over the area under a system of permits. Every hunter checked out, left a record of his hunt, and had his kill examined at the laboratory.

In the first year of hunting, the average kill for the area was 10.8 cock birds per hundred acres, and this harvest was produced by hunting pressure that averaged 99 gun-hours for the same land unit. (One hunter out for one hour is a gun-hour.)

This appeared to be intensive shooting; but to obtain a standard for comparison, in 1940 a survey of private farms was made by means of records kept by 136 selected farmers in the vicinity of the city of Lansing. It was thought that these farms represented heavily-hunted land, but results showed that gun pressure averaged 43 gun-hours per hundred acres—less than half the hunting done at Rose Lake.

Pheasant production was about the same in 1940 as it had been the year before, and the Rose Lake kill was nearly the same—10.2 cocks per hundred acres. But another factor was much different: Hunters had learned about the area and came in increasing numbers. Hunting pressure for the season was 176 gun-hours per hundred acres! With pheasant numbers about the same and three-fourths again as much hunting, the kill was nearly identical to what it had been in 1939.

We will skip a year and consider 1942. The pheasant population was much like that of the first two seasons. The kill was 11.2 birds per hundred acres. *But hunting pressure was 234 gun-hours per land unit.*

Here are the figures, side by side:

Year	Kill per 100 acres	Gun-hours per 100 acres
1939	10.8	99
1940	10.2	176
1942	11.2	234

Did these figures mean that you could increase the hunting pressure without increasing the kill? It sounded ridiculous, but there it was. Another area, the Prairie Farm, which was 8,000 acres of excellent lowland pheasant range, showed 6 out of 7 years with fairly uniform production. And the annual harvest evidently correlated more closely with numbers of birds available and conditions during the hunting season than with the *amount* of hunting. Prairie-Farm statistics were as follows:

Year	Kill per 100 acres	Gun-hours per 100 acres
1938	14.8	168
1939	15.6	256
1940	13.0	179
1942	16.9	206
1943	12.6	125
1944	17.6	183

On both of these areas it appeared that there was a point of *diminishing returns* beyond which additional hunting was largely unrewarded. At Rose Lake it probably took about 100 gun-hours of hunting to harvest the available surplus of birds. In an average year that represented roughly 75 percent of the cocks, which in turn meant about 10 cocks per hundred acres. Beyond that it was possible to pour in almost unlimited hunting without markedly increasing the kill. It meant that in Michigan's 22-day season, under the excellent cover conditions existing at Rose Lake and the Prairie Farm *it was practically impossible to shoot out cock pheasants.*

Evidently it works this way: The harder you hunt, the more wary and difficult the birds are to get. Also, the carrying capacity idea seems to be involved. It appears that a given cover pattern will preserve about a given number of cock pheasants in the face of unlimited hunting. To a surprising extent, *hunting is self-regulatory.* That this also applies in large measure to other species was indicated by the fact that neither rabbits nor squirrels were overshot under the heavy hunting at Rose Lake.

A consistent trend of hunting pressure was evident through every season: about half of the hunting was done the first week, 30 percent the second week, and 20 percent the last 8 days. Roughly 70 percent of the pheasant kill was taken the first week, 20 percent the second, and 10 percent the last 8 days.

What does this mean in terms of season length? Obviously, adding another week would mean little in the way of additional kill. Hence, when pheasants went down in the mid-forties and hunters were calling for a closed or drastically curtailed season, the Michigan Game Division opposed it on the grounds that the few cocks it would save meant nothing in terms of breeding stock. "It would be OK," they said, "if you *needed more cocks* and could cut off the *first week*."

The year that was left out of the above figures, 1941, was one of exceptionally high production on both of the study areas. The yield per hundred acres at Rose Lake went up to 17.4 cocks, and on the Prairie Farm it was 20.6. Hunting pressure on the two areas was 245 and 199 gun-hours respectively. Hunters killed more birds because there were more available when the season opened.

It was evident that the taper-off in hunting effort toward the end of the pheasant season was a result of difficulty in getting birds. An abundance of targets attracted heavy shooting, and conversely, few birds meant correspondingly less hunting pressure. That had been proved in surveys of the state and it also was proved when pheasants declined at Rose Lake as a result of a succession of poor breeding seasons. From 1943 to 1945 the annual crops per hundred acres were 6.9, 6.8, and 2.8. In '45, hunting pressure reached an all-time low of 91 gun-hours. When pheasants decline, hunting eases up.

Is it any wonder that pheasant investigators are becoming increasingly complacent about the effects of legal and legitimate hunting? Especially when it is being demonstrated on such areas as Pelee Island and the Prairie Farm that pheasants do just as well with a 1-to-10 sex ratio as with a ratio of 1 to 3? In fact, near-equal numbers of cocks and hens are no longer regarded as desirable. In Iowa, W. E. Green studied varying sex ratios and concluded that "hunting, as an instrument of management, may be desirable, as it helps maintain a more favorable sex ratio." In Michigan, Charles Shick found that one mating of a cock and hen was effective for an average of 22 days.

Shortages of cocks are reported commonly by hunters who go out late in the season and see a large proportion of hens. Or in winter they may encounter flocks of hens without seeing small groups or individual cocks that also are present. Come spring, however, it is almost a sure thing that cocks will be standing on the hillsides, as usual. The years 1943 to 1945 were seasons of poor hatch in California and hunters were reporting a shortage of cocks. It was said that harems numbered 15 to 20. Accordingly, state technicians ran some counts to test out the reports. They found harems ranging from 1 to 14 hens, with an average of 3.07. A sampling indicated high egg fertility.

Sportsmen and some game commissioners have not yet grasped the full significance of recent work in terms of the ability of this bird to care for himself. It might be well to point out, however, that we have dealt exclusively with legal hunting of cocks. When pheasants go down in numbers, there usually will be no reason for closing the season or drastically restricting the hunting of males. But if reduced numbers give rise to increased lawlessness (as is usual) and result in widespread shooting of hens, then measures will have to be taken; for the preservation of hens probably will do more for pheasant production than any other single measure.

In considering hunting kill in relation to population level in the pheasant, we can assume that a given hunting pressure will take a much higher *percentage* of a high population than of a low one. Let's say that available cover and other conditions permit cock birds to be shot down to a level of about 5 birds per hundred acres. If we started the season with a pheasant per acre, and half were males, then we would be shooting 90 percent of the roosters. But if we started the season with 40 birds to the hundred acres, and half were males, then a harvest of all but 5 would mean we were shooting 15, or 75 percent of the males.

Obviously, you can't carry this idea too far. If you started the season with only 5 fresh, un-shotover birds, some of them would be killed before the rest were "broken in" enough to assume that *n*th degree of elusiveness that is characteristic of the last survivors of a high population.

Half males? That doesn't sound like the sex ratios that are quoted for pheasants, does it? But there is nothing amiss here, because the common disparity in ratio comes in winter and spring. On nearly any area, before shooting, the ratio is likely to be near 1 : 1.

Figure it out: If in spring the average cock has a harem of 3 hens, and these hens bring through an average of 6 young apiece (optimistic, but round numbers), then by fall the sexes would add up this way:

	Cocks	Hens
Young	9	9
Adult	1	3
	10	12

Ratio   1 : 1.2

This calculation allows for no adult mortality, of course, and that would even things up still more.

In the case of pheasants, spring sex ratios are a good clue to the extent of the hunting kill—that is, if shooting is restricted entirely or principally to male birds. In Michigan, where hunting pressure on land around Lansing was only 43 gun-hours per hundred acres, it appeared that a substantial portion of the available crop was not being taken. In fact, it was reasonable to conclude that if sportsmen were killing one and a quarter million birds at that time, the kill could easily have been two million without any loss of breeding productivity. Sex ratios commonly ran about 1 cock to 3 hens.

As has been suggested, hen shooting would be ill-advised in an area where every effort must be made to produce more pheasants. However, there are conditions under which hen-shooting would be good management.

If pheasants are consistently undercropped and winter survival high, there is a good possibility of having a spring surplus of both sexes. If breeder hens are twice the number necessary to produce the maximum crop of young an area can rear during the warm months, the "drone" hens and cocks may as well be harvested. By increasing the kill, a higher turnover rate and productivity are brought about. In this connection, where many tracts are closed by landowners, it might well be good business to shoot hens on open land.

What the ultimate possibilities are in a state like South Dakota requires some wide-open thinking. Spring sex ratios there probably have approached 1:1 more consistently than anywhere else, which would indicate that a conservative proportion of the cocks was being harvested. A summary of conditions in the state was given by Bernard A. Nelson at the Midwest Wildlife Conference in 1946:

"The 1945 kill by licensed hunters was determined to be 7,500,000 birds. Add to this the kill by unlicensed residents, the illegal kill and the number of birds crippled or killed and not recovered, and the total kill would probably exceed 10,000,000. Considering that the number of hunters was 200,000 and that the pheasant range embraces some 50,000 square miles, hunting pressure actually was not great, and it seems unlikely that hunting took more than one-fourth or one-third of the birds. If these data and assumptions are correct, one is forced to conclude that the pre-season population in 1945 was between 30 and 40 million birds, or 6 to 8 hundred birds per section. As stated before, the 1945 population was probably only half of that of 1944. What the population was in 1944 is better left to the imagination."

Hens were shot in South Dakota through 1946, and in that year a check of bags showed about twice as many cocks as hens. This factor would affect observed spring sex ratios, yet it is evident that even the tremendous kills that were taken were only a part of the possible harvest in years through 1945.

Where pheasants are truly abundant, hen shooting is not only permissible; it may be mandatory. Too many of any kind of wildlife is likely to mean crop damage of one kind or another.

A study of published information to date leaves us with some rather startling conclusions on pheasant hunting:

1. There appears to be no biological objection to shooting 90 percent of the cocks—that is, male birds can be hunted to a point where spring sex ratios will be of the order of 1 to 10.

2. With any reasonable amount of escape cover present, legal hunting, however heavy, practically never results in the overshooting of cocks.

3. Season length is of little consequence, since heavy shooting results in a greatly reduced kill as the season advances.

4. When pheasants are low, hunting diminishes, and returns are low. There is no reason for restricting *the legal hunting of cocks.*

5. We haven't mentioned it, but a season limit means nothing at all. A daily bag limit helps distribute the easy early-season harvest among more hunters.

These principles will explain many attitudes of your state pheasant specialists. But they apply only to legal hunting in those parts of the country that realistically can be called pheasant range. Where only a semblance of shooting is being maintained by costly artificial methods in marginal range—we can forget such rules.

THEY'RE EXPENDABLE

It might be thought that in large measure the pheasant is a special case, since shooting can be confined to cocks and the bird is conveniently polygamous. These characteristics are a decided management advantage in most range. However, it will be found that nearly any species can sustain a generous toll by the gunner *in habitats where it can achieve a large annual increase.*

There is an important relationship between range quality and the allowable kill. The situation on two rabbit areas in Michigan illustrates this:

At the W. K. Kellogg Farm, near Battle Creek, a 3-day rabbit hunt was held on a 500-acre tract in December 1936. A total of 126 cottontails were shot. This was no ordinary hunt, for in the previous 6 weeks, 102 rabbits had been caught in boxtraps and marked with numbers tattooed in their ears.

Among the shot rabbits there were 57 with numbered ears, just 6 more than half of the marked rabbits. Offhand it was evident that the 126 rabbits bagged must have represented a little more than half of all rabbits on the tract. A high school boy might work out the proportion as follows:

$$\frac{\text{Marked rabbits shot}}{\text{Total rabbits shot}} = \frac{\text{Total rabbits marked}}{X}$$

$$X = 226 \text{ (pre-hunting population)}$$

Thus the kill constituted 55 percent of rabbits on the ground when hunting started. On a basis of our past conditioning that seems like overshooting and some besides. But there is good evidence that this crop was not too large: The fall shoot of the year before had taken 154 out of a population of 228, or a kill of 67 percent!

The breeding stock on this farm was perhaps 30 pairs of rabbits, which, if there were no mortality at all, could produce a fall population of about 600. Our December population of 226 was what *actually survived* from that potential.

About 40 miles from the Kellogg Farm was another rabbit study area, this one on poor sandy soil, in the Allegan State Forest. It supported a sparse, drouthy, ground vegetation and blocks of second-growth scrub oak. It was poor rabbit country; in fact the best it could do was about one-fifth the fall population found on the better farming area. At Allegan the spring breeding stock little more than doubled itself by fall.

Under these conditions, it's plain enough that to take half the fall rabbits would leave no "padding" between the hunting crop and the breeding stock. That probably would be overshooting, because some leeway to allow for natural mortality seems prudent.

For an area of ruffed grouse range in Minnesota, Ralph T. King calculated precisely how much leeway it was necessary to have. He found that it would insure the *maximum possible* number of breeders that his area could accommodate in spring if 40 percent of an October population were taken in hunting. Another 12 percent also would be excess and these birds would be accounted for by natural winter mortality, leaving the maximum effective breeding stock.

The percentage of a population that can be shot and the number to be left in allowing for natural "contingencies" undoubtedly varies greatly with location and species. There is no doubt that, to a great extent, hunting before winter will reduce the population to a point nearer the "security level" and thus actually cut down winter losses. If winter carrying capacity were a precise figure that could be determined beforehand, it would be possible theoretically to calculate the annual surplus, take them all by hunting, and then expect the breeding stock to come through to spring without losses.

We aren't likely to attain this ideal, of course; but in an Oklahoma quail study something comparable seems to have happened. The hunting harvest actually constituted practically the entire winter loss.

F. M. Baumgartner took inventories three times a year for five years on two tracts, one of which was hunted and the other closed to shooting. A winter die-off complicated the picture for two of the years studied, but figures for the other three probably are representative of trends on the two areas.

During three years, the hunted tract supported breeding populations of 11, 12, and 11 birds per hundred acres, respectively. Similar figures for the non-hunted land were 9, 12, and 13, indicating that the two units could winter about the same number of quail.

Fall populations, however, demonstrated that the shot-over area was better habitat; it carried 25, 25, and 19 birds, respectively, in the three years, as against 13, 15, and 15 on the closed unit.

The point of interest in this comparison is that on January 1 each year the number of quail left by gunners on the shot-over land was within one bird of the April inventory of breeders! In other words, by heavy shooting, this population was reduced to the point where only one bird per hundred acres was lost to natural mortality between the hunting season and spring breeding period.

Of course, another point that should not be missed here is that quail did not show a significant year-to-year increase on the area closed to shooting; they operated according to the same annual cycle as on the hunted unit.

An experiment at Virginia Polytechnic Institute further indicates how hunting fits into the annual-loss picture of the bobwhite:

In the fall of 1947, the college farms were divided into two areas roughly equal in acreage and numbers of quail. One tract was hunted and 39 percent of the birds removed. The other was left undisturbed.

On the following April 1, each area supported 21 quail. On hunted land there had been a winter loss of 49 percent, but on the non-hunted tract losses had been 60 percent. The number of birds involved was not large, but there is little doubt that they show the trend. That part of the annual surplus not accounted for in hunting tended to be taken by other factors.

These examples are part and parcel of the *compensation* principle. If we fail to take a hunting harvest, Nature does it for us. It is quite possible, and usual, for the hunter to get in ahead of natural mortality factors and convert the annual surplus of game to his own use merely by taking it before something else happens to it.

In the Virginia studies it was found that fall populations averaged about 11 birds per hundred acres. On a basis of experimental shooting it was found that the October harvest could be about seven quail per hundred acres, but if shooting were delayed until January, only two birds would be available to hunters. The difference, of course, represents what Nature would do to the population in the meantime.

Compensatory trends are observed frequently in the operation of natural mortality factors that assume different weights in different years. On two non-hunted areas of Iowa farmland, pheasants suffered heavy losses to blizzards and deep snow in the winter of 1935-36. The total mortality for that season was 48.2 percent.

The following winter was mild, and weather had little effect on the birds, but various other causes brought about losses of 40 percent. In still another winter, 49 percent of the population disappeared before spring, and that year heavy poaching and some predation were largely responsible.

The average winter toll in this habitat was 46 percent, and that reduction appeared to occur regularly irrespective of what caused it. Naturally, this does not mean that it's futile to try to eliminate limiting factors. It does emphasize that excess population present in all good habitats in the fall will be eliminated anyway and to use it as a hunting crop is just good business.

This probably is another way of saying that for small game species in the North the carrying capacity of a land unit usually declines during the cold season and the population is pinched down to fit a late-winter bottleneck. The size of the breeding stock that can winter successfully is to some extent a characteristic of local habitat, although this can vary markedly from the norm as a result of extremes in such variables as weather (as witness the two years we dropped in discussing the Oklahoma quail).

If this is true—and it is—we can see how, for some species, *shooting actually is beneficial* in the production of a new crop.

Does this sound far-fetched, wild, and visionary? Then follow through and see if you don't agree:

In some ranges winter appears to be an easy season for the pheasant. But in others, like the Iowa prairie country referred to, winter losses are heavy and regular. Now, if carrying capacity is expressed by a wearing down of numbers to a breeding stock the size of which tends to be somewhat constant, then *the elimination of a large number of cocks in the fall should allow correspondingly more hens to survive the winter.* This would raise the productive potential of our breeding stock—if that means anything in the particular area.

The fox squirrel furnishes another example, as illustrated by conclusions from a Michigan study:

"In this connection it appears that our late hunting season may well have another value. All squirrels are busily burying nuts in September and October. October and November hunting removes half-a-million-plus animals from the population and leaves their stored food safely underground to nourish those which are left through winter and spring. The hard winter of 1940 showed that little food means few young; and conversely, more food very likely means more young. It seems logical that this large fall kill is beneficial to the production of a new crop, since it removes early in the season a part of the yearly surplus which would otherwise be eliminated in the competition of the cold season."

In other words, hunting can replace natural losses, and in the absence of hunting, natural factors will compensate for what the hunter did not do. That accounts for the poor storage properties of game crops. If you don't take it when it's ripe, you've lost it. And that applies equally to closed areas and closed seasons.

YOUR SHARE

This portion of our discussion was started with a consideration of how large a toll could safely be taken from the fall population without reducing next year's crop. We noted that this proportion is larger in good range than it is in substandard range.

However, that may be a poor way to leave the question. Most of us hunt land that will qualify as somewhere around average for the species concerned. It may help to have some average figures.

In his book on quail in the Southeast, Verne E. Davison recommended that 6 or 7 birds be left in each covey. Since coveys will average 12 to 15 at the beginning of the hunting season, this means that approximately half the population can be considered the hunting crop.

After a six-year study of the bobwhite in Iowa, George O. Hendrickson and his students concluded that ". . . in normal years a breeding population of 400-800 bob-whites may be expected to increase 200-300 percent by autumn to provide a shootable surplus of 500-1000 birds on the 7713-acre area." That also appears to mean about half.

In Missouri, a 2,000-acre area showed hunting-season losses of 43 and 47 percent in two successive years.

In the light of all evidence, it seems realistic and conservative to conclude that a fair and safe quail crop for the hunter is half the fall population. It is easy to regulate this in the case of the bobwhite, for it comes neatly packaged in coveys and a covey size of 6 or 7 can be the indicator.

The cock pheasant already has been considered, and in effect we concluded that it is safe to shoot all the birds you can during the open season. That may mean a reduction by 90 percent and spring sex ratios of 1 to 10. But it works.

Determining just what portion you are shooting is more difficult for other small game. On productive areas rabbits will thin out and become much more difficult to get by the time you have shot 50 to 60 percent. That is not too many to take and it is especially difficult to overshoot an animal that produces a potential 20 young per female. Where cover is well distributed, you aren't likely to overshoot. Where cover is in small, far-between patches, your share is less and over-shooting much more likely. This is particularly so because rabbits from large areas of open fields tend to concentrate in available cover after frosts kill the annual vegetation.

Studies of the fox squirrel indicate that a kill of 40 percent of the fall population is not unusual and that this probably can be increased by 10 percent without harm to crops that follow. As we have seen, it's likely that the breeding stock is especially benefited by a fall thinning, since the species breeds in winter when it is largely dependent on stored food.

In the case of ruffed grouse, it is likely that there are few large areas where more than 15 to 20 percent of the population is being taken by hunters. There is no doubt that an allowable kill would be at least twice this number.

These kill percentages must, of course, include game lost through crippling. Such mortality often is difficult to estimate or measure. It is likely that waste is greatest where game is most plentiful and hunters have less incentive to use care in shooting and marking down. In general, we probably should not try to harvest our game so closely that errors in allowing for crippling loss will make the difference between a safe kill and overshooting.

CHAPTER 9

Frozen Asset

THE history of American game conservation has been marked by many a bitterly fought controversy, but for heat and lasting quality the wrangle over our deer herds is near the top. From California to Maine and Texas to Ontario it has smoldered and flared. In some states a measure of order has emerged from a welter of prejudice, misunderstanding, scientific fact, and economic interest. But on a broad front the situation still is unsettled and the old issues regularly revive. Every state and the border provinces of Canada have deer "situations." Essentially, our deer troubles are a harvest problem—the question being, how much and how?

The low point for deer in this country probably was reached in the first decade of the 1900's. Seton estimated that there were half a million whitetails at that time. On a basis of incomplete records collected from the various states by the Bureau of Sport Fisheries and Wildlife, prehunting numbers of this species probably were near 7 million in 1960. Including blacktails and mule deer, the national herd was around 12 million, of which roughly 15 percent was being taken annually by 4 to 5 million hunters.

A decade earlier, the national kill probably was nearer 10 percent of prehunting numbers, and this figure seems to inch slowly upward as biological management makes progress. It naturally raises the question of how far we have yet to go.

A well-situated breeding stock of deer will show a spring-to-fall increase of 35 to 45 percent. That is, by hunting season about 4 out of 10 deer will be fawns. If the range is fully stocked (as most ranges are), then annual losses must match increment. Using the prehunting herd as a base, the annual turnover of numbers is near 40 percent. But under a continuing bucks-only regulation the legal harvest of males is nearly always less than 10 percent. So, if the annual loss is

40 percent and the sportsman is getting only 10 percent, a major portion of the available crop is being wasted.

It is now well demonstrated that nearly any deer herd can furnish an annual harvest of at least 25 percent of its fall numbers. But this can be done only by taking a substantial share of does and fawns. The increase in the national kill percentage is largely a measure of the extent to which states are getting away from a hard-and-fast buck law and providing for the shooting of antlerless deer. There is a similar trend toward multiple limits where these are necessary to crop local herds.

In 1959, a California survey of deer regulations in the 50 states showed that only 3 states had no deer hunting, 12 hunted bucks only, and 35 had some provision for harvesting antlerless deer. Unfortunately, among those 35 states, many had made only a small start toward adequate cropping. There are important sections of deer country where public opinion has not kept up with vital statistics, and there is perennial resistance to the kind of regulations that would give the best return from the deer resource and keep ranges in productive condition. How this came about is a colorful, frustrating story, yet it holds good promise for the future.

WHITE MAN'S DEER

As we have seen, most forest wildlife is produced, not in stands of mature timber, but in early brush and sprout stages. The great primeval woodlands were not good deer range except where broken up by fires or Indian clearing for agriculture. "Edge" and variety were favorable, and old growth contributed benefits in the form of oak, beech, and chestnut mast. Some deer were present in a vast amount of country that is now entirely in farms. On the other hand, northern pine forests that held practically no deer have become productive range since they were clear-cut and then invaded by hardwoods.

Around early settlements heavy shooting soon brought the whitetail to a point of local scarcity. The first closed season was declared in Rhode Island in 1646—just 26 years after Miles Standish helped the lovely Priscilla ashore at Plymouth Rock.

As the pioneers moved westward and opened up new country, deer were acted upon by opposing forces. Widespread lumbering and land clearing for farms destroyed extensive stands of forest. The edges and cutovers became high-quality range, but the good effects did not last. Repeated burning left "plains" of grass and bracken in the debauched pineries of the Lake States. In the Northeast, large tracts were laid bare in futile attempts to farm soils that should have remained in forest. Wherever there were deer, the market hunter was active. He furnished meat for lumber camps and sent carloads of venison saddles to the cities. Records of the railways show that in the fall of 1880 more than 100,000 carcasses were shipped out of northern Michigan. Buckskin was likewise in demand, and in rugged back country the meat frequently went to waste.

Destructive forces snowballed, and the deer declined. In Pennsylvania and country to the north and east they were nearly wiped out. In much of the West and in the primary whitetail range from Minnesota to Maine, deer were generally scarce by 1900. Sportsmen and conservationists of every stripe were concerned lest their mass-production big-game animal should disappear altogether. Seasons were reduced and bag limits were cut, first to five deer, sometimes to three, later to one. Then came the masterstroke in deer management, the buck laws —California 1901, Pennsylvania 1907, New York 1912, Utah 1913, Wisconsin 1915, Michigan 1921, Oregon 1923.

Old-timers said you couldn't hunt deer that way. If you shot only antlered bucks you would get no deer at all. They had hunted deer all their lives and they knew about such things. They stormed and fumed.

It did work, and it helped build back the herds. A patchwork of refuge areas were set aside in all the big deer states. Fires were brought under control and law-enforcement agencies set up. Large predators such as the wolf, panther, and bobcat were drastically reduced in number or eliminated.

By the middle twenties recovery of the deer was evident on all sides. Hunters rejoiced. They shot the bucks and saved the does. The buck law had been sold to them as good management and good ethics. It had become a matter of morality. Poachers and hoodlums shot does; but to a self-respecting sportsman that "rack of horns" symbolized his prowess in the chase. He hung it over his fireplace and bragged about it in the barbershop.

JUST BROWSING

Further, and critical, developments affecting deer from coast to coast grew out of the seasonal habits of the three species that furnish our hunting: whitetail, mule deer, and blacktail, in the order named.

The deer is primarily a browsing animal. Its digestive tract is built to handle a coarse diet of leaves, twigs, and buds. In spring and summer all species eat a wide variety of green stuff, but they do not thrive when reduced exclusively to grass, herbs, or hay. A period of fall feeding on mast is ideal for sending the animals into winter in good condition, but mast crops are undependable. On most ranges the winter diet is mainly sprouts and tips of hardwoods or foliage of such preferred conifers as northern white cedar and hemlock.

In summer, nearly everywhere, deer are spread out over a large, and usually adequate, range in the uplands. In autumn, western "muleys" and blacktails migrate down-country to the foothills, where they concentrate on long-used wintering areas. Some movements are extensive, such as that of the "interstate" deer herd, in which 15,000 mule deer move as much as 100 miles from high summer range in Oregon southward to join a concentration totalling some 28,000 animals which compete with livestock on the wintering grounds about Clear Lake in Modoc County, California. Elsewhere in the West there are numerous mule deer herds that follow migration routes of from 10 to 60 miles.

In many areas there is a drastic pinching down of range from summer to winter. In the St. Joe National Forest of Northern Idaho there are 658,000 acres of summer range, but in February and March the deer occupy only 17,000 acres of this, or 2.5 percent. In the Logan Canyon area of Utah's Cache National Forest, wintering grounds constitute only 6.1 percent of the summer range. Usually, whitetails are not considered migratory, but the seasonal shrinkage of range is equally impressive. In the Upper Peninsula of Michigan about 10 percent of the land is suitable for wintering, and New York's Adirondack deer spend the cold season on 10 to 15 percent of their occupied area.

In open winters deer may remain well scattered and avoid major difficulties. It is winters of deep snow that bring trouble, for the animals gather in cedar swamps, ravines, and sheltered stream bottoms and tramp out a maze of paths. This creates the well-known "yard" where the herd usually remains until liberated by spring thaws.

In snow country the carrying capacity of deer range commonly depends upon food available in these winter concentration areas. When a herd becomes too numerous, a browse-line appears. Vegetation and low branches above the snow are taken clean, as high as a deer can reach—and that means the tallest bucks. Fawns with less reserve fat and a shorter reach regularly form the bulk of the winter kill. In the winter of 1950-51 an estimated 50,000 deer starved in Michigan, and about 45,000 of them were fawns. On depleted mule deer ranges, winter fawn losses of 25 to 50 percent are not unusual, and the figure goes much higher when the snow is deep and lasting.

Deer are strongly influenced by habit in their movements to winter range. There may be food in a swamp just across the ridge, but they won't go to it. They stay in the long-used yard, and next winter they will be back again, many to leave their bones among the high-skirted cedars.

The beginning of range deterioration usually is evident only to the specialist. It involves gradual reduction of the most palatable woody plants and their replacement with species that deer do not like. An insidious destruction of habitat takes place while people delay and bicker. The professionals are practically unanimous in their recommendations: Take more deer in the fall rather than send that big annual surplus onto winter ranges to be whittled away by malnutrition and disease. But the woods is still green, and to many people talk about starving deer has all the earmarks of an unconvincing hoax.

ILLS OF ABUNDANCE

In the West, fire and forest cutting have had their part in creating deer range, but another influence is widespread and important. By the early part of this century, destructive overgrazing had turned many a flourishing grassland into a stand of brush.

This was deer habitat, and the deer responded. Today, deer and livestock occupy many of the same ranges, and competition for forage is potentially greatest in foothill areas which are used by both in spring and fall. There is overlap in the food habits of deer, sheep, and cattle —although deer commonly take only minor quantities of grass and weeds (not true on all ranges), while livestock make a somewhat heavier demand on browse. After studying this situation in Utah, Julander concluded that "more wild land values can be produced on most ranges by grazing both deer and livestock, in proper numbers, than by grazing either alone." Properly adjusted uses may actually be complementary, since deer pressure on brush can have good effects on grass, and browsing by cattle on woody plants unpalatable to deer can help the growth of important deer foods.

When all animals are stocked within the supporting capacity of their favored forage, there is no problem. But deer-livestock competition grows directly as the range is overused by both. When grass and herbs are in short supply, cattle increase their consumption of woody plants. On a heavily used Arizona range, it was found that on a year-long basis a cow eats 4.4 times as much browse as a deer.

Since overgrazing by stock and overpopulation by deer are common in all western states, it follows that the allocation of forage on public and private lands is a real issue. In a pilot operation the committee studying the interstate deer herd in Oregon and California allocated the use of key forage species on the winter range to livestock and deer on an equal basis. Of course to make this effective you must have both grazing quotas and deer hunting under full control, and the California deer harvest has been particularly inadequate.

One of the major evils of too many deer is the effect on tree reproduction. It needs to be recognized that a reasonable thinning may have no detrimental effect—the woods may still be adequately stocked for growing a crop of timber. But a forest overrun with deer will show suppression or elimination of sprouts and seedlings, and through differential browsing it may be converted to a stand of largely unpalatable species.

Conditions in New York illustrate this: "Among the species ruined are oaks, ashes, hickories, basswood, magnolias, pines, willows, maples, yellow poplar, cedars, hemlock, yellow birch and walnut. The repeated browsing that ruins these future trees allows species which are not utilized by deer to grow up as the future trees of the forest stand—alder, hophornbeam (ironwood), blue beech (muscle wood), American beech, aspens (popples), white and gray birch, fire cherry and thornapple."

In 1946, Wisconsin began a far-reaching and detailed analysis of what effect deer were having on timber production—the industry, of course, being of prime importance in the land of Paul Bunyan. Walter Scott summarized the results of this study:

"It was found that forest tree reproduction in northern Wisconsin, due mostly to browsing by deer, was about 20 per cent below a very minimum desirable average of 500 stems per acre, and in central Wisconsin it was 60 per cent below this figure. The annual damage to natural seedling production in the forest areas was calculated at 650 million seedlings as compared with approximately 15 million planted from nurseries each year. This damage to forest reproduction was reported to be 100 times more serious than the State's forest fire losses of 1947, which burned one in every 500 acres of protected land."

After a study of deer exclosures and control plots in several Pennsylvania forest types, it was concluded that "good forest management . . . depends upon protection against excessive deer populations, and this can be accomplished only through a regular and adequate harvest of both sexes during the open hunting season."

The days of the purist, saw-log forester who sees only one value are largely gone. Forestry schools nation-wide are teaching the principle of "multiple use," which means that watershed protection, hunting, fishing, and grazing are to be recognized and managed values on most of our timberlands. Certainly the game manager and forester are finding a meeting of minds, but public insistence on too many deer has helped make things rough for an otherwise beautiful friendship.

The farmer and his county agent likewise have their viewpoints on exploding and overpampered deer populations. In western New York and southern Michigan it was landowners who spearheaded the legislative pressure that made possible in those states the first antlerless deer hunting. The farmers were fed up with inroads on truck crops, seed alfalfa, buckwheat, and other cultivated greenery which deer by dozens and hundreds gathered to enjoy in their fields. This situation has deveolped in many states. A Pennsylvania economic survey in two counties alone showed crop damage amounting to $188,751 in 1951!

Under such circumstances the permit shooting of nuisance animals by landowners is a necessity, and the total of deer so destroyed is huge. Latham remarked that it amounted to many thousands each year in

Pennsylvania, and individual farmers "have been known to kill up-wards of 100 deer in a single growing season." Some states have laws requiring payment for agricultural damage (Michigan and California have managed to avoid this), and it has been a substantial drain on game funds as well as an administrative headache. The costs of such a program in Maine (including administration) were close to $200,000 in 1949. Wisconsin began such payments in 1932, and through 1954 had expended $426,259 for damage claims and the construction of "deerproof" fences, exclusive of costs involved in investigation and settlement. The game funds of several western states have carried a heavy burden of this kind—which cures nothing.

People who think it is humanitarian not to shoot deer surpluses in the fall simply are uninformed about what happens to the animals later. Malnutrition and winter weather bring a combination of stresses that predispose an individual animal to all manner of ills, including the swarming of parasites, shock, and disease—pneumonia usually being the last stage. In primitive times natural predators such as the wolf and panther probably helped to cut down and scatter unhealthy con-centrations. But in his wisdom (!) the white man has wiped out the wolf (except for a few in the northern Lake States) and in vast areas reduced other enemies to the level of a minor influence. This over-protection of deer has produced ills of the range, for which the sports-man himself will pay in the long run.

The penalties are not restricted to deer hunters, for small game is much involved. In Pennsylvania it became evident that the cottontail is first to go when ground cover is reduced. Latham described an area of excellent rabbit cover which was fenced and stocked with a few deer. After the deer built up to the point where artificial feeding was necessary, rabbits were practically gone where previously 20 or 30 could be seen almost any evening on a mile of road.

Heavy deer populations literally scour the earth for mast, so that squirrels, grouse, turkeys, raccoons, and other species are deprived of a food supply vital to winter survival. Destruction of the nesting and rearing cover of game birds may be even more important in some areas.

One of the major delusions in deer protection has been the assump-tion that to shoot less is the way to have more. The truth is that thinning a herd of deer nearly always gives a boost to reproductive vigor —it's that "inversity" relationship so frequently encountered in all species. The outstanding work done on this phase of deer management by New York biologists has received nation-wide recognition. In 1947, E. L. Cheatum reported on a highly significant study:

New York's Adirondacks have winters with piled-high snow that is excellent for skiing and bobsledding but which also concentrates the deer. The growing season is short and soils are poor. In hard winters many deer die in overbrowsed yards. In contrast, the southern tier of agricultural counties has been invaded by deer only in recent decades, and the herd has been cropped under either-sex regulations. There the animals are in good condition, and the main problem has been crop damage. State biologists collected a series of does in both of these regions and compared their breeding status.

Their findings were striking: In the Adirondacks, 78 percent of the does were pregnant, as against 92 percent in the southern zone. About one in 24 of the Adirondack doe fawns had bred in its first fall season, but in the southern counties more than one in 3 had bred. Eighty-one percent of the Adirondack does had single fawns, as compared with only 33 percent in the southern zone. Correspondingly, in the mountains 18 percent had twins and there was but one set of triplets. But in the farming area 60 percent of the does had twins and 7 percent triplets. Even among the 37 pregnant fawns examined from the agricultural region, two bore twins. The study showed that the well-nourished southern does produced more egg cells in their ovaries, and obviously the percent fertilized and successfully developed was much higher.

Further studies in New York have shown that the ability of does to produce fawns varies widely and is correlated directly with food supply. In good range where herds are heavily cropped, the yield may be as high as 20 fawns per 10 adult does—the level found in western counties. Deer in the central Adirondacks show about half this production rate, and in local, extremely poor ranges the number of fawns per 10 does may be as low as 4. Incidentally, this index of herd productivity includes the contribution made by fawns breeding in their first fall season.

These range relationships are being verified in every state where studies are made. In the overbrowsed, northeastern section of Michigan's Lower Peninsula (where the buck law was long sacred), the deer herd yields 13 fawns for every 10 adult does. In the heavily hunted southern agricultural region the comparable figure is 20 fawns per 10 does—a level that is seldom exceeded anywhere.

Findings for western mule deer and blacktails show the same trends, although the percentage of doe fawns breeding is much smaller than in the whitetail. There is no doubt that food on the winter range is vastly important in determining reproductive rate. However, the quality of summer forage also plays its part, as indicated by a study of two mule deer ranges, one severely overused by livestock and the other in excellent condition.

The depleted range was the Antimony unit of south-central Utah, and it was compared with the Sublette unit of southern Idaho, one of the best summer ranges in the region. The examination of does taken during the regular and special hunts, after the breeding season, showed a lower ovulation rate (by 33 percent) on the Antimony unit and an embryo count averaging only 1.19 per doe as against 1.85 for the Sublette unit. On the overgrazed area all age groups were significantly lighter in weight than the well-fed animals on the better range.

This weight relationship to food supply is present everywhere—it might have been mentioned that western New York deer outweigh Adirondack animals, age for age, by an average of more than 20 pounds. In overbrowsed Pennsylvania forest lands some young fawns were captured and reared in pens on a plentiful, high-quality diet. At one and a half years of age they weighed as much as 265 to 280 pounds—nearly twice the poundage of their wild brethren!

Deer quality is always a meaningful consideration for sportsmen— not only weight and condition but antler development. Since antlers are shed each winter, it is a considerable physiological drain on the male animal to accumulate enough calcium and phosphorus from its food to have a new set ready for the November rutting season. Also, is has been noted in feeding experiments that the demands of growth and body maintenance are met before minerals go into antler development. This means that those "buttons, spikes, forks, and rocking chairs" are a fairly sensitive reflection of food quality and forage conditions.

Most deer hunters get no opportunity to appraise this situation for themselves—they have had little experience with truly well-fed deer. Nearly all male fawns have nothing more than skin-covered "buttons" in their first fall season. But when nourished properly, the young buck should have some kind of "rack" at 18 months of age. It may be anything from forks to as many as 10 points. The antlers are small in beam and spread, but they are respectable headgear as compared with spikes. In succeeding years the rack develops weight and span, and usually more points.

The condition of 18-month-old bucks is a critical question, since this is the age group that most commonly produces the "spike horn" on poor ranges. Actually, many such animals will be "antlerless" and illegal game under the various types of buck-law regulations (3-inch minimum, "polished" horn, one fork, etc.). Again, New York statistics are useful. A hunting season brochure had this to say: "During the majority of Adirondack winters in the past 24 years the deer population of the central Adirondacks has existed on such a scarcity of winter food that 50 percent of the yearling bucks and possibly 15 percent of the 2½-year-old bucks have not grown legal antlers. This results in about 25 per cent of the bucks that should have legal antlers being classed by the hunters as antlerless deer. When these antlerless bucks are added to the fawns and does only about one deer in five or six . . . has legal antlers."

Hunters who find spike-horned deer to be common should recognize this as abnormal and a symptom that range is on the downgrade. It calls for remedial action before conditions get any worse—but *what kind of action* is best left to the professionals who are being paid to know about such things.

WINTER HANDOUT

We have not yet recognized an important issue in the deer controversy: In the minds of many people the thing to do for starving animals is to feed them. Early in the game professional men saw this as a dangerous blind alley; but the public did not, and state after state had to go through costly and farcical demonstrations of the obvious. When deer are snowed in during hard winters, the vast bulk of the range is inaccessible, and even if it were not, the job of feeding hundreds of thousands of animals is too expensive to be practicable.

Worse yet, feeding only concentrates deer still more and insures the complete wiping out of all palatable browse. A test of supplemental feeding was made on the Cache National Forest in Utah for 7 years beginning in 1935. During this period 195 tons of hay and 11 tons of other feed were distributed to wintering animals. Each hunting season for three years about 20 percent of the herd was shot, including bucks, does, and fawns. Fall numbers were held to about 5,000, but there were still too many deer, and pressure on native vegetation was not lessened by the feeding. The conclusion was that further reductions were the only possible solution.

During the early forties, in response to public demand, the State of Colorado was spending $30,000 to $40,000 annually to winter-feed mule deer. The results showed that deer could not live on stock feed alone. They died with their stomachs full of alfalfa hay, and losses were highest where the largest amounts of artificial feed were consumed. Hay helped the deer only when they could get sufficient native browse to form the bulk of their diet. This, of course, only helped destroy the vegetation. Carhart, who reported this study, described the situation as follows: "The deer do like the taste of the domestic stock feed. They come in to the grounds. They concentrate instead of dispersing over areas where there might be sufficient browse to maintain them. They eat out all browse adjacent to the feeding areas. No such amount as is needed is available for the deer that haunt the feeding areas. The browse supply goes down. Deer have empty stomachs. They fill up on alfalfa. They cannot handle it—and they walk away from the troughs, weak from malnutrition, the bots or lung worms deal the last blow, and they die."

In 1956, a Fish and Wildlife Service news release told of a different kind of feeding program, this time in the Black Hills of South Dakota. Two experimental feeding stations were established to hold the deer in the high country in an attempt to head off winter damage to hay and other produce on valley ranches. The deer were fed alfalfa, ear corn, and a special deer concentrate. The operation went well until a heavy snow in January. Then the whitetails left their abundant rations in the hills and trekked down into the low country as was their custom. There are some things a deer won't do even for an easy meal.

In the early days of Wisconsin deer management, their biologists knew well what winter feeding was worth. However, the legislature earmarked game funds for this purpose, and at the same time issued a mandate for crop-damage payments to farmers. In 8 years before 1948, the State spent $235,000 of the sportsman's money for feeding deer and $106,000 for the acquisition of yarding areas. In the winter of 1947-48 alone, nearly 1,000 tons of alfalfa and concentrates were fed to about 23,000 deer. If we add that year's $55,000 for damage complaints, it's obvious that deer-herd housekeeping was getting expensive. As Walter E. Scott stated, nowhere else in the United States were sportsmen spending "so much hard, cold cash to accomplish, according to wildlife management standards, a result to their own present and future disadvantage."

Deer feeding as an alternative to deer cropping has not worked anywhere, and in that sense there is no reason to think that it ever will be part of a practicable plan to manage these animals as a public resource. However, we should not overlook the benefits of a kind of "feeding" that occurs when trees are cut for pulp or timber. The tops and limbs become available immediately as deer food. In Michigan the cutting of an average acre of hardwoods yields a quarter-ton of browse, and an acre of cedar swamp provides more than a ton of high-quality feed. In the winter of 1955-56 cutting permits were issued covering some 58,000 acres of state land, and it was estimated that the range carried through 100,000 deer that could not have survived otherwise.

It needs emphasis that feeding "with an ax" is no formula for maintaining an overpopulation of deer. But in a cut-over area, winter carrying capacity is raised immediately, and it is likely to remain high as a result of the sprout growth that follows. Of course, these benefits will be lost if the oncoming reproduction is repressed at once by heavy browsing! Every practical management measure depends for success on the principle that herds must be subjected to an adequate annual cropping with the gun.

"WASTE IN THE WOODS"

This was the title which Stanley G. DeBoer put on an article in the Wisconsin Conservation Bulletin in 1957, which largely marked the beginning of a new era of enlightenment on an old deer-management question—illegal kill. In areas overrun by hunters, it was common knowledge that standards of behavior deteriorated and that a substantial toll of illegally killed does and fawns was being left for the foxes. Speculation varied widely on the magnitude of this waste, but there were reasons for believing that local losses might sometimes at least equal the legal harvest under buck-law regulations.

The remains of dead deer are easy to miss in the woods. Counts of winter-lost animals must be made as soon as possible after the snow melts. To obtain figures meaningful for a large area, a total count must be taken on a sample large enough to be representative. The work reported by DeBoer was done in eastern Jackson County, west central Wisconsin, and it involved personnel from six divisions of the Wisconsin Conservation Department, as well as local sportsmen. They used lines of men spaced only 66 feet apart, and they covered a total of 7,684 acres in March, 1957.

The crews found 86 deer carcasses, of which 78 were judged to be illegal kills of the previous hunting season. In eastern Jackson County bucks killed during the hunting season had been registered, and this legal kill totalled 1,714. But when the figures on illegal kills were projected to this area, it was concluded that more than 3,000 does and fawns had been shot and left to rot. The buck harvest was 3½ per square mile, and the dead-deer count was 6½ per square mile—nearly two-thirds of the kill never went home to the food locker. A deer had been wasted for every 100 acres of range!

Obviously, in such counts mistakes could be made as to what caused the death of an animal, but work done the following year does much to fortify the conclusions. In 1957 hunting regulations in central Wisconsin provided that during the regular buck season any party of four hunters could buy a permit for a "party" deer of either sex. A repetition of the March survey in 1958 showed a startling change in the statistics:

The registration of legal bucks and antlerless animals in the fall of 1957 was 4,287, or 9 per square mile—two and a half times the kill of the year before. Based on the dead-deer count, animals left in the woods totalled 1,892, or 4 per square mile. Of all deer presumably killed by the gun, only 36 percent were legal and used in 1956, as against a legal kill of 69 percent in 1957. This was accomplished by a simple relaxation of restrictions. Yet DeBoer emphasized that still another thousand deer could have been taken from Jackson County without reducing the effective breeding stock.

By request of sportsmen, another survey was made in 1958 in Eau Claire and Clark Counties, which adjoin Jackson County on the north. This is a region of fewer deer and lower hunting pressure. The illegal kill was found to be lower also. The party deer regulation applied, and 82 percent of the deer crop was utilized. It is evident that, under bucks-only regulations, the heaviest illegal kill occurs where competition among hunters is greatest.

Reasonably accurate figures on illegal kill are difficult to come by, partly because law enforcement officers have been reluctant to make their own findings available. To many people the wanton killing of does and fawns might suggest that field personnel were not on the job, but this is not realistic. In some heavily hunted areas, the trigger-happy gunner seems always to be found, and the best of law enforcement probably will not prevent him from doing his irresponsible deeds. This is increasingly recognized as more facts come to light.

One of the most comprehensive surveys of deer lost in fall and winter was taken in Michigan in April and May, 1956. By a statistically distributed sampling, it provided figures on the entire Upper Peninsula.

"Of the total over-winter loss of 74,000 deer, 19,400 had starved to death; 900 were victims of dogs, predators, or accidents; 24,400 had died of unknown causes; 7,300 had been shot; and 22,000 were placed in the 'cause of death unknown' column, but the time of the death could definitely be put at 'fall or early winter.' Convincing but circumstantial evidence suggests that most of those 'died in fall or early winter' deer were shot. Some were unrecovered legal bucks but most were does and fawns."

It seems entirely logical that there are vast areas of deer country where losses through illegal killing are inconsequential. But regions of heavy hunting are where the most efficient use of the harvest should be made, and in some of these, at least, it appears that buck-law regulations are not "saving" anywhere near the proportion of deer herds that is commonly assumed. Many does and fawns are dying during the hunting season, and many more are dying on winter ranges. The mechanics of that annual turnover are becoming clearer year by year.

REGULATIONS PROGRESS

In the North and East, the largest deer herds have been found in Pennsylvania, Michigan, and Wisconsin. At some time between 1925 and 1945, each of these states supported somewhere around a million deer. In all three, deer have declined (as game biologists predicted) principally because of two factors, (1) the widespread overbrowsing of winter ranges, and (2) the natural progress of forest succession by which brush ranges favorable to deer become tree stages of lower carrying capacity.

It appears that realistic statewide inventories and estimates lagged somewhat in parts of the South and West. But in the fifties, both Texas and California were reporting well over a million deer, and it appears likely that these states will remain alone in that fascinating category for many years to come.

In the rapid progression from deer poverty to plenty, Pennsylvania led the nation, and this state's experience could have been a pilot run for the country if game-management agencies of other states had been free to profit by it. Plentiful deer are a particularly valuable asset in regions of heavy human populations, but this combination begets political pressures, and public understanding always lags behind technology. In the absence of other checks, deer simply increase until they destroy their food supply, their own numbers, and many other values along the way. The gun and the sportsman are the only reasonable means of preventing this.

By 1906 Pennsylvania deer were so depleted that in the next 18 years more than a thousand animals were imported to fortify the breeding stock. After 1910 the herd found practically ideal conditions in the brush-stage forests that sprang up as a result of fire protection. Already in the mid-twenties large areas were growing into sapling and pole stands, and food supplies declined. In 1930 the carrying capacity of Pennsylvania's range was estimated at a deer per 20 to 40 acres. The state should have had a herd of about a quarter of a million, whereas the actual number was nearer 800,000!

Richard Gerstall carried out food studies in which he found that hardwoods in the 7-year age class produced more than 200 pounds of potential deer food per acre. Similar samples in a stand averaging 35 years yielded less than 35 pounds. It was established that wintering deer require about 2 pounds of browse daily per hundred pounds of body weight to hold them in "fair" condition. Assuming a state herd of only half a million, more than 250 million pounds of feed would be required to support the population from December through March. "Since all would have to be produced on roughly eight million acres of forest land, much of which is in a state of development wherein less than twenty-five pounds per acre are being produced, and since during the severe weather the deer utilize only a fraction of the total range, little is the wonder that a food problem exists!"

In the face of terrific opposition, the first antlerless deer season was held in 1923, and 14 more were declared during the next quarter-century. But the killing of more than a million deer of both sexes failed to relieve pressure on the range. Under the system followed, mature bucks would be shot for 2 or more years while the herd built up to intolerable numbers. Then an antlerless season would be held, with everyone turning out for the easy meat. The cropping of 60,000 to 150,000 animals would be followed by widespread lamentation over the "wiping out" of Pennsylvania's great game resource. Such was the public reaction that the buck law would be invoked for another period.

The Commission persisted, and gradually the Pennsylvania sportsman began to learn by experience. From 1941 to 1950 there were 4 hunting seasons when no does and fawns were legal game and 2 more seasons in which the take was less than 5,000. The total deer harvest in that decade was 492,594, of which 199,449 were antlerless. In the 10 years after 1950 the picture changed: There were only 2 seasons entirely closed to does and fawns, and the total harvest was 706,143, of which 335,982 were antlerless. The pattern established was for an antlerless season of 1 to 3 days (with special licenses sold on a county quota basis) following the regular buck season. It worked—the kill held up. Relative to an old problem, in May, 1960, Executive Director M. J. Golden commented, "There is no doubt that winter kill would have reached disastrous proportions during the winters of 1957-58 and 1959-60 had harvests of antlerless deer not been accomplished in 1957, 1958, and 1959." Fortunately, during those three seasons Pennsylvania hunters had taken more than 300,000 deer!

This kind of erratic progress is evident in most of the big deer states and many lesser ones. Frequently game departments have been forced to retreat after achieving the kind of any-deer regulations toward which they were working. It happened after Wisconsin's heavy antlerless deer harvests of 1949 and 1950, after Michigan's special season in 1952, and following California's first general antlerless deer hunting in 1956. After 6 years of highly successful "hunter's choice" shooting in selected counties, the West Virginia Commission went back to bucks only in 1957. It was frankly to head off a "county option" plan that threatened in the legislature. This idea, of putting deer regulations in the hands of county boards of supervisors, has been used as a club over the heads of game administrators in several states. Obviously, it would result in chaos from which no one would profit.

In Michigan, California, and several other states the crux of the deer-hunting troubles is that legislatures withhold from game commissions the full authority to set seasons and bag limits. In doing so, they respond to a vociferous minority of public opinion. It is only when organized sportsmen and other responsible groups have studied the issues and waded full-force into the controversy that things begin to move in the right direction.

The biggest problem in managing a statewide deer season under liberalized regulations is hunter distribution. Local overshooting may occur in easily accessible areas while back-country problems are not helped. This was part of Wisconsin's trouble in 1950.

Actually, if food is present, overshot deer will recover quickly with a season or two of restricted hunting—just as they did in the 'teens and twenties. The most outstanding example yet known of total violence done to a deer herd gives reassurance that the animals can "take it" on a favorable range: "During California's attempt to stamp out foot-and-mouth disease (1924-25), one of the requirements was the destruction of all two-toed ungulates, including the deer, over a sizable area. A half million dollars was spent in employing skilled hunters to shoot 22,000 deer. To this sportsmen added an estimated 12,000. They were successful in eradicating the disease, but sufficient deer remained to restock the region in a remarkably short time. It is interesting to note that it cost $23 each, to kill deer under these conditions."

This attempt (which lasted more than 18 months) to exterminate the herd of the Stanislaus National Forest through the use of strychnine-poisoned salt, shooting, and other methods fell considerably short of getting all the deer. Correspondingly, the danger of "wiping out" deer through sport shooting is almost nil. However, on an easily hunted range (plenty of roads) under any-deer regulations, a concentration of hunters can reduce a herd to the point where shooting is poor for a season or two. This thinning is temporary, and in the meantime browse supplies are recovering.

Standing somewhat apart, amid the pulling and hauling over the buck law, a scattering of states, such as Massachusetts, Maine, New Hampshire, Minnesota, and Idaho, never protected does. They harvested deer irrespective of sex, confident in the quality of female venison and aloof to the morality of murdering mothers.

At the North American Wildlife Conference in 1951, Hilbert R. Siegler told how "Both bucks and does have been hunted by the white man in New Hampshire for over three hundred years with no apparent harmful effects on the deer population." The open season was the entire month of November (the primary rutting period), and the last restriction had been in 1925, when the bag limit was cut from two deer to one.

Even under these conditions there are overbrowsing troubles and declining deer herds in remote areas where hunting is light. Most deer hunting is done within a mile of a road—so, a part of the answer has been to open up old logging trails to provide better access to the range.

The pattern of the future probably is best shown in several western states that once had buck laws but now have sensible deer regulations, established and working, year after year. Notable in this respect are Colorado, Utah, and Oregon. They went through all the old troubles, but they survived, and they have a system that seems here to stay.

Colorado is divided into 98 management units—largely natural watersheds—in each of which deer and hunters are managed according to local needs and opportunities. In 1956, Game and Fish Director Thomas L. Kimball described the devices used to balance hunter pressure against the number of deer to be taken:

Since "opening day" has a long-standing charm for deer hunters, the opening is delayed for 5 days in ranges nearest the large population centers; hunting begins in the more distant areas where deer need to be harvested. In remote areas of deer depredation and overpopulation, where it is difficult to attract any hunters at all, the device is a special "pre-season" with two deer allowed to a single license. "Post seasons" (sometimes extending to many months) may also be declared after the regular hunting period to allow for a mopping up of surplus deer in underharvested hinterlands. During the general hunting season, in easily accessible areas of high deer population, the limit is one deer of either sex per license, *but a hunter may purchase any number of licenses.* Because of these multiple limits, Colorado hunters enjoy the highest success in the nation—about 100 percent! The state kill approximates 25 percent of the pre-hunting herd.

The division of states into hunting and management units was the most significant development of the fifties, and it will be much in evidence in the future. It recognizes that deer ranges and herds must be handled according to local conditions in the field. The system must be flexible, as it is in Colorado—the Commission can change regulations on 48 hours' notice. This obviously means that full authority for the Commission is essential, and where that does not exist, a great step in deer management is still to be taken.

PRODUCING MORE DEER

These days, with the general increase of human population, public agencies are much concerned with mass benefits. As applied to big-game hunting, this concern is with deer, and with producing a maximum crop consistent with other uses of our wild and semi-wild lands.

For 30 years (after 1930) the public of many states was bemused with the question of shooting female animals. This delayed the program of managing ranges for greater production. The size of that annual deer crop has now become evident, and it is obviously better to use available forage in nurturing a new generation than to expend it in keeping alive unused animals from older generations.

It is likewise evident that those herd surpluses from years past will prevent any management of the range itself. They will forestall improvement of the browse supply and hence any build-up of deer numbers. Already in the thirties, the Pennsylvania Game Commission was using bulldozers to open up even-aged woodlands, and they sold timber at the rate of 13,000 acres a year. But overabundant deer wiped out the sprout growth, and the operation failed.

A more recent and much larger operation in Michigan greatly improved winter survival, but it too fell short of supporting the state's carry-over of unharvested animals. In 1960 Bartlett told how public and private logging was cutting 200,000 acres annually, but this was only 1 percent of the northern deer range, and it failed to offset the natural aging of timber stands. A large-scale waste of deer was evident. "Surveys indicated that in 1956 winter losses totaled over 100,-000 of which nearly 40,000 starved. Similar surveys indicated a 1959 loss of nearly 70,000 with 16,000 of these starved, and a loss this last spring of 87,000 with 20,000 starved. These were surplus deer, not taken by hunters, and wasted because they were left on an already overpopulated range."

Michigan was waiting for better deer regulations, but management was in the right direction. In that state and elsewhere, in low-grade forest areas biologists were experimenting with aerial applications of herbicide to set tree stages back in favor of brush and sprout stages. In southern pine lands controlled burning is well established for the management of both timber and game. Fire is being used in brush ranges of California to improve the quantity and quality of deer browse. It may be combined with mechanical clearing, controlled grazing, herbicide treatment, and the seeding of herbaceous plants to bring about the desired conditions. This sort of experimentation is going ahead in many parts of the country, and the steady improvement of methods can be confidently expected. Here is where the biologist knows his ground, for managing deer in the open is merely a matter of knowledge, imagination, and hard work. It is hands-down more rewarding than trying to manage these animals in the legislature!

A major asset in long-term efforts to get deer management on a durable and paying basis is the increasing recognition of economic values. This especially involves landowners interested in another crop and businessmen with a growing appreciation of the tourist industry.

There are vast areas of the semi-arid Texas hill country where deer management is a sounder and more profitable enterprise than cattle grazing. A state survey showed that the deer season brought to each of four counties about half a million dollars in business, and one "rancher" sold hunting rights for $23,500 in two seasons. Annual business returns in Utah's well-managed deer hunting are about $13 million. It is patently far-sighted and profitable for a state with surplus deer to lower out-of-state fees to an attractive level and "sell" a portion

of the annual cron to people from beyond the border. The brought-in
dollars will not all be in the game and fish treasury, but they will help
to stimulate and confirm the interest of all citizens in a proper handling of the public resource.

The great deer controversy probably has helped many states to learn
the facts and clarify their policies. Despite backsliding here and there,
one success builds upon another, and the result is progress. Considering all the possibilities, it is reasonable to expect the figure on national
deer kill to go on increasing for some years to come.

CHAPTER 10

It's the Limit

THE conservation literature of twenty years ago featured no more classic situation than that of the conscientious sportsman teaching his basically rapacious boy to return little fishes to the water. How many of us had law and morals invoked to wrest from our eager clutch the first trophies of childhood!

The moral was good, the sportsman's ethic was sound; but we know now that frequently the law had its shortcomings.

Here and there in previous chapters we have brought out the fact that fish partake in those almost universal characteristics of animal populations—high productivity and rapid turnover. In considering game birds and mammals, we found there was a crop to be taken, and if we failed to do it, somehow it got taken anyway and our only recourse was to grow another one.

It is all to the good that fish are not exceptional in this natural scheme of things. A critical application of the facts of life is giving the mid-century fisherman a new and revised testament on which to shape his philosophy and align the thinking of his offspring. Many of those little fishes, we find, might better have been knocked on the head.

Certain of the life-scientists whose specialty was fish were seeing the portent of their findings by the mid-thirties. Fifteen years later their facts were being discussed in commissions and even seeping through to legislative committees. Considering our limited means of communication, this is not long; it is good progress.

Fishery biologists had their ideas and theories, but they had to be circumspect about going out and trying them. Conservationists were nothing if not conservative. Restrictions and limitations had been important in righting the wrongs of the old free-and-easy days, and neither the sportsman nor the scientist was sure where they had to stop.

In 1944 the opportunity appeared for a large-scale experiment with liberalized regulations, and a biologist with knowledge and vision was there to make the most of it. The scene was Norris Lake, one of the TVA reservoirs in Tennessee. Several states in the South had loosened up on seasons and limits prior to this, but the TVA work was needed proof, and it served to extend the movement rapidly.

It had all begun back in 1940 when studies of tagged fish indicated that game-fish populations were being subjected to a hook-and-line drain of only about 10 percent. This was far less than the available crop, and other work showed that large numbers of mature fish were disappearing from the population without being accounted for. In other words, natural mortality was taking more of the large desirable game fish than was the sportsman!

Bass, for example, grow rapidly in these warm southern waters, and they do not live so long as the slower-growing northern fish of the same species. R. W. Eschmeyer, who directed this work, stated that "At the age of three years, bass in Norris have the same length as bass in Wisconsin waters ordinarily attain in six years. However, very few bass in Norris reach an age of six years; in fact, relatively few reach the age of five years according to numerous records col lected."

The indications were that unless one of these mature fish was caught before it was five years of age, it would never be a part of the useful fish crop.

Since the fish harvest by sportsmen was so obviously inadequate, a revision of regulations appeared to be in order. Previously, Norris Lake had been closed to fishing from April 1 to May 29. Following the suggestion of TVA biologists, the Tennessee Department of Conservation eliminated the closed season in 1944.

They never went back to it. In the 59-day spring period, anglers took nearly 275,000 pounds of fish from Norris Lake. This was nearly twice the catch during the regular season and in addition to it. Fishing during the summer was just as good as in previous years. Eschmeyer concluded:

"Enough evidence is now available to show definitely that most game fish in Norris Lake have ordinarily been wasted. Most of these fine fish, of desirable size and species, never reached the frying pan. They died a natural death."

From the standpoint of the angler, spring is his best fishing season, for at that time of year the baits he presents are not competing with large natural food supplies. Following the spawning period, in productive waters huge numbers of fingerlings appear and provide such carnivores as bass with unlimited provender. Amid such abundance, the large fish have little reason to be attracted by shoe spoons and wooden facsimiles of nothing a bass ever saw. That is the reason for the taper-off of fishing returns during the warm part of the summer; but at that time the new generation of young fish are being thinned out and grow rapidly. By fall they are larger, more difficult to catch, and require a greater feeding effort on the part of the bass. Then fishing picks up again.

Some of the preparatory work at Norris Lake had included a study of the effect of catching male bass off the nest in spawning time. In 1942 the season was late and the bass had barely begun to spawn when the season opened on May 30. This same situation was repeated in 1943, but both years an excellent crop of young bass was produced. Observations showed that the male bass guarding a nest would merely "bump" a plug or other object brought near the nest. Relatively few of the fish actually were caught off the spawning beds.

It is becoming widely evident that a fish population can be productive only when heavily cropped. When its numbers are high, large quantities of food are used merely to keep alive, and the individual fish does not get enough to put on much weight. But when anglers thin out older fish, the younger ones find food enough to grow rapidly and the turnover rate is increased. Under these conditions a fish may be of desirable size a year or more sooner than would be the case in a dense population.

Heavy fishing usually divides the crop among more fishermen and the success of the individual may be unsatisfactorily low. Nevertheless, the water in question may be much more productive than it would be under light fishing.

Although E. S. Russell was referring principally to salt-water species, his statement on this subject applies to practically all fish populations: "It is clear . . . that, up to a certain point, fishing is good for the stock. It clears out the accumulated stock of old slow-growing fish, enables the remainder to grow more quickly, and makes room for the oncoming broods so that they can survive in greater numbers and grow more rapidly. A stock under the influence of fishing utilizes the available food more efficiently, through increased rate of growth, and renews itself more rapidly."

For many a fisherman it will be difficult to assimilate the idea that fishing may, on occasion, help to produce more fishing, but we will repeatedly find situations where that is the case. The crux of the matter is that the harvesting of a fish (or game) crop must be tailored to fit a specific situation. By adopting such a discriminating approach, we can make available knowledge pay off to a maximum extent in fuller creels and more sport.

DEFICIENT FISHERMAN

How present conditions affecting fish populations differ from those existing in primitive times has been described by George W. Bennett, Illinois fishery biologist.

Originally, it was the young fish that bore the brunt of predation by a wide variety of enemies for whom they were a staple food supply. Such young fish would, of course, be taken in proportion to their numbers and consequent availability. The high reproductive rate of nearly all fish is geared to this heavy natural mortality of the early age groups. Since large fish are less vulnerable to attack by most enemies, they tended to accumulate and become plentiful.

The occupation of this continent by man brought about conditions not in keeping with primitive adaptations. Fishermen select (when they can) the larger fish, and they have long done battle with competing fish predators. The effect of most stocking (limited, to be sure) was to add to the numbers of small fish, and minimum size regulations had a similar effect.

"Because the high reproductive potential of the fishes has remained unchanged, there has been a great increase in the survival of young fish, resulting in added competition for food and space, in over-population of waters and in stunting of fish. Intensive interspecific competition among the fishes themselves may be the key factor responsible for eliminating or reducing populations of many of the more desirable game fishes in some waters, because the young of these species are unable to compete with the young of others under crowded conditions.

"A common belief among anglers is that, in lakes in which the annual yield of game fish has declined over a period of years, intensive fishing is responsible for the progressively poorer catches. In most instances in which an actual decline may be proved, no data are at hand as to the kinds and quantities of fish that remain in the lake at the time of low production. However, in 22 artificial lakes in Illinois, most of which were censused at a time of low production, only one showed a decline in yield associated with intensive fishing."

As a matter of fact, a search of fisheries literature indicates that this single case, having to do with Onized Lake, is the one published account describing the reduction of a fish population below carrying capacity by hook-and-line fishing.

Onized Lake is a 2-acre artificial pond used for recreation by the employees of a glass company near Alton, Illinois. After construction in 1933, the pond had been stocked with several species, including bass and crappies. A creel census in 1939 indicated that heavy fishing had removed nearly 700 pounds of fish from the lake. The catch in 1940 was smaller by about 1,000 fish.

It should be pointed out that, as far as reproduction is concerned, a few individuals spawning successfully could have far overstocked the lake. But the food supply probably was not sufficiently large to replace in one year the poundage removed in 1939. It appeared that the number of fish attaining desirable size declined and hence fewer were removed by anglers in 1940.

The crop in 1939 weighed 350 pounds per acre and in 1940 the catch was 143 pounds per acre. Yet in 1941, when the entire stock of the lake was poisoned out, it was found that there were still 47 bass of legal size, including 12 ranging from 3 to 6 pounds in weight!

The overfishing was not "depletion" in the ordinary sense, but a temporary reduction below carrying capacity. In his conclusions on the study, Bennett made the following significant statement:

"In spite of heavy fishing, the natural spawn of fish was obviously sufficient to insure replacement of those fish removed, and under reduced fishing intensity the lake would have returned to its former carrying capacity."

Elsewhere, Thompson recorded that following the reduction, the growth rate of fish in Onized Lake increased greatly and the production of young was unusually successful. He remarked that "this supports our belief that lakes recover from overfishing much faster than from underfishing."

Evidently sport fishing of even the heaviest intensity is not likely to result in any permanent damage to the resource. In the northern states it usually takes three or four years for a fish to grow to desirable size for the angler. In the meantime it has spawned one or more times and thus fulfilled its biological function. It would seem that there is almost no chance of cutting down annual reproduction by such cropping. As Moyle explains it, when a part of the large fish are removed, "there is ample food for the remainder. The fish are not hungry; they do not bite, and fishing declines. Usually enough adult fish of all kinds are left to perpetuate themselves."

In the South it has been shown that in both natural waters and artificial ponds it is possible, by hook-and-line fishing, to take only about half of the available harvest of adult bass and bluegills.

That this is a general situation is indicated by other findings in Illinois. Figures on artificial lakes in that state show that such waters can maintain an annual yield equal to about half their carrying capacity, or 100 to 150 pounds per acre, when the population is limited to species that take the hook readily.

For eight years, catch records on a 14-acre lake operated by a fishing club in Macoupin County averaged 98 pounds of bluegills, largemouth bass, crappies, and bullheads. For three years, an 11-acre lake in Douglas County produced an average of 80 pounds; and an experimental pond where only bass and bluegills were present yielded 162 pounds under heavy hook-and-line fishing. When 22 isolated ponds and artificial lakes in central Illinois were drained or poisoned, it was found that they were supporting an average weight of all fish of 600 pounds per acre. Of course, that included minnows and rough fish.

Angling has almost universally fallen far short of taking the place of natural predation in reducing the numbers of small fish. Detailed population studies on the game fishes of two Indiana lakes for 2 and 3 years respectively indicated that the total pounds per acre of legal fish varied from 113 to 232 and that the harvest by fishermen accounted for from 5 to 36 percent.

It is seldom the case with land animals, but Ricker and his co-workers found that the number of fish dying of *old age* probably was greater than the harvest by sportsmen!

They also investigated what effects the war had in its reduction of fishing pressure on stocks of lake fish and found that there was no discernible effect at all. A lake in which 31 percent of the legal blue-gills had been taken previously yielded only 20 percent during the war. But the total turnover in this population was 70 to 75 percent per year—the difference was natural mortality. It can hardly be doubted that in the past there has been a greatly misplaced emphasis on seasons and size limits in the management of warm-water fish. Eschmeyer summed up the situation in this way:

"The hook and line is such ineffective harvesting machinery that ample brood stock generally is present regardless of fishing intensity. Therefore, the major purpose of fishing regulations, other than those limiting the gear, is to provide fair distribution of the fishing and the fish crop. In general, the major concern of fishery administrators has been over the question of preventing the 'fishing out' of our waters. There is now ample evidence to suggest that it is extremely difficult, in many of the larger lakes and streams, to 'fish out' a water to the point where inadequate brood stock remains. Fishing becomes too poor to be attractive long before such extreme decimation of the population is effected."

In other words, it is the diminishing-returns phenomenon that similarly prevents overcropping of many game species.

RATIONING RETAINED

That heavy sport fishing does not actually "deplete" the fish population is something of an academic fact if it results in a condition under which a large proportion of anglers go home unrewarded.

That this applies to large carnivorous fish in the North is a common observation. The productivity of many a northern lake, especially those on infertile watersheds, is low to begin with. Owing to the short season, low temperatures, and meager food supply, fish grow slowly. Any concentration of angling effort removes the larger fish and their replacement takes time. The division of the crop among many fishermen reduces the share of an individual, even though the lake may be *producing more pounds* of fish than when fishing was good for a few sportsmen. This trend of events undoubtedly has occurred on many of the popular resort lakes of northern United States and southern Canada.

It seems evident that under these conditions there is a valid need for regulations applying to seasons and limits that will permit more anglers to share in the available harvest. There are other situations in which limitations on the catch are of even more vital importance.

The fact that a single spawning fish ordinarily produces from a few thousand to a million or more young, would seem to guarantee against any serious thinning out of breeders. But when it does happen, the depletion of breeding stock becomes the most serious kind of overexploitation. Higgins indicated the reduction of shad on the Atlantic Coast and sturgeon in all waters as the best examples of this. "Were it not for adequate protective measures, the salmon of Alaska would be another outstanding example. . . . If other kinds of fish were as easily depleted as shad and sturgeon commercial fishery production of most species would have declined as severely as has the production of these species. We all know that this is not true. On the contrary the total production of fish in the United States and Alaska has increased."

Heavy commercial fishing may result in uneconomic use of the resource by removing too many fish in the smaller size classes. Reduction of fishing to permit greater size development will result in the catching of a greater poundage. The striped bass in Chesapeake Bay is a case in point. The standing crop is larger when intensity of commerial fishing is held to the proper level. The total yield is better and fish are larger when 40 percent of a large standing crop is taken rather than 80 percent of a small one. "At the low rates of fishing more fish are allowed to spawn and thus still further increase the stock of fish . . . All this is accomplished without any sacrifice on the part of the fishing industry."

In this connection, the establishment of catch quotas for specific waters is better than creating laws to make commercial fishing more difficult. The latter expedient only increases costs and the price to the consumer.

From these cases, it is apparent that there are types of fish harvest that threaten not only the immediate supply, but the very existence of certain fish stocks. However, this applies almost entirely to large-scale commercial operations. Sport fishing does not appear to threaten any species, although it has helped to create poor fishing in some waters under the wrong kind of season, size, and creel limitations.

PROLIFIC PANFISH

The various kinds of sunfish are typical of small, "forage," or prey-type species. With them we can class the crappie, perch, rock bass, and their kin and call them all "panfish."

Some are to only a minor extent herbivorous, but all feed near the bottom of the food chain—if not on plants directly, then on small organisms that do feed on the drifting green cells that convert dissolved minerals into living tissue and thus support all life in the water. On the fringes of this arbitrary classification are species like the catfish, suckers, buffalo, and some kinds of shad, ordinarily considered "rough" fish.

The panfish and rough fish have high reproductive rates and their abundant young form a part of that small-animal key industry which is the aquatic counterpart of the mouse, vole, ground squirrel meat-ration of the terrestrial predators. The main difference is that in the water large carnivores like bass, walleye, trout, and pike are the game fish so dear to the heart of sportsmen.

Public preference for the kind of fishing that is done with large minnows, frogs, plugs, spoons, and bucktails has stepped up the removal rate for big fish and eased predation pressure on the panfish. In our examination of the carrying-capacity phenomenon we saw that a given body of water will support a given poundage of fish, and that poundage can exist either as a small population of large fish or a large population of small fish.

When panfish are not thinned out, they become too numerous for the food supply, stop growing, and by competition with the young cut down further effective reproduction of the carnivores. That is overpopulation.

Too many panfish is one of the commonest troubles where sport declines on formerly productive waters. From south to north it is becoming widely recognized that the harvest of such fish should be encouraged in every way possible—especially by removal of season, size, and creel restrictions on hook-and-line angling.

In referring to the former overprotection of panfish in Louisiana,

Viosca pointed to the need for regulations that would aid in keeping the predator-prey balance:

"In some areas in which the standing population may run as high as a thousand pounds of fish in an acre of water, the large majority are frequently stunted sunfish, very few of which may be of legal size, which means that here we have fish which are outnumbering our desirable species by many pounds to one, and by several hundred individuals to one, and yet relatively few of them are available for human consumption under the law."

That this problem is by no means restricted to southern states has been indicated by other reports. Thorpe found what evidently were comparable conditions in Connecticut. He recognized that the productivity of a body of water for the sportsman does not depend solely upon the poundage it can support, but rather, "upon the ability of an angler to catch some reasonably good fish. It appears that the majority of Connecticut lakes do not now meet this requirement primarily because of the balance which exists between species and between age classes. The cause of this unsatisfactory balance is a matter of speculation but the evidence indicates that it is the result of unwise stocking and overfishing under improper catch regulations."

The story of too many small fish of the wrong kinds is most frequently told of productive waters. "This state of unbalance," said Thorpe, "more often than not is exaggerated in the rich lakes apparently as a result of ideal survival conditions for young of all species and a scarcity of large carnivorous fishes." Of course, no fish population becomes crowded unless conditions favor its reproduction.

Here we might pause to recall that not many years ago we were paying fish-management dollars for the operation of hatcheries to stock warm-water fish in waters where there were too many of the same or other kinds already. Now, after some realistic appraisals, we are coming to understand that the real problem is to find ways of overcoming the terrific productivity of some of the very species we stocked. There is little cause for wonder that this complete reversal "threw" the sportsman and that now he has to start over and develop an entirely new set of standards.

The heavy stocking programs were not sponsored by the biologists. They originated by assumption in legislatures and administrative offices, often with the help of political pressure. But they were official policy and that policy is rapidly changing its spots. Public understanding has been severely taxed by liberalization of hook-and-line regulations, but it is likely that even more radical measures will be needed under some conditions.

NET PROFITS

The question of how to cure overpopulation ills is not one to be answered off-hand. Fish scientists have by no means worked their way through the wide range of these problems and their conclusions will be different from one part of the country to another and even from one lake to another.

It is clear that there will be no need for many of the restrictions of the past and that more sport will result when these are relaxed. It may be that in many waters proper regulations alone may tip the balance in the right direction.

However, as we have seen, the angler is not very effective with his hook-and-line gear where there is a big job to be done. If conditions are highly favorable to panfish, he is not likely to make much headway in reducing them; and likewise, the mere retention of closed seasons and limits on game fish probably will not generate sufficient predation pressure to do the job.

That future fish management will consist of realistic seasons and limits, plus other measures where they are needed was indicated by Greene in discussing the situation in New York. He mentioned the intensive selective fishing for popular game and food fish as a good reason for retaining limitations on the harvest of such species:

"Even with restrictions to limit such selectivity, it still results in poor fishing and in waters poorly adjusted for the production of their naturally successful, desirable species. Admittedly a perfectly balanced harvesting of fish is an unattainable ideal. But if we can avoid selecting only desirable fish and approach the harvesting of all species according to their capacities to produce, we shall progress toward fully realizing the capacities of our inland waters."

Taking New York's Black Lake as an example, he indicated the need for protecting the wall-eyed pike, smallmouth bass, largemouth bass, northern pike, and muskellunge. "The taking of rough fish and undesirable species should be encouraged in various ways. For example, perhaps seines of specified dimensions should be allowed for the taking of bullheads, catfish, rock bass, suckers, and sunfish. The edible qualities of gar pike and mooneyes should be given publicity and ways of taking them should be made available. This would leave the minnows, and probably even these should be harvested in quantity if the highest yields of food fish are to be maintained."

A systematic job by management crews may get some of our maladjusted fish populations started in the right direction. In some small lakes or ponds where seining or poisoning can be carried out efficiently, good results have been obtained by such methods at least temporarily. A pilot project of this kind was carried out in Michigan on Standard Lake.

This lake, at the junction of Cheboygan, Charlevoix, and Otsego Counties, long had a reputation for poor fishing. Its two halves, of about 16 acres each, were connected by a narrow channel, and the south basin was poisoned in 1937. Reflecting the infertile conditions of the watershed, the lake was found to be carrying only 22 pounds of fish per acre, of which an average of less than three were legal game fish. After poisoning, the undersized rock bass in the lake showed a conspicuous increase in growth rate. Such an operation would make more legal-sized game fish available to the fisherman.

In Massachusetts a 265-acre pond was heavily overstocked with white perch. The fish were stunted and measured 4 inches when state fish-management crews netted 2½ tons of them for removal in 1949. A year later when they went back to net 3 tons more, the size of the fish had increased to 5 inches. Massachusetts has a full-scale reduction campaign on panfish and has advertised a list of lakes and ponds where sportsmen are urged to concentrate on such species as yellow perch, white perch, bullheads, black crappie, bluegills, and sunfish. Said a state news release:

"Unless panfishes are harvested in much greater numbers than ever before, pond fishing will continue to deteriorate. Springtime fish kills, often resulting from diseases and parasites running rampant among overcrowded, undernourished panfish populations, will very soon become a wide-spread public nuisance."

Where a lake is small enough to be poisoned out completely, or where drainage is possible, a frequent expedient is to destroy the entire fish population and start over. Wisconsin biologists were getting persistent requests for the stocking of more fish in Stewart Lake, a 7-acre artificial pond, because of the poor quality of the fishing. They investigated and found it to be dominated by a crowded population of 5-inch crappies plus an abundance of bluegills and bullheads. They could find no evidence of predatory fish.

Stewart Lake was drained down to about an acre and then seined and poisoned. There were 279 pounds of fish to the acre, and the fish ran nearly 12 to the pound! The entire pond contained just 15 largemouth bass. After destruction of the population a new breeding stock was introduced. It consisted of 722 fingerling bass and *two pairs of adult bluegills.* Two years later the pond was opened to fishing. The first day's catch by more than a hundred anglers was estimated at 300 bass, ranging from 13 to 15 inches, and 2,000 bluegills of from 5 to 8 inches. There was no guarantee that the population would stay in balance, but good fishing had been restored.

Conditions in many a lake have so deteriorated that the cure will have to come through individual prescription by fishery biologists. But a big improvement might be brought about in some waters and much imbalance prevented by a more general and practical program that could easily be self-supporting. Thompson mentioned that in Illinois fishing seems to have been better in the days when there were no licenses or hook-and-line restrictions and when commercial operators were allowed to handle any species of fish. He indicated that more recently a few hundred commercial fishermen were taking a crop aggregating several times the catch of the state's 400,000 resident license-holders. This despite the restriction of market fishing to certain waters, species, and sizes.

In 1942, Viosca laid the matter directly on the line in commenting on the overpopulation problem in Louisiana: "The only way to tip the scales in favor of the black bass is to commercialize or outlaw the bluegill sunfish and related species. Here is a potential supply of human food many times the total production of largemouth black bass, that is barely scratched under the present laws of our State."

The idea has grown steadily that commercial cropping is to play a part in the management of sport fishing. During the war, when all food supplies were being intensively utilized, the Director of the Fish and Wildlife Service urged the increased harvesting of neglected stocks of fish: "The great middle section of the nation in particular has untold quantities of buffalo, carp, drum, gar, bowfish, catfish, suckers, and other varieties which make up the group designated as 'rough' fish. Practically all of these are edible and of high food value, but they have been unable to overcome long-seated prejudices . . . There is no hesitancy in advocating a . . . campaign in this connection because of the fact that taking and consuming the less desirable fresh-water varieties of fish will be good wildlife management as well as a boost for the national food economy."

The average angler is highly suspicious of the commercial fisherman, yet the man in business removes fish that are occupying waters largely to the detriment of game-fish populations. Carrying capacities being what they are, and considering the high breeding potential and objectionable habits of such species as carp, it appears that the angler can only profit by any activity that will in some measure reduce the numbers of rough or panfish.

MORE AND BETTER FISHING

It would be imprudent to generalize as to just where fishing restrictions should be liberalized. But the trend in this direction is evident. In 1943 only three states permitted year-'round angling for warmwater species, and by 1949 the number had increased to fifteen.

Many states were experimenting to learn how the principles applied to their conditions and also to convince the public that it would work. Pilot runs were in nearly all cases reassuring, such as the one on Escanaba Lake in northwest Wisconsin. This lake was opened to unrestricted hook and line fishing in 1946, with a creel census providing year by year catch records. After 10 years it was evident that the harvest of game fish was more than twice the catch on comparable waters under the old regulations, and there was no sign of depletion.

Ohio was the first northern state to "go liberal" in all inland waters. Their experiments on the question began in 1945, and by 1952 all lakes and streams were open the year around and without creel and size limits. Director Dambach voiced their satisfaction: "These actions have made possible millions of hours of worry-free fishing pleasure for the citizens of Ohio. There is no evidence to date that it has hurt fishing of any kind for any species."

In 1957 Indiana eliminated size limits and the closed season for all warm-water fish. In preparation for the certain public objections, fishery biologist H. E. McReynolds circulated a questionnaire to get a nationwide summary of regulations. Of 40 states replying, 17 had no creel limit and 31 no size limit on panfish. Thirty-eight were open all year for panfish and 35 for bass. A limited loosening up of regulations was evident in many more. It seemed especially significant that the biologists in all states (that answered the question) were in favor of liberalized fishing and the sportsmen of 27 states were considered to be generally for it.

An important benefit of the year-'round open season, where it is adopted, will be to permit farmers to manage their fishponds realistically. A heavy harvest is essential in managing a pond if it is to be kept in balance, and intensive fishing around the calendar is called for. A fertilized pond is an agricultural enterprise and this fact is being increasingly recognized, but there have been plenty of troubles along the way. J. Hammond Brown described how Missouri got around the principal difficulty.

"Those landowners who had fair sized fish ponds with a nice crop of fish were up against state laws that told them when they could take the different species and how many they could take in a day. Then there were the problems of trespass and of the dictum of public fishing on waters publicly stocked. This last problem came from the fact that in many instances the landowner was aided in his stocking by the state." After a public hearing the Missouri Conservation Commission made a move that can well be a model for other states where the problem arises.

"Along with the annual promulgation of the regulations for the taking of fish in Missouri waters, the following amendment to the section of the law dealing with the taking of fish was adopted. It reads:

Excepted Waters.—Farm ponds, and other natural or artificial impoundments which are not stocked by or subject to stocking with fish from overflow or from other waters of the state and to which the owner, occupant or lessee thereof has the exclusive right of access.

"This definition of 'excepted waters' relieves the landowners of such waters of the necessity of following the state's regulations as to the time and manner of harvesting whatever crop of fish may be in such waters."

The farm pond program still is far short of its potential, but its growth has been rapid, and well over a million ponds have been built. Farmers have taken to the idea so well that pond construction has outrun the technology of managing them in practically all parts of the country except the Southeast. Private ponds will add to the total fishing water of a state and reduce fishing pressures on public lakes and streams. In the South, commercial ponds and club ponds are being successfully managed. As Homer L. Swingle frequently has pointed out, a farm pond is a means of catching runoff water from a farm and taking a final crop from its dissolved fertility before it finds its way into streams and, eventually, the sea.

Although we have stressed the need for a heavy harvest of some kinds of fish, these are the less desirable ones that the average angler has been neglecting. There is increasing competition, year by year, for the supply of game fish. As brought out previously, restrictive regulations are serving their primary purpose in distributing the catch among more fishermen.

In the year 1959, compilations of the Fish and Wildlife Service showed that fishermen in the 50 states spent $50,347,832 for more than 22 million fishing licenses and permits. As the popularity of angling grows and the number of fishermen increases, the equity of each in the supply of desirable fish diminishes. Any means of augmenting the acreage of available waters is all to the good. Likewise there is increasing thought on measures to obtain more sport per fish caught.

In treating this subject, Hazzard traced the trend of reduction in Michigan's trout limit: "Late in the 19th century a limit of fifty was imposed, which was reduced to thirty-five and then twenty-five and finally fifteen. These later reductions came with increased angling, particularly with the advent of the automobile and good roads." He remarked further that "The trend in all progressive trout states has been toward lower daily limits, thereby placing the emphasis on the sport value rather than the meat value of trout."

For Michigan's trout streams it was concluded that the limit of 15 trout, but not more than 10 pounds and one fish, was satisfactory, since there was no evidence that they were being overfished either before or after the war. Research information showed that in spite of heavy pressure, the catch of northern streams held up throughout the season—which averaged about 130 days.

Where legal-sized trout were being released in either streams or lakes the story was different. When conditions were favorable for feeding, fishermen who got to the planting spots shortly after the hatchery truck had no trouble in filling the limit. "If the number of legal-sized plantings in streams and small lakes is to be increased, a lower limit is necessary in order to make these plantings yield the maximum amount of sport."

Certain lakes in Michigan have been found favorable for trout, even though they have no connecting water suitable for spawning. These have been stocked with trout and in the absence of competition (other fish have been removed) excellent survival and growth is obtained. In these lakes also, it has been easy for fishermen to make a killing. "Catch records from lakes planted with marked trout show that from 80 to 94 per cent of the survivors of previous fall plantings of legal-sized fish are caught out *on opening day*, leaving little for angling the rest of the season. On larger lakes trout are not taken so rapidly."

An extra trout license supports the legal-sized planting program in Michigan, but it has been a problem to extend the sport provided in this way much beyond the week after stocking. Special limits applying to individual waters is a method that is proving workable and gaining in favor.

A logical extension of this experience has been the establishment of the "special regulation trout pond." Impoundments at state hatcheries and on small spring-fed streams have been stocked with brook, brown, and rainbow trout and opened under a regulation permitting a catch of only two fish per day and fishing with flies only. No boats are allowed.

In spite of the pessimistic predictions of old-timers, the trout pond program appears here to stay and is growing. Records on seven such ponds from 1944 to 1947 showed that fishermen caught 44 percent of all fish planted and there was a good carry-over of residue fish from one season to the next.

Such methods are, of course, best adapted to heavily populated areas, and the number of people who can be served will depend largely on the number of sites suitable for the impoundment of water sufficiently cool for trout. Hazzard pointed out that spring feeders far too small to be stocked and fished could be converted into ponds that would accommodate a fairly large number of fly fishermen without crowding. An acre pond is equal in surface area to a mile of stream averaging 8¼ feet in width.

The old days of virgin streams harboring many years' accumulation of "family-size" game fish are rapidly fading into limbo. If we are successful in bringing about more far-sighted and conservative use of watersheds in mountain grazing areas and wilderness timber lands, a steady improvement in the productivity of cold-water fish will result. But it is likely that the most positive management will always be through regulations that spread the resource among many people.

Management of game fish by regulation will be still more intensive in heavily populated regions, and special waters and special restrictions will make it possible to serve more people with more sport, in spite of the fact that their catch poundage may be small. As we have seen, however, there is a tremendous supply of fish now considered less desirable. These can be managed far more efficiently than in the past by making the annual surplus available to the kid with the cane pole and the man with the rod.

As fishermen learn the facts, they will get the hang of things. They will see that there is a right and a wrong place for the limit, and that their own specialists are the ones to decide how and when it should be applied.

CHAPTER 11

Greener Grass

IT needs but a superficial examination of the fauna and flora of the earth to affirm that living things have developed in communities, of which the plant and animal components display a high degree of dependence on one another. On large land masses or in extensive water areas many species have retained a wide range of versatility that has enabled them to survive with many competing species and in the presence of numerous actual or potential enemies. Such enemies might, of course, be predatory forms or those that cause diseases.

In restricted ranges, animals frequently have been exposed to relatively simple community organizations and sometimes to extreme conditions of one kind or another. This has led to specialization and the loss of powers that would have been necessary for survival elsewhere. It is the reason why we find blind fishes in caves and flightless birds on remote islands.

Before men took over intensive regulation of the earth's lesser inhabitants, mountain and desert barriers and broad stretches of ocean served to isolate one life complex from another; and over geological time periods, plants and animals reached mutually tolerable adjustments by virtue of a large-scale and drastic weeding out of misfits. Through this process a vast number of creatures never seen by man became extinct and others became better adapted to their ranges because they constantly produce genetic variations, and those that have survival value tend to be preserved.

This was the world of life as man found it; but he couldn't leave it that way, for he himself was in many ways a generalized animal, tied to no specific set of environmental conditions—a natural cosmopolite destined to inherit, not just a part of the earth, but all of it.

Wherever they went, men have had a restive inclination to reshuffle the fauna. And nothing has been so evident as their complete failure to perceive that the original condition was one of intricate organization and that their changes might set off a long chain of faunistic reverberations.

There has been much argument, pro and con, on the advisability of introducing foreign species to the fauna or flora of any country. In terms of the primitive condition, it probably would be for the most part inadvisable. But primitive conditions do not hold for long after the invasion of Caucasian man, and by the time he has thoroughly overhauled the pattern of plant life it stands to reason that he may have prepared habitat niches which no native animal can fill adequately and for which there is something made to order on the other side of the world. It is true also that natural environments have existed in which the introduction of something new and useful did no apparent harm to anything important to human interests.

It probably is human nature to overlook the blessings close at home and to be forever appraising the seemingly greener grass across the fence. But that's the way it is, and the question of introducing exotic game and fish is perennially in the news. It is a many-sided issue and one on which thinking needs to be straight and clear. A long history of experience with such activities should furnish facts applicable to future policies.

THINGS OLD AND NEW

In the United States, success with three exotic game birds has provided some of our most convincing evidence that something is to be gained by the introduction of animals from beyond our own shores. All three, the pheasant, Hungarian partridge, and chukar, have a wide distribution in the Old World and many locally adapted races. They typify the kind of animal that stands the best chance of making good in a new range.

Pheasants had found their way to Europe from the Caucasus as early as 1000 B.C., and they probably invaded England with the Romans half a century before the Christian era.

The stock of birds that was brought to eastern United States was for the most part, if not entirely, from England. Richard Bache, son-in-law of Benjamin Franklin, introduced pheasants on his New Jersey estate on the Delaware River in 1790, but they evidently did not persist. In 1880 Pierre Lorillard liberated large numbers of pheasants in northern New Jersey, and in 1887, Rutherford Stuyvesant began stocking on his Tranquillity game preserve at Allamuchy, New Jersey. John C. Phillips reported them well established in that region by the early nineties.

Phillips himself was involved in bringing a strain of "nearly pure, old, dark-necked English pheasants . . ." to North Beverly, Massachusetts, in 1897-98, an introduction that immediately caught on. From there they spread into New Hampshire, Maine, and Vermont.

Probably the first outstandingly successful planting of pheasants in this country was made with birds predominating in Chinese ring-neck blood which Judge O. N. Denny, Consul General at Shanghai, sent back to Oregon. The first shipments never arrived—it was rumored that one lot was eaten by the ship's crew at a holiday celebration—but in 1881-82 several dozen pairs were liberated in at least two locations (the records do not agree) in the Willamette Valley. Conditions evidently were just right, for the birds "took" and spread rapidly. In ten years there were enough of them for an open season.

Subsequently, pheasants were stocked in practically every part of the northern half of the country and in many areas of the South. This far-and-wide distribution has followed the scatter-gun pattern, and it is likely that the species now occupies every sizable unit of range adapted to its needs. The records show that many of the plantings failed, but here and there a few birds became acclimated and survived to breed. When conditions were right, it required only a few.

In 1908, Fred J. Green, of Calgary, Alberta, brought the Hungarian partridge to the northern Great Plains. He studied the country and selected his area; then, with the backing of a small group of sportsmen who raised about $3,000, he imported wild-trapped birds direct from the plains of Hungary. There were 7 pairs the first year and 95 the next. Ten pairs more came in 1914—and that is the story.

"Huns" were introduced at a time when the small-game cycle was on its way up, and climatic conditions were favorable. The bird and the environment meshed and the breeding potential went to work. They spread through Saskatchewan into Manitoba and south into North Dakota. In 1924 additional releases were made in North Dakota—about 7,500 in all, and these, plus infiltrations from the north, formed the basis of a population in that state estimated in 1942 at 8 to 10 million.

As might have been anticipated, the Hungarian partridge has proved best adapted to the northern plains, although it was one of the first birds to be introduced, unsuccessfully, in eastern United States (1790). It has had periods of comparative prosperity at various locations in the Lake States, southern Ontario, and the Northeast and has been tried in 42 of the 48 states. In both Europe and America the southern limit for this species is about the 42d parallel, which in this country is represented by a line drawn through Cape Cod on the east and the California-Oregon border on the west. There is no gainsaying the fact that the hunky has been one of the most valuable of foreign additions to the roster of American game species.

The chukar partridge is our most recent acquisition from abroad, and it is doing well, in spite of discouragement with early trials. A systematic attempt was made to establish this bird in Missouri in 1934, but it developed that the strain in use had come from the mountains of Nepal, India, at altitudes from 6,000 to 10,000 feet. Of 22 subspecies of the chukar in Eurasia, this one appeared *least* likely to make the grade in Missouri. The augury was sound, for the birds failed.

This job, however, was not a complete loss. The work was planned well and the results studied. The report on it is a chapter in our book of progress.

Tests with the chukar in Nevada had a more favorable outcome—incidentally, this was the state's first Federal Aid project. From 1939 to 1943 pen-reared birds were stocked in 25 locations. The scenery in Nevada was much different from Missouri, but even there the plantings on plains and farmlands disappeared. The birds hung on in rugged semi-desert, from 5,000 to 7,000 feet up, and there they prospered. Nevada had the first chukar hunting season in 1947.

The project to introduce chukars has been carried out since 1950 by the Fish and Wildlife Service, stimulated by a committee of the International Association of Game, Fish and Conservation Commissioners. The birds are now well entrenched in western states, with a race from Turkey helping to broaden the range. Experimental releases have shown promise as far east as North Dakota and Texas. Actually a few chukars were established in the early thirties in California's Owens Valley and Mojave Desert. In spite of stocking in all but 4 of the state's 58 counties, the only success has been in arid country.

Introduction of the chukar has been widely supported on the important basis that the birds are not known to compete with desert quail or any other native species. There is no such assurance in regard to another Asian game bird that received extensive trials during the late fifties. The "coturnix," or Japanese, quail is a small, migratory bird with varieties widely distributed in the Old World. It has a fantastic breeding rate, several generations being produced in the same year. Initial stock was propagated at the Missouri game farm, and by 1958 several hundred thousand had been released by some 19 states. Sportsmen generally considered the bird to be inferior to the native bobwhite, and biologists were restive because coturnix seemed to have a bobwhite outlook in its choice of habitat. There were sincere sighs of relief in many quarters when, by 1960, it seemed that Japanese quail (the strain in use, anyway) had failed to naturalize.

Still another failure was a cause for thanksgiving far and wide. It was the case of the "San Juan" rabbit. These animals were descendants of domestic rabbits established during the last century on the San Juan Islands of Puget Sound. Domestic rabbits are derived from the wild European rabbit which, as M. O. Steen put it, ". . . has a long and notorious record as a pest of very serious proportions in the areas throughout the world where it has become successfully established." (See pp. 31 and 191.)

As early as 1949 dealers in the State of Washington were selling San Juan rabbits to clubs and dog trainers in eastern states. Probably no responsible state official ever favored this, but many of them seemed powerless to stop it. The federal Lacey Act (1900) prohibited the importation of exotic animals except under permit, and likewise interstate shipment contrary to state law. But the San Juan animal was already here (i.e. not foreign), and many states had no laws controlling such things; in 1958 at least 20 states still lacked such authority. In other cases existing laws were not enforced.

Despite repeated warnings by biologists and administrators, this creature was widely stocked by people who could not see the obvious alternative—managing for more cottontails. Occasionally, the animals were reported to have over-wintered, but except on Santa Barbara Island, California, there do not seem to be any self-supporting populations. This fiasco points up the need in every state for a law governing the liberation of non-native animals, and for good enforcement thereof.

It is possible that in this country valuable work is still to be done with exotic game birds. A pheasant adapted to a warm, humid climate might well extend pheasant distribution far southward of the present range of the ringneck. In 1956 Gardiner Bump of the Fish and Wildlife Service (in charge of Foreign Game Introductions) obtained two promising races in a particularly difficult collecting expedition to Iran on the Caspian Sea. The build-up of these birds on game farms will permit trials in several states, and other pheasant races offer additional possibilities.

Other game birds secured by Bump and undergoing field tests in the West are the Spanish red-legged partridge, gray francolin, seesee, and black partridge. The Reeve's pheasant, a long-tailed, spectacular, forest bird, has had some success in France, and it is being stocked experimentally in southern Ohio. Many such attempts have failed, but this work is more carefully planned than ever has been the case in the past, and there is no foretelling what may come of it.

VACANT NICHES

The profitable introduction of animals to new American habitats has by no means been limited to foreign species. Important work of this kind has been done with native stock.

The mountain goat—not a goat, but a near relative of the chamois— is one good game animal to which Nature does not seem to have done complete justice. Some excellent ranges were left without a breeding stock.

From its principal stamping grounds in British Columbia and Alberta, a narrow tongue of occupied range extends southward along the western side of the continental divide into Montana and Idaho. East of the divide there are plenty of mountains but, originally, no goats. They seem never to have crossed the intervening valleys to populate what appears to be ideal country for them.

In 1941 the Montana Fish and Game Department began a project to stock vacant goat ranges. Their first catch of four animals were hauled 350 miles to Sweet Grass Canyon on the east slope of the Crazy Mountains. That year and the next a total of 21 animals were liberated in this area. In a week's check-up in 1946 two men counted 56 goats, including 7 yearlings and 12 kids. Nearly all were within five miles of the point of release.

From 1941 to 1948 a total of 62 mountain goats were captured in the Teton drainage west of Choteau, making possible the establishment of three, and possibly four, new herds. Blindfolds and drug injections proved to be effective in reducing shock during the large amount of handling that was necessary. It was also found expedient to loop a piece of garden hose and cement it over the two horns of an animal; then, with feet tied, it could be moved. From a catch of 25 goats in 1943, 13 were carried 7 miles down a mountain stream in a rubber boat, loaded into a plane and flown as near as possible to the new range, then packed into the mountains on horses.

In 1924 an accident resulted in a mountain-goat herd on Harney Peak in the Black Hills of South Dakota. Several animals escaped from an enclosure at Custer State Park and disappeared into the Harney Range. Five years later goats were being seen, and in 1940 the new herd was estimated at 200. After 1950 numbers evidently levelled off at about 300, which was thought to be the carrying capacity of the range. This herd is being used as a nucleus for further trapping and transplanting to other areas.

The goat episode recalls the establishment of wild hogs in Tennessee. The original stock (probably) came from the Hartz Mountains of Germany and the animals were kept in a confined area. They too escaped by accident.

The taking over of the semi-arid West for cattle raising and agriculture resulted in the elimination of the pronghorn antelope (not an antelope, but a unique American species) from much of its primitive range. When land use became more stabilized, it appeared that there were large areas that could be producing pronghorns without compromising other interests. Accordingly, the animals were systematically trapped and moved to new territory. Texas, New Mexico, and Montana have been especially successful in starting new herds, and by 1960 antelope were being hunted in 14 states. Research indicates that the pronghorn feeds much more on weeds and sage than upon grass and only occasionally competes to any significant extent with range livestock.

It probably is true that since the glaciers melted enough time has elapsed so that most species of our wildlife **had** spread to all of the range that was naturally suited to them. However, as we have seen, there are exceptions. Another good one is the case of the Merriam wild turkey in Wyoming. This bird did not previously exist in Wyoming, but an area in the Medicine Bow National Forest looked suspiciously like turkey range.

Accordingly, in 1935 a swap was arranged whereby the State of New Mexico sent wild turkeys and quail to Wyoming in return for some planting stock of the sage grouse. The deal was closed, and in the spring of that year nine hens and six gobblers arrived at their new home on the George Waln ranch about four miles northeast of Laramie Peak. One of the hens killed herself at the liberation, but the rest of the flock remained in the vicinity and were fed by Mr. Waln for two winters. Three broods were reared the first year, and the second spring the flock departed, taking all the tame turkeys of the ranch with them.

It was reported that other domestic birds were lured away from their owners by the Laramie Peak flock, and how many were added in this way was not known. But by 1942 the wild population was well established and numbered between 400 and 600 as a conservative estimate. They had spread over 16 townships in 7 years.

Much of the turkey transplanting that has taken place in the United States in recent years can be classed as "restoration." This species, like the deer, had been removed entirely from much of the country to which it was native, but protective laws and the regrowth of forests in the present century made available suitable areas of made-over range. Many states in the East and South have moved in new breeding stock and now have the turkey reinstated and making progress on its own account. From 1938 to 1945, Texas alone distributed turkeys to 73 areas in 65 counties and estimated the state population at 100,000 birds.

The transplanting of a native species is frequently worth trying and stands much more chance of paying off than where a completely "foreign" form is used. The climate and vegetation are more likely in such cases to resemble the range to which the animal is naturally adapted.

An exotic species that does make good in a new range may appear to be well adapted to it; but it would not be surprising, in the passage of time, to see animals in the new colony taking on characteristics somewhat different from those of the parent stock. In one case, this appears to have happened far sooner than would be expected.

The mouflon is a wild sheep found originally only on the mountainous islands of Corsica and Sardinia in the Mediterranean. In 1869 a herd of ten mouflons were transferred to the Tribec Mountains of Slovakia, where they multiplied and became well established.

About the year 1910, it was observed that a distinctly different sheep was preponderant among the Slovakian animals. About one mouflon in four was of the original type—red in summer and chestnut in winter, the old rams having a whitish saddle-patch and horns with divergent tips. In the new subspecies (for such it is) the rams are darker in summer and nearly black in winter. The saddle patch is gone, and the horns are short and thick with *converging* tips. The new range has produced a new race. This, incidentally, is "evolution" under our noses.

Past work in the redistribution of various mammals and birds is now highly significant to the American sportsman; but nothing done with furred and feathered species can compare with the extensive reshuffling that has taken place among North American fishes. It is well exemplified by the record for our five species of Pacific salmon. Originally, they were almost entirely confined to the temperate waters of the North Pacific.

A survey by the Bureau of Fisheries showed that from 1872 to 1930, eggs and young fish aggregating nearly 50 million from California, Oregon, Washington, and Alaska were shipped to 17 Atlantic-Coast states and 16 foreign countries. All of the plantings failed except those made in situations where both fresh- and salt-water conditions were similar to the original home of the salmon. New runs were established successfully in Maine and Canada on the Atlantic coast and also in New Zealand and Chile.

Waters of the western states were far less well supplied with a native fish fauna than those of the eastern half of the country; and as a result, most of the species movements have been toward the Pacific. About 25 new kinds of fish have been introduced into marine and fresh waters of the Pacific Northwest, and 21 of them are established and producing. In spite of the large amount of sport furnished by trout and salmon, in 1938-39 the Washington Department of Fisheries calculated that 44 percent of the fresh-water catch in the state was composed of introduced species.

The yellow perch made up more than 22 percent of this yield. First plantings of this popular cane-pole fish were made in 1890, and it is now present in nearly all of the lowland lakes of Washington and Oregon. Except for the land-locked sockeye (silver trout) it is the fish most commonly caught by Washington sportsmen.

It has been reported that some 39 species and subspecies of fishes have been stocked in Nevada since 1873, and 24 of these now are found in the state. An economic appraisal of the introduced fishes of California shows that the annual commercial value of shad, striped bass, catfish, carp, spiny-rayed fishes, and trout exceeds 13 million dollars. Sport fishing for the brought-in kinds "is equally as important as the fishing for all of the native fresh-water and anadromous fishes . . . The cost was only a few thousand dollars and from all available information the returns have been worth many millions of dollars."

The brown trout, or Loch Leven (from Europe) found a place of usefulness in California's streams, since it does well in the slow and weedy stretches of trout streams not well suited to (native) rainbows. Similarly, the eastern brook trout thrives in "high mountain lakes with very cold and short summers, and it is able to spawn more successfully than rainbow trout in spring seepages in the bottoms of such lakes, thus maintaining itself naturally where the rainbow has difficulty. Like the Loch Leven, therefore, it utilizes a portion of the trout habitat which would otherwise be wasted."

The striped bass is one of the most valuable native marine fish of our Atlantic coast. It did not occur in the Pacific until 1879. That year, and again in 1882, two shipments of yearling fish totalling 435 crossed the country on the new transcontinental rail line and were liberated in San Francisco Bay. The California coast now offers some of the best striper fishing in the world, and the species migrates between the southern part of that state and Oregon. The maximum commercial yield, of more than 1¾ million pounds, was taken in 1915, but since 1935 it has been exclusively a sport fish in the Pacific.

A transcontinental fish-haul in those days was no small undertaking, and an even more delicate venture of this kind was successfully carried off by Seth Green, pioneer fish culturist, nine years before the stocking of the bass. On June 20, 1871, with one assistant, eight tin cans, and 15,000 just-hatched Atlantic shad, he left Rochester, New York headed for California. After 7 days and many changes of water, he reached Sacramento with a gratifying number of hungry survivors.

Shad are like salmon in that they tend to spawn at their point of origin, so the fry were put aboard the California and Oregon Railway and taken up-river 275 miles to Tehama. There Mr. Green dipped up a glassful of water from the Sacramento River and found it full of food organisms. The temperature being right, he released his fish.

The appearance of mature fish in the stream two years later indicated establishment, and the spread of the shad from that time on was a continuing success story. In 1880 they were appearing in the Columbia River, and 20 years after the initial plant, adult fish were being taken in the Fraser River, British Columbia. The range of the shad is now spread over 3,000 miles of coastline, from Kodiak Island, Alaska, to San Diego.

The carrying of newly-hatched ocean fish across the great buffalo ranges on the slow and laboring Union Pacific appears to be a prodigy of accomplishment, but an even more amazing feat was the first introduction of trout to Tasmania.

For 12 years it had been tried repeatedly, but the eyed-eggs had to be shipped from Liverpool half way around the globe, through the heat of the tropics, in a slow-going sailing ship, and kept cool all the way. It had been too much.

But after a decade of study, this epic of acclimatization was accomplished by T. A. Youl in 1864. He moss-packed both trout and salmon eggs in a box under 9 feet of ice, in an especially constructed compartment of the hold of the ship *Norfolk*. She sailed on January 20 and arrived at Melbourne on the 15th of April. From there the eggs were sent south to Hobart, Tasmania, where they arrived after 91 days of travel. They were hatched successfully in the River Plenty.

From this beginning, trout were carried to suitable waters in Australia and New Zealand, where they have thrived and furnished abundant sport. The salmon of that shipment, and many a one since, hatched and were stocked in suitable streams. But when the smolts descended to the sea, the tale ended. They never came back. More recently, Pacific salmon have done well and runs now are established in a number of New Zealand streams.

One of the possibilities in the vacant-niche kind of stocking is that of replacing a valuable native species that has become extinct. With the advent of logging runs and the energetic introduction of trout to all available waters, the grayling, Michigan's jewel of northern streams, disappeared completely. There now is no doubt that the sub-species formerly found in that state is extinct.

Fish specialists have been hard put to find physical differences between the Michigan grayling and the Montana grayling, which is available for use in Michigan waters. In the decade beginning in 1926, about two million fry and half a million yearling fish of the Montana grayling were distributed in various lakes and streams of Michigan. All but one of the plantings failed, and this one was in a small lake where all other fish had been removed. It is now conceded that the grayling cannot be brought back to Michigan streams. The waters that proved to be unsuited to the native fish appear to be no better for the introduced one.

The examples cited here and a multitude of others unmentioned show that in many circumstances much is to be gained by the *proper use* of non-native species. It that were the whole story, there would hardly be an issue, but unfortunately there is another side that is not so favorable.

The trouble is that nearly all of the acclimatization work of the past was done purely as a matter of trial and error. Comparatively, the trials were legion, the errors frequent, and the successes few. The introductions that went wrong show that it would be poor business to keep the movement going on the old basis.

INFILTRATION

The "English" sparrow and starling are known over much of the nation, and have made clear to many people the undesirability of many of the alien species that might be brought to our shores. Other errors of faunal transfer are less generally recognized, but the idea is gaining ground that with animal imports there is always the possibility of introducing parasites and diseases that will find just the host they are looking for in one of our valuable native species.

A shipment of game birds arriving in California from Hong Kong, China, was found to be infected with Asiatic Newcastle disease, a virulent malady of poultry and game birds which thus far, and at some cost, has been kept out of North America. As a result of this importation, the disease had been spread to five game and poultry farms before authorities of the University of California and the Bureau of Animal Industry caught up with it and eliminated the sources of infection.

The matter of disease is not to be taken lightly, but the possibility of infiltrating native game stocks with "inferior blood" may in some cases be of equal concern. It is possible that a problem of this kind has resulted from the repeated stocking of Texas (Mexican) bobwhites. From 1910 to the present, these birds have been scattered freely from south to north over eastern states. In the first 15 years, records of the Biological Survey showed that more than 233,000 Mexican quail were brought into this country. From $1.50 the price rose to as much as $36 per dozen.

These quail went to points as far north as Nova Scotia and Ontario. The severe winter of 1904-05 wiped out the bobwhite over large areas of the North, and after this disaster reinforcements from Texas and south of the border arrived in a steady stream. In 1928, Phillips opined, pessimistically,

"This period probably marks the end of the big northern birds that were able to withstand climatic conditions well up into southern New Hampshire, southern Vermont, southwestern Maine, and southern Ontario. Investigations by the Bureau of Biological Survey and by others have shown that Mexican birds in Pennsylvania mate with, and undoubtedly will eventually change materially the character of, the native stock . . . The writer has seen a large series of present-day Pennsylvania and Georgia specimens that show various gradations from eastern-looking to the pure *texanus* type. There is little doubt that the native northern stock will be swamped out."

It is a moot question whether or not this has occurred, since the bobwhite has been in serious trouble in parts of the East for several decades. The failure of present quail populations to reach the high peaks of northern birds in some areas at the beginning of the century probably can be accounted for by habitat changes. Ordinarily, it seems probable that a small infiltration of inferior blood would quickly be eliminated from a population by the selective dying off of weaker birds. But it is possible that particular conditions have altered this.

Roger M. Latham and C. R. Studholme studied the situation in

Pennsylvania and revealed facts that may have key significance. Pennsylvania quail were drastically reduced by the hard winter of 1935-36, and they have failed to recover since then. In the period following the reduction, there were heavy importations of Mexican quail. These, coming at a time when native stock was at its numerical low, would have had their maximum effect in degrading the northern birds. Latham and Studholme had indications of physical changes which were strongly suggestive that this had happened. If it has, many years of annual turnover and natural culling may be necessary before the population regains its former thrift.

That the danger of this kind of "race pollution" is not limited to small animals is witnessed by the fate of local populations of two European species of big game. As a result of depletion during the late war, it has been estimated that the various herds of ibex in European mountains now aggregate less than 2,000 animals. Early in the last century this wild goat became extinct in one of its native ranges—the High Tatra Mountains of Slovakia. In 1901 they were reintroduced from Austria, and some years later two Asiatic goats, the Bezoar-goat and the Sinaitic-goat were stocked in the same region.

These two exotic species interbred with the ibex and produced a creature considerably different from the native form. Worse yet, physiological changes were induced, and the breeding season of the ibex was shifted until the young were being born in February and March, a time of year when survival was impossible. In 1951 it was reported that "there now survive only four female Ibex-like creatures as the last monuments of a once-powerful animal in the wild parts of the High Tatra mountains."

The introduction of a nearly-related form to a range already occupied by a native species appears to be an especially pernicious kind of biological boondogling. Ordinarily there will be nothing to gain in such a measure, as is witnessed by one of the most ambitious experiments of its kind—introduction of the Lapland reindeer to Alaska. The reindeer is a caribou from Asia where it has been domesticated by many tribes of natives across the northern fringe of the continent. To provide a more reliable means of support for Alaskan natives, a herd of 1,280 animals were brought to the Seward Peninsula between 1891 and 1902. Under the care of Lapp herders, these built up to a maximum estimated at between 600,000 and 1,000,000 animals. The herds were concentrated in the coastal area from Point Barrow to the Alaska Peninsula.

It developed that this importation was a direct threat to the great, migrating populations of barren-ground caribou. Wherever opportunity offered, the reindeer would join wild herds of caribou and interbreed with them. Olaus J. Murie stated that "The caribou's greatest menace is not the wolf, nor the hunter, but man's economic developments, principally the raising of reindeer." He pointed out that there was no need for replacing the abundant and thrifty herds of the interior with the animal from Asia, and the caribou certainly needed no infusion of domestic blood.

The possibilities for overenthusiastic promotion of the reindeer were apparent in the first detailed bulletin on the new industry published by the Department of Agriculture in 1922. At that time it was estimated on a basis of preliminary reconnaissance extending to all parts of Alaska * that the territory would eventually be able to support from three to four million reindeer. Nowhere was there any perceptible consideration for what would happen to the admittedly superior caribou.

As it turned out, when the Eskimos took over complete care of their herds, it became evident that they were hunters and not keepers of livestock. But the stage already was set for their failure. The lichen ranges had been vastly overstocked and their carrying capacity reduced. This undoubtedly accounts in large part for the decline of the reindeer to some tens of thousands by 1950. At the First Alaskan Science Conference, Murie called attention to the critical importance of the lichens in maintaining caribou numbers. He also made this observation on recent suggestions that there be other additions to the Alaskan fauna:

"Certain well-meaning people have proposed that elk be brought into interior Alaska. I can think of nothing more dangerous to Alaska's game animals if the elk should succeed in establishing themselves. Elsewhere we have found elk competing with mountain sheep and moose. Some years ago I had several sacks of reindeer lichens shipped

* And with little realization of the low grazing capacity of the slow-growing lichen tundra. Once depleted, the lichens may take 30 years (or much more) of complete rest to recover.

from Alaska to Wyoming to try out on elk. Though this was strange food to the elk, and it had been dried a long time, they ate it. We cannot afford to add to the caribou problem by introducing another herd animal that would deplete their favorite food.

"Unfortunately, there are also proposals to introduce the coast black-tailed deer into the moose range on the Kenai Peninsula. Here again the present program aims to keep a famous moose herd in balance with the browse supply. Such worthy effort should not be thwarted by placing there a competitor."

Probably one of the great but hidden attractions of foreign introductions is the expectation of getting something for nothing. People without a knowledge of big-game ecology and the realities of food-supply limitations might well imagine that there is plenty of room in the forest for another species. That is why the carrying-capacity idea is stressed over and over again by the biologist.

DISPLACED FAUNA

Over the face of the earth, no more startling examples of the far-reaching effects of the introduction of exotic forms of life can be found than those in New Zealand. From 1774 on, beginning with the efforts of Captain Cook himself, a wide assortment of mammals and birds were brought to the two islands.

In its pristine state, New Zealand was a land of primitive flightless birds and a few fish, although two species of bats were there originally, and the Polynesian rat and dog had accompanied the great fleet of canoes that brought Maori colonists from Raiatea, near Tahiti, in the fourteenth century. The early introductions featured goats, hogs, and sheep and were intended to make available a food supply where there had been practically none before.

The flora of New Zealand had developed in the absence of any plant-eating mammals, and the native birds had been free from the attention of mammalian predators. This obviously rendered the old adjustments highly vulnerable when the white man established his "acclimatization" societies and began to bring in anything and everything during the second half of the 19th century and the early part of the present one.

The vegetation has been radically altered by the new grazing economy (that included widespread burning and overstocking) and the introduction of more than 600 species of plants, including gorse, Scottish broom, American blackberry, and others, that "ran wild." The endemic birds were so susceptible to predation by small carnivores imported as a follow-up to oversuccessful rabbit stocking that many people became resigned to the idea that the entire pattern of living things would have to be done over.

European rabbits became a part of the fauna in 1870. After two or three false starts with small numbers, the effort was increased and the animals became established. As in Australia, this rabbit now has become a major liability. On one 1,600-acre sheep ranch, 96,000 were trapped in 5 years. They now kill more than 16 million rabbits annually in the two islands. The export of rabbit skins and carcasses brings in more than $5 million a year, but the animals do damage estimated at twice that figure.

Of 130 introduced species of birds, about 24 have become established. Of 48 species of exotic animals, all but four were brought in intentionally, and 25 now are living in the wild. An herbivorous opossum from Australia "seems to be eating the forests and orchards from the top down, while the deer, goats, and rabbits, are denuding the land from the ground up."

New Zealand imported the red deer, Himalayan goat, Virginia white-tailed deer, Japanese deer, and deer from other parts of the world. They have increased so rapidly and done so much damage to vegetation that there now is a year-'round open season on big game. No license is required, and the government will supply ammunition to anyone who will shoot these animals. In one year a single hunter is known to have killed 2,400 head of big game.

The red deer, in particular, has assumed the position of a major pest—a situation practically inconceivable to many American deer hunters. Forest and agricultural damage has been widespread, and the species now is looked upon principally in terms of "control."

Early in the century, stunted deer and malformed heads were appearing in the kill, and "new blood" was prescribed as the cure. More deer were brought in. Later it became evident that range was deteriorating and the deer themselves were showing the effects of malnutrition. Protection was removed from this species in state forest plantations in 1927, and bounties were paid until 1932. The control job then was taken over by the government Forest Service.

Beginning in 1931, "parties of experienced deer hunters were sent every year to the various districts where assistance in coping with the growing numbers of deer was most urgently required. The deer-killing parties were under experienced field officers and worked on basic wages plus a bonus per skin." In recent years skin exports have been about 100,000 annually. Present concern over the red-deer threat and the commercial position of the species are brought out in Wodziki's further statement:

"Although the Department of Internal Affairs has performed a great work in destroying deer it is doubtful whether the recent reduction in the deer population could have been achieved without the intervention of private hunters attracted by high market prices. It is to the credit of the Department that it has reduced the cost of deer control by utilizing the services of private hunters. This has been effected by such measures as the supplying of cheap ammunition, the sale of army rifles, technical advice on preserving skins, the purchase of skins by the Department and the leaving of accessible areas for private hunters. Thus it has been made easier for the private hunter to shoot deer, preserve their skins and dispose of these at a profit."

He comments further that "Owing to difficulties of transport and other reasons no commercial use is made of the carcasses. The ancient belief that some animal organs are particularly potent and have a miraculous influence is still prevalent in China, and deers' tails, antlers in velvet, testicles and sinews are eagerly bought by Chinese merchants in New Zealand for their fellow-countrymen."

New Zealand colonists came to a land that offered few of the wild-game assets that contributed so abundantly to the support of early comers on the continent of North America. It was natural that they should think of bringing in what they lacked. No one understood the existing life communities—and now no one ever will. Trial and error were the only recourse, but as we have seen, in this field the mistakes may be costly. We have had proportionately fewer of them elsewhere only because conditions were different.

People interested in game seldom do much redistributing of the world's carnivores, but such species have come in for a measure of attention. The mongoose of India, a weasel-like animal best-known for its propensity to kill outsize cobras, is a naturalized citizen of numerous sugarcane-raising islands of the Caribbean and Hawaii. In the period following our own Civil War, damage from rats was costing the cane growers of Jamaica alone an estimated half-million dollars a year. In 1872 an enterprising exponent of biological control, one W. Bancroft Espeut, procured nine mongooses from India and set them free in a land of plenty.

The mongoose liked Jamaica and soon spread to every part of the island. In ten years damage from rats had declined to half; and by that time other effects of the introduction were appearing. The ground dove, quail dove, a native petrel, and the cony became scarce. The bobwhite quail, which had been imported successfully, was nearly wiped out. Snakes, frogs, turtles, crabs, and domesticated stock such as poultry, pigs, lambs, pups, and kittens suffered heavy inroads. Ticks and several insects became severe pests because of the destruction of their enemies. Twenty years after, it was decided that operation mongoose had miscarried.

In the eighties, the mongoose cure was applied to a rat problem in the canefields of Hawaii, where it brought about some initial benefits, but the animal soon had a price on its head. Among other misdeeds, it occasioned the rapid reduction of the Hawaiian goose and Hawaiian duck, which are found only in those islands.

True to what can be expected of any too-prosperous animal population, mongoose numbers have tended to decline and fit into the somewhat disheveled life pattern of the areas upon which it has impinged. It is by a special benefaction of Providence that we are not contending with the beast in this country. In February, 1892, an irresponsible report was circulated that the Department of Agriculture was about to bring in the mongoose as a means of destroying gophers on the western range. This erroneous rumor had a good press and attracted widespread notice.

People familiar with mongoose exploits elsewhere made frantic protests to the government. Less well-informed individuals liked the idea and set about aiding the project by unilateral action. It was only through the most strenuous efforts that importations from Hawaii were prevented.

The menace passed, and gophers and government breathed easily once more. So far as is known, the animal has not become established on this continent, although strange things happen. In November 1920,

Thomas May, a farmer near Midway, Kentucky, noticed that some-thing had been running under his haystack. Thinking it might be a mink, he set a trap and caught a creature entirely new to him. The skin finally ended up in the National Museum, and the verdict was —a mongoose.

Although this affair turned out well, others have by no means done so. There is widespread regret over the introduction of the Argentine nutria or coypu, an oversized marsh rat which was liberated, or allowed to escape, in various states by discouraged fur breeders. Separate colonies were established in Washington, Oregon, California, New Mexico, Louisiana, and probably other areas before 1940. On Gulf Coast marshes from Alabama to Texas the species is an arrant nuisance. It destroys great areas of marsh vegetation used by muskrats (sometimes this is a benefit to waterfowl) and is the subject of increasing "control" operations because of extensive damage to agricultural crops. Fur prices have been so disappointing that many trappers do not bother to skin the animal.

Likewise, little good is to be said of the wild goats and pigs descended from those brought in by the Spanish Padres, that are now found in the Coast Range and on islands off Southern California. Burros that escaped from prospectors have given rise to a wild stock that is competing with bighorn sheep around desert water holes. Even camels were released there but failed to make the grade.

If a poll were taken on the popularity of various alien animals that have become a part of the American wildlife scene, the Asian carp undoubtedly would find little justification for its existence in the New World. Pond-raised carp have been an important article of diet in China and Japan for more than 2,000 years and were brought to Europe before the year 600 A.D. Culture of the fish in ponds had spread widely on the continent and in England by the 16th century. The United States Fish Commission brought carp to this country in 1876 and a year later stocked them in American waters.

Spencer F. Baird, United States Commissioner of Fisheries, encouraged the spread of this species and the bureau furnished many states with fish. The original breeding stock of 345 carp was kept at Baltimore and Washington and multiplied rapidly. "By 1880, 50,000 carp had been distributed, and within a few years fish by the hundreds of thousands were being sent out annually."

The hardy Oriental has been eminently successful in competing with our native warm-water fish. Eggs laid by a female may average 24,000 per pound of body weight. In the way of sustenance, all is grist to the carp. It is primarily a bottom feeder and consumes great quantities of organisms that are a principal dependence of other fish. Much of this provender goes into growth, since carp are slow-moving and have a low metabolic rate. They use up little energy in getting about, but rather root in beds of vegetation, which they destroy as a habitat for more desirable species. They muddy the water, excluding sunlight and reducing plant growth thereby. Once established, this plaguey creature is almost impossible to eradicate.

The species has become a similar nuisance in other countries, as is indicated by a case history related by George S. Myers:

"Fifteen years ago a great to-do was made in Brazil about the great success to be had with the pond-culture of carp. The man (now deceased) who made the noise was a very good zoologist but had had no practical experience in pondfish culture and (at that time) knew little either of carp or of the tremendous variety of excellent food fishes existing in Brazilian rivers. As a result, carp ponds were pretty generally sprinkled over southeastern Brazil. The result? Few of these carp ponds produced as much as had been expected, and interest subsided except for sporadic outbreaks. In 1944, the writer stood on the banks of the majestic Rio Iguassú at Porto União, watched gigantic schools of carp sweeping along, and heard the laments of the local fishermen, who said that many of the better fishes were becoming incredibly scarce. Nobody wanted carp!"

It is unfortunate that the layman sometimes is advised on technical matters by people in authority who do not recognize the limits of their own knowledge and in fields well removed from their own specialties. Myers cited another case in point:

"On another occasion the writer was told by a member of the Department of Agriculture of Trinidad that his department had approached an agency in the United States for advice on some freshwater basslike, game fish which might succeed if introduced into the lowland waters of that British West Indian island. Small forage fishes were abundant there, but no larger game species of good food quality was present.

"It happens that Trinidad is only a few miles off the delta of the great Orinoco River of Venezuela, which river possesses (among three or four hundred others) two species of tucunaré, which are good-sized (15 to 20 inches) basslike fishes. They rise to a plug or even a dry fly beautifully, fight hard when hooked, have breeding habits very much like those of our black basses, and have been pond-raised in Brazil. In addition, they are celebrated as the finest food fishes among the 3,000 or more species of fresh-water fishes in South America! Finally, they live under ecological conditions exactly similar to those of the lowland Trinidad Streams. After all, they are found within 50 miles of Trinidad!

"What did the agency in the United States recommend for introduction into Trinidad? Why, North American largemouth bass, of course!"

GILDED LILY

The history of introductions of foreign species to North America encompasses a wide variety of animals and not-small expenditures of time and money. Many of the attempts are unrecorded. We have a tendency to remember the few successes, such as the pheasant, hunky, and chukar, and forget, as Leopold said, "the planting of Tinamou, Curassow, Chacalaca, ocellated Turkey, guinea fowl, ptarmigan, willow grouse, blackgrouse, capercailzie, hazel grouse, elegant quail, red-leg partridge, francolin, bamboo partridge, painted quail, Egyptian quail, Chinese quail, and a score or so of assorted pheasants, doves and pigeons which have died out, but which have served to put off for fifty years the day when we shall face the question of doing something real for the game species already in our coverts."

The latter point is the real question in weighing our future policy on exotics. This continent was provided with a complement of birds, mammals, and fish exceeded, in the aggregate, by no other land in the world. All the raw materials are here for a superior program of public benefits through good wildlife management.

Our trouble is the old and universal trouble that we have not mustered the social discipline to study what we have to the point of true and intelligent understanding. We took the grouse and turkey, the rabbit and deer, for granted as commonplace. When we struck a snarl that was beyond us, it was easier to avoid the issue than to cope with it. We could simplify the problem by calling for something new, strange, and hence better.

Experience has amply demonstrated that even the most desirable appearing foreign species can become an arrant liability, and this should rule out any continuation of hit-or-miss importations. Caution and thorough study of all possibilities are clearly indicated before we do any more adventuring with exotics. For supplying the few situations where there is need and a truly vacant environmental niche, only limited projects will be required.

As we have recognized, there are places where such work might pay dividends, but it is a low-priority job. For every such case, it is easy to see a dozen where work with excellent native animals stands a better chance of producing safe, sane, and profitable results. We have commitments at home, and we will do well to stand by them.

CHAPTER 12

Turned-Loose Game

THE historian of the twentieth-century conservation movement will take a broad view of the whole and assay the outstanding trends for various periods. He may well consider the first thirty years as a period of retrenchment—when, with many a body flung into the breach, we managed to stall the most flagrant and large-scale waste and when citizens at large began vaguely to suspect that the freedom to destroy could not be a permanent feature of American mores.

The next twenty years, from 1930 to 1950, may be called the "propagation era." Imbued with the outlook of the mechanical age, we set up our assembly lines and vowed we'd put a game crop where there wasn't any. Some said it couldn't be done, that we'd be back to Nature sooner or later; but that was a defeatist and reactionary attitude unworthy of a true progressive who knew that in all things science must prevail and that the impossible took only a little longer.

It was a turning-loose technique that brought the pheasant to northern farms from the Great Plains east and to islands of suitable range in the West. The method also accounted for the huns on the northern prairies and new colonies of valley quail as far north as Washington. People were pleased and wanted more of the same. They confided in the philosophy which Michigan's P. S. Lovejoy characterized this way:

"Originally we had no pheasants. They were introduced. For twenty years we have had one medium sized game farm putting out birds and eggs . . . Doesn't it stand to reason that if one got us fair hunting, that two game farms would make hunting twice as good?

"If a good man on three meals a day, can buck up a cord of wood, does it follow that if the man gets six meals a day he can buck up two cords? If 40 apple trees per acre will pick 500 bushels of fruit, does it follow that trees planted 80 per acre should yield 1,000 bushels?"

Probably many didn't reason it out this way. They just wanted more pheasants and more quail and called for the only thing they thought they knew about.

By 1950 many a game farm still was operating and many thousands of rabbits still were being trapped in Missouri for shipment to the East. But policies were changing both in sportsmen's organizations and in state agencies. The total propagation and stocking budget in all states was around three million dollars, but there were widespread frank admissions that the bulk of it was waste.

THE LOGIC OF IT

The kind of game stocking we are discussing here might be called annual-maintenance stocking. It is the attempt by artificial methods to produce pheasants, quail, and rabbits to hunt. It includes nearly any kind of turning-loose in areas where the species in question already is established.

No discredit is reflected on anyone by the fact that, as in this case, there has long been widespread support for what now appears to be, for the most part, an unwieldy and unprofitable method. The sportsman followed where he was led, and state commissions built up a program that appeared to have no workable alternatives. It is true that, even thirty years ago, a minority of professionals in this field were pointing to habitat improvement as the best bet in management. But there seldom was a clear-cut demonstration of workable habitat improvement, and this slant on things was something few understood and still fewer could defend to a public devoted to action and figures.

Many a thoughtful conservationist has reflected on the inconsistency in some of our popular ideas on management. For some species, such as ducks, grouse, and squirrels, we know that large-scale propagation is out of the question and we are not especially bothered by the lack of it. Over large areas these animals furnish good shooting for lots of hunters without any artificial "put and take." But the common attitude toward several other species is entirely different. Suggest giving up the rearing of pheasants or even the stocking of cottontails and the idea is likely to be greeted with consternation. Especially in parts of the densely-populated Northeast, artificial methods dominate thinking to such an extent that any other approach is instinctively considered to be gambling with theories.

The typical wildlife specialist habitually takes a dim view of any kind of management that involves the one-by-one handling of animals. In fact this attitude is so characteristic it looks suspiciously like prejudice to the average sportsman. Without knowing the reasons for it, he may write off as channeled and biased the very science that, by definition, should be free of such weaknesses.

If he had no experimental evidence at all, the wildlife biologist still would be likely to come to the conclusion that annual restocking is not the way to produce animals for public hunting. Here is what he would put into the hopper and what he would get out after the wheels had turned:

There are all kinds of pheasant ranges—good, poor, and everything between. The good areas are doing all right. The poor ones are not productive because of limitations that reduce their capacity to support pheasants. In unproductive areas the trouble lies not in the quantity or quality of breeding stock, but in the fact that the bulk of the annual crop of young becomes "surplus" because it lacks the means of survival. Now, when we try to cure this ill by liberating more birds we simply add to the natural overproduction that already is taking place.

In the final analysis, stocking animals in occupied range must be fundamentally limited by operation of the carrying-capacity principle. Even in the event of major declines, it is likely that population adjustments take place on *almost* a year-to-year basis because of the potentially high productivity of even a small number of breeders. We observed previously (p. 52) that when a bad winter wipes out most of our quail, a surviving remnant is able, in the understocked habitat, to bring through a greatly increased percentage of young for a season or two until numbers are restored to "normal" for the area.

Such being the case, we must assume that nearly any game area is supporting what it can under existing habitat and weather conditions in a given year. The wild breeders normally carry on a stocking job considerably in excess of carrying capacity and everything beyond a certain number is "expended."

That is the way the biologist figures things out on the basis of what he knows or thinks he knows. A knowledge of natural history and some cost accounting population-wise will take him that far. But the game scientists never have been able to get any great number of sports-

men to put much stock in this kind of reasoning. It is too easy to label
as theory and brain-trust logic. So they have gone ahead on a try-it-
and-see basis. One of the ideas they have tested is the expectation that
birds produced under conditions of domestication are less able to compete and survive after liberation than the wild stock already afield.
That probably should apply also to a rabbit taken from the home range
in which it learned to make a living to be turned out in country entirely strange and with wild-reared natives already established on the
"corner lots in the best part of town."

It appears to be characteristic of young animals that they wander
about and after much trial and error settle into situations where their
wants can be satisfied with reasonable effort. Conceivably it's like the
marbles in a pin-ball machine which are batted from here to there
until they finally come to rest in unoccupied holes in the board. Some
young fox squirrels tagged in Michigan during the summer were
found to travel more than forty miles before winter. Others remained
in the woodlot where they were born.

Obviously, one of the most important deterrents to any animal
settling down will be the prior occupation of a desirable situation by
other individuals. Population pressures (p. 50) being what they are,
we can expect it to be normal for many maladjustments to exist and
that the unlucky creatures who are wandering or in "marginal" locations will be the "expended" portion of the annual production.

The follow-ups on game stocked in occupied territory help to fill in
this picture and show what actually happens in terms of the fate
of individual animals. A study in New Hampshire brought out some
of the unhappy realities:

In April, 1938, an 800-acre state game refuge had a population of 15
wild pheasants, 9 cocks and 6 hens. To these were added 94 pen-
reared birds feather-marked for easy recognition in the field. Only
31 of the introduced birds were seen after release. Wild cocks drove
all but one of the game-farm males out of the area.

Predator inroads began immediately after the release and accounted
for 28 of the stocked pheasants, great-horned owls, foxes, and house
cats getting the bulk of the easy prey. Five males established crowing
areas (territories) on the refuge and one of these was a game-farm
bird. One out of the 6 nesting hens also had been stocked. In July

there were 8 adult hens and 6 cocks on the area. In other words, the population had been adjusted to about the pre-stocking level.

Some indication of the relative ability of wild and propagated birds to survive is given by an experiment on a private hunting club by biologists of the California Division of Fish and Game. Three banded samples of valley quail were released on the area in the fall and winter of 1942.

One sample was composed of native birds trapped on the area and released in the same place. Another sample represented wild quail trapped elsewhere and liberated on the club land. The third group was game-farm quail stocked on the area. The following fall, returns on the three groups were as follows: Native birds—7.7 percent; wild-trapped introduced—1.7 percent; game-farm birds—0.

It's plain enough that any animal *not on his native range* is at a big disadvantage. However, released pheasants seem to do somewhat better than quail. On an area in Wisconsin, Buss trapped and banded wild pheasants and released game-farm birds for comparison. In the year following he carried out trapping operations that indicated about a 9 percent carry-over for natives as against a survival of 4 to 7 percent in the releases.

The turnover of wild individuals in an established population is a drastic weeding out of animals that are either unfit or unlucky. This takes place on a large scale every year that is favorable for breeding. If we toss more animals into this system, one of two things must happen to a released individual. Either it is eliminated along with the naturally-produced surplus, or it can survive as one of those individuals most fit and favorably situated. If it does survive, it probably does so *in place of* a wild individual that might have been there otherwise.

As would be expected, this is a matter of degree. If stocking is done early in summer, the adjustment will be more complete by hunting season than if it is done later in the season.

In good range there seems to be a better chance of the stocked animals making the grade and meeting competition. This is indicated by results of an experiment carried out in Pennsylvania: The land where liberations were made was classified roughly as first-, second-, and third-class pheasant range. For nearly 2,000 banded cocks stocked in the fall of 1936 in the first two range classes, returns were 29.6

and 8.9 percent respectively. In 1937 slightly less than 3,000 cocks were stocked in all three classes and yielded reports on 35, 15.9, and 11 percent respectively. It probably is significant that results for second- and third-class range are comparable to stocking jobs done more or less indiscriminately in many states. Such land does not produce the best hunting and there the demand for stocking is greatest.

In estimating the significance of animals that survive, the in-place-of idea usually is ignored. If a good return on stocked birds is secured, it is considered to be all profit. This is not entirely realistic. Game-farm birds could have survived at the expense of wild birds or they could have been shot instead of wild birds. We need the full story, and we seldom get it.

To be consistent in this reasoning, however, we can recognize situations in which the carrying-capacity phenomenon would make stocking much more effective. In good habitat where a wintering population has been reduced to a low level, there is no reason to doubt that stocking healthy breeders would help bring fall numbers up toward normal. This was indicated during a quail investigation on a 3,000-acre tract west of Stillwater, Oklahoma, from 1939 to 1941.

This work involved the release of 1,064 birds in an area of fairly uniform range. It so happened that the winter of 1939-40 was a bad one for quail. Evidently all the released stock was killed off and wild breeders were badly depleted. The following spring, June-stocked quail showed fairly good survival and establishment and probably speeded recovery of the population.

By the following year, however, quail numbers were definitely up, and when more game-farm birds were added to the high population of 1941, they largely failed and resulted in little increase. The habitat appeared to be supporting its full complement of birds. Where the maximum effective breeding stock already exists, even a liberated bird that produces a brood may not increase the available shooting population.

The functioning of carrying-capacity limitations in this way is indicated by the outcome of a 3-year stocking study in Missouri. The Conservation Commission was familiar with the principles involved and with work in other states, but they were under pressure for more quail rearing by people, who, true to their principles, had to be shown. The job was given to the wildlife research unit at Columbia, and they proceeded to set up a program in the spring of 1942.

In Boone County they selected two similar areas of farmland, each of more than 2,000 acres. For three successive springs they stocked 60, 60, and 63 pairs, respectively, of banded quail on the West Ashland area; which additions more than doubled the wild population. As a "control," on the New Salem tract no birds were stocked. Both areas were censused with dogs before covey break-up in spring and again before hunting season in the fall.

The results of the experiment were definite: All three years the unstocked New Salem area carried a higher fall population than the stocked land. Obviously, it was a better area for quail. But it might be expected that, over the long period of this work, the tract which had the number of breeders more than doubled each spring would show an increase in birds; instead, fall numbers of quail on the West Ashland range were 305, 210, and 252 for the three years, respectively. The number of birds actually was smaller each fall, in relation to those on the check area, which had 452, 312, and 442.

The real pay-off in this job comes when you consider the seasonal changes in numbers on the two units of range: On the stocked area quail increased just to the extent that would have been expected *if only the native brood stock had been present.* Evidently liberated birds added nothing, whether or not any of them lived to breed. That few of them did survive is indicated by the fact that during three years not one band was recovered from the 366 game-farm birds.

Sometimes a statement is heard to the effect that "We have the range; now what we need is the birds." This is most frequently heard from the raise-'em-yourself school of game management. It ignores the fact, says the biologist, that the real measure of range carrying capacity, over enough years to rule out temporary variables, is *how many birds a given area produces.* A quail is a much better judge of quail habitat than a hunter or a biologist. To say we have the habitat but not the birds substitutes human judgment for the only sure-fire yardstick we have for measuring the quality of conditions on the land.

We also hear much about the stocking of "depleted" areas; but on careful study it will be found that game populations usually are depleted because conditions no longer favor them and that pump-priming liberations on such land are no different from anywhere else.

In a Virginia study they deliberately shot off all wild quail from two areas and replaced them with banded game-farm birds. The first experiment was in fall and the second in spring. Of a total of 73 released quail, only one band was subsequently recovered. A low survival of stocked birds was evident, but it also was evident that the shot-out land was repopulated immediately from outside. From this work ". . . it is apparent that it is not necessary to stock quail, even on areas entirely devoid of birds where habitat is suitable and native birds are present on adjoining areas . . . Actually, there seems little point in stocking quail even in large areas, such as counties where the native population is seriously depleted. Probably better results could be obtained by carefully protecting the few remaining birds and improving habitat."

The report on this project makes the further significant statement: "One of Virginia's neighboring states recently released 13,500 banded quail and offered to pay $1.00 each for all bands turned in; only 152 were recovered."

WE TRIED IT

A game farm is a going enterprise that anyone can understand up to the point where animals are turned out into the world to fend for themselves. Up to that time they are something visible and concrete. From there on they become statistics—which also are impressive if, come fall, you can go out and get some shooting.

One trouble has been that many an area has not produced good shooting even though sportsmen knew it had been stocked by the state. And many a club has put time, effort, and money into rearing projects on pheasants or quail and released them personally on familiar ground—with no visible results.

The principal support for game-farm programs stems from the usual willingness on the part of hunters to assume that what they are shooting had its origin in an incubator or under a setting hen. However, in many places sportsmen themselves have become restive after digesting annual state statistics on "produced" game birds and witnessing no improvement in shooting. This observation has led in some cases to suspicion that somewhere figures on liberated game got multiplied by "factor X" just to reassure the consumer.

To protect themselves from this uncomfortable (and doubtless unjust) suspicion, the State of Washington Department of Game adopted in 1935 a painstaking procedure to convince sportsmen that stocking statistics actually were stocked birds. Following advance notification, the representative of a local sportsman's organization would witness each release. Birds were transported at night and liberated at dawn. In testimony to the validity of the operation, the witness signed an affidavit that he had counted the birds and seen them turned out, and further that he was not connected in any way with the State game department and that he, John Jones, had been officially delegated by the Happy Hours Hunting Club to serve as planting inspector.

The obvious way to determine the results of stocking is to band the birds and check returns from shooting. Technicians long have urged clubs to do this and many have carried out such projects. The results usually have been disappointing.

In the summer of 1942, the State of Indiana helped 48 cooperating conservation clubs in an experiment to determine the effectiveness of their pheasant propagation work. These were small rural clubs that would be stocking their birds locally in 35 different counties. Approximately 4,000 cock birds were banded and the work given good publicity to help get bands returned. The results were compiled by six districts, and recoveries varied from 0.6 percent to 9.7 percent. The statewide average was 6.4 cocks shot for every 100 released.

These results probably are representative for summer stocking with 8- to 12-week-old birds. Late-summer banding of more than 11,000 cocks in Ohio resulted in returns of 7.9 percent. Of a sample of 15,520 cocks banded and released in Massachusetts in 1944 and 1945 the percentage of recovery was 9.1. In New Jersey, hunters reported 8 percent of the bands from 14,050 pheasants liberated on "open lands" in the summer of 1946.

A part of this poor showing is due to the fact that some hunters shoot marked birds and then fail to return the bands. Information from Wisconsin indicates that it might be realistic to double the figures. In 1941 and 1942, Buss made an intensive follow-up of the stocking of 8-week-old pheasants in Dunn County. He found that each year about 20 percent of the birds were recovered by hunters.

On two carefully controlled areas in New York the kill percentages on stocked pheasants were 18.5 and 16.2.

From 1922 to 1946 the State of Utah reared and stocked approximately 145,000 pheasants. Little thought was given as to whether the work was really effective until 1940, after which groups of birds were banded each year. Experimental releases were studied from 1945 to 1947 on areas where hunters were checked and the success of both wild and reared pheasants was investigated.

Some of the more pertinent results were: "Average hunter returns of bands from banded males on carefully checked areas was not higher than 7.5 percent of the total released while wild stock of males in Utah was reduced by hunting to . . . approximately half of the preseason numbers."

Heavy mortality occurred among stocked pheasants, dogs being the most important single cause of death. "Game-farm birds constituted not more than about one-half of one percent of the annual state-wide pheasant harvest during the period of study . . . Only a small percent of the game-farm birds survive the winter to enter the breeding population the spring following liberation."

The record for large-scale operational stocking in summer is a discouraging one. But it is true that small batches of birds on favorable areas may show a survival far above average.

In the exceptionally favorable summer of 1948, Wisconsin biologists brought through well over half of an August planting of 614 young cock pheasants stocked on a public shooting area. Hunting-season checks showed that 58 percent of the birds were shot. This phenomenal success was by way of considerable pampering, special handling, and the provision of food on an area offering favorable cover and water conditions. But it shows that with enough attention to detail nearly anything can be done on a small scale.

THE PRICE

The ultimate question in evaluating any management method that will produce some shooting is how much it costs. If the expenditure of land, labor, and capital is sufficiently low, we could expand almost any kind of program to the point where it would render *public* service.

Naturally, the cheapest way to rear and stock birds is to use modern incubators and brooding devices and turn out the "finished" product at 8 to 10 weeks of age. Most stocking has been done in this way and, as we have seen, the results have been poor. Birds put out in summer are exposed to the same natural mortality factors that operate to reduce the wild crop progressively from the time of egg-laying to the hunting season. There is no doubt that, if other conditions are equal, the earlier a bird is released, the less chance it has of being on hand in the fall.

The natural production mechanism involves huge losses and still yields good hunting. Presumably we could do the same—except that our birds come at "retail" prices.

A review of the results of Indiana's stocking program on game birds since 1899 indicated that ". . . each quail bagged has cost the Department of Conservation a tidy sum of $40." On the same basis it appeared that pheasants had been considerably better (!), since ". . . each male pheasant bagged had cost $20." These calculations were based on quail recoveries averaging 3.1 percent and pheasant returns of about 6.4 percent. It was concluded that ". . . artificial propagation is not the answer to Indiana's bird problem."

In Oklahoma the State Game Department found that on two experimental tracts about a third of the quail stocked in September were taken in November. The cost to hatch, rear, and release each bird was $1.75. On this basis each quail bagged would represent a purchase price of $5.25. Very likely this comes close to representing quail stocking at its best.

Cost figures on summer-stocked pheasants in Michigan indicated that every reared bird that reached a hunter's bag cost the state $16.20 —and that was in the days when a pheasant could be turned out at 12 weeks for 90 cents.

When the establishment of a quail hatchery in Texas was under consideration, the Game, Fish, and Oyster Commission made a thorough investigation of the possibilities. They studied costs, weighed the results of experimental work in neighboring states, and consulted national authorities for advice.

It was calculated that to serve the entire State properly would require 10 hatcheries costing $100,000 each and that their operation would entail an annual expenditure of half a million dollars. Then, if Texas could obtain results ten times as good as those of any other state—*the shootable population of quail could be increased by 10 percent!*

They decided that "More quail can be produced for the hunter's gun if the money is spent for education and encouragement of better land use practices that will improve the quail environment, and for experimental work to learn what specific quail management techniques can be applied to Texas conditions and Texas wild quail populations."

Based upon reports published in 1948 and 1950, it appeared that the national bill for the propagation of game birds and out-of-state buying of rabbits was in excess of three million dollars. State sportsmen's organizations in Michigan, New York, Missouri, and elsewhere were publicly supporting the reduction of stocking expenditures in favor of more range improvement work; and there were widespread stirrings of minority opinion in this direction. Much of the stocking still was helter-skelter, but the increasing recognition of its inefficiency was bringing about revisions of policy designed to get more for the propagation dollar.

All evidence indicates that to get the most out of pheasant stocking, *large numbers* of birds should be turned out on *limited areas* that are *heavily hunted.* By this method the hunter stands the best chance of getting a high proportion of cocks before something else happens to them.

State-operated public shooting areas near large cities probably fulfill these requirements better than any other land that can be stocked. Urban populations in the Northeast create a demand for hunting targets that in some areas is out of all proportion to the available habitat within easy driving distance of large cities. Such conditions mean posted land and low sportsmanship standards.

The operation of artificialized shooting preserves by states has been a sort of next-best expedient. Returns have been higher than in any other kind of stocking, but the cost of holding cocks to fall is added to that of hatching and rearing. On two Wisconsin hunting areas it was found that about a third of the cocks released during July and August were taken during the hunting season, but late September plantings were twice as good. Probably the highest recovery obtained in large-scale work was in Illinois where, as a general figure, it was reported that 69 out of every 100 stocked birds were harvested on public shooting areas. This may be explained by the fact that pheasants were turned out *each night* to insure a supply for the next day's shooting.

In regard to this kind of shooting, New York's Deputy Commissioner, J. Victor Skiff, observed: "One thing is certain—it is not economically possible to stock directly for the gun when the operation has to be financed solely from fees paid by hunters for their small game licenses. Before the war, on a number of special experimental areas set up for public gunning, known as our Landowner-Sportsmen Areas, the cost of pheasants brought to bag proved to be several times the price of an individual hunting license. Those who hunted some of the better areas were well pleased. They should have been, because it took the license fees of several sportsmen to give them one day of pheasant shooting."

The operation of such mechanized "hunting" preserves recalls the pigeon shoots of yesteryear wherein trapped passenger pigeons, or domestic birds, were liberated from cages directly in front of the gun. Wealthy men have long used hand-reared ducks or upland birds as targets, but there is an important reason why you and I don't do it. It would seem to be reasonable for public preserves to charge a fee that would cover the cost of artificially-reared birds. But whether they could stay in business on this basis is an open question. When costs are entirely public, the system becomes a lottery whereby funds of several hunters are pooled to produce a limited and temporary satisfaction for one.

Essentially, there's nothing wrong with such a lottery if all the parties are willing, but nearly every state has a large and long-term job of range improvement waiting to be done. This program represents an *investment* whereby funds will draw interest for increasing numbers of sportsmen year after year. In the face of this sober obligation, spending our money on birds to shoot seems a bit like going to the races when the kids need shoes.

FAR-FETCHED RABBITS

The cottontail furnishes more shooting than any other species of North American game, the likelihood being that between 30 and 50 million are taken in an ordinary year. Above all things else, the rabbit needs cover well distributed over the land, and the widespread destruction of farm hedgerows and thickets has reduced this species drastically in many areas. This development led to the obvious expedient of turning rabbits loose to replenish the "depleted" supply.

If rabbits could be reared in captivity, it would long ago have been a thriving business. From 1931 to 1934, Pennsylvania tried various methods of producing the cottontail in range fields, and they got a few, but at a cost and never in sufficient numbers to make impressive statistics. The confined animals were subject to infestation by fleas, ticks, lice, bots, roundworms, tapes, and bladderworms. They produced fewer young than healthy rabbits in the wild.

Ohio also tried this and had particularly significant experience with a large range field. A tract of 270 acres was surrounded with a "vermin-proof" fence and 9,000 imported cottontails were stocked. What was to be expected actually happened and practically the entire population, introduced and natives alike, died off. In the following winter it was difficult to find a rabbit on the area. But subsequently this tract was developed into a unit of good range by food and cover plantings. The result was that it became productive of rabbits without any stocking.

The cottontail was not amenable to assembly-line treatment, but supplies were available in certain midwestern states and could be had on an across-the-counter basis. This was the sort of thing people understood, and thrifty Missouri farm boys were trapping rabbits for shipment east at a time when the Ford car still had a brass radiator.

The most thorough shaking down ever given the rabbit-importation program was done in Pennsylvania by Richard Gerstell, who published the results in 1937. From 1916 to 1936 the state had purchased nearly three quarters of a million cottontails. A study of stocking and kill records for individual years indicated that results were not evident. The releases had not produced larger kills and their only accomplishment was cited as ". . . that psychological reaction created by the liberation of hundreds of thousands of paper rabbits each cut out of a one-dollar bill."

New York stocked "western" rabbits during the thirties and reached the maximum of 22,000 in 1937-38. Importations then were banned as a result of a tularemia epidemic. The ban was lifted to permit clubs and individuals to resume such stocking in 1942. A general decline of rabbits followed, and this stimulated interest in more state stocking. A research project was set up to assay the efficiency of the method.

Returns were discouragingly low even on rabbits stocked on heavily hunted areas during the open season. Many animals died soon after being liberated, and those that survived to be shot or to breed cost $6.98 in purchase and shipping costs alone. Joseph Dell, who did the work, concluded that "It is not feasible for the State to carry on a program of cottontail importation and also that it is very expensive for local clubs to do so in view of the low rate of return." Emphasis in New York's rabbit program is now on better range conditions.

This is the trend of events in Pennsylvania also, although the state has had a never-say-die adherence to the idea of trapping and trans-planting—from cities, parks, cemeteries, and improved "rabbit farms." Their excellent research through the years has produced convincing evidence that the way to have rabbit hunting is to build up the range and grow the animals where they are to be shot.

State-to-state shipment of cottontails declined rapidly in the early fifties. Demand fell off because tularemia was all too frequent in the Midwest, and then supplier states cut off the shipments. In some cases, beagle clubs turned to the "San Juan" rabbit, but this too is on the downgrade. Producing cottontails is largely a matter of developing favorable cover, and the results of such work have been spectacular where carried out under knowing direction. The rabbit is likely to be our first American game species that comes under a general program of sound management.

CHANGING TIMES

Year by year, research results have piled up the evidence against one-by-one methods. A review of the situation in the range of the bob-white quail showed that in 1948 one state still was stocking about 60,000 birds annually and another 36,000. Three states stocked from 5,000 to 9,000. One state distributed eggs as a "public relations" measure, two never had game farms, and nine had either reduced their programs or abandoned them completely.

In the winter of 1948 a combined committee of the National Re-search Council and The Wildlife Society published a report on the proper use of natural resources. Here is what the document said under the heading, "Artificial Propagation of Wild Game":

"There is little or no evidence that any permanent increase in game resources can be brought about by artificial propagation of birds and mammals. Money spent for artificial propagation often is diverted from useful enterprises to their detriment or non-support. It is therefore felt that the Wildlife Society, game managers, state game departments, and the Fish and Wildlife Service should carry forward educational campaigns among sportsmen as to the probable futility of artificial propagation as a means of building up the game supply. On the other hand the value of such time-tested methods as habitat improvement should be emphasized."

We should realize, of course, that the failure of one method has no relationship to the workability of another. It should be especially emphasized that artificial propagation and habitat improvement are not necessarily alternatives. It seems to be evident that game farming is a poor way to produce public shooting of any kind; but it also is true in the case of pheasants that there has been little progress in the development of effective methods for improving conditions on the land. Every technique must be judged on its own merits, and we can save money on anything that does not produce results. In many cases, it will not be for us to decide what a given land unit will produce—we will be wise to manage the species to which it is naturally adapted. Results on a vast scale are possible where conditions are right and we can learn to use natural production possibilities; but there are conditions to be met.

Ideas are the power behind all progress. For many years there seemed to be an almost insurmountable inertia in public thinking, but it would take an incurable pessimist to doubt that truth is rapidly coming to the fore. Healthy change calls for evolution rather than revolution. Our game farms will serve valuable experimental uses for many years, but we will see a rapid decline in the delusion that they can support public hunting.

CHAPTER 13

Deep End

THE artificial approach to wildlife management has nowhere been more intensively utilized than in our handling of fishery problems. For many years, the fish culturist was the only professional man in the field—a situation that persisted in some states until 1950, when the Federal Aid in Fish Restoration Act was passed. The fishery biologist is now active everywhere, and among other accomplishments, he has complicated issues once considered rather simple.

These complications have been especially significant for the administrator. A large segment of public thinking has not yet been disturbed by them and continues in its total allegiance to the industrial revolution and assembly-line tactics. A clear exposition of the situation was made by a Connecticut biologist at the Northeastern Game Conference in 1948:

"Few sportsmen will question a management program if it includes stocking. The appearance of the hatchery truck seems to lull people to sleep and all critical analysis of the situation vanishes. All fish men are familiar with the soothing effect produced by the stocking of a few fish. There will continue to be some stocking which serves no other purpose than good public relations until such time as the sportsmen, themselves, learn the fundamentals of fishery management. The questions that come to the desk of every fishery administrator indicate to him that stocking is the criterion by which the angling public is judging his value to them. Fish men are human, too, so after a time the administrator may get weary of explaining the facts of life to unappreciative audiences and ship a few fish to the human trouble spots. This wins for him the high regard of the sportsman and it matters not whether the stocking cannot possibly improve fishing. When sportsmen start asking their administrators, 'What do you propose to do to improve fishing and why do you believe your program will show results in the creel?' instead of 'How many fish do you stock?' it will indicate that they are awake at least and that a new day in fish conservation has arrived."

The biologist has questioned, and in some cases succeeded in getting abolished, many a time-worn stocking practice. He also has discovered new and effective uses for the hatchery. In terms of numbers of fish, artificial production decreased by 61 percent between 1936 and 1958. But the largest decline was in fry—the smallest size. Production of legal-size fish greatly increased, and the total weight of fish stocked in 1958 aggregated more than 13 million pounds. In the 22-year period, state hatcheries increased from 383 to 482 and federal hatcheries from 88 to 95. The national's annual fish-rearing budget had grown to nearly 18 million dollars.

This is obviously a big management venture. And here, as with every major and costly effort in the wildlife conservation field, we must ask the question: Is it paying off?

Not unexpectedly, the final answer will be yes, and then again, no. It's another situation that calls for discrimination and understanding. Important changes in ideas and programs now are in progress. Moves in the right direction will need vigilant protection by people who are properly informed. Utah's Superintendent of Fisheries called the turn:

"Plans based on study and the understanding of the broad principles underlying animal ecology are now replacing the old 'legislative' type of biology and a more comprehensive management program is the result. Fish culture will adjust itself to a measured rather than an assumed need."

DREAM FISH

The early work of fish-culture stations was concerned largely with the reception and propagation of fish stocks from abroad and the rearing of native fish for the widespread introduction of such species into new waters. Many of these ventures were highly successful, since small plantings into barren aquatic habitats frequently produced spectacular fishing within a few years. From there the transition into maintenance, year-to-year stocking was easy.

Twenty years ago there was heavy emphasis on the stocking of fry (newly-hatched fish), much of it with pan and game fish in warm-water lakes and streams. Such tiny morsels of life bulked large as statistics and were highly impressive on paper. But they became less so when investigators began to demonstrate the propagation records of *individual* wild fish.

For example, a project was carried out in Deep Lake, Michigan, to count the fry produced in nests of several warm-water species. R. W. Eschmeyer and W. F. Carbine, who successively carried on the work, marked individual nests with colored marbles. After a few preliminary trials with the method, Eschmeyer began to suspect sabotage. The marbles were disappearing from rock-bass nests. Some lying in wait and careful watching of nests gave the explanation. Male fish, who were guarding eggs, objected to the marbles. They would pick them up, carry them to the edge of their territories, and dump them.

After other problems were dealt with, these studies continued for four years, and they gave a picture of natural productivity and waste that is something to contemplate: The average largemouth bass nest produced more than 6,000 young, a rock bass nearly 1,500, a pumpkinseed sunfish over 6,000 and a bluegill in excess of 16,000. In this one 15-acre lake the 4-year production of bluegill fry was about 37 million! For each million bluegills that reached the free-swimming stage only 416 lived to maturity. Production of black bass was around 860,000 of which 714 survived to breeding age!

Other work showed that the northern pike, which lays its eggs in flooded marshes, yields about 32,000 eggs per female, and less than one quarter of one percent of these produce young fish which leave the marshes for deeper waters.

If we were to get into the figures for certain ocean fish, the statistics would be even more fantastic—it is not unusual for more than 99.9 percent of the eggs to be regularly "expended," only one individual in many thousands living to reach maturity. With this sort of reproductive potential in operation, it is clear to anyone that in most cases ultimate population levels depend *entirely* on the capacity of waters to support fish. One large female walleye could, by depositing half a million eggs, stock a large lake far beyond its habitable level for this species. A Minnesota study showed that "assuming minimum survival of pike perch fry from natural spawn one of our large lakes produced almost as many fry annually as the entire hatchery plant of the state produced and distributed in several hundred lakes."

With mortality so high, what becomes of the few thousand dearly-bought fry or fingerlings that our hatcheries can "liberate" in lakes and streams to maintain fishing? Is Nature less severe on them than on the wild stock of her own production? Counts of populations show that the ratio of old to young fish is such that it would be necessary to stock bass or perch fingerlings at the rate of 2,000 per acre to increase legal-sized fish by *one per acre*. The stocking of small fish in waters where the species already is present and reproducing implies the assumption that Nature is not turning out enough of them to keep up with our rate of harvest. In a previous chapter we learned that with maximum fishing intensity it is possible to take only about half of the standing crop of mature fish. Measuring this fact against the breeding potential of even one pair of adults indicates that the stocking of occupied waters is a game in which we can't win. A summary of statewide stocking in Michigan from 1936-45 showed that bluegills had been planted at the rate of 35 fingerlings per acre in 1,138 lakes, largemouth bass at 2.4 per acre in 687 lakes, and smallmouth bass at 1.9 fish per acre in 308 lakes. Yet seining in 12 lakes showed an average of 742 wild fish per acre.

Fishery biologists have had to go no further in demonstrating the uselessness of maintenance stocking of warm-water fish. A few trials with marked fish have borne out the expectations. From 1946 to 1948, an Indiana biologist liberated fifteen samples, of about a hundred each, of fin-clipped fingerling bass in three streams and then tried to recover them in seining operations. He could account for only about one percent of the fish after stocking and it was evident that the hatchery product could have no effect on fishing.

As would be expected, our former primary effort in trout stocking was likewise with small fish—usually fingerlings. But when such plantings came under serious scrutiny, the results that had been taken for granted were far short of the facts.

A good example of numerous projects of this kind is an investigation of the (then) federal Bureau of Fisheries in the St. Mary River, Virginia, in the mid-thirties. After exhaustive tests of the suitability of the stream, the planting of more than 11,000 marked fingerling brook and rainbow trout, and a careful creel census, the conclusion was that little had been gained by the plantings. Only 268 fish were recovered by anglers, giving a 2.4 percent return. "The stocking of fingerling brook and rainbow trout in St. Mary River has not resulted in any improvement in the abundance of the population. Further stocking of fingerlings in this or other similar streams in the region does not appear to be advisable."

Eliminating fry from consideration, it is obvious that the most economical way of stocking trout is to rear them through the first summer and then stock in the fall as fingerlings. Carrying them beyond that period adds materially to cost, and hence the method has been given every opportunity to succeed. On the Pisgah National Game Preserve and North Carolina state lands, stocking experiments were carried on for four years with marked fish. Five fall plantings of 6- to 8-inch rainbows showed returns of 2.8 percent in the following fishing season. Five-inch brook trout gave a recovery rate of 3 percent and brown trout 10.6 percent. On a basis of such poor results, the stocking of small fish was greatly reduced.

Michigan carried out extensive experiments with all types of stocking. In 1945 it was evident that many practices needed revision, and a brochure reviewing research results was issued for public information. It made use of data from three other states and indicated that in 19 plantings of marked brook trout the average return to the creel was 1.16 percent. "In 12 experiments with rainbow fingerlings an average 2.02 per cent survived to the fisherman's basket. Five experiments with brown trout fingerlings resulted in an average recovery of 3.4 per cent."

That such results are not restricted to eastern streams is evident from work on Convict Creek in California. There P. R. Needham and D. W. Slater studied the food relationships of stocked and wild trout and it was shown that introduced fish are at a distinct disadvantage. Winter mortality of the hatchery product was from 50 to 70 percent. They concluded that "plantings of fingerlings are largely ineffectual in streams containing numerous wild trout, since competition and predation prevent any significant survival."

This viewpoint now is generally accepted among fish specialists and recent years have seen a steady reduction in expenditures for the stocking of small fish in waters where natural spawning is possible. There is no question that by the use of such methods in the the past large expenditures of the fisherman's legal tender have been made with little, if any, real return. By way of hindsight, it is not difficult to see that some logical thinking population-wise and a few well-conceived experiments could have shown the error of these ways years before that actually was done. But that was not our method of going about things, and the best that can be done now is to profit by past experience.

FINGERLING PAY-OFF

It is a curious fact that the use of hatchery-reared fry and fingerlings in occupied waters is our poorest stocking investment; but such fish introduced into suitable aquatic environments can yield better returns than any other kind of planting.

As applied to trout, "suitable environments" usually are lakes where there is *little or no competition* and where there are no gravel-bottom feeders for natural spawning. Such waters cannot support a wild population, but young stocked fish may show excellent survival and growth. In this case, the fingerlings are being placed in a practically vacant environment, and they are converted into keeper-size fish at a rate far exceeding the efficiency of natural reproduction in occupied waters.

In Michigan extensive surveys were carried out on lakes where temperatures and other conditions might be suitable for trout, and which were landlocked and adapted to the poisoning of existing populations of less desirable fish—stunted perch, for example. Success was attained with brooks, browns, and rainbows, according to conditions. The small investment required for the production of fingerlings and the fact that such small beginnings can populate an entire lake with mature fish, makes this a highly satisfactory kind of stocking, even though regular inoculation with more fish is necessary to keep the lunkers coming. This is lake "rehabilitation," and the states are doing more of it each year.

Some northern lakes are found with deep areas suitable for lake trout or rainbows where these species can be stocked and furnish sport, even though the shallower water is populated with warm-water fish. There are, of course, all degrees of competition and food supply in lakes. Whether stocking will pay and the kind and size of fish required can be determined only by an expert—and some trials.

This is stocking after enlightenment, and its success depends entirely on the fishery biologist. Somewhat similar is the work being done on a "corrective" basis. According to Moyle, "Stocking, especially with fingerling game fish such as walleye pike and northern pike, is now being used to restore the natural balance between the large voracious fishes and the forage fishes. In this way lakes overrun with small perch and sunfishes can again be made to produce fishing for the larger game fishes." Conversely, where food species are deficient, there is the possibility of establishing populations of forage fish (especially minnows) to feed the game fish.

An obviously profitable use of hatchery stock was the establishment of salmon runs in New Zealand streams; and similarly, the product of the "fish factory" can be employed to good advantage in bringing back killed-out salmon stocks in our own streams where conditions suitable for spawning and growth have been restored.

We have northern lakes, also, where the entire population is winter-killed by deep persistent snow covering the ice in winter. This cuts off sunlight and kills the plants that normally liberate oxygen used by the fish. Where this happens only occasionally and conditions are otherwise favorable, it may pay to restore a breeding stock of suitable species via the hatchery. In many shallow lakes winter-kill is frequent and stocking would not pay.

Projects of this kind have a good future, and the way is open to expand the work for many years to come. But in terms of quantity production it is far overshadowed by what is being done at present with warm-water fish, principally bass and bluegills, in man-made ponds.

As has been mentioned before, the farm-pond program received its great impetus through the imaginative and well-supported research of Homer L. Swingle in Alabama. Success in southeastern states led to experimental work elsewhere. After 1940 the idea swept the country, and the Soil Conservation Service, Fish and Wildlife Service, and many state conservation departments have aided hundreds of thousands of farmers in constructing, stocking, and managing small, private impoundments for fish production.

There are good reasons for this popularity. An average, one-acre farm fishpond will yield an annual harvest of 200 pounds of fish and provide about 400 man-hours of high-quality sport. It is one of the most immediately practicable and satisfying wildlife management operations that has yet appeared.

This program is due to bring about a tremendous increase in available fishing waters and they will be scattered over the land in a manner that will serve literally millions of people. Already in 1943, a Soil Conservation Service survey in 12 northeastern states indicated a need for approximately 86,000 ponds. That would be one for every eight farms. Not all would be adapted to fish production, but it was expected that the aggregate would be about 65,000 acres of water suitable for fish management.

Five year's experience showed that the estimate was far short. Farmers liked ponds and were asking for them. By 1947 a pond for every nine farms had been planned, and in the last year of this period the rate was one per 4.3 farms. The new revised estimate for the Northeast was 380,000 ponds with 126,000 acres of new water for fish management.

As of 1956 there were more than a million and a half ponds, averaging an acre apiece, on American farms, and the rate of construction was at least 100,000 per year. Of course, every such impoundment requires an initial stock of fingerling fish. For the Southeast the going formula has been 1,000 bluegills and 100 largemouth bass per surface acre. In other regions management practices are less well established, although in warm waters the bass-bluegill combination is being widely used in the absence of precise knowledge of anything preferable. In cold northern waters, trout and other species are better possibilities. Research in this field has not caught up with demand, but it is going forward rapidly.

It is evident that this program will keep the hatcheryman busy for the indefinite future. Many farmers have had to wait for fish, and in the meantime some have impatiently put available wild fish in their ponds. This is almost invariably a mistake and results in fish populations that are "out of balance" and unproductive. It often necessitates draining the pond and starting over. Overpopulation with stunted bluegills is a common trouble, and stocking and fertilizing practices developed for southern states have been designed to prevent this.

A moot question has been whether public hatcheries should be used to stock private ponds. As of 1956 there were 24 states where laws and policies did not allow the use of state fish for this purpose. In fact, some were pouring the products of their warm-water hatcheries willy-nilly into lakes and streams as an alternative. This had a plausible look to an uninformed public, even though it might have little real use-fulness.

Of course, federal hatcheries stepped into this breach, and in the year mentioned they sent out some 58 million fry and fingerlings to warm-water ponds, lakes, and reservoirs in 42 states.

As policy making becomes more realistic, it is likely that more states will be using their bass, bluegills, and possibly other species in ponds. An initial breeding stock is all that is required, and the few small fish are not a large investment. These new waters represent good land use and good conservation. A point frequently neglected is that, although they are not public waters, the public does fish them. How the State of Missouri came out on this question has already been described (p. 171). Such a minor subsidy of the landowner certainly is in the in-terest of all the people—something that cannot be said for many of our subsidies.

KEEPERS

The most fire and smoke in the fish-stocking picture is being gen-erated over the problem of maintaining trout fishing. Since before the time of Izaak Walton, the (proper) taking of trout has been quite the "gentlest" type of angling, and it has been comparable to grouse and turkey shooting in the recruitment of loyal and militant sup-porters.

Particularly in the heavily populated Northeast, there is many a stream where we would have no trout fishing at all without regular visits by the tank truck of the fish culturist. Here fry or fingerlings will not do at all, because there are few wild trout of catchable size to bear the brunt of the sport, and statistics do not rise well to a fly. It has been shown beyond all doubt that survival to legal size is prac-tically nil among young planted fish where competition is present, and stocking has more and more come to be a matter of hand-feeding them to creel proportions and presenting them for catching in one easy lesson.

This is the serious truth of the matter, for hatchery trout are not difficult to take, and they usually boost fishing success in a stream for from two to four weeks after replenishment. They are not up to the natural product in either fight or flavor, but they are a satisfactory next-best for many fishermen. A particularly unsatisfactory aspect of this kind of production is that tank-bred trout seldom survive the winter, and even in summer a great many more commonly are poured into a stream than ever come out. As Moyle indicated, "Trout streams so managed are not being planted in the sense that farm crops are planted. They are being used as temporary holding reservoirs in which the hatchery trout are kept until taken by anglers."

Fisheries investigators have done enough quantitative work with legal-length fish to have a good evaluation of this kind of management. The results have been variable but consistent with conditions.

In the main, there are two ways of stocking legal trout—during the fall, to permit them to become "wild" over winter, and during the fishing season directly in front of the rod. Experiments with both kinds of planting have been carried out in many states.

On the Knife River, Minnesota, 500 brown and 500 brook trout were planted in the fall of 1942. The following April a similar release was made and a nearly complete creel census obtained in the open season. Fishing was not intensive on the river, and a total of 1,239 fish were accounted for. Not quite 2 percent of the fall planting appeared in fishermen's creels, as against 14 percent for the spring stocking.

The Salmon Trout River in Michigan's Upper Peninsula was another lightly fished stream on which a 3-year creel census and tagging study was made to determine the best method of stocking 7- to 9-inch brook trout. From 1938 to 1940, fall-planted fish gave returns of not more than 1 percent, whereas a maximum of 19.6 percent of spring-planted fish were recovered.

From results elsewhere, it is to be suspected that returns on these northern rivers would have been higher if fishing had been more intensive. This probably is an important factor in explaining some of the variability evident in recoveries of stocked fish. Exceptionally high return figures were obtained on the Deerskin River, one of Wisconsin's good trout streams, in a complete creel census by CCC labor for the first 9 weeks of the 1941 season. During the previous December and in early May a total of 1,002 brook and 1,621 rainbow trout were planted in about 17 miles of stream. The fish measured 7 to 15 inches and were marked by fin clipping.

The total catch during the census period was 3,438 fish, of which 71 out of every hundred were "wild" and 29 were hatchery trout. In all, 82 percent of the brooks stocked in May and 28 percent of those turned out in December were brought to creel. Of the rainbows, anglers took 48 percent of the December fish and only 30 percent of those stocked in May. None of the released fish was taken in a later season.

The time-lapse factor has appeared consistently in most stocking jobs—the longer fish are in the stream, the fewer of them ever reach the landing net. On the Gila National Forest in New Mexico they planted 2,000 rainbows of 7 to 9 inches 10 days before the opening in 1939. A creel census showed that 40 percent of them were caught by anglers—mostly in the first three weeks. A planting of 6- to 8-inch fish in the Pecos River gave returns of 58.8 percent. This stocking was done 3 days before the season, and it can be compared with another plant made 40 days before fishing began in the following year. In this trial the yield to fishermen was considerably reduced, being slightly more than 28 percent.

In Michigan's Pine River, plantings were made at monthly intervals during the open season of 1937. Each release consisted of 3,000 brooks and rainbows, and after every replacement fishing improved for a period of 2 to 3 weeks. Fishermen took about 20 of every 100 brook trout stocked and about 18 of every 100 rainbows. Few of the fish survived to another season.

Unexpectedly, this work showed that wild fish would bite more readily after the stocking of hatchery trout. Evidently, adding more individuals per unit of stream increases competition for food and shelter, causing native fish to forage more widely and making them take the lure more frequently. This might appear to be an advantage at first sight, but there is a serious objection to it. Since the liberated stock do not winter-over to any extent, the net result is a depletion of breeding fish and a reduction of the wild population in years to follow. Hazzard and Shetter reached the conclusion that "the eventual fate of a stream stocked with large trout would be somewhat as follows—few or no legal trout left to breed, few fish in the stream except those just planted from the hatcheries, and very few if any 'lunkers' to provide the thrill anticipated by all trout fishermen while catching the 8- to 10-inch fish for the pan."

A summary of Michigan research is fairly representative of the effectiveness of ordinary stocking operations in streams containing wild fish. Biologists there carried out 68 experiments involving 40,000 marked trout of three species in 11 streams. "The average recovery of legal-sized trout planted in the spring or open season was approximately 25 per cent for brook and for rainbow and 12½ per cent for brown trout."

As elsewhere, fall-planted fish have made a poor showing in most of the tests—Michigan returns averaged between 4 and 6 percent. By expensive and painful experience, the futility of attempting to overstuff aquatic habitats for any appreciable length of time has become manifest. This kind of stocking is diminishing rapidly.

In the artificial planting of trout to catch, we are back to the same principle that was revealed in our study of game stocking. "Liberated" animals as a means of building *populations* will not work. Population levels on the land or in the water are under strict natural controls, and surpluses of any kind are rapidly eliminated.

If we are to produce trout artificially, it must be done on the same basis that pheasants are stocked: Turn them out and get them quick, before their natural fate overtakes them.

The efficacy of this policy is evident in the high returns on heavily-fished waters. During the wartime gasoline shortage, a Connecticut stream near large population centers was stocked with about 1,400 each of brooks, browns, and rainbows. The heavy fishing pressure produced recoveries of 83, 79, and 83 percent, respectively, for the three species.

The federal program of trout stocking on the Pisgah National Forest has followed the same evolution of policy that is evident in the states. Fall release of tens of thousands of 7½-inch fish had little discernible effect on fishing in the following seasons. Recoveries averaged only about 9 percent for such plantings. Real improvement in fishing was not evident until in-season releases were made. From these an average of more than 47 percent produced fishing, and individual lots of fish showed recoveries as high as 82.7 percent. As a result of the heavy stocking, fishing pressure increased greatly on the Pisgah, and releases before the rod are deliberately calculated to meet it.

It is in lakes that the survival and recovery of keeper hatchery trout has been highest. In fact, it has developed into such a quick and obvious put-and-take that there has been little satisfaction in it for anyone but the meat fisherman who shadows the hatchery truck. Even fall-planted rainbows in Michigan lakes returned from 23 to 73 percent, and spring plantings gave a yield of 90 percent or more. This would be excellent, except for one disconcerting fact—it has been evident that early comers (repeatedly) take limit catches so easily that within a few days the harvest is in and only a few fishermen are benefited. Needham summarized figures from 36 research papers describing studies of "catchable" trout planting in the United States and Canada. He found that "Between 65 and 85 percent of most state budgets for game fishes are allocated for the propagation of trout." Nevertheless, using California as representative, only about 30 percent of the anglers fish for trout. Of those who try for the legal-size hatchery product from 65 to 75 percent come away empty handed, and over half the fish are caught by about 10 percent of the anglers. As for cost, Needham said:

"Many of us who prefer the quiet of a wild stream are taxed to support the catchable program without sharing its benefits. Assuming that catchables cost $0.20 apiece as they are planted, and assuming a 50 percent mortality after planting, then each fish placed in the creel costs some $0.40 apiece. If your angling license cost you $3.00 then, theoretically at least, you have had more than your money's worth after you have caught eight of them."

Eschmeyer observed that "The ever-expanding trout rearing programs must eventually be financed exclusively by the trout fisherman. When this change is made the program will probably expand less rapidly." In terms of poundage, a Pennsylvania fish culturist remarked that "on a cold business basis, the trout that are stocked in the streams have a cash value, on the average, of 55 cents a pound." Of course, the value of a pound of fish *in the creel* would be much greater—according to Smith's calculations, from $1.50 to $12.50. Such costs are understandable when we consider that from egg to stream a hatchery trout is under the care of the fish culturist for from 18 to 24 months.

Again we see the essential similarity of stocking "legal-size" pheasants before the gun and trout before the rod. Under both methods comparatively few of the consumers are getting the bulk of the returns. In the case of trout, as previously pointed out (p. 172), this effect is augmented by the fact that limits are generally high. A lower limit would distribute the catch among more anglers provided fishing is sufficiently intensive to take the crop before Nature gets the job done.

Fishing usually is not so concentrated in areas where natural waters are plentiful and productive. Of course, a scattering of angling pressure permits a higher standard of sport. Under these conditions the catchable program is least necessary and may be a liability to wild waters. Put-and-take stocking probably is more defensible in such a state as Connecticut, where trout fishing on large rivers is maintained almost solely (under insistent public demand) by the stocking of 8- to 12-inch fish. A greater emphasis on sport, the objective of Michigan's program on special-regulation trout ponds (p. 173), would greatly increase the benefits per trout caught. Needham emphasized this idea as an alternative to the all-out stocking of catchables:

"Recent trends towards setting aside certain lakes, streams or sections of streams for fly fishing only or where 'catch-and-put-back' areas have been designated, will do much to improve the quality of angling. If artificial lures and barbless hooks are required in such areas, a lot of fishermen will be able to enjoy quality sport, including the experts. And that, basically, is what we are trying to provide."

The setting aside of waters for particular kinds of fishing is frequently opposed on the grounds that it is undemocratic and discriminatory. Of course, many Americans once considered it a violation of their "rights" to have any kind of hunting and fishing regulations. Increasing controls over the activities of individuals is a price we will be paying in ever greater degree for the privilege of expanding our own population. This is the same kind of "discrimination" we practice in restricting deer hunting to the bow and arrow in certain areas at certain times, or when we set a limit of three shells per gun in the taking of waterfowl. These are devices for increasing the sport and spreading it out among more people. Healthful recreation is our greatest justification for taking any kind of wildlife, and harvesting methods must be tailored to make the supply last.

In spite of the unfavorable economics of the program, the release of trout more than 6 inches long has shown no evidence of curtailment. In the late fifties California had the largest program of this kind, with an annual stocking of more than 10 million trout. The State of Washington was planting 7 million and Colorado nearly 5 million. New York and Oregon stocked more than 3 million, and six other states were roughly in the 1- to 2½-million class.

This much we can say for it: Fishing can for a time be improved by this method, and there is no other way to achieve the same immediate result. The program probably will never be entirely self-supporting—the trout fisherman could hardly afford it—but Michigan's dollar trout license (in addition to the regular fishing fee) is a recognition that in a state with many kinds of fishing it is not quite fair that the bulk of the revenue should be used to satisfy a few trout-stream specialists. Fisheries men recognize, however, that the stocking of legal trout is popular and that it will need to continue until the average fisherman (1) is much better informed than now, (2) sees some workable alternatives in spending his money, and (3) becomes much more discriminating in his conception of what is sound and unsound in public management. In some areas of few streams and many people better methods may never be possible. In others it is likely that painstaking research will show preferable ways to spend fish-license money. But research is slow, and to achieve this result the sportsman will need to be willing to have more of today's money spent for tomorrow's fishing.

THE OUTLOOK

In spite of the vast waste of funds that has attended the use of artificially propagated fish, it is clear that certain kinds of stocking will pay off and that these have a future. The sorting out and evolution of policy now are in full swing. The informed sportsman is the one who will decide how long uneconomic phases of fish stocking will persist as a concession to public demand.

Considering all the trends, it is quite likely that for many years to come our fish cultural stations will be serving the purposes outlined by Clarence Cottam at the annual meeting of the New York State Conservation Council in 1948. As Assistant Director of the Fish and Wildlife Service, Cottam probably expressed the trend of thinking of federal biologists when he gave five categories of justifiable stocking:

1. Stocking for new introductions, or re-introductions, of needed and desirable species.
2. Stocking fish for farm ponds under a planned program.
3. Stocking salmon and other anadromous fishes where high dams have eliminated much or all of former runs.

Deep End

4. Stocking for "put and take"; i.e., planting fish in waters favorable for growth and development but where there is no spawning, or perhaps where fishing pressure far exceeds the productivity of the stream.
5. It may be economical and justifiable to plant predaceous fish in some waters overpopulated with stunted fish.

That probably is as far as anyone can go in making present policy and looking into the future. Fish propagation and stocking are worth all this attention because, like the young cowbird in a nest of warblers, they have come to dominate the scene and hog the nourishment. Public thinking is ever in terms of hatcheries, despite the fact that of the fish caught, only a minuscule portion ever started life in a tank or rearing pond.

Our great dependence for angling sport is on the yield of naturally productive waters, and to increase such natural yield is the most promising aim of management. Like nearly all our conservation efforts, this turns out to be a problem in land-use ecology, the solution to which will require intelligent and sustained attention. We could do far better than we are doing now; but there is no point in pessimism, for the constructive trend is here and well on its way.

CHAPTER 14

Varmints

THIS chapter and the next will be devoted to a subject inherently complex as a purely biological problem. But, as if that were not a sufficiency of trouble, it is further complicated beyond all reason by inherited prejudice, vested interest, and genuine economics.

In no other phase of wildlife management do the professional and the amateur come so soon to a parting of the ways in their thinking. No subject in this field can approach that of predation in stirring men's blood, even to the extreme described by J. Frank Dobie—who told of a sheepman on the Frio River in Texas who would saw off the lower jaw of a trapped coyote and then liberate the animal to be killed by his dogs.

Of recent years there has been a noticeable resurgence of "practical" writings which call down the vengeance of Heaven on the visionary biologist for his maddening refusal to apply simple mathematics to the predation phenomenon.

Perhaps the biologist has reason in his view. It may make sense if we know enough about it. And in an age when even an atom has no privacy it is not unthinkable that responsible sportsmen may want to acquire a working knowledge of predator-prey relations.

Even a few years ago this would have been utter presumption. But the war of the forties vastly changed the public attitude toward both abstract and applied science. Time was when it was easier and more comforting to take a tonic to thin our blood in the spring and call every ache rheumatism. A more discriminating identification of our troubles and the painstaking development of remedies based upon precise knowledge has taken time and it has taken the practice of medicine out of the hands of herbalists. There are few who wish to discard scientific gain in this field or go back to "practical" therapy. Nevertheless, even today, there are a minority who do not "believe" in doctors just as there are farmers who do not "believe" in fertilizer.

Of course, neither of these modern amenities is a matter for belief at all. Both are a measurable benefit where properly applied. That they may be involved in mistakes does not invalidate their position as a part of modern civilization.

Consistent with this medieval hangover in other disciplines, in wildlife management it is not uncommon to have "horse sense" brought into vital issues to the exclusion of what professionals look upon as fact. Horse sense is, perhaps, good enough for a horse, but that does not admit the frequent implication that it is good enough for anyone. For some time there have been unmistakable indications of man's diminishing reliance on the horse.

FLESH AND THE DEVIL

We will fail completely to develop a realistic view of predation and predator control unless, first of all, we face the fact that we are hopelessly preconditioned on the subject. Predation, of a sort, occurs in human society and people have developed a positive and long-standing opinion regarding it. Quite commonly this attitude is carried over into their thinking on animal relationships.

Of course, killing for food is a part of our own formula for survival, and the average person accepts that as justified. To an extent that is personally satisfactory he has put his own house in order, but he looks with contempt at the killing in the animal world about him. He reacts with cold fury at the bobcat who waylaid a deer for breakfast—a doe fawn, no doubt. Maybe in the twentieth century any creature should be above such conduct. However, the bobcat feels no qualms of conscience and keeps right on being an uninhibited carnivore. He has his own standard and he won't change his way of making a living just because the world's most successful biped has taken to wearing pants.

It is true that some of the carnivores have not come along very fast, although it could be pointed out in our own case that it took six thousand years to develop the square milk bottle. A measure of charity and humility would become us, but instead, intolerance and a predator phobia have been built into our moral code from the beginning. It seems to be perpetuated in this way:

One of the first tales to impress us, as we graduate from kiddie-car to tricycle, concerns the miscreant wolf whose one aim in life was to get a tooth into the plump physique of Little Red Riding Hood. That the wolf never connected implies the ascendency of virtue over depravity—and, perhaps, lays the groundwork for a measure of disillusionment.

Another tall one deals with a family of bears and a well-known blonde. Then there is a whole series of harrowing chronicles that feature the little-pig threesome or certain rodentia like mice and rabbits * who are forever being pursued by foxes and similar beasts of ravin bent on nibbling ears or worse. In the standard formula the carnivores consistently seek their protein on the trail of innocence and grass-eating helplessness. By the time Junior enters kindergarten he has acquired something besides long pants: It's a fixation that a creature which eats anything built to kick and squeal is a villain of the animal world.

As Junior progresses, his fixation will not lack nourishment. Professional writers learned long ago that the atrocities committed by gore-fed carnivores are among their most merchantable material for the magazine trade. Happily there is a growing roster of exceptions, but a common type of writer still seems above responsibility for accuracy in his product, and some of them even operate in the name of science.

From the first, war on the carnivores has been one with game production. Not so long ago wildlife management was a trade rather than a profession, and you served apprenticeship among the brooders. To old-timers so trained, game farming was game management, and their whole lives and economic interests were tied up in it. Outside fences and in range fields they trapped innumerable hawks, owls, skunks, raccoons, and foxes attracted by the unnatural concentration of easy-come prey. As a result of such experience, the perpetual abatement of predators became an integral part of the picture.

Many people think like our old-timer, and they have their effect on Junior. To them a carnivorous animal is not wildlife; he is the enemy of all honest wildlife. The wolf doesn't live in the forest; he *infests* it. You don't just kill a predator; you execute him. You don't hunt him for sport; you track him down in a crusade for moral reform.

Likewise, people who have a dispassionate interest in eagles, wolves, and mountain lions are commonly looked upon as queer. Those who

* I know, Professor, but he's mighty like a rodent, isn't he?

claim values for predators are eccentrics—poet naturalists whose notions can be disregarded by all good, down-to-earth realists. Scientists who want more facts are just stalling or balled up in theories. And besides, added facts would be irrelevant, "because we're going to do it anyway."

A part of Junior's conditioning comes from the older naturalists, who habitually colored their writings with graphic accounts of how the flesh eaters tore into their prey (i.e., unnecessary roughness) or killed just to be doing something. Nearly all of the so-called popular descriptions of raptorial birds dwelt at length upon the sinking of the owl's talons into the back of the helpless rabbit and the slow and lingering demise thereof. Others described with excruciating pleasure the alleged vampire-habit of the weasel in "sucking" his victim's blood. The "cowardly" coyote regularly makes news not questioned as to authenticity, and the "cruel" wolf is an accepted villain from the first shudder of childhood. Mankind generally looks with the eyes of Colonel Roosevelt in describing a cougar treed on the rim of the Grand Canyon: ". . . the big horse-killing cat, the destroyer of the deer, the lord of stealthy murder, facing his doom with a heart both craven and cruel."

Even some of the well-meaning souls who have gone out to tell the "other" side of the story have pointed out that a hawk may now and then take a chicken or a pheasant but we must not condemn them all because a few are "outlaws." As a matter of fact it may happen in the best of (herbivorous) species. Commenting on some incriminating observations, the great Seton wrote:

"Many fair-minded observers point out that, though some Redsquirrels are bloodthirsty little ruffians, these are the degenerates, the freaks. Others are blameless citizens of the woods." *

My grandmother summed up the plaint of humankind when the dog next door killed her favorite cat:

"Oh Lord," she asked, "why can't they be nice?"

VICE AND VERSA

Just so we understand one another, you will not find here any one answer to the "control" question. But we will examine the position

* Reprinted by permission from *Lives of Game Animals,* by E. T. Seton. Copyright 1929. Doubleday & Co., Inc.

of representative predators in the communities they occupy and review some situations that should make us chary of taking everything at its face value. We will try to estimate the problem in its true proportions and gain perspective in judging its various phases.

No one seems to approve of predation but, like sin, it is not often that anyone succeeds in stopping it for an appreciable length of time. It's a universal phenomenon in communities of living things. Many a hunter visualizes a simple formula something like this:

$$\text{Fox} + \text{rabbit} = \text{fox}$$

A rabbit taken away would seem to be one less, but we observed in our review of "the one-year plan" that animal populations are padded annually with a surplus that is inevitably eliminated. It is a fair question, of course, whether the predator needs to get any of this surplus and whether we cannot do all the eliminating ourselves.

To begin with, it must be fully appreciated that we are dealing with adjustments of long standing. The herbivores and carnivores "grew up" together through eons of evolution. Many species have fallen by the wayside and become extinct. Those that are left have stood the test of time and of one another. Most of them show amazing adaptability and resilience. It is evident that they got by successfully in a primitive fauna, the problem being whether they can continue to do so in the world as it is today.

Many people, no doubt, think that freedom from predation would be the life beautiful for nearly any of our game. One of the classic tests of this idea was made on the Kaibab Plateau, which includes the north rim of the Grand Canyon in Arizona.

In primitive times the Kaibab was an isolated and productive deer range. It had long been a favorite hunting ground of the Navajos and Piutes who annually killed a few hundred deer in laying in their winter stores of skins and meat. In addition, the area supported a thrifty population of mountain lions which also made inroads on the deer.

The plateau was a complete range, with summer, spring-fall, and winter units to which the deer moved seasonally and which provided ample year-'round forage. In 1882, geologist C. E. Dutton described the area in glowing terms: "We, who through successive summers have wandered through its forests and parks, have come to regard it as the most enchanting region it has ever been our privilege to visit . . . There is a constant succession of parks and glades—dreamy avenues of grass and flowers winding between sylvan walls or spreading out into broad open meadows. From June until September there is a display of wild flowers quite beyond description."

In 1906, by presidential decree, the Kaibab portion of the Grand Canyon Forest Reserve was made the Grand Canyon National Game Preserve.* Deer shooting by the public was terminated and government hunters began a systematic clean-up of predators. During the next 25 years the total known predator kill was reported to be 781 mountain lions, 30 wolves (which were exterminated in the area), 4,889 coyotes, and 554 bobcats, plus an unknown number of eagles. Uncle Jim Owens, a federal warden, was credited personally with removing more than 600 of the cougars.

The Kaibab was early recognized as a good livestock range and about 2,000 cattle were placed there in 1885. This number grew until 1913 when 15,000 cattle and 5,000 sheep were being grazed on the area.

The "protected" deer increased also. The herd numbered perhaps 4,000 when the game preserve was created, and thereafter the annual build-up averaged nearly 20 percent—while it lasted. In 1918 the Forest Supervisor reported a declining food supply and too many deer. But too many deer was something no one understood. Public sentiment and state injunctions opposed any killing. As an alternative solution, cowpunchers actually tried to herd deer off the area. Numbers continued to pyramid as investigators who visited the plateau reported impending disaster. Where else, on a summer evening in 1924, could you see *seventeen hundred* deer in one meadow? The total herd now numbered perhaps 100,000.

That winter the vegetation made its last stand and went down in defeat. Deer died by thousands and ". . . those that lived ate every leaf and twig till the whole country looked as though a swarm of locusts had swept through it, leaving the range (except for the taller shrubs and trees) torn, gray, stripped, and dying." In many areas, 80 to 90 percent of the forage was gone.

* This area north of the river now comprises the Kaibab National Forest and Grand Canyon National Park, totaling somewhat more than a million acres.

In 1923 the government predator control program was terminated, but sport hunting of lions and fur trapping went on. An author who described the situation in 1928 commented: "Despite the fact that deer are too abundant on the Kaibab, nine lions were killed in 1927 . . . I believe it is about time to establish a five year close season on lions."

In 1924 hunting of deer was again permitted on the national forest and for the next five years about 1,000 were taken annually. But the physically degraded deer continued to die each winter, and breeding productivity went down. By 1930 there may have been 20,000 left, and in the decade to follow even this number was halved.

The affair Kaibab is cited frequently as an example of mismanagement. Yet, at the time, it had almost universal acceptance as the proper thing to do. As Ben H. Thompson summarized its implications in the second National Parks Fauna: "It was done then with the idea that proper wilderness utilization would consist of killing the blood-thirsty animals so that people could enjoy the gentle ones. But we have seen what happened to the gentle deer of the Kaibab and Grand Canyon. Unfortunately, the Kaibab was only the type case; the same thing happened in many places throughout the West in both national parks and national forests where deer and elk have been protected and their enemies destroyed. The whole difficulty arises because we have learned to appreciate only a few wilderness aspects."

To begin with, policy-makers in our national park system acted on the same assumption that motivated the Kaibab deer fiasco. For the first forty years of the existence of the system, trappers, hunters, and even poison were used to rid the parks of a wide assortment of "vermin." Most of these public areas were purged of mountain lions, and wolves were wiped out in all parks outside Alaska.*

Yellowstone Park is another example of what happens when big game gets—protection. With cougar and wolf eliminated and the coyote reduced, hoofed animals outgrew their food supply. Thousands starved, and the range was so damaged it will need decades of restricted usage to recover. "While other factors were involved, such as grazing and disruption of age-old migration habits north of the park,

---

* During the forties, wolves found their way from Canada to Isle Royale National Park in northern Lake Superior, where they are now established and helping to keep the formerly overpopulated moose in check.

the normal population of predators would probably have prevented, or at least mitigated, this catastrophe."

The relationships of big game to seasonal ranges and to their enemies gradually came to be better understood. As large carnivores disappeared, they were more appreciated as one of the important elements of primitive fauna that would have to be preserved in the parks if at all. By the mid-thirties routine control operations had been discontinued by the Park Service and a new policy had developed, providing:

"That every species shall be left to carry on its struggle for existence unaided, as being to its greatest ultimate good, unless there is real cause to believe that it will perish if unassisted;" and "That the rare predators shall be considered special charges of the national parks in proportion that they are persecuted everywhere else."

No doubt many people feel that if a species is preserved in one spot on the continent it is adequately provided for. What is commonly overlooked is that our native fauna existed in regionally adapted varieties, each differing from others and of interest in its own right. Such races are not always suitable, and never so satisfactory as the original form, for establishment in areas where the species has been wiped out. At one time the Western states supported varieties of the grizzly bear that were exterminated even before they could be described. The park predator policy provided further:

"That no native predator shall be destroyed on account of its normal utilization of any other park animal, excepting if that animal is in immediate danger of extermination, and then only if the predator is not itself a vanishing form."

The next logical question is, what was the result of this "visionary and unrealistic" attitude toward predators? Have they returned to the parks and decimated our big game? We can follow through on Yellowstone. Here the most effective checks on hoofed animals, the wolf and cougar, were gone, but long-time coyote control had also been considered necessary there to the continued existence of the antelope, bighorn, and muledeer.

In the spring of 1937 the Park Service assigned Adolph Murie to a 2-year study of the relationship of coyotes to other species in Yellowstone. This intensive field investigation gave the best picture yet obtained of the place occupied by the coyote in the natural economy of the big-game ranges to which it is native.

Findings that will surprise many people are that a fairly large number of coyotes actually starved to death in the midst of herds of bighorn and deer. Disease was another evident check on the coyotes. The population in 1937 and 1938 evidently was not much different than it had been previous to 1935 when control measures were in effect. Murie states:

"In Yellowstone, after 4 years of absence of artificial control, it is apparent that coyotes have not multiplied according to mathematical expectation. The evidence shows that the population spread has been very limited and has been only into areas adjacent to the park boundaries." In this connection, he points out elsewhere that coyotes ". . . rarely travel any great distance and that the majority remain with the game herds in the vicinity of the park boundaries. Forested areas adjacent to the park already carry a permanent coyote population. Trappers along the north side of Yellowstone National Park welcome the appearance of coyotes outside of the boundaries."

As to what the coyotes lived upon, Murie's conclusions were based upon the analysis of more than 5,000 droppings interpreted in the light of year-'round spying on the home life and social relationships of undisturbed animals in the wild. It was evident that "during spring, summer, and fall, rodents constitute by far the most important part of coyote diet, the majority of these being field mice and pocket gophers. The percentage of birds taken is relatively small and there is much evidence to show that many of the birds were obtained in the form of carrion. As a matter of fact the percentage of insects, particularly grasshoppers and crickets, computed on the basis of occurrence, is more than double the percentage of birds in the diet. Considering these items, together with a long list of miscellaneous species and materials, we must conclude that the role of the coyote in the fauna is not a harmful one during these seasons of the year.

"In winter . . . the big game herds furnish most of the coyote's food. This is chiefly in the form of carrion, [offal left by elk hunters was especially important] and, particularly in the case of deer, of weakened animals fated to succumb before spring."

The coyotes killed some newborn elk calves, and they cleaned up the remains of others born dead—these cases were difficult to separate;

but in any event the sum-total of pressure on the elk was negligible. Further conclusions were that "no appreciable inroads on the populations of deer, antelope and bighorn are taking place. On the other hand it became clear that the big game species are seriously handicapped by a poor, crowded range. Several big game species are competing with the bighorn and this situation requires continued attention."

Before leaving this subject let's make something clear: It has nowhere been said that coyotes do not sometimes kill perfectly healthy deer or the healthy young of elk and other big game. The point is that individual cases are not necessarily significant in judging the over-all population effects of a predator on its prey. It's the mass influence that counts and that can be determined only by sustained gathering of both positive and negative records at all seasons. Also, how the coyote lives in Yellowstone does not necessarily apply elsewhere, although it furnishes valuable clues as to what the probabilities are.

It might well be added that a reappraisal of former predator policies is by no means limited to the National Park Service. Many of the states have gone through a similar evolution where such technical matters are in the hands of long-term personnel.

SHEEP AND FACTS

General notions, it has been said, are generally wrong, and this seems to apply to game management as well as anywhere else. For a sportsman or game technician to be consistently "for" or "against" predator control is like a garage mechanic saying that he either believes in, or does not believe in, the blowtorch. He may need it sometimes for a particular purpose, but he can't use it for everything.

There are situations and times when a specific job of predator control, by methods that will get results, is called for. But it is obviously a waste of effort to spend our resources on predators unless they constitute an important and primary limiting factor for the game species we are trying to increase. An attractive path of least resistance is to assume without benefit of proof that they do.

Ask any rider of the range what has happened to mountain sheep in the West. The chances are good that the answer will feature the coyote, golden eagle, or some other flesh-eater. This might be factual under some conditions, but to be sure about it takes a lot of intensive work backed up by a kind of savvy you don't often get just by riding the range. It will be interesting to find out what most of the professional inquiries on bighorn sheep boil down to.

It has been estimated that in 1800 there were about two million of these animals, which to the old prospector, were (and still are) the primest meat in the mountains. The bighorn at one time ranged the grassy foothills and valleys and could be found in bands of 30 to 50 in the backlands of the Missouri Valley. On the first steamboat trip up the river in 1832, George Catlin found them numerous on the steep bluffs and hillsides. This was in country that was well populated with wolves.

Needless to say, the situation has changed. In his 1960 monograph on the bighorn, Buechner calculated that total numbers of the four races remaining within our borders were between 15,000 and 18,200. Obviously, something has gone against the sheep.

The situation in central Idaho has been carefully studied and probably is fairly typical. In the Salmon River drainage early explorers found an abundance of bighorns, a situation that persisted at least into the 1850's. About 1870 a major die-off began, evidently resulting from an on-set of scabies, after which the sheep never approached their primitive numbers. Scabies and a hard winter probably accounted for another drastic reduction about 1890, and further losses were reported in 1910. It is likely that livestock competition was catching up with the wild bands during this period.

For a quarter-century after 1917 Idaho sheep did not show good increases (they did better after 1945), and lamb losses were common. Here, as elsewhere, there was a popular idea that eagles were preying heavily on first-year animals. In the course of his studies in Idaho Dwight Smith decided that eagle predation was infrequent and of minor consequence. Buechner considered available records for the entire West and reached the same conclusion. Likewise, he reviewed impressive evidence that bighorns are not highly vulnerable to coyotes and that control programs have little to offer in managing wild sheep.

In a field study of the bighorns of Yellowstone Park in 1934-35, Harlow B. Mills found the animals to be suffering from mange, lungworm, a deficient range, poachers, and poor survival of lambs. He reached a definite conclusion about predators:

"The destruction of predators that attack the bighorn is not to be desired. Bighorn are notably susceptible to disease. The value of many animals lies in the fact that they are scavengers, destroying the bodies of animals which cause pollution of food and water, or otherwise aid in dissemination of disease. Predators that kill and devour the sick or weak individuals while they are highly infective and associating with healthy susceptible animals, are of more value than are the scavengers."

About 70 percent of Montana's bighorns died in an epizoötic in 1924-25. Investigations in the forties showed that sheep still were not increasing. Couey reported that some herds "build up to fair numbers and then suddenly die off from disease. This fluctuation has been reported as occurring for the last fifty years, probably since white men came in and reduced their numbers by hunting; then they were crowded into small areas where they had to compete with other game, man and his livestock. Their low resistance to disease, coupled with a drain from predators and poachers, has been enough to keep their numbers in check." Pneumonia was found to be the most important cause of death—possibly induced by lungworms, which are common in nearly all herds.

Colorado was plentifully supplied with Rocky Mountain bighorns at the time of early exploration and settlement. Unrestricted shooting, and scabies introduced with domestic sheep, probably brought about a drastic decline that occurred late in the 19th Century. Hunter and Pillmore indicated that with the effective control of scabies in domestic sheep, this scourge largely disappeared from the bighorn bands after 1900. But the continued history was one of build-up and crash. One of the finest herds in the state, on the Tarryall Range southwest of Denver, was said to have largely died off of hemorrhagic septicemia in 1923-24 (lungworm could have been involved). This herd built up again and was in excellent condition in 1940. Under protection from hunting, and with good range management by local ranchers, some 400 animals were healthy and largely free of predation.

Three herds of this region, Tarryall, Kenosha, and Pikes Peak, continued to increase—to about 1,500 animals in 1951. A year later, it was evident that a die-off was in progress. The Colorado Game and Fish Department had realized the need for managing bighorns, and they had authority for a sheep license. In 1953 they declared an open season under a limited permit system. This was against violent public opposition—it was the first legal hunting since 1885.

The hunting was too little and too late to prevent a heavy loss from disease, but the autopsies of animals shot made it possible to demons rate the wide prevalence of lungworms and resulting "verminiferous pneumonia." The conclusions were that, even on a generally favorable range, the sheep had reached a concentration of numbers that induced the disease outbreak. The three herds of the Tarryall and Pikes Peak region were down to about 145 animals in 1954.

I spite of recurrent troubles, today's bighorns are holding their own —and slowly gaining ground—in western states. Emphasis in management must be on protecting critical winter ranges from damage by livestock and other big game species. By trapping and transplanting, new herds are being established. Hunting must inevitably be a part of the picture, to hold the herds at healthy densities on the forage available.

The bighorn is classically range-sensitive and disease-vulnerable. In the history of our western herds there are strong implications that this species needs the cullling of its ancient enemies, the wolf and cougar. This may be particularly so since the introduction of new diseases. The predators are natural regulators that do a job which the gun seems unlikely ever to duplicate. How important this is, only the future can tell.

It must occur to anyone who reviews the status of our wild sheep that a study under primitive conditions would have been highly rewarding. Fortunately, this has been possible in the far North—with the wolf on hand and the domestic sheep absent. It was another job by Adolph Murie—this time in McKinley National Park, Alaska.

By far the most thorough of its kind, this 2-year inquiry resulted in a publication that is one of our best examples of sound ecological reporting. A particular objective of the Park Service, which sponsored it, was to determine the effect of wolves on numbers of the Dall sheep.

Previous to 1929, sheep were abundant on Mount McKinley, but that year, and again in 1932, there were hard winters with crusted snow of unprecedented depth. The sheep died of starvation in large numbers and there probably was heavy wolf predation at the same time. Sheep have not been abundant in the park since 1932, and wolves were generally plentiful in the region until the late forties.

Murie concluded that the wolf was a definite limiting factor to the sheep, and his observations on its hunting success indicate the intensive weeding-out process to which a prey species may be subjected.

If sustained through the ages, as it undoubtedly has been, it could hardly fail to render the stock more vigorous and more efficient in using the protective features of its environment.

For example, it was repeatedly observed that a sheep at the base of a steep rocky slope was not alarmed at the approach of a wolf, since it was perfectly aware of its ability to escape in such terrain. Even the lambs could ascend the rocks at a pace that the wolves recognized as beyond their endurance.

On the other hand, the sheep were careful not to allow a wolf to get above them on a narrow slope, since from such a position they might be driven down onto more level ground where the wolf considerably improved his chances. It was evident that deep snows narrow down the area of safety in a given unit of range.

Murie's work in the park demonstrated conclusively that for some combinations of predators and prey, at least, the oft-repeated idea that predators take the weakest first is no fable. In common with other big-game animals, sheep in the park were markedly susceptible to one or more fungus diseases of the mouth which cause a deterioration of soft tissue and bone and a loss of teeth. The condition might cause death or so weaken the animals that they were more easily run down and killed by wolves. More than 800 sheep skulls, both old and recent, were picked up and studied. They showed that most of the sheep dying in this area belonged to the old-age group or were young animals showing signs of disease. Healthy sheep in their prime seldom succumbed to wolf predation or other mortality causes. A young animal was likely to be weakened by its first winter, and there was consequent heavy mortality among yearlings. The hunting habits of the wolves indicated a perpetual screening of the sheep for exposed individuals:

"It is my impression that the wolves course over the hills in search of vulnerable animals. Many bands seem to be chased, given a trial, and if no advantage is gained or weak animals discovered, the wolves travel on to chase other bands until an advantage can be seized. The sheep may be vulnerable because of their poor physical condition, due to old age, disease, or winter hardships."

Caribou calves were a common food of wolves during the spring, and although young animals were easily captured during their first few days, after that they became more nearly capable of holding their own with the rest of the herd. The caribou bands were numerous at times and did not appear to be particularly alarmed by wolves unless actually chased.

"The wolf's method of hunting calves seems to give an opportunity for the elimination of the weaker animals. Usually the wolf chases a band of cows containing several calves. The speed of the calves is only slightly less than that of the wolves, at least on level terrain, so they make the wolf do his best, and the chase continues long enough for a test of the calves."

Although many sportsmen are likely to see red at the thought of a fine game animal such as the Dall sheep ending up as wolf feed, it is very likely that the wolf has played a part in making the sheep what it is. And by holding the population at a level below the carrying capacity of the food supply, they may be preserving both the sheep and the range in good condition. In discussing the effect of deep snow, Murie states:

"A large population quickly devours the food available on ridge tops and they must all go down to the deeper snow [where they are exposed to wolves] in search of food. A smaller number might find sufficient food on the ridge tops to pull them through a severe winter. This is an example of one of the regulatory devices of Nature."

It is evident that in an area like Mount McKinley National Park there is an ultimate point at which carrying capacity would be limited by the food supply but that it would be extremely precarious for the sheep to build up in numbers to that point. The actual carrying capacity is determined at a lower level by the extent of the type of terrain that represents comparative security from wolf predation. Of course, the density of wolves has something to do with this, since two or more wolves can catch sheep in territory where one would be ineffective.

The build-up of wolves in Alaska during the forties * was the subject of some highly salable magazine articles. The early demise of our big-game herds was forecast. There is no doubt we could have done with fewer wolves, but from a purely cold-blooded viewpoint this periodic abundance has its redeeming features. It is hardly to be doubted that caribou, moose, and sheep have survived periods of wolf

---

* By 1950 they seemed to have declined considerably.

prosperity many times in the past and that these are periods of respite during which vegetation has an opportunity to regenerate.

The general increase in carnivores which became evident in the early forties was the cause of grave alarm among people interested in the future of big game. Since our wild sheep have fared badly in so many areas these animals were the cause of particular concern. In 1943-46 a study of wolf-prey relationships in the Rocky Mountain National Parks of Canada gave a good appraisal of conditions that can be compared profitably with those already described.

This field study, by Ian McT. Cowan, covered five parks in British Columbia and Alberta comprising an area of more than 7,000 square miles. Bighorn sheep were abundant in the park region, yet they were undergoing little predation from a wolf population estimated, as a maximum, at one animal per 87 square miles of summer range. Most of the sheep ranges had good grazing associated with escape topography in the form of steep, rocky slopes, but in other areas the animals were feeding "far removed from any terrain offering natural protection. . . . The behavior of these sheep certainly leaves one with the impression that wolves occupy an unimportant place in their lives. Few wolf kills have been found on this area, though wolves have been present every year."

One area of range with few protective features and little available food was supporting a band of sheep in the face of year-'round hunting by wolves. However, these sheep were barely holding their own and showed a low survival of lambs. In regard to the over-all status of sheep and wolf, "the evidence seems to indicate that the Jasper Park wolves seldom hunt sheep, that the animals taken are those that from time to time [are] surprised away from escape facilities."

The region of this study was overpopulated with big game to such an extent that serious food depletion was evident on the winter range. The total stocking of sheep, mountain goat, elk, moose, caribou, and mule deer aggregated 30 to 40 head per square mile, or roughly 300 to 400 animals per wolf.

These big-game herds contributed 80 percent of the wolf's annual diet, the heavy population of elk alone making up 47 percent. Elk were obviously being hunted in preference to sheep, and in this case all age classes including prime animals were being taken. Yet the annual production of all species was such that the wolf was not an evident limitation.

"Vital statistics for game herds living with and without wolf pressure reveal that there is no discernible significant difference in the survival of young, or in the sex ratios within the two groups.

"It is concluded that under existing circumstances the wolves are not detrimental to the park game herds, that their influence is definitely secondary, in the survival of game, to the welfare factors, of which the absence of sufficient suitable winter forage is the most important."

Here, evidently, is another case where the wolves might have done a service if their toll on browsing and grazing animals had been sufficient to hold numbers at a lower level. Conditions at the time of this study point to ultimate reduction of the game—but through depletion of the food supply rather than through wolf predation.

It is probable, of course, that game animals rendered "surplus" from any cause will have their last rites celebrated by the wolves. The frequency of wolf kills in this, or any similar region, would make a sensational report for any man's magazine. A few case histories, with blow-by-blow descriptions of the final act of carnage, would convince the most apathetic reader that here was an emergency of the first order.

THE SORTING OUT

From the foregoing it appears that it is a natural function of predators to keep big-game range from being destroyed by the animals it supports. Sufficiently intensive and well regulated hunting could (and should) do this also in certain areas.

Game birds and mammals present a wide variety of predation adjustments, many of which are complex and misleading at first sight. It will be well to get some of the possibilities in mind.

How predation becomes involved with other mortality causes is suggested by an observation during the die-off of fox squirrels in Michigan's Allegan State Forest in 1940. In midwinter a dog was intercepted in the woods carrying a still-warm squirrel. It readily gave up its victim for examination and the squirrel was found to be in poor condition and to have more than half its fur missing as a result of an infestation of scabies mites.

The questions that can be asked about this squirrel well illustrate the inadequacy of straight-line thinking. What killed the squirrel? Was it the dog? Or was it spring weather conditions which prevented the oaks from bearing mast? Did a lack of belly fat kill the squirrel, or was it the exceptionally hard winter with deep snow which sealed off what little food remained buried in the ground? Or, again, was it the scabies mites that "took over" a weakened, emaciated animal and helped in turn to render it vulnerable to the dog?

What conclusion would have been justifiable if we had found the bones of this squirrel in a fox scat that winter? The ifs, ands, and buts of the biologist are tedious at times, but they may also be realistic.

It is not new, but becomes steadily more evident, that disease and parasitism are important means by which prey animals, which may have been comparatively secure otherwise, are made available to their enemies. The analysis of thousands of stomachs and scats of hawks and owls, foxes and coyotes, is futile and misleading if the work is done indiscriminately and published without qualification. This fact is gaining recognition, and food studies of the carnivores now are regularly confined to specific areas where populations are under careful surveillance for the period involved.

In northwest Wyoming in 1940 a careful job on the Rocky Mountain bighorn indicated a relationship that never would have been apparent to superficial observation. The lamb crop of that year was reduced by half by the 15th of August. Both field work and laboratory studies showed that a type of epidemic pneumonia was killing lambs which otherwise were in good flesh and condition. In this case a control program on coyotes served at least one useful function. It permitted the primary cause of the losses to be determined:

"The control of coyotes on Crystal Creek was continued until August 15. This program was no doubt responsible for much of the accomplishment in the solution of lamb loss because it enabled the party to observe sick lambs and to find two dead lambs. From the observations made a year ago it was clear that coyotes were eating lambs and removed the sick and dead animals before they were seen by the field party . . ."

Another statement from this account is representative of usual findings in such situations: "Reconnaissance of the Hoback Mountains has shown the immediate problem to be competition between domestic sheep and the bighorn sheep. Domestic sheep are at present utilizing the entire winter range."

Whether or not, in this case, a food shortage was directly responsible for pneumonia among the lambs, it is true that a common progression of events can be represented thus:

Range depletion→ disease→ predation

It is habitual with many observers to describe predation as the primary factor and fail entirely to see the more fundamental ills of the game population.

Local catastrophes are almost always characterized by increased predation and carrion feeding by meat-eating birds and mammals. In his long-term studies of muskrat populations in Iowa, Paul L. Errington found that muskrats are fairly secure from the mink under favorable conditions of food, water, and health. But when marshes flood or dry out, or disease spreads in the population, a first evidence of trouble is increased success in the muskrat hunting of the mink.

For small-animal populations it has become increasingly evident, as the results of research accumulated, that numbers ordinarily are not determined by predation pressure. This reality has both favorable and unfavorable features in terms of action management. First, it is true that we cannot depend upon our remaining carnivores to "control" rodent liabilities such as orchard mice and ground squirrels on the range.* But neither do they *primarily* determine the population levels of rabbits and game birds, so direct predator control seldom is called for as a small-game management measure. "Direct," as used here, means control by killing individuals as distinguished from control by manipulating the habitat, which may be entirely practicable.

The relative independence of population trends of the coyote and rabbit was demonstrated at the San Joaquin Experimental Range of the Forest Service in California. In 1935-36, as a result of calf losses, a program of coyote reduction was carried out. At that time the cottontail also was plentiful on the area. A drastic thinning of coyotes had no discernible effect on the rabbits; in fact, during 1939-40 rabbits underwent a marked slump in numbers despite relative freedom

---

* "Control" here means keeping the population within limits such that economic damage is unimportant. Unless the rodents actually are on the increase, something obviously is controlling them even though they are abundant.

from the attentions of coyotes. The latter undoubtedly had been taking part of the annual production of rabbits, but it can be assumed that this portion of the population was a part of the expendable annual surplus, and when coyotes were removed from the picture some other fate befell the rabbits. Biologists of New York State observed a similar occurrence in their work on the grouse of Valcour Island in Lake Champlain.

LIVING WITH IT

These examples indicate that in judging effects we need to look well beyond the mere fact that a predator and a prey species occur on the same land unit. The numbers of each, the prevalence of disease, food supplies, the presence of competing species, and the amount and quality of cover are factors that must be thrown into the equation. The final effect of the carnivore is an expression of all of them. Predation occurs in terms of the environment, and effective control, where that is practicable, usually will be achieved by treating causes and not symptoms.

In the case of the San Joaquin rabbits, it was determined that taking a predator away resulted in no evident benefit to the population. Similarly, in a good habitat it may mean nothing at all when a predator is added. The rabbit and fox were involved in such a situation on a 500-acre farm near Battle Creek, Michigan:

A kill record on rabbits was kept for this area from 1932 to 1947, and the species was intensively studied for 3 years in the mid-thirties. Two annual kills at that time were 125 and 135. During this period the tract rarely was visited by a fox and none was resident in the immediate vicinity. In the early forties foxes became much more plentiful in the region and were regularly found on the farm. Yet the status of the rabbit showed no change as a result of fox predation (it almost certainly occurred). In fact the largest rabbit harvest in 16 years was taken in 1941 when 172 animals were removed. That was an exceptionally favorable year for rabbits all over southern Michigan—at a time when foxes were on the up-grade.

Studies of fox food habits on two areas in Iowa showed that during spring and summer young cottontails were a common food under ordinary conditions. However, during the summer of 1940, pressure on the rabbits was released considerably by the ready availability of muskrats exposed to easy hunting by lowered water levels resulting from drouth.

In terminology sometimes used, the muskrat would be said to act as a "buffer" for the rabbits—since it was more available and absorbed the punishment. At the time these facts on the rabbit and muskrat came to light it also was observed that in sparsely populated "marginal" range, pheasants evidently were more vulnerable to foxes than in better range that supported higher densities. In this better range the sum-total effect of predation does not appear to have been important. The careful field studies of Errington and the Hamerstroms indicated the situation to be as follows:

"During the breeding season, remains of pheasants may be found in varying numbers in the den debris (including scats) of red foxes . . . and in the nest debris (including pellets) of great horned owls . . . However, the heaviest pressure was commonly borne by pheasant populations of such high density that the net effect upon reproduction may not have been great. In northwestern Iowa localities where adult pheasants were serving as staple food for foxes and horned owls under observation, the pheasant nesting seemed to continue much as usual, and these localities were among those well known to sportsmen for the excellence of the pheasant hunting they supplied."

In spite of flat assertions to the contrary, it *is* possible in many situations to produce a game crop and have plenty of predators around at the same time. Considering the situation in the prairie states, one observer wrote:

"Quail and foxes both exist in high numbers in southern Iowa and in Missouri. Foxes and coyotes are present in Nebraska's better quail territory. Coyotes are numerous in the world's best pheasant range in South Dakota, Nebraska, and North Dakota. Both coyotes and sharptailed grouse are numerous in Nebraska National Forest."

With an abundant population, however, and with the character of vegetation changing with the seasons, it is logical that some rabbits will be "spilling over the edges" of the best situations and will be getting by, for a while, in marginal locations. These are the animals most likely to become fox feed, and even if that isn't their fate, they probably will be marked "surplus" anyway and eliminated before spring.

In a given unit of range there probably will be an optimum density level where the population of prey animals will be reasonably safe from predation (i.e., the carrying capacity phenomenon). But variable factors, such as weather, may alter the condition of this range unit, for better or worse, in a given year. In such case the percentage of a population taken by natural enemies may vary widely simply because availability varies. In discussing game birds, one author described the situation this way:

"Predation is a normal and necessary check on game bird populations. However, some workers have found that at times predators take a greater toll of birds than at others. Strange as it may seem these times are not when the predators are most numerous, but rather when the game birds are most numerous. Thus a high population density of grouse or pheasants suffers a proportionately greater loss to predation than a low population."

Do we need predator control? The answer is, "certainly," but a little enlightenment calls to question the one-by-one war of attrition that we are wont to carry on season after season.

Hunt the predators? Those, like the fox and crow, that are prolific and plentiful, yes. They provide sport and some wear fur. But should we pay an outsize fee to try to get rid of the annual crop of foxes a little sooner than Nature will do it? If our primary interest is rabbits, wouldn't it be more effective "control" to work on the rabbit cover by way of a permanent operation?

THE FABLE BUSTERS

Predators are sometimes referred to as one quantity in that well-known but little-understood equation, "the balance of nature." It has been a favorite sport in recent years for writers, technical and otherwise, to debunk this idea. It's all a lot of tommyrot, they say, because man has taken such liberties with the flora and fauna of this, and other, continents that no semblance is left of the original natural balance.

The fallacy here is that even in primitive America there was no *status quo* of the kind implied. The northern hemisphere was recovering from the ice age and many changes were occuring. Vegetation types were following the glaciers northward and animal species were flowing hither and yon as they found favorable conditions developing. In many cases new local varieties of animals appeared that were specialized to fit a given set of conditions, and other varieties and species became extinct when they could not adapt * themselves to change. There was plenty of flux in what the pilgrims found here, although it was taking place over time periods that could not be observed easily during one human life.

Another line of attack on the balance of nature is that there never has been such a thing—because look at the constant ups and downs of both herbivores and carnivores. They vary from periods of great abundance to near-disappearance. Now one species is prosperous and now another—where, oh where, is the balance of nature?

Probably the answer to all of this is that you can define any idea in such a way that it is discredited. In nature nothing is so constant as change, but practically everywhere there is a system of checks that prevents individual species from becoming abundant beyond certain limits and also prevents them from declining to extinction. A community of plants and animals is a system that contains both constructive and destructive forces. But since one species does not gain permanent advantage and destroy the system, then certainly a balance exists.

Anyone who has studied wildlife populations in various habitats will have observed that practically everywhere animals live in communities complete with herbivore and carnivore components. This is true even in our most artificialized environments. In fact, it may seriously be questioned whether an animal commuity can exist for long in anything but relative balance. If such a condition developed, there would be a rapid and catastrophic wiping out of something and then the infiltration of new species which would come to a tolerable adjustment with one another. This is automatic, since the ones that don't fit the new pattern just don't last.

Most of our farming country in the East is representative of an environment that differs radically from the primitive condition. Many of the animals it supports were not present in the original forest. Yet an appraisal of the species association as it is today shows a balance quite as complete as any that existed half a millennium ago.

Within animal communities there is a *fluctuating balance* like the teetering of a pair of scales. It is constantly being reestablished among

* Not particularly good terminology, but this is a complex subject that we will not go into here.

new species as conditions are changed. It involves such dynamic and competitive elements as vegetation, herbivores, carnivores, and diseases and parasites, and it exists within limitations imposed by climatic extremes. It adapts flexibly to artificial conditions such as land-use practices and the cropping of certain species for game and fur.

The balance of nature is a useful and realistic idea, *as long as we apply it to what actually exists.* There would seem to be little point in giving it an impossible Mother Goose connotation and then tossing it out as useless.

A surprisingly precise balance of predator and prey fish populations was brought out in a study of five Florida lakes. For lakes with comparable conditions the poundage per acre of largemouth bass was found to be a constant proportion of the total weight of the fish. The "supporting" populations varied in species composition from lake to lake, but their weight relationship to the bass was the same. It was notable that in lakes where garfish occurred, the bass were correspondingly reduced.

In these fish associations it took about three pounds of "forage" fish to support one pound of predator. If it were possible to measure populations of land animals over large areas, it is likely that some such average relationships would be found, but the constant change that is characteristic of terrestrial habitats makes it well-nigh impossible to reduce the equation to simple terms.

Adaptations among species naturally associated are such that there is little danger of a predator actually exterminating its prey. If this were to occur anywhere, it might be expected in the case of the lynx and snowshoe hare in the far north. On the upswing of their cycle, the hares become vastly abundant for a period and the lynx, with easy living, builds up its numbers to a corresponding peak. Then the hares suddenly die off to a point of rarity. For a time, with their food mainstay gone, there are hungry cats to spare scouring the land desperately for food. Even under these conditions, enough hares survive to build up to abundance again within a few years.

With regard to this same subject, a Canadian biologist made some pertinent observations on the effect of wolves on Ontario deer:

"Some hunters are afraid that the wolves are gradually exterminating the deer and are telling alarming stories about wolves killing large numbers of deer. It is true that wolves kill deer regularly and that in the spring, when the snow is crusty, they can often kill as many deer as they want to. However, instead of becoming exterminated, deer have greatly extended their range in Northern Ontario in the last half-century and are in most places more numerous than they used to be thirty years ago . . . Apparently the deer population of Northern Ontario can stand as well a certain amount of hunting by wolves, maintain itself, and even steadily extend its range into the wolf country northward."

It begins to look as though we have nourished a misplaced and in some cases a lethal sympathy for our fed-upon wildlife. As individuals they don't stand a chance anyway and racially it's their enemies that keep them in business. This was strongly suggested in Murie's studies of the Dall sheep and wolf. For the mule deer and mountain lion, Thompson speculated as follows:

"Deer and cougar lived together for countless thousands of years before white man came along to protect the helpless deer. The part the cougar played in developing the deer into an animal with its particular type of fleetness, grace, alertness, and cunning—the very characteristics which make the deer a deer and not a cow and hence desirable for recreation and game—we can only conjecture. We do know this, however, that in areas where deer have had the predatory menace entirely removed, they have largely lost both the game and the aesthetic values."

Although it is difficult to prove this relationship, there can hardly be any doubt that it exists—not only among birds and mammals but in practically all living things. Karl F. Lagler applied the idea to another creature of primary interest to sportsmen: "One might go so far as to say that the gaminess of such a fish as the smallmouth bass is due to the survival of those best fitted to escape their enemies during many centuries."

HARUM SCARUM—BUT NOT BAD

To a great extent, we have considered the relations of carnivores to our game-prey animals from a narrow and purely arbitrary viewpoint: Could we have more game and better hunting if we got rid of what at face value appear to be our competitors? A sampling of specific cases seems to indicate that in most situations predators have a place in the scheme of things. In any case we should be convinced by now that action without investigation often leads to waste and sometimes to catastrophe.

Discarding this orthodox meat-hunter reasoning, let's look at it from another side. After all, we are interested in other birds besides quail and ducks, and we are interested in animals other than those that wear horns and chew their cuds. For a while in the fall we hunt, but the rest of the year we are outdoors too, and we get a lot out of animals that are never taken home. Carl L. Hubbs has put his finger on this idea in regard to creatures that eat fish:

"Fish predators within reason should be tolerated, giving due regard to the value or interest of the predators to others, . . . There are those who would rather hear a kingfisher rattle his way down a stream than to catch a trout; their desires and rights should be respected. The development of fish management, I believe, will be hastened and rendered more sound, if fish managers compromise and counsel with the preservationists."

That brings democracy into it, doesn't it? Another statement by Karl F. Lagler, put it this way:

"The concentrations of young game fish in large numbers in hatchery waters attract unusually many predators. In the United States this has accounted for the destruction of as many as thirty thousand predatory animals annually in the name of protecting these fish. Unfortunately, the role of fish culture in improving angling becomes less and less significant as we learn more of the natural requirements and capacities of game fish in wild waters, and thus such slaughter of predators is unwarranted; particularly unwarranted, since by so doing, not only are we sacrificing potential checks against overpopulations with resulting stunted fish in nature, but we are robbing Peter the bird lover supposedly to pay Paul the angler."

Breathes there the man with soul so dead that for a few more limit kills or a few more trophies in his lifetime, he would once and for all erase the fox track from December snow, the eagle and osprey from the mountain air, the wolf song from the brittle arctic night? (Going soft, aren't we?) Let's not be deluded. Our public press still is full of the kind of smug anthropomorphism which cannot refrain from describing the morals as well as the features of the cougar, he of the . . . "massive broad flat head, malignant yellow eyes, muscles and sinews like coiled springs of steel wire, the hate of a demon, a cunning that passes understanding, viciousness personified . . ."

There are some whose dream world is peopled only with decent, upright vegetarians. But most of us will feel better to string along with something a bit more sane, if sinful. We have use for the carnivores. They are game too, and they are something besides. Most of us will back the sentiments of elder-scientist and conservationist Charles C. Adams, who waded into this subject at the annual meeting of the American Society of Mammalogists in 1930:

"I think that we can afford to have mountain lions somewhere in America besides stuffed specimens in the museums. If we were a poor country and did not have millions of dollars that we waste on trifles, we might say, 'We cannot afford a few mountain lions.' But we are probably the richest nation on earth, and what would be the cost of maintaining one hundred mountain lions in North America? Would it stagger American civilization? We have millions of acres in National Forests, in the Public Domain, and in the National Parks. Some of the areas could be managed in such a fashion that some of these animals could be preserved and eat deer meat! Why shouldn't they?"

In 1946 a Missouri farmer, who was much more than a farmer, stood before the 8th Midwest Wildlife Conference and told of 25 years of development for *all* crops on a tract of "stubborn Missouri soil."

He told of building fertility, cattle, and quail, and he had a slant on the predator question:

"Every time I kick that big owl out of her tree to see the crows chase her, I am convinced I am not a wildlife manager but just a farmer with silly ideas like that one which just flew out of the tree. Better not try to shoot that owl, I know she does some damage, but I will protect her just like I would a flock of prairie chickens. Perhaps it's because I like to hear that hoot split the quiet prairie night, or perhaps it's because, in learning to grow 600 head of cattle where 15 grew before, I have also learned to wonder, if perhaps the same Mother Nature who made room for me on this 1800-acre farm didn't also think there was room enough for an owl."

Practical? Yes, I think so. With J. Frank Dobie I suspect that this curious, impartial sympathy toward *all* creatures, regardless of their diet, is an attitude of the cultivated mind. It is a measure of a man's civilization. If ever we are to achieve a reasonable concord with the earth on which we live, it will be by our willingness to recognize, tolerate, and employ the biological forces and relationships both in our own numbers and in the living things about us.

CHAPTER 15

Under Control

AS has been implied, there is practically no situation where it would be desirable for a rapidly multiplying species to be free from natural enemies. Conditions that call for predator control are exceptions rather than the rule, but this does not eliminate the measure as a part of wildlife management. We undoubtedly have man-dominated environments into which some predators do not fit without catching at the corners, and there are situations where it can be demonstrated that control operations will show a clear profit.

A good example of the latter was revealed a few years ago in an experiment carried out by the Fisheries Research Board of Canada as a part of sockeye salmon investigations in British Columbia.

Adult sockeyes migrate up from the sea to Cultus Lake where they spawn in fresh water. At one or two years of age the young fish ("smolts") leave the lake and move downstream to complete their growth in the wide open spaces of the ocean.

Fishery biologists found that survival of eyed eggs in the lake was little more than 3½ percent, and of free-swimming planted fry slightly over 4 percent. That seemed low and there was a strong suspicion that an unduly large proportion of young sockeyes were being expended to nourish less desirable denizens of the deep.

To test the idea, a systematic attempt was made to reduce important enemies of the salmon. For three years gill nets were operated intensively. Squawfish and char (salmon predators) were thinned out to about a tenth of their original numbers, and fairly large inroads were made on other species.

Coincident with reduction of predation, the survival of sockeyes increased. Almost 9 percent of the eyed eggs came through and more than 13 percent of the fry lived to go downstream. It was calculated that the control operation in the 3-year period added 3,800,000 smolts to the seaward migration. Calculating that 1 out of 10 would reach the fisherman's net, the gross value of the additional catch would be $90,000. Since the cost of control was about $10,000, the operation showed a neat entry on the right side of the ledger.

We should bear in mind that this project was set in motion by fisheries experts who saw a situation where they thought they might succeed, and by careful follow-up they discovered something that probably could be used elsewhere.

In the foothill region of California's San Joaquin Valley, the Beechey ground squirrel is the most important nest predator of the valley quail. A study indicated that squirrels break up more than 30 percent of the nests. A 300-acre area where the ground squirrels were poisoned in two successive years provided a test of whether egg-predation really was reducing the quail. Apparently it was, for the poisoned area showed more birds consistently after the operation was carried out in May 1936. Late winter (February-March) populations of quail were as follows:

	1936	1937	1938
Poisoned area	90	229	220
Check area (no poison)	90	135	90

In a case like this we have a good indication that effective ground-squirrel control would increase quail. Whether it would produce enough quail to pay the cost of control measures, of course, is something else. If there are other reasons for reducing squirrels, then we can count more quail as one of the values to be gained in judging the feasibility of the operation.

A somewhat comparable situation existed in the thirties on the Lower Souris Waterfowl Refuge in North Dakota, which is an important breeding ground for blue-winged teal and certain other species of ducks. Skunks also were quite plentiful, and in 1936 they put about 30 percent of the duck eggs to their own use. About 55 percent of the ducks hatched successfully.

Accordingly, in a 9-month period 423 skunks were taken out of circulation on the study area. The result was evident. Only 7 percent of the eggs were taken by skunks and 69 percent of the ducks hatched successfully.

How a prey species reacts to reduction of its enemies depends in part upon its numbers, as is shown by a series of controlled experiments carried out by the New York State Conservation Department.

The job was done in the early thirties and the object was to determine effects of intensive predator control on ruffed grouse populations. Mammal and bird predators, such as foxes, weasels, hawks and owls were much reduced on experimental tracts, and comparable land units without such control were kept as checks.

It was found that heavy predator control reduced nest losses consistently, but whether such reduction actually resulted in more birds in the fall depended upon other factors. In 1931 grouse were on the up-swing of their cycle and numbers had not yet reached the peak. Under these conditions intensive predator killing produced about 25 percent more grouse in the fall. However, even on the check area where no predators were taken, the grouse continued to increase, and the following year they reached a maximum for the region. With grouse at their high point, the reduction of egg mortality failed to result in more shootable grouse in the fall, populations being much the same on both areas.

As has been indicated elsewhere, there are fairly numerous cases where the elimination or drastic reduction of natural enemies has been followed by the increase of big-game animals far beyond the point of health and thrift. Such abundance frequently was the direct result of vast increases in food supply (following forest cutting and burning), but a natural coterie of predators might have helped to hold their prey at more reasonable levels. A cooperative study by the Forest Service and Fish and Wildlife Service on the Los Padres National Forest in southern California indicated that plentiful coyotes probably were holding a heavy population of deer in check. It was evident also that killing off the coyotes without substituting heavier hunting for predation would mean too many deer and a depleted food supply. Currently this is one of the biggest objections to predator control in the nation's deer ranges.

In the early days of antelope restoration in the West it appeared that coyotes might be preventing the build-up of herds in areas where pronghorns had been drastically reduced. Gabrielson described the results of a long-term coyote-control program on this plains animal in the territory where California, Nevada, and Oregon join: "In that region a small herd remained in 1920 and 1921, when the species had reached its lowest ebb there. The antelope were protected by state game laws, and there is little evidence that any considerable number were killed illegally. After their low point in 1920, when the animals had decreased noticeably from disease and possibly other causes, predator-control operations were undertaken by the Biological Survey, and between January 1, 1921, and June 30, 1934, a total of 7,595 coyotes and bobcats were removed. While this reduction of the predator population was being carried on, the antelope herds, which had for several years been stationary, with comparatively little success in rearing fawns, gradually increased from about 500 animals to their present population of 7,000 to 8,000. Now the antelopes are numerous enough for the same or even greater predator pressure to be of less importance than formerly, and other factors affecting the herd may become more serious." *

As in this example, predator control is practical as a temporary, pinch-hit measure for the protection of a breeding stock on an adequate range from which a game animal has been nearly or wholly eliminated. This would be justifiable even at high cost if the final result was the establishment of a productive population. It is assumed that emergency protection from natural enemies would be accompanied, when necessary, by restoration of the environment to a point where the population could attain productivity and survive on its own.

It is by the same logic that we can condone control of local predators amid concentrations of nesting waterfowl on refuges or island colonies of other nesting birds. These areas have been set aside for intensive (and expensive) management. The predators concerned are not in danger and may be considered expendable.

This, however, is a far cry from the wanton shooting of all hawks and owls which has been so widely acclaimed under the guise of "varmint hunting." Probably there is no category of wildlife so generally appreciated by people who enjoy the out-of-doors as birds of prey. A growing awareness of the high esthetic value of these birds is behind an increasing trend toward total protection in progressive states—a trend well supported by responsible sportsmen's federations. The at-

* Reprinted by permission from *Wildlife Conservation,* by Ira N. Gabrielson. Copyright 1943. The Macmillan Company.

tempt in certain states to protect some predatory birds while others (especially the Cooper's hawk) are left unprotected is meaningless and completely ineffective. The average gunner does not know one from another, and if he ever became interested enough to learn the difference, he would not want to shoot them anyway. Laws protecting hawks and owls always make provision for the elimination of nuisance individuals where these are doing economic damage. This is as it should be.

It is evident that there will need to be a general protection of predatory birds if such rare species as the larger falcons and the bald eagle of the East are to be preserved at all. The pressures of habitat change are on these remnants of our primitive fauna, and we cannot afford the shooting that goes on year after year.

In the same manner we cannot afford extermination of the wolf in the Lake States. It has too much value for those who camp, canoe, and hunt in the north woods and to whom the species is one of the attributes of wilderness—not to mention its value as a co-habitant of too-numerous deer.

Attempts to use predator control as a year-after-year force in the economy of a wildlife population seem to be almost universally unsound. In healthy wildlife habitats wildlife communities take care of themselves, and sustained excessive predation can in most cases be taken as a symptom of deficient cover or some other semi-permanent condition. The word "sustained" is not to be passed over lightly, because temporary predation to excess is a valid reason to suspect such temporary population ills as disease, intolerable weather extremes, or lowered water levels (where these are important to such species as ducks or muskrats).

This discussion deals exclusively with the need for predator control as a *wildlife management measure*. It can be stated without qualification that stock and poultry raisers must have protection from depredations in areas where such use of the land is sound national economy. How they are to get such protection and who is to pay for it is not the subject of interest here.

Predator control undoubtedly is most efficient when carried out by public agencies with trained personnel maintained year after year for this purpose. But any routine program for wildlife protection on an area as large as a state should be immediately suspect as beyond the requirement of problems *that are characteristically local and temporary.*

The matter of harvesting the annual surplus of predators is a subject little understood but fraught with implications. In Chapter 3 we observed that breeding stocks of animals are healthiest and most productive when the population is thinned out early in the season and competition among breeders is minimized. This undoubtedly holds true for carnivores as well as herbivores.

In the early forties foxes became far too abundant over much of the nation. Many states were under public pressure for intensive control of foxes. It is almost universally the case that these programs do not get down through the annual surplus of animals and actually reduce the breeding stock; and if they did that the breeding stock might rise to the occasion and be even more productive.

So what does such control mean? Are we actually keeping the fox healthy by taking off excess numbers each year and thus creating favorable conditions for producing next year's crop? Are we delaying the reckoning that Nature has in store for the fox—such decimating agents as rabies, encephalitis, and distemper?

It is likely that we are, but it is hardly justifiable at present to adopt a leave-the-fox-alone policy to hasten his decline. Until much more is learned about the timing of such things, it will be better to hunt and trap for all we are worth to get the most out of foxes and similar carnivores in years when they are plentiful.

Our best evidence indicates that in many cases the most effective way to control predators is to provide their prey with a better habitat in which to live. Curiously enough, in the case of big game this may involve reducing the prey rather than the predator. A favorable range usually produces in spite of predators, and on poor range no amount of control is likely to send hunters home satisfied.

This sketchy appraisal of the carnivore menace indicates that an attitude of caution toward control programs is realistic. However, it will be well to identify some of these large-scale efforts specifically. They are among our most costly wildlife management endeavors and are of concern to those who pay for them.

G-PROGRAMS

William Penn is credited with hiring the first government predator-control agent when he put a professional wolf hunter on Pennsylvania's payroll in 1705. The last known wolf in the Commonwealth was killed in Clearfield County just 187 years later.

As long as environmental conditions remain favorable, the larger carnivores show a remarkable ability to persist in the face of year-'round hunting and trapping—even when this is done by efficient full-time professionals. However, wilderness disappeared before the advance of the settler, and with it went wolf, bear, and panther. That was the history in much of the East, but west of the prairies both wilderness (of a sort) and its inhabitants were able to persist much longer by virtue of the sheer vastness of the country. Now, habitable parts of the West are filling up rapidly, and modern methods of killing the carnivores make anything possible. If there are reasons for something less than total elimination of the large predators, we need to know it and bring proper policies to bear.

The settler who had the stubborn fortitude to establish his home on the frontier was perpetually warring against the flesh-eaters to protect his few domestic animals. Sometimes he suffered ruinous losses. His bitter attitude toward the carnivores was understandable, and to this day it persists in the less-settled parts of North America.

In the West, characteristic wildlife problems are interwoven with what has happened to the grass. Rabbits and rodents have become abundant, in violent and periodically recurring cycles, on areas where at one time they were much less plentiful. This has led to extensive poisoning campaigns to reduce this competition for forage. To make way for stock-raising, the wolf, cougar, and grizzly had to be eliminated from much of their former range, and many people would pursue these species into the last wilderness areas and eliminate them entirely—a process now well under way.

In the face of traps, dogs, and strychnine, the adaptable and prolific coyote held its own and even extended its holdings, but the appearance during the war of sodium fluoroacetate, compound "1080," completely altered the outlook. Widely spaced injected carcasses are deadly baits to the far-ranging brush wolf, and its extirpation in large regions is now but a matter of time. Even national parks and monuments are being emptied of coyotes by the placement of baits outside their borders.

Coyote inroads on calves and sheep have been prohibitive in many ranch areas and they necessitate control. Where such control is to stop has become an issue, since it now is recognized (by the biologist) that predation is a force that should not be eliminated from the annual regimen of big-game herds.

In general, there are two points of view that are pulling and hauling in roughly the western half of the country. One is that enough traps, coyote getters, and poison will hold both rodents and predators at such low levels that stock-raising can be carried on profitably wherever there is water to grow anything. The counter claim is that range misuse is a cause of some of the troubles and that less poison would be necessary, for rodents and rabbits at least, if grasslands could be maintained in a healthy, productive condition. Although little enough has been done on it, western biologists have made a few investigations that are highly suggestive and indicate that the ideal of "biological control" (through good land use) is worth looking into.

When soil is laid bare on the plains, there is a predictable year-to-year succession of plant types starting with annual weeds and proceeding in orderly sequence (when undisturbed) to a final or "climax" grass stage. Investigations of recent years show that such animals as rodents, rabbits, and antelope largely depend for their livelihood upon weeds rather than grass. Overgrazing sets vegetation back to early stages of succession, and hence ground squirrels, pocket gophers, woodrats, hares, and rabbits are most plentiful on misused land. Likewise, from what we have seen previously, more of such prey species may well contribute to coyote abundance.

Some investigators of rodent-livestock competition have called to question the benefits or practicability of poisoning. In connection with woodrat studies, Vorhies and Taylor concluded that artificial control measures were unnecessary and would do no good on the open range. An 8-year job on rodents and rabbits at the New Mexico Agricultural Experiment Station indicated some benefits from control but it was concluded that the profits probably did not offset the costs.

The few studies that have been made of stock losses to predators have raised other questions. It is well known that popular reports in support of government control programs are not distinguished for be-

ing critically impartial. In a Utah investigation of coyote-sheep relationships, it was found that reported losses were about double actual
losses. On the San Carlos Indian Reservation, predation by coyotes on
newborn calves was shown to be related directly to the depleted range
and poor condition of the cattle.

The little research done is no adequate basis for understanding
what is taking place on western grazing lands. Yet it indicates that
the situation is not so simple as it has been defined, and it suggests
that good land-use practices might help to bring some measure of
harmony to areas where perpetual control now seems to be the rule.

Our chief concern here in regard to these programs is that control
for game-management purposes is regularly wrapped up in a single
package with the poisoning of coyotes and the hunting of cougars
for stock protection.

In some western states the political weight of stock-raising interests
has managed, by legislative action, to have state game funds added
to the support of predator-control programs carried out by the federal
government. State administrators have opposed this, questioning its
value to sportsmen whose funds were being pried loose in the name
of game conservation. As we have seen, there are good reasons for such
an attitude.

The most constructive thought that now can be offered on the
control impasse is that no solution will be forthcoming until a much
more serious attempt is made to unravel some fundamental biological
relationships. In the meantime the sportsman can be quite certain
that he has no need for indiscriminate control of the carnivores. His
problems are few and local, and they can be handled locally, after
proper study, by his own funds and personnel.

REWARD OFFERED

In connection with the assumed need for predator control, the long-
standing instrument for common action has been the bounty. Offering
a reward for the social enemy is something anyone understands (or
thinks he does) and the method is ideally adapted to mass resolution.

There is a long and historic record on bounties, which we have no
space nor need to review in detail. But even a hasty look at the evidence indicates why the bounty system is in such a sad state of dis-
repute among all who have studied it. In practical operation it has been

a means of subsidizing the taking of an annual surplus of predators that would be eliminated naturally anyway. With one or two possible exceptions (See note p. 373), it is unlikely that bounty payments ever have inspired sufficiently heavy hunting or trapping of a predatory species to clear away the annual "padding" and get down to the breeding stock.

De Vos pointed this out in discussing the wolf in Ontario· "It should be realized that only two pups in a litter must survive to reach maturity and breed if the population is to remain constant. Normally the surplus is killed off by disease and other factors. Apparently the effect of the bounty system is not great enough to upset the normal balance of the wolf population."

In ten years Ontario paid more than half a million dollars in bounties on wolves and coyotes, but the latter species went through its customary 10-year fluctuation and at the end of the period the total wolf population was greater than before. E. C. Cross calculated that to bring about an actual reduction it would be necessary to kill more than 30 thousand wolves at an annual cost of more than 400 thousand dollars.

He pointed out that in the face of a fairly stable wolf population and increasing numbers of brush wolves, the white-tailed deer had spread northward some 300 miles. "Not only have these deer penetrated this wolf infested territory, but they have established themselves there, increased in numbers and have continued to spread out in the very teeth of the wolf pack. . . . Failure to control or reduce the wolf population of Ontario at the present time is not a matter of any importance. It is a serious matter, though, that for many years a very large proportion of all expenditure which should have been directed towards bettering game conditions has been wasted in this useless harrying of the wolf."

Bounty hunters operate most intensively when profits are high—in the fall. The thinned-out population of spring would be more vulnerable to a really all-out effort, but results are so meager in animals taken that the effort never materializes.

The obvious answer to this might be that the rate of payment must be high in order to guarantee a profit for such work. But experience has shown that high payments only bring on "management" of the predator resource (by the liberation of females, etc.) and ingenious frauds of many kinds.

In an excellent bulletin on the fox, Clayton B. Seagers of the New York State Conservation Department evaluated bounties in this way:

"In the first place, large sums must be expended for bounties on foxes *which would be taken anyway* before a penny can be expended on foxes taken *because* of the bounty. Here's how it works. Assume that an average of at least 19,000 foxes have been taken *without a bounty* each year in New York for the past quarter-century. This would mean that a minimum of $57,000 would be spent on foxes which would be taken anyway. Since the *reported* take of foxes is estimated at from 20% to 50% less than the *actual* take . . . it is reasonable to assume that more than $75,000 would be spent uselessly, before bounty money began to cut any figure at all!

"To sum up, there's not one shred of evidence to indicate that the bounty system does anything but increase private incomes from the take of fox pelts at the expense of either the taxpayer or the sportsman's license dollar, according to who pays the bounty freight."

In 1946 a similar conclusion was reached with regard to the fox bounty in Iowa:

"It can be flatly stated that any reasonable fox bounty paid one winter will have little to do with the number of fox the next winter. For nature has wonderful ways of making up for winter losses until populations reach, or approach, maximum densities. (It is believed the fox in Iowa is reaching this point.) Then her methods of elimination are no less mysterious and spectacular."

The bobcat is another species which has been a favorite target of bounty fans. Actually, numbers of this animal in the East frequently have been too low to suit the snowshoe brigade who are learning to like the ring of hound music in a snow-clogged northern spruce swamp. Bobcat hunting is gaining as a sport rather than as a livelihood.

Vermont had a bobcat bounty of long standing, and in the 50 years following 1893, a total of $40,754 was paid out of the State Treasury for this purpose. At the end of this period it was evident that bobcats had not been reduced. A state biologist concluded, "There is no justification for continued bounty payments because the cat probably exercises no definite control over any wild game species in the state." It was particularly noticeable that when the Vermont bounty was reduced from $10 to $5, the bobcats bountied in that state decreased, but a corresponding increase occurred in New Hampshire where payments were higher.

In New Hampshire there also was an interesting variation in bounty payments on bears among the several counties involved:

"After paying a substantial bounty on bears for many years, the state treasurer . . . in 1894, called quits. In exasperation, he said that if the various counties continued to be successful in breeding bears for the bounty, in proportion to their tax levy, it would require a state levy of nearly two million dollars to pay the claims. Similarly, New York had a bounty on bears, but withdrew it half a century ago, not because such a bounty had become unnecessary, but because the number of animals killed increased steadily each year."

In Michigan the total of annual bounty expenditures grew from $232 in 1870 to $371,236.44 in only 9 months of 1922 and ". . . is a story of increasing taxation, indifferent disposition of public funds and fraudulent practices that can have but one ending."

With regard to illegitimate claims, the state's Biennial Report for 1922 used vehement language:

"The payment of bounties for the killing of such predacious creatures as may be destructive to the wild life and domestic stock of this State had of recent years become so saturated with fraud, collusion and trickery that our legislators sought some means of substitution for this expensive and worthless system.

"Since 1869, there has been paid in legitimate and illegitimate bounty claims, the staggering total of approximately $1,117,160.42. In 20 years, from 1897 to 1917 the state paid bounties totalling $177,-507."

To the bounty already existing on the wolf, the legislature of 1897 added the wildcat and lynx. In 1917 the list was enlarged to include the fox, owls, hawks, and weasels. Two years later crows and woodchucks went on the blacklist. By that time it had become too rich for the treasury and in the legislative session of 1921 all bounties were repealed except those on the crow and woodchuck, and they were cut in half. With left-over claims the total bounty bill for 1920 and 1921, plus 2 months of 1922, was more than half a million dollars.

"A dealer in coyote pelts in New Mexico, solicited certain individuals in the Upper Peninsula who, as records attest, claimed and received thousands of dollars in bounties, offering these men coyote skins at $7.00 each. His letter stated:

'Upon recommendation of Mr. . . . . . . and of . . . . . ., I am offering you several coyote skins with scalps on, at $7.00 each. Other trappers in your territory are taking advantage of this, why not you?'

"Certain members of a train crew on the D. S. S. & A. Ry., are alleged to have made a practice of bringing into Michigan scores of coyote pelts from the Dakotas, Minnesota and Wyoming, which cost around $3.00 originally and which were sold to Michigan taxpayers at $35.00, the bounty thereon."

"Trappers of the old school openly boasted they never killed a female wolf or coyote if she could possibly survive the injuries sustained when trapped." One phenomenally successful "trapper" was investigated after the Boards of Supervisors of Iron and Gogebic Counties had paid him $5,000 in bounties in less than two years. His tangible assets were six traps and a partner. It was found that the two men had bountied 248 wolf and coyote pelts in four counties in nine months at a profit of $8,680!

Increased efficiency in the bounty business was evident in county catch records. In 1915 Gogebic County redeemed 27 wolf pelts, and thereafter the number steadily increased to 335 in 1920. In Ontonagon County the average verified catch for four years was 52. In 1919 claims were presented on 133. In 1920 the figure rose to 220 and in seven months of 1921 to 235. At that time the law was repealed.

"The history of the Michigan bounty law on predacious things is dotted with the work of those who padded bounty orders, manufactured woodchuck scalps by sewing ears on pieces of pelts, collected bounty on housecats claiming them to be 'wildcats'; of substituting blackbird heads for baby crow heads; of claimants stealing from township clerks the once bountied and discarded scalps and heads, of others who purchased Wisconsin weasel, where no bounty is paid, and collected a bounty in Michigan on them, falsely swearing they had been captured in this State."

Our capacity for learning is called to question by the fact that in 1958 Michigan paid $226,700 in bounties. In the fiscal year 1958-59 the Game and Fish Protection Fund faced a large deficit, necessitating cuts totalling $75,000 in research, public fishing sites, and lake and stream improvement.

The Pennsylvania bounty system is justly famous and notable, as it has continued without interruption since 1683. This despite the fact that Pennsylvania experience and research have given the world some of its most clear-cut information on the futility of bounties.

In 1913 the Commonwealth established a hunting license and provided that collections were to constitute the Game Fund, half of which was to be set aside for the payment of bounties. Payments were first made by County Treasurers, but this gave rise to such unbelievable chicanery that the act was repealed.

In regard to this early phase, Joseph Kalbfus, executive officer of the Game Commission, made the following statement in response to an inquiry from Michigan, "Pennsylvania repealed the bounty law (1915) because so many frauds were perpetrated that payment for bounties became a burden upon the State. There were so many unfair and unjust claims that those controlling our State funds realized that unless something was done in the matter of bounties, our State would become bankrupt . . . I have gone over the claims made for bounties in several counties of this State and believe that I am safe in saying that one-third of the amount paid has been deliberately stolen."

In spite of this repeal, surcease from bounties was not to be. In 1915 a new act made the Game Commission solely responsible for payments and provided that all expenses involved were to come from the Game Fund. This left the baby on the doorstep of the Pennsylvania sportsman who, in the biennium 1958-60, still supported it with a payment of $214,610.

Perhaps the most important benefit of this program was the analysis of its effects by Richard Gerstell, published (creditably) in a Commission bulletin in 1937.

The record of payments in the 20-year period from 1915 to 1935 indicated a total bounty expenditure of $1,879,600, of which 63 percent was for weasels and 24 percent for gray foxes. The trend of payments for weasels by 5-year periods was as follows:

1915-20	36,816 weasels bountied
1920-25	49,029
1925-30	54,707
1930-35	68,423

Total payments for weasels (20 years) $1,209,500.

Gerstell's comment on this was that ". . . it appears that the bounty system has not to any noticeable extent, if at all, controlled the weasel even though two-thirds of the system's cost has been expended in payments on the species. A summary of the control effected by the system on each of the species involved would seem to indicate that as a predator control measure, the payment of bounties has proven generally inefficient as it has placed under control only one relatively small species population [the bobcat kill was down to 97 animals in 1935-36], while its effect on five others has been negligible."

As to future events and what this long indoctrination had done to the thinking of the sportsman, he divined correctly that ". . . the system has educated the public to the necessity for predator control. Unfortunately, this may prove an ill-directed and misspent activity in which vast amounts of time, money and energy have been wastefully expended, while if instructed in a deeper knowledge of animal ecology, those same forces might have been far more gainfully employed by all concerned."

In spite of this report, representing an investigation supported by the Commission, bounty payments in Pennsylvania went on. A summary in 1948 showed that in 28½ years the cumulative total of such expenditure had reached $3,377,043, which represented nearly ten cents out of every dollar disbursed from the Game Fund. For the first half of the century the sportsmen of the Keystone State contributed more than 1½ millions in subsidizing those who harvest the annual crop of weasels—a species which can have but little, if any, effect on the bag of game.

Disillusionment over the bounty system came early to the State of California: In the 80's there had been a welter of county bounty laws disagreeing in form and substance. As is usual in such cases, the bulk of the business was going to counties paying the highest rewards. Also true to an oft-repeated pattern, the counties appealed to the state for a uniform system and, incidentally, for a footing of the bill.

The legislature complied and enacted a law setting a price on coyote scalps in March 1891. As early as July of the same year there were objections. In the San Joaquin Valley an overproduction of jack rabbits was thought to have some connection with the reduction of coyotes. Also there was some discontent over payment for scalps shipped in from Mexico, Arizona, Nevada, and Oregon.

After nine months it was reported that $101,495 worth of coyote scalps had been purchased at $5 per. The unforeseen magnitude of the operation caused a move in the legislature to overhaul the law, cutting the price in half and providing for the witnessed destruction of scalps. But the law did not pass and the payments went on. In June 1893, when the total expended for coyote rewards had reached $187,000, the State Board of Examiners reneged. There had been no appropriation for the bounty binge and the state was feeling the pinch.

But hard-earned claims were still outstanding for a total of $129,000 and others were coming in rapidly. The collection of scalps had become a smoothly operating interstate industry and it was evident that there would be an imminent need for some hundreds of thousands of California dollars to redeem the crowning glory of coyotes from all over the West. Early in 1895 the governor used his authority to sign a repeal bill and stopped the business.

There were renewed efforts in the legislature to have funds provided for payment of claims made prior to the governor's moratorium. In 1901 a measure passed providing for restitution to petitioners bringing suit within one year. The claims had gravitated to a few individuals and in 1902 the superior court in Sacramento entered judgment against the State for $126,505. Other courts made similar awards, but the money was not forthcoming until the Supreme Court handed down a decision in September 1904 compelling the State to settle claims in the amount of $287,615. The total cost of coyote bounties between March 1891 and June 1893 was a neat $475,000. Thus did the coyote, for a time, control California.

In March 1944 Utah passed a new bounty law that allowed payment on all animals taken after September 1943. Up to August 1944 the cost was more than $70,000—of course not counting administration. It was a curious fact that 71 percent of the predators presented for bounty were taken in Utah counties bordering other states. Conspicuous exceptions were two counties adjoining Wyoming and Colorado but not readily accessible from those states. The interior counties were heavily populated with coyotes but stockmen there were hiring their own predator-control agents. Paid hunter-trappers of the Fish and Wildlife Service noted a large increase in thefts of traps and animals in 1944 when the law went into effect. In 1943 in the Salt Lake City district 61 trapped animals were stolen, and in the year following the figure was 255.

Based upon the law in Utah, a uniform 10-state system of bounties was proposed for the purpose of ironing out discrepancies and reducing interstate commerce in redeemable carrion. However, the public was becoming informed.

The plan called for a tax of 25 mills per dollar on sheep and 10 mills on turkeys in order to provide funds for a $6 bounty on coyotes and bobcats and $15 on wolves and mountain lions. In Utah an additional 5 mills on sheep and 2 mills on cattle was allocated to organized predator control. Thus the total levy on Utah sheep was 30 mills.

The records of the Nevada State Sheep Commission showed that the state's 452,881 sheep were worth $2,370,913. A tax of 30 mills on this amount would yield $71,127.39 as a bounty fund that would provide payments on 11,854 coyotes and bobcats. However, private fur trappers were already taking more animals than this, and hence a tax subsidy of the amount planned would add nothing at all to the control effort.

The realistic outlook of the average trapper in managing his bounty-fur resource was fully appreciated by those who would be paying to maintain the industry. A businesslike view of the plan was taken by the president of the Nevada Wool Growers Association:

"Naturally the individuals engaged in taking predatory animals for bounty are interested only in financial returns and arrange to harvest the surplus predators with the least possible operating effort or expense. It is poor business for a trapper to take coyote pups or adults during the spring and summer months for $6 when the same animals can be bountied and in addition yield a prime pelt worth from $6 to $10 during the fall and winter months. The successful fur or bounty hunter governs his activities to perpetuate his income, at all times husbanding his resource and being careful to preserve an adequate breeding stock which, from his standpoint, is good herd management. To the man engaged in this occupation coyotes are potentially of greater value than sheep and the production cost much less, for the gross returns from a prime coyote will amount to about $14 ($6 bounty plus $8 per pelt).

"It is neither good judgment nor good business for a trapper to devote any considerable effort to taking a few coyotes that might be causing serious damage on a lambing or summer range, for the cost of such work is in excess of the financial return. It is far more profitable to crop the surplus in the fall when furs are prime. Under such a plan the wool grower, in effect, is contributing lamb, mutton, and funds to a competing industry.

"Nevada has had a bounty system and wants no more of it. Many instances of hunters releasing female coyotes and other abuses could be cited. One might be related as typical. In eastern Nevada some years ago, a fur trapper was employed by a group of sheepmen and permitted to retain the fur. This man took a great many coyotes yet there was no apparent reduction in sheep losses. However, when he was later replaced, his successor took 27 pegleg coyotes in sixty days, of these 23 were females. This indicates that the first hunter was releasing females to assure a sustained yield of coyotes."

There are few phases of wildlife management on which the conclusions of investigators have been so much in agreement and so positive. Some states thought they had progressed beyond the use of bounties, but in the early forties the carnivores were building, continent-wide, to a peak of numbers. Legislators had not heard of wildlife science, and a rash of new and bigger rewards on foxes, coyotes, wolves, and lesser beasts broke out across the nation. In 1959 a nationwide survey showed that the laws of 31 states still made provision for the payment of bounties on predatory mammals and birds.

During this last resurgence of the system some enlightened sportsmen's organizations opposed the use of their funds in this manner, and in a few cases (notably New York) they made it stick. But the issue still is with us. Conscientious leadership will need all the facts it can find to oppose a bounty dip into their conservation treasury. A wealth of information is available, and if they review it they probably will find it easy to agree with Gerstell in his conclusion that "it is as yet impossible to prove that any system of general predator control can properly be included in a sound and comprehensive wildlife management program."

Unfortunately the bounty is well adapted to the needs of the poorly informed, politically minded administrator or the table-pounding fireball in a sportsman's club. It is likely to be used, and once it is entrenched, the profits enlist loyal supporters.

As for our general outlook on the question of whether to control or not to control, we must judge individual cases on a basis of a full understanding of the biology and economics involved. There is no single rule around which all right-minded citizens can rally. The answer, as we have seen, is sometimes (locally and temporarily) yes, but more often (and in the long pull) no.

And it's likely that this always will be the answer.

PART III

The method and the outlook

CHAPTER 16

Lead Kindly Light

THE view is widely held that a body of knowledge becomes a science when its facts are a reliable basis for predicting the future. In other words, wildlife management will be a science when we know enough about it to call our shots in growing wildlife crops.

It's fair to estimate that by the middle of the 20th century we did have a science on our hands. Its birth in the late twenties marked the end of an era of taxation without representation for renewable resources. The new era employs the concept that the condition of such resources is a public concern in order that maximum taxation without deterioration shall be possible. Not only are we coming to appreciate and preserve the goose that lays the 14-carat eggs, but we see profit in feeding her vitamins.

Any review of action management in our first half-century provides abundant evidence that, more commonly than not, the results of past programs were not predictable. Our thought-up remedies were misapplied to ills we could not even diagnose.

The improvement of knowledge came partly through unfortunate experiences with the intuitive approach. And the rest of it came largely by virtue of a well-conceived but faltering research effort.

There are three stages in the acceptance of an idea, says C. Leonard Huskins: first, we do not believe it; second, it is of no importance anyway; and third, we knew it all the time. In wildlife affairs we have seen this sequence repeatedly, but we have seen also that as each new truth finally batters its way into the public mind, it wears away a bit of resistance for the one to follow.

It would be difficult for anyone to deny that ignorance, specific and general, is basic to most of our conservation troubles. Authorities have long agreed on this. When Harold Titus was to retire (temporarily) from the Michigan Conservation Commission in 1936, he admitted to deep discouragement: "I am overwhelmed by the magnitude and ramifications of the problems which confront conservation authorities, State and Federal, and bowed down by the conviction that not until many years have passed—perhaps the span of generations—can we in America hope for a *continued and general* betterment of conditions for Nimrod and Angler." The first obstacle to better fishing and hunting, he stated, was "biological, ecological ignorance."

In one way and another we seem to have established the principles of wildlife management, but how successfully we apply them will depend upon detailed know-how which only high-quality investigational work can produce. It is clear that range improvement usually will represent the best approach to the problem of larger populations of game and fish; but in order to doctor habitat ills for a given species in a particular part of the country you must be able to define the important local characteristics of good range. What has been done in other types will help, but it is seldom that a pattern of management can be transported very far without clipping the corners and fitting in a new piece here and there.

This accounts for the almost never-ending need for investigations, studies, finding-out programs, follow-ups, or whatever else they have to be called to get them approved by people who would shy away if they were frankly referred to as "research." That's what they are, of course, and in the 20th century A.D. such subterfuges shouldn't be necessary.

It is an odd fact that, with the "scientific age" all about us, many otherwise astute individuals pride themselves on a kind of "hard-headed realism" that won't see through any technology more complicated than a double-play and which tends to write off the scientist as a chair-warming academician. They would feel much better if it were possible to stick to the simple system of yesteryear under which the answer to every conservation problem was another hatchery, a bounty, or to import something. It was a case of all cats being gray in the dark.

Frequently enough, the wildlife brand of biologist is just a guy who liked hunting and fishing so much he found a way to make hard work of it. Many such men today have had not only their technical training but 10 to 30 years of highly "practical" experience. Their opinions are not all theory. They are far from having the solution to

plenty of our quandaries, but they do have *the means of learning
whether or not there is a practical and satisfactory solution.* The all-important tool, of course, is research.

It is, unfortunately, true that many technically trained people are
so thoroughly channeled in their own interests that they are unable
to back off and relate their corner of scientific thought to other
branches of knowedge. More especially, they are likely to become so
dependent on the idiom of their specialty as to be incapable of putting
what they know into terms that an average citizen can comprehend
without danger of cerebral hemorrhage. The greatest threat to public
enlightenment is the scholar, enamored of long words and abstractions,
who writes to please himself, assuming that those who fail to follow
are mental pedestrians unworthy of concessions. A minor example,
perhaps, is the catchy lead of a lively government bulletin on life-climate relationships:

"Bioclimatics," it says, "is a science of relations between life, climate, seasons, and geographic distribution. It deals with fundamental
laws, principles, systems, and methods of application in general research and economic practice, and has special reference to the major
and minor effects of the major astronomic and terrestrial laws of
causation, as represented by the variable phenomena of life, climate,
and seasons, relative to the geographic coordinates as expressed, measured, and interpreted in units of time, temperature, and distance."

If, betimes, wisdom comes slow to the people, and if they harbor
untoward suspicion of the man of science, or him so identified, it
might be possible for one with sympathy and understanding to assemble materials and make out a case for them.

PILOT PROJECT

Wildlife investigations are the means of keeping the cost of our
failures down. They are small-scale trial-and-error through which we
develop methods and try out our theories before applying them in
large operational projects. Every state and the federal government
have carried out ill-advised programs that went wrong and resulted in
lost time, money, and resources. Much of this could have been avoided
by foresight and modest appropriations for research.

Control programs, far and wide, are perhaps the best example of
operations without benefit of investigation. Insecticides and herbicides

are being spread willy-nilly over land and water without any prior knowledge of whether their harmful effects will not be greater than their benefits. It is only since 1958 that the federal government has had a reasonable effort in this field—largely as a result of the fire-ant fiasco in the South.

Predator control has long gone forward at its face value, any real appraisal being either avoided or ignored. Elsewhere we have noted how the Pennsylvania bounty system has continued without interruption despite the findings of a competent study which showed it to be practically worthless to the sportsmen who have paid for it. In regard to a situation in Ontario, E. C. Cross had this to say:

"The relationships of wild animals are exceedingly complex. The problems of game management and general wild life management of Ontario can only be solved by intensive studies in Ontario. If the money now being used in 'wolf control' were to be used in finding out what our natural resources in fur and game need, and meeting that need, it would return dividends instead of deficits."

Charles T. Vorhies, long an authority on the relationships of range fauna and flora, made this thought-provoking statement at the Second North American Wildlife Conference in 1937:

"Notwithstanding the real need for rodent control which appears often in many places, it is a little disturbing to note that such control was exercised on 32½ million acres in 1935-36. I certainly have no means of estimating whether this was 50 per cent necessary, 75 per cent necessary, or 100 per cent justified. But I have seen in my own region some extensive control which I do not believe was either necessary or economically justifiable, and I do know that such work has been proposed on the basis of 'something to do' for CCC Camps. At the risk of drawing fire it might be suggested that if the control division of the Biological Survey were itself placed under a bit more of the control which might be exercised as a result of coordinated life history and ecological research we might see a better balanced program in relation to range wildlife." With the advent of vastly more lethal toxicants since the early forties, the need for evaluation and studies in range ecology is even greater than before.

The difficult position of the Forest Service in attempting to carry out their complex mandate on the management of millions of acres of land for watersheds, timber, wildlife, and grazing is evident in this statement made in *A National Plan for American Forestry*, in 1933:

"One of the greatest handicaps, if not the greatest, is the insufficiency of scientific data on which management can be based. There is need to know more about the extent to which the important species of vegetation can be grazed without injury; how depleted ranges can be restored most effectively and most rapidly under use; what adjustments in normal stocking of ranges must be made because of recurring droughts, or critical timber, game, or watershed situations; and many related questions. These all involve intensive research, pending the result of which we must of necessity resort to trial and test."

To this day, the magnitude of this problem in land-use ecology has not been faced and an adequate research program provided for.

When we considered the periodic coming and going of certain game and fur animals in the North, one fact stood out above all others: We can expect a recurring disaster that will reduce this primary wildlife crop by millions every decade—but no research effort yet mustered has been equal even to explaining the cause of these tremendous losses.

With reference to one species, Kimball indicated that the pheasant depression in the Dakotas resulted from factors which prevented the production and survival of young (also true elsewhere). "If a small fraction of the millions of dollars lost because of the pheasant decline had been spent studying these factors our problem would be nearer solution." If we multiply this situation by the many species probably participating in the northern game cycle, it is beyond doubt that a boat has been missed somewhere.

These big, broad problems are everybody's responsibility and therefore no one's. The history of our stocking programs is another story of operations without investigation. For lack of any evaluation there is a record of large-scale and expensive bass stocking in Wyoming dating back to 1881. In 1938 the State Fish Warden asserted that in spite of this long-continued effort, only four lakes were known to contain bass in numbers great enough to permit fishing.

"Sportsmen continue to demand bass fishing in waters which are obviously not suited to this warm water fish. The general failure of bass in Wyoming is of special significance because, of course, it indicates that bass are not adapted to most of the supposed bass waters of the state, and points out the tremendous amount of effort wasted in attempting unsuccessful introductions."

It is almost needless to indicate that the suitability of such waters for bass could be determined by nearly any fishery graduate for a relatively nominal expenditure. Such men were not easily available, of course, in the early period of the work. Another pertinent fact is that sportsmen would not have been pleased by the answer. Research biologists probably would be more popular if it had not been their duty to report that many a trusted cure-all wouldn't work!

We will have to face this. In the words of Iowa's fish and game chief, Bruce F. Stiles, "The aim of research is to know the truth. Even unwelcome truth is better than cherished error, and the welfare of our wildlife resources depends upon the extension and diffusion of knowledge."

Many a fact turned up in our "finding out" will need to be filed to await the additional truths necessary to give it meaning and practical use. This is the long-term view, and sustained progress and efficiency will depend on its adoption. However, much of the gain in theory and basic biology will be accomplished not by deliberate plan but in the process of tussling with our immediate problems. The word "research" to some signifies something abstract and theoretical, but in the wildlife field much of the effort is going directly into things the sportsman is asking for and about.

It was the investigations of TVA fishery biologists that demonstrated the excellent sport fishing available in those waters during the spring months and also the fact that fish populations could hold up well under a year-'round open season. Eschmeyer pointed out that "the research which led to an increased catch of several hundred thousand pounds of fish in Norris Lake in 1944 paid . . . dividends."

Considering that these studies were the forerunner of liberalized regulations and bigger fish crops throughout the South, and to a considerable extent in the North, the results assume even greater significance.

Along these same lines, a neat bit of investigation in Nova Scotia pointed the way to better salmon fishing:

It was found that the catch of Atlantic salmon in rivers like the Margaree is related to spring freshets. The rise in water level permits fish to leave the ocean and pass shallow tidal estuaries into the stream.

This introduced the idea of creating artificial freshets and inducing a run of fish according to planned schedule. This could be done, under some conditions, by the release of impounded water.

On the Moser River a trial of the method worked. When temperatures were not too high, the creation of small but sudden artificial freshets resulted in double the expected numbers of both salmon and brook trout entering the stream and gave good angling.

This is a kind of research that requires little selling to fishermen.

THE MEANS

In Chapter 3 it was evident that many of the successful or promising management techniques involved in habitat programs were developed or discovered in the course of investigational work. Their further refinement will depend largely on the continuation of such sifting of facts and testing of ideas.

The distinction frequently is made between long-term, "basic" research and short-term "practical" studies. To some extent this is realistic. The first implies a steady searching out of information which will fill the blanks in our knowledge of the lives, habits, and requirements of important animals and the composition of environments. This is the process by which we learn enough about a given species to make intelligent guesses as to what might work in the way of action management. The trying out of such theories in short-term (if possible) experimentation is usually looked upon as practical. Nearly everyone agrees that both types of inquiry are needed.

In the United States, research on wildlife * problems is done principally in state conservation departments, colleges and universities, and the Bureau of Sport Fisheries and Wildlife. To a lesser extent it also is supported by private institutions and individuals. Cooperative projects have tended to erase the lines of cleavage and give all agencies

* Somewhat tardily we might point out that the term "wildlife" may be used to cover all animal life. In the sense that is coming into wide usage, however, it refers most specifically to birds, mammals, and fish—i.e. the groups of greatest economic interest. The plan sent to President Roosevelt in 1935 for consolidating the Bureau of Fisheries and the Bureau of Biological Survey called for a new agency to be named simply the "Wildlife Service." In deference to those who thought the Bureau of Fisheries was losing identity, the President added the words "Fish and," thus creating what to many is a redundancy in the title. In 1956 the service was divided along the old lines into two Bureaus—Sport Fisheries and Wildlife, and Commercial Fisheries.

something approaching a common front in getting the job done. Two developments have been of chief significance in this respect:

The program of the Cooperative Wildlife Research Units represents a combined effort by the Bureau of Sport Fisheries and Wildlife, land-grant colleges (where the units are located), state conservation departments, and the Wildlife Management Institute.*

The purpose of the units was fourfold: (1) to train competent men in the wildlife field, (2) to conduct research on wildlife resources, (3) to promote public education in wildlife management, and (4) to provide technical assistance to state wildlife agencies. The units have distinguished themselves in carrying out these functions and have added to wildlife literature a long succession of reports, bulletins, and papers on the results of investigations on management problems in the states concerned.

Another development of critical importance was passage of the Federal Aid in Wildlife Restoration Act (Pittman-Robertson Act) in 1937 and the Federal Aid in Fish Restoration Act (Dingell-Johnson Act) in 1950. Under the "PR" program returns from the 11 percent manufacturer's tax on sporting arms and ammunition are held in the treasury until appropriated by Congress for disbursement to the states for wildlife restoration purposes. "DJ" funds come from a similar (10 percent) tax on fishing tackle.

States must match the federal money in the proportion of 1 to 3, or 25 percent. Apportionment in the wildlife program is made on the basis of land area and hunting licenses sold. In the fish program the basis is total water area and the number of fishing license holders in the state. The Bureau of Sport Fisheries and Wildlife is charged with administration of these acts and has a Federal Aid Branch to handle the job. States submit projects consisting of land acquisition, development, maintenance, surveys, research, and administration. The Bureau reviews such proposals for conformity with the law. As of 1960 tax collections and appropriations to the two federal aid programs were running about 20 million dollars per year, of which roughly 15 million was for wildlife restoration and 5 million for fishery projects.

This work is lumped into four categories by federal aid administra-

---

* A non-profit, private organization supported by industries, organizations, and individuals. Its objective is to contribute to national welfare by promoting better use of natural resources.

tors, and in the fiscal year 1960 projects approved for the states and territories under the Pittman-Robertson program were as follows: land acquisition—273, land and water development—298, investigations—207, coordination (administration)—46. The federal report stated that "Investigational projects were active in 48 States and all the Territories and constituted 26.7 percent of program obligations. . . . Fruits of this research effort in 1960 were 362 publications covering the diverse activities of this wildlife program."

A similar summary of fishery work indicated 42 projects for land acquisition, 97 for land and water development, 110 for investigations, and 42 for administration. Of the investigational projects, many comprised overlapping functions. A total of 81 included survey and inventory work, and 61 the evaluation of management techniques.

There is some question whether year-to-year surveys, commonly a basis for regulations, should be classed as research at all. It is likely that well over half of the "research" being done by state fish and game agencies is in this category. It could more properly be called "management inventories" or something similar, since the terminology used tends to give the public (and commissions and legislatures) the wrong impression of how much is going into the development of new knowledge in the wildlife field.

The federal aid programs provided a much-needed stimulus to all kinds of investigations in the states. At the time the acts were passed, some states were doing no research at all, whereas all of them have such programs today. The quality of the work depends much on the quality of the supervisory and field personnel that can be hired under existing salary scales—in other words how much the employing agency is able to pay for the intensive academic training and years of experience that the best men bring to bear on research problems. Salaries for investigators frequently are low, just as they are for the men who hire such personnel.

Civil service organizations commonly fail to appraise and rate research positions realistically, and this has been a serious impediment to administrators. Many a wildlife research man has gone into other allied fields when he found it no longer possible to advance in his chosen discipline. The cause of wildlife conservation does not, in these cases, receive the full benefit of money spent for training a man. To be perpetually breaking in new trainees, only to lose them when they become most valuable, has been a source of inefficiency and discouragement to the directors of conservation programs.

A measure of the importance accorded to wildlife research in the federal government is found in any annual budget. The appropriation to the Bureau of Sport Fisheries and Wildlife for 1959 showed these amounts under "Management and investigations of resources":

Management of fishery resources	$4,365,050
Extension and training	169,700
Fishery research	517,000
Administration of wildlife resources	3,281,825
Control of predatory animals and injurious rodents	2,053,000
Wildlife research	1,058,875
Soil and moisture conservation	205,950
River basin studies	840,100

We get a bit more perspective on these figures by checking the breakdown under the various headings. "Management of fishery resources" is practically all for the fish hatchery program. In addition, about half of the fund appropriated for fishery research is for *propagation* research. Relative to the generous item for predator and rodent control, at the Senate hearings the Director of the Bureau indicated that western states and private agencies would be making an additional contribution of $3,200,000 in 1960. It is notable also that about a quarter of the wildlife research funds were for *control methods* research.

In both state and federal wildlife programs it is evident that basic research on population mechanisms, environmental relationships, and habitat manipulation—that is, ecological research—is one of the last items to be supported. In times of stress it is one of the first to be cut.

Considering how little is known about some of the large operations now in progress, a striking disproportion is evident. Eschmeyer properly evaluated the situation when he stated: "It is easier to plant fish, to make laws and to introduce exotic species than it is to determine whether these activities are sound conservation. Likewise, in connection with environmental improvement, the most recent factor in fish management, it is easier to install an 'improvement' than to determine whether that 'improvement' is beneficial or injurious."

It is characteristic of the resource-management field that research needs seldom are recognized until some crisis is at hand or a large developmental program is under way. Then the investigator is called to counsel on problems which he has had no opportunity to study. Leopold was impressed with this fallacy in 1937, and it is with us in undiminished proportions today:

"Half a dozen New Deal bureaus are spending a score of millions on wildlife work, but not a red penny for research. They come to some research unit whose total budget would not pay their office boys and say: 'Please give us the facts on which to build our program.' Naturally we can't. Nor could we if we stood with them under the financial cloudburst. Facts, like pine trees, take not only rain, but time."

THE METHOD

When research is up for a hearing, questions frequently asked are: "When will it be finished? When are we going to be satisfied with our answers? How long must investigations continue?"

The scientist's reply is without apology. Only in minor matters will it ever pay us to stop looking for more knowledge and better ways of doing things. In any large and continuing enterprise, efficiency demands the maintenance of some form of investigations—indefinitely.

In resource management, this need is pressing because applied ecology (the science of relationships between living things and their environments) is a relatively new branch of study. The natural laws and principles applying to it will be elaborated steadily and the end is not in sight. For that matter, the same can be said of the oldest provinces of human endeavor. Mathematicians, physicists, and chemists are nowhere near the end of their accomplishment. The limitless mysteries of the universe undoubtedly were in the mind of Vannevar Bush when he called science "the endless frontier."

In spite of many fine accomplishments, there is little doubt that wildlife science is having research troubles. Most of these stem from misconceptions of how research is done and what to expect of it. The administrator is a key man in the picture, and if he knows what is right and fights for it, the chances are good that his showing will be creditable. It will be well, however, to face the fact that he is not a free agent. He is responsible to commissioners who only rarely are scientists and to a public who are much more impressed by action than by technically sound policy.

Much of the field research now being done on wildlife problems is in the hands of men at or near the bottom of the pay scale in their organizations. They are men just out of college, many with limited graduate training. Under supervision of high professional caliber, they would pay off. They could learn the inscrutably critical application of the scientific method that is the mark of a good research man.

They seldom have such leadership. They are on their own, and the wonder is that they do so well. But in the main, such a system results in many a beaten path being trod again and old facts being paraded under a new coat of varnish. The investigator is financially insecure. Within a few years he will have acquired family responsibilities that lead him out of fact-finding into better paying positions in administration or management. Then a new crop of trainees takes over.

A common fault in handling research men is the inclination to use them as extension agents and in trouble-shooting. A few such assignments lead to more, and before he is aware of it the investigator has been converted to an errand boy or public relations specialist. But on the budget, his job still is charged to "research."

There is a discernible feeling among some responsible officials that one whose business is wildlife research should spend every day cruising the land amassing "records." Notes are something that can be written up evenings, and final reports can be prepared week-ends after the party of the second part has been shifted (frequently with little warning) to a new, and "hotter," assignment.

The result is that even good studies may never be written up or only sketchy, perfunctory reports filed. Publication of a technical paper is out of the question. In a few instances the results of field studies have been deliberately suppressed and publication forbidden because the findings were contrary to existing policy. Occasionally, also, a job is carried out the conclusions of which appear to have been reached beforehand by a sort of deliberate incompetence. Fortunately, this sort of thing is not common. Most of the mistakes are honest errors—the result of immaturity in conservation agencies. And here and there we see a high standard of performance, toward which the whole field, we hope, is developing.

To speed up such development we should understand how good research is done and how it is administered. The selection of men with proper training and aptitudes is the first requisite. There are differences in individuals, and many a good man will not do a good job of research. What the investigator has is mainly a state of mind. In the words of Charles Kettering, "It is the problem-solving mind as contrasted with the let-well-enough-alone mind. It is the composer mind instead of the fiddler mind. It is the 'tomorrow' mind instead of the 'yesterday' mind."

In their book on *The Organization of Industrial Scientific Research,* Mees and Leermakers (of Eastman Kodak Company) described the results of questioning the directors of a number of laboratories in regard to what they considered of prime importance to successful operation in this field.

Morale of the staff was considered to be the most important single factor, with cooperation between workers second. The authors' further remarks are of special interest:

"Perhaps the two most important factors in maintaining high morale of the laboratory staff are as follows: (1) Recognition of the individual's accomplishments by others, either within or outside the laboratory. Men should be permitted to publish their findings in order to build up their scientific reputations, since those interested in fundamental research usually receive recognition in this way. (2) Adequate salaries for scientific work. Scientific men should be rewarded as well as the men in the development, production, and sales departments of the company. Practical results are more easily appreciated than fundamental science, but if fundamental research is to be carried out, it must be attractive financially. This situation is now recognized in most large laboratories, and policies are established for paying as much to scientists doing successful fundamental research as to men in administrative positions or in developmental work." *

In regard to the latter point, keeping a good man working in a given region on a given set of problems will be worth all it costs. Ability and experience will be our best investment over the long haul. We need mature judgment and imagination to get at the inner workings of the natural world.

Such a man must be a top-flight scholar. He must have good library facilities and time to use them. He must have time to study his data, work them over in many different ways, and write them up. Before he

---

* Reprinted by permission from *The Organization of Scientific Research,* by C. E. K. Mees and John A. Leermakers. Copyright 1950. McGraw-Hill Book Company, Inc.)

is through with a given assignment, he will have spent at least an hour in the office and laboratory for every hour spent in the field. The man who does not is slighting the drudgery part of his job, but that is the part that makes his field work profitable. Unless he is exceptional, writing is the hardest work he will be called upon to do.

Many a wildlife problem will need the team approach. It will require the combined knowledge of men with such specialties as birds, mammals, plants, pathology, soils, and others that fit a particular problem. The ecologist puts all of these specialties together, but he can't know them all. Part-time work by some personnel, and cooperation between agencies may go into the forming of a research team.

Several years ago an editorial appeared in *Michigan Conservation* defending the state's game research work. It quoted an official of the United States Rubber Company who indicated that only about two percent of the research done by that company paid dividends. But that two percent, he said, "is what keeps United States Rubber in business. The company which does not carry on incessant research is headed for the rocks."

Likewise, we should not expect every wildlife inquiry to result in some momentous discovery. But surrounded as he is with unknowns, a good man nearly always turns up usable facts, and it is likely to be that way for a long time to come.

To boil it all down, progress in wildlife conservation will require the best research program that can be organized. It is essential, and we cannot afford the time and money wasted in second-rate performance. The era of guesswork management is past.

Trails into the unknown are broken in one way: We need to get the best man available, and then give him time to think. With Davy Crockett, we must first make sure we are right—and then go ahead.

CHAPTER 17

Biopolitics

IN many a state sportsmen and other conservation-minded people pridefully point out that long ago they removed their fish and game affairs from the political arena. And on every side we see that good progress has been made; yet, it must be admitted, this is a relative matter.

There was a period when each time an administration was overturned, all personnel down to the last warden packed up and went home to await the return of democracy. Today there are few places where such primitive abuses are possible. But it will be interesting to ask two questions of any conservation administration: (1) how do management policies originate? and (2) how rapidly can they be applied? A complete answer to these queries is likely to reveal that procedures are not so objective as we might have supposed.

The deer problem is a case in point. By the middle or late thirties, states with the largest herds had employed technical staffs to work on deer. These men quickly saw the dangers in overpopulation and the proper function of the gun in preventing it. There was good background material to draw upon, and this, plus local investigations, brought about a relatively good understanding of management; but almost without exception, deer specialists have worn out their welcome asking for the privilege of doing this, their logical job.

It is to be suspected that within a few years we will see relatively good deer management in nearly all parts of the country; but today there is many a forest area where these animals cannot be cropped realistically because research and management are not operating on the same shaft. In some states it still is true that investigations are being carried out by technical game agencies, but *deer are being managed by the legislature.*

Of course, the legislature has access to data collected by any state agency; theoretically, on such problems they should be able to come out about as well as the Conservation Commission. The trouble is, they are not geared to work at that level. Their multiplicity of issues and the speed with which these must be handled preclude a good job on minor year-to-year matters such as regulation of seasons and bag limits. Of necessity, legislatures are alert to attitudes, but they are incurious about unpopular facts. There has been a common and superficial public prejudice against shooting does and fawns. There-fore these sacrosanct creatures have not been a part of the game harvest, even though a sketchy review of available information will show that they are dying of other causes anyway.

Some would say, "But this is the will of the people as expressed through their representatives. And, after all, isn't that democracy? Do we want it to be any different?" That is persuasive logic, but we're in shallow water and we'll move out a way before we anchor. Take another example:

At the federal level, the Fish and Wildlife Service has been dele-gated responsibility for fixing regulations on migratory birds. In large degree, this has been an effective system. The plume hunters, whose atrocities have become legend, are no more. The punt gun, formerly used in the mass killing of waterfowl, has been eliminated even on Maryland's eastern shore. Largely through a widespread public inter-est in birds and the cooperation of local enforcement agencies, our songbirds are no longer used for target practice or hunted for the pot. These things we take for granted, but they did not come about by chance.

A few years ago, at a Maryland waterfowl meeting, a federal judge indicated publicly that he would not enforce a statute against shooting of waterfowl over baited grounds because he believed it did not have the support of "the people." And, encouraged by this, at the same meeting an assertive young lawyer arose and asked in effect who these dictator-minded federal bureaucrats were to tell "the people" how they should or should not hunt ducks. "Let's vote," he said, "and decide whether we want to kill the ducks or not. They're our ducks, and if we want to shoot them, why not?"

That would, undoubtedly, be the will of *some* people, just as *some* of the people would never kill any deer. But reflection suggests that public officials who have been given a job to do—even though it involves reducing the kill of waterfowl or liberalizing deer regulations —represent a prior interest and the prior intent of *all* the people. A judge and a lawyer might, conceivably, be right about certain details of management, but no one has given them that responsibility. Meetings can be packed and rigged, and the rights of those not present are easily forgotten.

To put it somewhat differently: Has not the ultimate and studied will of the whole public had its rightful expression in the creation of an agency and a system for (1) gathering technical data on technical questions and (2) using this information to formulate and administer regulations? Such agencies were created by representatives of the people in Congress and in legislatures, and their budgets originate through those same representatives.

Conservation agencies will not always be right—as has been demonstrated frequently—but over the long haul, if the system is at all reasonable, it is quite likely that they will work their way through to the truth of our issues and equate our conflicts more efficiently than can be done purely on a public-opinion basis.

METHODISTS ALL

We gave the public-opinion system a thorough trial for several decades and, by hindsight, the pitfalls now are evident. Looking at our wildlife-conservation record we see that it would be difficult to imagine a field more ideally adapted to misconception, sloppy thinking, ham science, and professional four-flushing. In spots the program still is such a confusing mixture of crudity and technology that the most sophisticated professional must hump to keep his sorting up to date.

When wildlife affairs first were brought under regulation we had no technology, and one man's opinion was about as good as his neighbor's. For long there was a prevailing conviction that "anyone can run a fish-and-game program," and most of our untrained administrators did it on a part-time basis. Theoretically, they should have got along well simply by giving people what they demanded, but the system could not guarantee even this.

An important weakness was that segments of public thinking frequently disagreed; hence, one could be played against the other when there was a deeper motive in by-passing an important issue. As we have seen, this was the situation that made possible the frittering away of our tremendous buffalo resource, and Hornaday was at some pains to publicize the facts:

"The slaughter of the buffalo down to the very point of extermination has been so very generally condemned, and the general Government has been so unsparingly blamed for allowing such a massacre to take place on the public domain, it is important that the public should know all the facts in the case. To the credit of Congress it must be said that several very determined efforts were made between the years 1871 and 1876 looking toward the protection of the buffalo. The failure of all those well-meant efforts was due to our republican form of Government. Had this Government been a monarchy the buffalo would have been protected; but unfortunately in this case (perhaps the only one on record wherein a king could have accomplished more than the representatives of the people) the necessary act of Congress was so hedged in and beset by obstacles that it never became an accomplished fact. Even when both houses of Congress succeeded in passing a suitable act (June 23, 1874) it went to the President in the last days of the session only to be pigeon-holed, and die a natural death."

We aren't advocating that our democracy be changed for a monarchy, nor did Hornaday. But it seems evident that if there had been an agency in the government with the delegated authority to guard and manage this resource—an agency of competent, career professionals —it is unlikely that even the Secretary of the Interior could have brought about the destruction of the buffalo to accomplish a political objective (subversion of the plains Indians).

Another drawback to the system was that the people were easily hoodwinked by sharp operators. Frequently they were sold a pig in a poke and then even forgot to look for the pig. Of this we can cite an amusing example from across the water. Human nature, it seems, is the same everywhere.

In the nineties, gray partridges were not doing well in England, evidently owing to a series of bad-weather breeding seasons. People thought the birds had "inbred" (a nonsensical notion that rears its head frequently in this country), and decided that new blood should be brought in from the plains of Hungary.

The demand for "Hungarian partridges" was good, and for a number of years a dealer in Holland did a vigorous business. He made connections with a receiver of poached and stolen partridges in England who was getting native birds but was having difficulty in marketing them. An arrangement was made whereby the English gray partridges were sent to Holland and transferred to the kind of baskets used on the continent. Then they were shipped back across the channel as Hungarians and liberated to improve the blood of the supposedly degencrate native stock. Evidently it worked, for English partridges have since had periods of obvious prosperity. No doubt the originators of the importation plan were well satisfied with their scheme.

From the very beginning of organized effort, people have displayed a particular gullibility in regard to the reward system of predator control. There always has been a St. George-and-the-dragon element in this which made the payee feel good. Likewise there is an undeniable charm in the simplicity with which an onerous problem can be resolved merely by placing a price on the head of an unpopular scapegoat. Under the ruse of the predator bounty millions of all-too-scarce wildlife dollars have been siphoned away as a subsidy to trappers and others who found it a convenient aid in living off the land.

The bounty was one of the three tools in the kit of the amateur game and fish manager. The others: artificial stocking and the importation of exotics. All three achieved an almost unassailable standing in the public mind. They were taken for granted for so long that it became almost heresy to question them; and they have had a strong carry-over into the period of our attempt to convert to a scientific basis of operation.

The game and fish regimes of the twenties turned to the help they had for advice and counsel. Their old-line game keepers and fish culturists were skilful artisans who had learned, through long apprenticeship, the trade of rearing game birds and fish. In public utterances they did not hesitate to interpret their (frequently excellent) turning-loose efforts in terms of on-the-land management, game in the bag, and fish in the creel. They got away with it because we, the sportsmen, did not know where their livestock-rearing knowledge ended and their ecological ignorance began. They didn't either, and they reacted instinctively against anything that appeared to call their art to question. No doubt you and I would have done the same; but the effect of it all was to put the biologist in a difficult position when he arrived on the scene and found things that needed to be changed.

The old-line political administrator had a job with inherent difficulties that we are only now beginning to realize. He had little to draw upon—except opinions on every side. He developed a fairly characteristic pattern for getting along. When fish were plentiful and game prospered, he pointed with pride. He modestly told the sportsman what a magnificent job he (the sportsman) had done. Since the latter knew, or suspected, that he personally had not done much, it followed by implication that someone had been on the job and there was an obvious place to put the credit. When something went wrong, the fish and game majordomo viewed with alarm, in public and repeatedly. He pounded the table and swore mighty oaths that all records would be shattered. He asked for more money, rolled up his sleeves, and his hatchery men went to work.

In our early efforts we stumbled onto some outstanding successes— like the importation of the pheasant and the transplanting of the striped bass. Our greatest failures were where they are today, in the routine management of native species on native range.

Public opinion and guesswork could not hope to handle such things, for the people, like their first administrators, were not trained for this technical job. They saw only the surface of conservation problems and were concerned almost totally with *methods* rather than with ground-level causes and effects. Sportsmen, game and fish administrators, legislators, "nature lovers," and many another category of would-be and well-intentioned wildlife promoters thought like poorly informed human beings and not like the creatures they were trying to manage. They did what others had done before them with little reflection as to whether it worked or not. They cherished slogans and obvious answers. They tolerated the spending of a minute portion (if any) of the conservation budget to learn the hows, whys, and wherefores. When things went wrong they forgot any real progress and revived the old panaceas "just to be sure." If the picking stayed lean, they went after somebody's scalp. When nature smiled, they beat each other on the back and took credit for a "grand job."

It would be a grave error to categorize too much or to generalize too broadly. *Any method* may, tomorrow, find a proper place for a time in a sound technical plan. But most of our expensive and profitless wrangles arise because a few people insist on applying the same old cure-alls to the same problems long after it has been amply proved that they do not work. Sometimes the technical man has no certified alternative; but if he knows what will not produce results, he believes that this knowledge, too, should be applied and that there is better chance for success in trying something new.

INEXACT SCIENCE

Most of what we look upon as political is a hang-over of our way of doing things 30 years ago. And in judging this, it is a natural tendency to take the most advanced system as a standard. But in a degree that we are likely to overlook, 30 years ago still is with us.

In 1946, at the North American Wildlife Conference, the late E. Sydney Stephens, pioneer of American conservation and chairman of Missouri's commission, gave a revealing analysis of the status of state conservation agencies. They could be judged, he stated, by the use of seven criteria: Adequate legal authority, employment of trained personnel, the development of wildlife environment, education, practical research, cooperation with landowners, and the support of citizen organizations.

On this basis, he found that "Twenty-five are lacking in adequate legal authority to administer wildlife resources or to regulate their use . . . Sixteen states employ no trained technicians whatever, or are not better than 20 per cent equipped or manned. Fourteen give no attention to the improvement or development of environment. Twenty-one carry on no cooperation with any group or individual. Fourteen make no effort whatever in the field of education, and twenty others do not claim to be more than 50 per cent efficient in that vital field; none is more than 70 per cent efficient. Twenty-three, or practically one half of the states, do not carry on research of any kind. Nineteen do not cooperate with any landowner or land-use agency. Five states maintain no forestry departments . . . Twenty-three complain of the absence of adequate support of organized groups.

"By these standards, the departments of 12 states are less than 25 per cent efficient, and 30 rank below 50 per cent; and only 5 have a 'passing' grade of 60 or better. The 12 states which rank less than 25 per cent efficient collect from sportsmen and expend $2,345,100 annually. Since they are so pitifully deficient in the application of so many sound practices; since they are expending money for outmoded and even detrimental practices; since they are dominated by politics, the money which they expend is wasted—all to the detriment of wildlife. They should be painlessly but promptly put to death. The next 18 might be given a stay of execution on their promise to reform."

This was a state administrator speaking—one of many years experience and one universally respected. His considered judgment was supported two years later by an even more detailed survey and study of the Wildlife Management Institute. They compiled a chart of functions and operations of State Fish and Game Departments, and it showed that only seven departments had as many as 85 percent of the functional and administrative requirements for effective operation. Thirty states were found to have less than 75 percent of the basic operating essentials.

Since that report there have been years of progress. But even today our grounds for optimism are a scattering of high-quality programs rather than mass achievement. Pressure groups still rule—sometimes in states where conservation functions have long been well organized. The pressures that cause trouble, of course, are those generated in favor of outmoded and unsound ideas. And these frequently come from intelligent people who have been highly successful in other activities. They do not realize that wildlife management is quite as complex as medicine or mechanical engineering, although we are far behind those fields because of a general failure to insist on the technological approach.

A detailed appraisal of our failures would lead a pessimistic critic to conclude that, conservation-wise, the affairs of state are in a sorry state of affairs. Yet we see steady changes for the better and new and encouraging marks on that chart of the Wildlife Management Institute. People with vision and a will for progress want to see the right thing done. In past chapters we have reviewed many of the foremost issues and tried to indicate the direction taken by our most enlightened programs. We know well the slogans of the amateurs and the biological cheesecake that pleases them. In this field the genuine politician is not hard to identify.

He is in a difficult position, for this is an era of change-over from wildlife-management midwifery to professional practice. The true politician wants to be eminently practical, so his every value tends to have a dollar sign. He wants credit for embracing all that is new and scientific, yet would wish to hang on to all that is old. He manages to be for everything and hence nothing, to say yes and then again no, and end up on that safe, sane, and inoffensive middle ground of neutrality where we waste *only a part* of our money "just to be sure." He stands resolutely for progress, yet he feels that "there will always be a place for" anything that can't be dropped easily, however useless. When the chips are down, he is for the things that he knows will win friends and he hopes will influence wildlife.

Politics, it is said, has been at the root of many resource abuses. One can hardly disagree with that. The path of conservation has been a rocky one, and we suspect that this cause might have been hallowed by the bones of a few more martyrs along the way.

But where does politics begin and end? In looking for the greatest good for the greatest number, our representatives sometimes sell into servitude legitimate values dear to the hearts of an intelligent and conscientious minority. Maybe they don't want to do it, but it's the lesser evil. Even more commonly, they may know what is right, and best for the majority, but *the people don't know any problem exists.* The mail and the pressure say do the wrong thing and, perhaps regretfully, it gets done. Is that politics?

What we call politics, as applied to wildlife and other resources, probably refers most commonly to the action of the man who does what he knows to be wrong because he would lose personally if he did otherwise. Sometimes he is right in saying that the public are not "ready for it." Then we must ask, is he telling people what is right? He may be overcautious and refuse to take any risk in the interest of progress.

However we reason it out, we must come back to the basic truth that it is the people themselves who play politics. It is your money and mine that pays for the support of fact-finders and administrators in governmental agencies. When pressure groups urge a particular idea, and year after year bedevil commissions and legislatures to override systems of management supported by study and good technical data, we have the commonest kind of politics. It can stall progress and cost us much.

It places a heavy responsibility on the citizen that he has an essential and unavoidable duty to pull for the right thing, and that he will do serious harm if he pulls for the wrong thing. As Glenn L. Martin put it: "In the use of the power that is ours, let us be sure that our demands are just—that they are in the interests of true conservation, and are not born of desire for self-indulgence detrimental to the common good."

This is no suggestion that the people should in any degree give up control over their resources. It is only to emphasize that we probably can gain in efficiency by doing as the executive of a large and complex modern industry must do. We have the means of employing competent men to handle the specialties represented in resource management. We should be able to entrust details of the program to them.

Naturally, we will be critical in appraising progress, but the question we should ask the administrator is not, "What will your deer regulations be?" Rather it is the query, "Are your regulations on deer and all other management practices based on sound inquiry and the use of information from all sources? Are you hiring men on a basis of merit and then giving them a chance to do their jobs?"

An enlightened public opinion now can find its most constructive function, not in trying to make technical decisions, but in seeing that the administrative mechanism is adequate to do these things well and that it operates in a congenial political climate. Many an administrator finds that a major part of his time is taken year after year in explaining the same things to the same people and in defending his staff from abuse. When this becomes an important public liability, then counter-pressure, likewise public, is called for.

Said Dr. Gabrielson: "Sportsmen's groups can do the greatest service to their own interests and to the interests of America by insisting that their state conservation department be free from partisan and personal political interference, that it have adequate authority, that it resist ignorant pressures from hunting and fishing groups, that it have an adequate law enforcement staff, adequate personnel to make accurate inventory of game stocks each season and trained research men to work on its problems, that it have a sound educational program, and that it devote its funds to sound basic work to produce more fish and wildlife.

"Sportsmen have every right to demand this kind of a program. Once they get it, they should fight to see that personalities, selfishness,

and greed do not interfere with that program. In other words, a conservation department that is doing a good job should be backed even
if sportsmen do not like the way the commissioners wear their hair or
the way the wardens drive their cars."

Any group action on behalf of a principle or issue can be considered political, and in that sense we must have politics and never will
be able to separate it from our democratic process. The self-interested
kind of politics is finding the going more difficult each year. Increasing numbers of people are looking beneath the surface of wildlife
issues. The sportsman, in particular, is losing his horse-and buggy
outlook on management, and perforce the politician is finding that
sound programs are politically expedient.

The word "politics" will lose much of its sting, when the things
people ask for and demand from their representatives are largely for
someone else. Men will make it possible to use resources wisely by an
attitude of mind. As Carl C. Taylor put it, "There must be millions
of them who are willing to measure what they do by what they *ought*
to do."

WATERED DOLLARS

No one who has read the newspapers in recent years can doubt
that our wildlife affairs are involved in political and social events on
a national scale. One gathers at times that renewable resources are
chiefly significant for their nuisance value when someone is preoc-
cupied with making the desert bloom or harnessing a river to overrun
another wilderness with kilowatts. The native fauna and flora have a
faculty for getting in the way, to be stepped upon or stumbled over,
when there is a "waste" area to be "developed" or "reclaimed." With
each great boondoggle, it seems, some fish or game asset is sideswiped
by someone bent on something he defines as progress, and left to
expire unnoticed. Maybe these are just impressions—or are they?

The great and lamented expansion of government since the mid-
thirties certainly has been no overgrowth of *real* facilities to investigate, administer, build up, and protect such national property as soils,
watersheds, range, forests, national parks, sport fish, birds, and mammals. In fact, when blanket cuts and reductions are made, the skin-
tight budgets and limited staffs that represent such functions shrink
still more, and that leaves the way a little more open to those whose

thinking has an ever-current date line and to whom "production" has become a fetish and an end rather than a considered means.

In the thirties it was common knowledge that a life-long conservationist, J. N. Darling, had resigned as chief of the Fish and Wildlife Service so he could work effectively, immune to the threadbare accusation of personal interest. In 1945 he swung hard at conditions that have perennial parallels:

"The Soil Conservation Service in the Department of Agriculture is the most valuable custodian of our No. 1 precious natural resource and is headed by one of the greatest authorities [Hugh H. Bennett] on land use and sound soil management in the world. His Service was cut to the bone in appropriations and personnel three years before the threat of the present war made such a sacrifice necessary.

"The U. S. Forest Service was without an authorized head, leader or chief for about two years, while the morale in that great agency of conservation fell to the lowest ebb in 25 years.

"The Fish and Wildlife Service . . . under as sturdy and able a conservation leader [Ira N. Gabrielson] as lives, has been so crippled by cuts in its personnel and appropriations that maintenance of many of its restoration and refuge projects will have to be curtailed.

"Economy? God bless it, yes. But one-fifth of the cost of the abandoned Passamaquoddy power project or the Florida Ship Canal would be more than all these curtailed conservation agencies ever dreamed of spending in their most ambitious years. And the so-called Florida Ship Canal, condemned by every scientific authority as more damaging than beneficial, is still on the authorized project list of the Administration."

In regard to "democracy" it is well for the thinking citizen to have his own standard and his own definition. These days the word is found in strange places. The same is true of "conservation." People who could not lick it joined it. Especially in connection with great reclamation developments, biological principles applying to the human population and its living standard are being ignored in favor of local and temporary dollar gains. In many cases what someone calls "expanding the economy" may well result in a new and precariously situated concentration of population, a reduction of living space, social problems, more pressure on all resources, and a depressed level of living.

Visionary? Yes, by common standards. The hooker is that there are ecological phases of the population-resource problem that are not being handled by ecologists. Such ideas as too many people or too much development are easily dismissed as fanciful. The logic against them may be persuasive. When a biological concept is stated by someone who does not understand it, the result frequently is ridiculous. When stated by someone who does not *want* to understand it, it is always ridiculous.

The average citizen may not know, nor does it matter much, that the government reports of conservation programs in which wildlife figures prominently would make a respectable library. But if he did know it, he might naturally assume that there must, somewhere, be a national plan for resource use and development in which such things as fish, mammals, and birds take their proper place.

It would surprise many to learn that there is no such plan nor any early prospect of having one. It would take a much larger book than this to review the present status of our important national wildlife issues. But we can see where we stand, in terms of politics and economics, by a brief look at one of them.

At Minneapolis you can take a plane across one of the great historic game lands of the continent to Spokane, Washington. The early part of this flight is along the border between North and South Dakota, and on a clear day in summer the traveler sees orderly sections of tawny wheat that stretch out from one horizon to the other. From 18,000 feet this doesn't look like duck country—but it is. This is the heart of the prairie breeding grounds, the "pothole country," that yields an important share of the continent's annual crop of blue-winged teal, pintails, mallards, shovellers, gadwalls, baldpates, and several other species.

The potholes are a feature of the country that immediately impresses the air traveler. The land is speckled with them, some dark and full of water and others that appear as smudges in cultivated land. The latter have been drained.

For many years it has been known that drainage in the prairies was destroying (as in many other regions) important waterfowl habitat. Under the potholes there is fertile soil—much of it washed from the surrounding upland. To cultivate it for agricultural crops is profitable once the water is gone.

These prairie depressions collect water from the snow-melt and hold it into summer. Where soils are "tight," it stands. During the great drouth of the thirties, farmers sank wells in their dried-up potholes—sometimes these were their only source of water. When that ruinous period gave way before increased rainfall and high wartime prices, they were ready to make the most of it. The forties were a period of faith, hope, and parity; and many potholes were converted from the raising of ducks to wheat, flax, and barley.

Drainage became easy through organized government assistance. The Soil Conservation Service was giving technical help to locally organized soil-conservation districts. A part of their function was to give appraisals of the agricultural potential of any land, wet or otherwise, and to make plans for drainage if it was practical from the standpoint of the farmer.

The farmers found that 60 percent of the cost of draining a pothole would be paid for through the agricultural subsidy program of the Production and Marketing Administration (later the Agricultural Conservation Program). The government guaranteed $1.90 a bushel for wheat, and the cost of a drainage project could be cleared in a year or two. Wheat filled the elevators and piled up in huge golden mounds on the ground. It went into the holds of retired Liberty Ships. But the farmers could not lose, and they grew wheat and more wheat.

This organized destruction of one resource while we overproduced another received national attention in 1949, when Clay Schoenfeld, of the University of Wisconsin, described it in an article in *Field and Stream*. His inquiry revealed that many resource authorities in the region realized that pothole drainage was not in the national interest, but in the face of dollar realism they could do nothing.

Generally favorable water levels in the early fifties tended to obscure the effects of drainage, but drought conditions were back again in 1958. In following years the situation deteriorated, particularly for diving ducks that nest over water. By 1961 the canvasback and redhead were in dire distress.

The "pothole controversy" has continued to be one of our most bitterly fought wildlife issues. The slogan, "Save America's Wetlands" was the theme of the National Wildlife Federation in 1955. In the prairie states citizen's organizations were raising funds to buy (a few) potholes. Congress allocated all of the revenues from the new 3-dollar

(1959) duck stamp to the acquisition of wetlands. A national small watersheds program was gaining momentum. The Department of Agriculture was retiring land from cropping under the the Soil Bank program—and "retiring" potholes from duck production in favor of more crops. Estimates of the wheat surplus in 1961 were 1.6 billion bushels. Each year Congress calmly ignored suggestions that drainage subsidies be discontinued.

The position of the average citizen is our present concern. His duck hunting was whittled down another notch. He paid for the technical plans and surveys that told a farmer what his pothole would grow and how to get the water off. He paid for much of the drainage through the beneficence of ACP. He paid for the piled-up wheat. He paid high prices for flour and bread. He also paid for the buying and flooding of land elsewhere (through his duck stamp purchases) to replace in a small way the duck habitat that had been drained.

The question is whether, in a period of footloose economics, when it is decided (somewhere) that an outpouring of tax dollars is in order, we must blindly stockpile one commodity when another, much in demand, is further reduced. Could we not benefit the farmers—and the public—more effectively by paying for the keeping, even reflooding, of potholes?

Such things are not possible under our present system, because there is no national mechanism for deciding what is in the interest of the whole public. At cabinet level the functions of government already are specialized, and it has been demonstrated beyond any doubt that, however good their intentions, bureaus with conflicting missions (such as drainage versus the creation and preservation of duck habitat) cannot decide at field level what is good for the nation.

This is the strategy that should be planned in higher headquarters. Only with such planning can the tactics of operational programs be completely effective. Unfortunately, in the higher echelons of government, politics is more important than good biology or good economy. The failure to provide sound guidance is evident in recurring wrangles between field staffs who try vainly to resolve questions of local versus national interest. In all such cases the most dollars will win, and people who represent such resources as wildlife seldom have anything but a principle to back them up.

Government agencies, of course, do not appropriate funds. That is done in the Congress by representatives of the people. And they do it because the people demand it. Some of our best authorities on resource management are in government bureaus; and some of our most conscientious and hard-working conservationists are in the Congress. But we still have no national plan. Pressures are in other directions.

A design for resource use would not be easy to make. It would require the best professional thinking the nation could muster. It would need to provide for change; but values in terms of *national need* could be placed in their proper order and guide lines for management and development created. It would need to be executed outside all political creeds and considerations. Some day this must come about, but how soon?

Certainly this is no suggestion that we have more of the kind of regional planning that projects impossible details far into the future, completely dissociated from the reality of budgets or organizational lines of cleavage. Only the rough outline of the future resource program can be sketched realistically, but its motives and principles could be defined. The crux of its operation would lie in the creation above cabinet level of a small, non-partisan commission to serve as a review board in resource issues.

Few would deny that we need a simplified, effective resource Magna Charta. But those who might formulate it now would be faced with a particularly difficult decision. We still have a few forests uncut which took half a millennium to grow. We have certain marshlands still undrained. We have dam sites (these are limited) still unused. We can collect certain types of interest on these as they now are. How much of such capital should be kept as a reserve for the future, possibly against national emergency? In case of real need we could liquidate all, but should we do it short of such need?

We have skimmed the field, and we can only indicate what might be found by a closer look. It is a certainty that wildlife as a public asset is being neglected, and that this is so because the people themselves have been taking it for granted and failed to make it an issue. Many of their representatives and their employees want only support to change this. When enough people make their will known, there will be changes.

CHAPTER 18

We'll Call It Yours and Mine

YOU and I own two kinds of property: that to which we have title as individuals, and that which we hold in community. Our tenure in both cases is acknowledged to be temporary.

It is an American tradition, with legal substance, that wildlife is a public possession even though it occurs in part on private land. Obviously, an individual landowner is under no compulsion to harbor or protect this common property if he chooses to do otherwise. It's a curious situation, and one of which the implications grow more difficult year by year.

Where are we to hunt and fish? The signs say "No Trespassing," and they multiply like rabbits. Where are we to camp and hike and picnic and just be alone? This year it's fenced. That used to be a lake; but the county drained it and now it's producing onions. Here was a boulder-strewn field, a corner of woods, and a spring; now there's a house, an acre of old automobiles, and a gravel pit. Wildlife belongs to the public, but so, perhaps, does the moon.

The continent is filling up with people. For three centuries Americans thought their patriotic mandate was to "develop" everything. They looked with suspicion on any idle resource or unoccupied space. But the past thirty years has changed all that irrevocably.

We have come to realize that many of the things we own in common must be as vigorously defended as what belongs strictly to you or me. We have seen such possessions, undefended, melting away before our eyes. There is nothing from coast to coast, of any value whatsoever, that someone whose slogan is "private enterprise" does not want. Where to draw the line on personal ambition and assert the claim of public benefit? No lawgiver ever endowed us with this one. We are working it out the hard way, but if it takes too long there will be nothing to decide. Those will win who git thar fustest with the mostest men.

309

At this stage of our inquiry it should be evident that wildlife will be managed for a greater contribution to our standard of living, or it will dwindle like the snows of yesteryear, according to what is done with land and water. In the last chapter we got an inkling of the great drainage issue that so vitally affects our hunting, trapping, and fishing. There are other similar issues that need recognition, and their handling for better or for worse hinges directly upon what we do or permit to be done on the real estate that is yours and mine.

In some cases it will be evident that certain assets are of the nation and of the ages. No one is likely to buy the Grand Canyon or the General Sherman tree; but conceivably an Indiana woodlot or a patch of Iowa prairie might have the same kind of public worth. Posterity, to be sure, will never do anything for us; but, on second thought, *we are posterity,* and there are grounds for suspecting that something is being done *to* us. As a nation we are being forced into responsibilities which require us to take a more-than-animal interest in the portion of the earth which we hold in trust. For, much as many people disdain the idea, as a species we are not immune to the kind of biological alternative that can be seen in many a western sheep range or northern deer yard.

Toynbee's scholarly study of world history gives little emphasis to a fact which grows on the inquiring reader nonetheless. The minds that manned the twenty "civilizations" which have disappeared or fallen into decay in the course of the human chronicle thought *politically.* In the mass flow and clash of populations we see responses to powerful *ecological* thrusts, but men had no background and perception to think or plan that way. For some it would have been no cure had it been possible, but for others it probably was a fatal weakness.

As we have seen, our own planning is largely political; and the dimension that deals in quantities of resources and numbers of people is waiting for recognition. It's a biological dimension, and an understanding of it is best grounded in the study of lesser creatures. Man is given the intelligence, though perhaps not the humility, to learn therefrom.

KEEP OFF

Up and down the land, wherever there are cities and large numbers of hunters, an issue has sprung forth with the certainty of sun-

The beautiful, deep-throated trumpeter swan, once on the verge of extinction, is staging a dramatic comeback on the Red Rock Lakes Refuge in Montana. In 1935 there were 73 of these splendid waterfowl in the United States; census figures for 1958 show a tenfold increase in numbers, to 735. (Fish & Wildlife Service.)

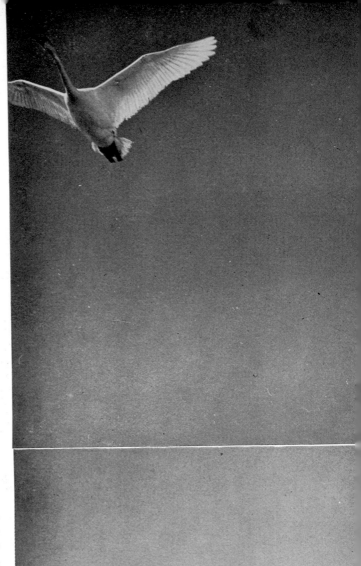

The supreme grace of bird flight: trumpeter swans on the wing, Red Rock Lakes Refuge, Montana. (Fish & Wildlife Service.)

Protected remnants of the once mighty bison herds that once swarmed over the North American continent. (Photo by the author.)

Mule deer browsing contentedly on winter range, Malheur Refuge, Oregon. Such a herd may increase by half every season. Below, a group of Rocky Mountain bighorn sheep in Colorado. This wild species suffers from strong range competition with livestock, elk, and deer. (Fish & Wildlife Service.)

A "big burn" on Snow Creek, Washington. In primitive times such burns were the home of the deer, rabbit, and quail. (Fish & Wildlife Service.) Below, a contour orchard in Berks County, Pennsylvania, showing diversion terraces and a farm pond for fish and recreation. (Soil Conservation Service.)

Above, left. Salmon jumping the falls in breeding time, Brooks Falls, Alaska.
Their needs are worth considering when we build dams across their spawn-
ing rivers. (Fish & Wildlife Service.) Below, what stream pollution by sugar-
beet wastes did to thousands of fish that deserved a better fate. (Fish &
Wildlife Service.) Above. In Michigan more than 2,500 deer are bagged each
season by those who, like champion archer Paul Jeffries, prefer to hunt
them with bow and arrow rather than with the gun. (Rex Gary Schmidt.)

Looking back over the trail leading to Charleston Peak in one of our national playgrounds, the Nevada National Forest. (Forest Service.) Below, a young follower of Izaak Walton waiting happily for a pull on his line along one of Wisconsin's "unimproved" streams. (Soil Conservation Service.)

rise. They call it "farmer-sportsman relationships," and it is reputed to be a perplexing and controversial situation. It is, no doubt, but it will be less so when we have dismembered it and looked at the parts.

Too many hunters tramping across any man's property, or unwelcome conduct by a few, will bring forth the signs that say "Keep out." It is the inevitable defense of you or me, whether we be farmers or not. It is the reaction of any city sportsman who buys a place in the country.

In terms of our American definition of property rights this seems to be fitting and as it should be. The conception of wildlife as a public asset stems from the days of few people and little competition for game and fish. No one has advocated strongly that the legal ownership of wild things should be changed—we have enough inherited conviction to keep that as it is. But such proprietorship never has carried with it the privilege of entry other than by consent of a landowner. Many troubles have grown out of the tendency of hunters to contest the basic and legal right of one who owns a piece of land to determine who will use that land and what will be taken from it.

There are places where this has given rise to genuine management difficulties. Extensive damage by too-plentiful deer has been a discouraging liability on many forest-edge farms and estates. Large levies on the game fund have been used (perhaps not wisely) in some states as compensation for such inroads. But when half the battle is won and regulations are liberalized, reduction of the herd through legal hunting sometimes is thwarted by great blocks of closed land. The signs have gone up in Michigan's orchard country, New Jersey estates, and other areas far and wide. Pennsylvania's former law permitting counties to abrogate state regulations prevented the reduction of deer where a cutting back of numbers was an economic imperative.

It will progressively become clear to individual owners that, for their own protection, they must find a means for the orderly cropping of big game. We can be confident that if legislation fails temporarily, the deer themselves can be relied upon to bring a meeting of minds and a way out of this particular trouble. But with small game the situation is different. The failure to hunt usually means only a wasted crop and dissatisfied hunters.

This is the real farmer-sportsman problem, and it is inherent that the burden of solution is on the sportsman. He needs good relationships if he is to be granted the favor he requests, and it is logical that he should take initiative in bringing this about.

The unhappy truth is that there are few places where a farmer has anything like adequate protection from vandalism. The more hunters there are, the more hoodlums there will be, and there need be only a few to precipitate the extensive closure of property. Surveys among farmers indicate that there is little objection to the hunter who hunts by permission only. There is rankling aversion to the climber of back fences.

Large and responsible state sportsmen's organizations are steadily assuming a more important role in American conservation affairs. They are not pressure groups in the old sense. Their leaders are not the fanatical and ill-advised go-getters of former years. Through lengthy and intelligent committee work, they are bringing study and analysis to technical problems, and they are coming out with understanding and sound policies. It is a new approach, and it is here.

It seems inevitable that the burden of leadership in creating better farmer-sportsman relations will devolve upon such groups; and they will need to recognize responsibility for deeds of the hoodlum even though he is not of their number. A first requisite to free entry and public hunting on private land is *easy and adequate protection for rights of the landowner.*

In 1950, the legal situation in the United States and Canada was surveyed by Seth Gordon, later Director of the California Department of Fish and Game. He found that only 13 states and provinces had laws prohibiting shooting close to buildings and that there was evidence of less land posting in those which gave the landowner this protection. Only 11 of the reports indicated that laws made possible adequate punishment for the destruction of property or personal injury. Just 21 had laws against the carrying of loaded firearms in automobiles. In only 5 could a field officer seize the license of a violator, and in 17 the administration had no power to suspend hunting privileges of violators.

There is widespread evidence that our legal mechanisims are far from adequate and that this is endangering our only means of harvesting game crops on private land. Trespass laws, in particular, should be so stringent and so well enforced that a farmer who needs protection and assistance can get it easily and quickly.

Much emphasis is rightfully being given to enforcement of game and fish laws. The poacher and the game hog, we are told, are taking a wildlife crop that belongs to you and me. But in terms of total populations and annual increase, the *n*th degree in cutting down such violations makes available much less game than is going to waste on closed or lightly hunted land. There is reason for thinking that trespass laws with teeth, sponsored by the sportsman, and with efficient enforcement for the period of the hunting season, would make available more game for legal hunting than any other single measure that we could back.

You can't make a man do anything, says Dale Carnegie. So it seems to be the logical and workable approach, if we would harvest wildlife surpluses on private land, to give an owner the legal status he wants and to which he is entitled. Then we can go to him, recognizing hunting for what it is—a privilege.

To face it, no such program is going to be the sportsman's message of redemption. It won't provide the shooting needed by thousands of gunners near New York, Detroit, or San Francisco. But it would mitigate a growing evil that bids fair to eliminate *all* free hunting in such regions. We will have to acknowledge that when people concentrate there are certain things they won't have in their backyards. If they would hunt, many of them will have to go where the hunting is.

The question of where to hunt is only a part of the greater yen of Americans for wild-land recreation. The "great open spaces" are no longer so great, and they steadily become less open. Florida is being ringed with cottages. The traveler to the north finds guides with union cards, metal boats, and motors. (We don't begrudge them that; we merely point it out.) Bannock gives way before the advance of Bisquick (which is better, of course) and sourdough is fading into the flavorsome past. All this we can, and must, accept as progress.

It is fair to ask, do we need to keep some country free of commercial clutter where there is half a chance of catching a big fish, seeing an eagle, or hearing a wolf howl? And should we have places, not too far from home, where, like Garbo, one can just be alone?

If we want such things, we'd better get them now. A few people still can afford to buy such luxuries for themselves, but privacy comes ever at a higher price, and personal wealth is no solution for the bulk of us. The question is, what land and how much should be dedicated to the casual (as opposed to intensive and private) use of all the people?

As a part of the answer, many states now are buying public hunting grounds and access sites on fishing waters. The game areas are officially and primarily "for wildlife restoration," and as such their purchase and development usually come under the federal-aid (Pittman-Robertson and Dingell-Johnson) programs.

A century ago, in eastern states, the settlers of new lands sometimes bought them sight-unseen, or they failed to interpret correctly the significance of forest types. They homesteaded soils that couldn't last in crop production, so they went out of business and their farms either reverted to public ownership in lieu of taxes or were held for other purposes. In large part it is such areas that now are being converted to public use. On the maps of land-economics surveys they are labeled "Forestry and recreation." Wildlife is important in the recreation part of it, and a calculated forestry program is essential to creature management. A prominent feature of such public game lands will be the impoundment of marshes, ponds, and lakes. These can hardly lose in the increased production of waterfowl, fur, and fish.

In the East we should get a good crop of forest game from these submarginal lands, and to the West the situation will vary greatly with rainfall and local fauna. With good management there is much we can do to better conditions for near-at-home hunting and other recreation, but it is true that the possibilities fall short of satisfying all requirements.

MEN AT WORK

Other public lands to which we as citizens hold title have a vital place as parts of the national playground. National and state forests of the East are well established in this function. Hunting, fishing, picnicking, sightseeing, and bird-watching (especially of spectacular hawk migrations) are an uncontested public interest in large stretches of landscape the length of the Appalachian mountain system.

In the West we have even more extensive holdings. For the most part it is the leavings of what was given away or sold at nominal prices. But that is not unique, for most of our private lands everywhere were at one time "granted" to someone. Rapid development was bought with a lavish giving away from East to West, and the policy produced a powerful nation in a phenomenally short time. Vast assets in timber, land, fur, and mineral rights went into the deal, and they lasted so well that a habit of thought developed with respect to national wealth. Lurking in the background of many a latter-day controversy is the hang-on feeling that anything owned by all of us is fair prey; and if it possesses tangible worth, it must eventually come in for a round of private ownership in order that the public sheep may be properly sheared.

Much in the news of recent years has been the case of certain western stockmen who hold grazing permits on public lands and who have attempted repeatedly to convert these, on almost a gift basis, into private ranges. This is by no means unique as a threat to our common property, but it recurs periodically and involves facts and issues which you and I need to know about. In this case the wildlife value is of key significance and the interest of the whole people seems clearly defined.

To get the background of it, nearly all land outside the original thirteen federated states was at one time federal property and was classed as "public domain." Roughly it has been 70 percent of our national acreage. Most of this passed into private ownership through grants, patents, sales, and military bounty. Some of it has been "reserved" by the government as Indian lands, national forests, reclamation lands, parks, game preserves, and wildlife refuges. The remaining public domain (lands not reserved for any particular purpose) now totals about 186 million acres. About 180 million acres of this lie in eleven western states, and nearly all of it that can be grazed has been used that way since the time of settlement.

In these same states, lands reserved from the public domain as national forests total approximately 134 million acres, of which more than 77 million acres have been used for grazing. The act under which a President is empowered to set aside actual or once-were (the usual thing) forest lands as "public reservations" was passed by the Congress in 1891. It came at a time when the complete wreckage of our native timber resource and the ruination of forested watersheds was in view. President Harrison reserved more than 13 million acres, and the process was continued by his successors. McKinley estab lished the Bureau of Forestry in 1901, which was renamed the Forest Service in 1905, and two years later the reserves became the "National Forests." Theodore Roosevelt, aided by his chief forester Gifford Pinchot, set aside 148 million acres.

National-forest lands were placed under federal administration and management to bring about two essential public benefits: (1) water-shed protection, and (2) timber production. A third interest, the grazing of domestic stock, was well established, and by a long and painful process it came under managment of the Forest Service.

During World War I, in line with the national need for meat pro duction, the already heavily grazed lands of the public domain and national forests were loaded with livestock. Stockmen demanded that national parks and game preserves be thrown open to similar use, and in a few cases they were successful. It is interesting to note that where this was done it required strenuous measures and about ten years to terminate the "war emergency."

The result of this onslaught was further widespread erosion and destruction of perennial grasses. Heavy stocking continued on into the depression period of the thirties, and conditions on the unreserved public domain reached a state of emergency, both for vegetation and graziers. The range was free and open to anyone. A Forest Service re port stated that "The serious conditions on it reflect the absence of management. A rancher must graze the range near his property as heavily as possible, from early spring till late fall, or year long if in the region of mild winters, in order to avoid having someone else crowd in on him. During the summer growing season 'tramp' herds may closely utilize feed that should, for the best interests of the in dustry as a whole, be reserved for winter. Such herds often come in and profit by whatever protection local stockmen have given the range."

The evidence was overwhelming that regulation of grazing on public-domain lands was an urgent necessity. No long-term policy existed for this national property, and a plan was considered under which such lands would be turned over to the states. It was rejected by the states themselves in 1932. Two years later Congress passed the Taylor Grazing Act.

In the words of its sponsor, Representative Edward T. Taylor, of Colorado:

"Overconfidence in plenty resulted in waste, which was followed by overuse of what remained. Free range and less grass resulted in poorer stock, economic loss, and loss of topsoil that will take years to replace. . . . We are all dependent upon this range in one way or another and have an interest in its proper use, management and preservation. . . . The public range, one of our vital resources, was being trampled to the dust through unwise competition and an utterly inadequate public-land policy."

In the title of this measure it was stated to be "an act to stop injury to the public grazing lands by preventing overgrazing and soil deterioration, to provide for their orderly use, improvement, and development, to stabilize the livestock industry, dependent upon the public range, and for other purposes."

The act provided for the establishment of grazing districts to be administered by a Grazing Service. Lands not in these districts would be handled by the General Land Office (agencies combined in 1946 in the Bureau of Land Management of the Department of the Interior). Both the Taylor Act and the Federal Range Code were written by and for stockmen, and the low fees charged amounted to a sizable subsidy for the minority lucky enough to hold permits on federal lands.

Fees for grazing districts were set at 5 cents per cow-month and 1 cent per sheep-month. The state received 50 percent of the fees collected in lieu of taxes, and 25 percent more went back to the districts for range improvement. Land Office charges averaged slightly less than 2 cents per acre, with a similar rebate. Forest Service fees were on a sliding scale and somewhat higher, with 25 percent returned to the states for use by counties on roads and schools. In addition, the Forest Service spent up to 20 percent of amounts collected in grazing fees for range improvement. Administration of all the grazing lands showed a substantial deficit in terms of collections accruing to federal agencies. From 1936 to 1943, expenditures by the Grazing Service alone were $4,768,681 more than the grazing fees available for administration. A similar situation prevailed in the General Land Office and the Forest Service at that time.

We will keep in mind that this subsidy out of the public treasury went, not to the entire livestock industry, but to a minority holding permits on public lands and that this gave them a distinct competitive advantage over ranchers operating entirely on their own property. Even the small fees charged were the subject of complaint, emphasizing that the grazing "privilege" (by federal statute) had come to be regarded as a right. Some estimate of its true worth is given by the fact that ranches sold by owners holding public-land permits have commanded a premium up to $100 or even more per head of cattle.

It would appear that the permit holders have had a fair shake, and better, but it has long been evident that they have more comprehensive ambitions. The shape of the program was well outlined already in 1926. An editorial in *American Game* entitled, "Impossible demands of stockmen," indicated plans being made for the public grazing lands:

"Demands are being made on Congress by the live stock interests of the West which, if granted, would undermine the very foundations of our National Forest and big game conservation structure.

"They ask for legislation that would give present grazing occupants of the National Forests and public domain perpetual property rights, inalienable and transferable, to the exclusion of all others and creating a private monopoly of the use of these public lands.

"They insist upon immunity from liability for all except *wilful* damage to all resources of the forests, including timber and game.

"They demand that grazing rights shall be granted on an 'area basis' which would preclude the United States government from safeguarding against over grazing.

"They stipulate that there be no further extension of present National Parks and that no new parks or *Federal Game Preserves* be created in the States of Arizona, California, Colorado, Idaho, Montana, Nevada, New Mexico, Oregon, Utah, Washington and Wyoming."

This attempt and others fell short of the ultimate accomplishment, but lobbies of the small organized group of big operators were perennially active in Washington, and they had a strong hand in the liberal provisions of measures taken to administer and regulate grazing. Many western stock associations have repudiated their machinations, and a relative few grazing permittees have had a direct part in the "land grab" move. Nevertheless, the promoters have never failed to identify their own interests with those of all cattle and sheep men and to cite the reduction of grazing quotas as imminent peril to the national economy.

Such reductions have been the only possible cure for the land sickness that long overgrazing brings about. In general, the paring down of grazing quotas was done more slowly than strict adherence to public interest would have dictated, but in carrying out this duty employees of the Forest Service, in particular, have been subjected to unbelievable personal abuse. Even their children have felt the stigma of community resentment. Yet recuperation of the range was for the ultimate good of the graziers themselves, if they had any long-time motive. Studies have shown repeatedly that the best production and profits are obtained from reasonable stocking on a thrifty range, rather than by the heavy stocking that soon results in a poor range and low yields of forage.

The political organization and pressure of the permittees grew with the years. In 1947, in *Harper's Magazine*, Bernard DeVoto described their progress: ". . . what the stockgrowers wanted was protection from migratory operators who had no base property and could undercut them by moving herds from range to range, and some kind of umpiring that would keep them from cutting one another's throats. When the Grazing Service began to discharge the further duties Congress had given it, repairing and restoring the damaged range, it was doomed. From 1941 on the pressure group made a sustained attack on it and by 1946 had destroyed it. Cuts in its appropriations reduced it to a skeleton force wholly subservient to the stockgrowers and it became a subsidiary agency of the Bureau of Land Management. . . .

"It was during the final stages of the attack on the Grazing Service that plans for a similar attack on the Forest Service were matured."

The drive was well-planned and it built up in a crescendo of vitriolic propaganda against the Forest Service. It was sparked by several members of a subcommittee of the House Committee on Public Lands, some of them stock growers and themselves holders of permits on the national forests. A series of hearings were held in the West, packed by demonstrative crowds of those who were to profit by the campaign. For a time, this determined group seemed about to succeed. They had the ball rolling, and opposition was drowned in the clamor. The public grazing lands, they thought, were headed for the last frame-up.

Aims of the grabbers, avowed and ultimate, were summarized in a brochure issued in June 1947 by several national conservation agencies. In brief, they were, first of all, that present holders of grazing permits (no one else) would have the privilege of buying at prices averaging about $1.25 per acre what they wanted of the 130 million acres of Taylor Grazing Lands. Further aspirations were evident in a statement by the vice-chairman of the Joint Livestock Committee on Public Lands, ". . . eventually stockmen hope to return [?] other public grazing lands in the West to private owners—the men who now utilize these properties. The total grazing lands include some tracts now in the national forests and even some tracts which never should have been included in national parks but have been placed there." This was ominous forewarning of what was in store if the current program succeeded. The brochure commented on a further statement:

"He pays his respects to all citizens of America who oppose this grab of our public lands for a mere pittance of its [sic] value in the following language: 'The Committee (of Stockmen) expects the baying of the pack of pool hall conservationists who will be needled into action by the threatened bureaus. Few of them (the pool hall conservationists) have anything at stake, or any constructive ideas. They are full of misguided information and a lot of enthusiasm and don't know what to do with it except howl.'"

Meetings at Rawlings, Wyoming, and Grand Junction, Colorado, went off as scheduled, with the opposition getting little recognition and even less time to voice their objections. But in other meetings, western newspapers, and livestock, game, and civic organizations met the challenge head-on. They had time to muster forces and they used them effectively. Supported by national conservation groups, they brought the long-standing record of chicanery into the open and gave the lie to false accusations against the Forest Service. In the end, the move to take over the grazing lands subsided. It went underground to lay more strategy and to allow the national furor to die down. There will be no cessation of effort—the stakes are too high. But the public has been awakened, and vigilance is evident wherever conservation forces are organized.

Vast numbers of citizens in our eastern metropolitan areas can know little of these problems relating to semi-arid lands of the West. Through long association, and especially by virtue of their pressing and immediate concern with water supplies, westerners have had to understand them, and they have shown a fortunate and proper disposition to defend their own and the national interest. But it is a part of the self-interest of each of us, and even an obligation of citizenship, to comprehend public values in land that still belongs to you and me. It is to be doubted that there is any longer a premium on private "development." We will hardly gain further strength by giving away what is left. This remaining property now has community uses of which wildlife and recreation are not the least. In this connection its past and future treatment is of further interest.

THE FOREST'S PRIME EVIL

It probably is true that our greatest grazing issue concerns the national forests. As previously stated, these areas were reserved to public use primarily as watersheds and forests. Yet in 1946, the year the great "land grab" got under way, 29,460 permit graziers had 1,293,-133 head of cattle and horses and 3,735,648 sheep and goats on the forests. There is much land in the "forests" which does not support trees and which is suitable for grazing. On the other hand, any heavy use by livestock is precluded in areas where a continued growth of timber is expected. The relative balance of major values was brought out by Mont H. Saunderson in his book, *Western Land and Water Use*. He listed them this way in terms of annual revenue:

Water	258 million dollars	
Recreation	20	" "
Timber	18	" "
Grazing	3	" "

On a basis of the three uses most easily measured, he estimated that an acre of national-forest land was worth $30 as a watershed for the irrigated agriculture that depends upon it, $3.50 for the lumber industry that depends upon national-forest output, and $2.00 for the investment in stock ranches that use the forests as summer range. This appraisal seems to hold, and on further consideration we will find that each value (including recreation) is likely to remain in the position assigned to it.

It seems indisputable that planning for future timber supplies must be done in terms, not of years, but of centuries. We need to know where we are going, and the program must be right at the start. There is reason for confidence that we do have a sound timber program in the national forests—if it can be administered freely to the best advantage of the general public. The value of these lands as a source of wood products can be expected to increase by virtue of regrowth, planting, and selective harvesting.

Headlong and destructive overcutting was long the status quo on public and private lands alike. In the Lake States, millions of acres reverted to public ownership in lieu of taxes under the old "cut-and-get-out" philosophy. Even today there is far too much of this kind of logging, and there is no immediate prospect of bringing sawlog cutting into balance with growth. Recent figures indicate that the annual harvest of saw timber is taking place half again faster than wood of this category is being produced. Unwise practices and rampant fires brought soil loss and desolation to many a mountain slope, and rehabilitation is a long and costly procedure for which all of us must pay.

For present purposes we have no reason to go further into forestry problems. We need only recognize that the national forests will have an essential function in wood production and that any use that inhibits this function will need to be examined carefully.

In their comprehensive 2-volume report of 1933, *A National Plan for American Forestry*, the Forest Service emphasized the growing importance of recreation and the need for national recognition of this use. They estimated that there were 506 million acres of commercial timberland in the United States, and of this total approximately 45 million acres could justifiably be withdrawn from commodity timber production and given over to the primary function of providing public recreation. This would be land in all types of administration, federal, state, and local.

On the national forests themselves, recreation is of many kinds, but hunting and fishing undoubtedly are paramount. The steady bettering of conditions for big game has been reflected in large increases for several species. In 1921 big-game animals on all national forests in the United States proper were estimated at 535,327. In 1950 the figure was 2,560,000. A break-down of this total for the most important species showed 2,200,000 deer, 198,000 elk, 77,000 black bears, 800 grizzlies, 27,000 antelope, 9,300 moose, 14,000 mountain goats, and 9,800 bighorns. The kill by sportsmen that year was 353,000 animals. Approximately 70 percent of the big game in the West and 30 percent in the nation as a whole is found on the national forests, which also include 81,000 miles of fishing streams and 1½ million acres of lakes and ponds. Access to this land is free, and hunting and fishing are regulated by the states.

Saunderson derived his figure on recreational income of the forests "by applying commercial rates to the figures of known recreational traffic or uses in the national forests." He recognized that many such uses are "elusive," being non-commercial and intangible. Elsewhere he says, "Recreational uses of these lands eventually will exceed in importance all other uses, excepting watersheds. Indeed, with this exception, the recreational values may now exceed all other values."

The forests are playing a feature role as national playgrounds, and their importance in this respect would seem to give big game a management priority over domestic livestock. Actually the game herds on these areas are under a serious winter-range penalty because "there are within the national forest boundaries private lands obtained under the mining and town site laws, and agricultural homesteads in the narrow valleys running up into the national forests or pocketed in the surrounding timbered areas." The extent of all private holdings in 1933 was nearly 25 million acres.

This situation has been a perennial headache for western game administrators. The fertile valleys are good grazing and agricultural lands, yet once they were the wintering grounds for large numbers of big game. The result is crop damage; invasions by hungry elk, in particular, have brought important financial losses to some ranchers.

Where there is no other satisfactory remedy, game herds will need to be brought into reasonable balance with available foods *outside* these farms and ranches. But where wintering areas occur on public property, it would appear that you and I have a right to expect that the food needs of our deer, elk, antelope, and bighorns will be a primary concern. We too are running animals on those lands, and every citizen is a "stockholder" in the enterprise. Permit graziers have, on occasion, blamed the sad plight of the forage on use by big game, and demanded that such animals be drastically reduced to make way for domestic stock.

As we have seen in former chapters, it is true that deer and elk have become too numerous in many areas, and they have depleted their own winter foods. In such cases they need reduction (by hunting if possible), but it should be done in the interest of health and productivity of the game herds themselves rather than to permit more domestic grazing pressure. Although some competition between game and stock does occur, food studies have shown it to be much less than was formerly assumed. Competition is least on the best range.

No generalizations ever can adjudicate these troubles. They must be handled on the scene in a spirit of fair play and with proper weight given to both private and public interests. Permit graziers have frequently displayed little concern for anything but an immediate desire to crop every available blade of public forage. They have gone farther than this, as is evidenced by a statement of the president of the New Mexico Game Protective Association at the annual meeting of the Western Association in 1947:

"Moreover, at the instance of one of the recognized leaders of the organized livestock associations, there was at the State's recent legislative session introduced a bill to divert the major portion of game department license funds to common schools, to roads, to the payment for damage suffered by property owners and what not, which proposed law, if passed, would have effectively emasculated the entire Game Department's program and activity."

This should effectively demonstrate the lengths to which completely self-centered commercial interests may go to destroy anything that stands in their way. Western sportsmen and their game and fish administrators have had a major part in fending off threats to public forest and grazing lands.*

In regard to water supplies, it would hardly be possible to overstress

---

* In this and other respects, as we look about the country and hear the words and witness the works of some of the senior administrators who came into the business largely unprepared and who learned their jobs by the bruising process of trial and error—we can only wonder that they learned and lasted as they did and hope that others to come will have a fiber of equal quality.

their importance to western states. High mountain land gets most of the rainfall and yields the bulk of water used for irrigation and domestic purposes. An alpine watershed may be far removed from the fertile bottomland where its yield of moisture is used in specialty-crop agriculture, but it is an integral part of the enterprise. Nearly 30 percent of the crops in 11 western states are irrigated, and this acreage produces more than half the agricultural income. National-forest lands west of the 101st meridian yield more than 147 million acre-feet of water per year, which is a major part of the supply available in these states.

In Colorado alone, mountain watersheds produce water worth 50 million dollars annually. Capitalized at 5 percent, for this purpose only, the land is worth 50 dollars per acre. This value would be seriously impaired by the kind of overuse that has been common wherever strict controls have not been exercised. Erosion not only ruins the land itself but the usability of runoff water is affected. Benefits from hundreds of millions of dollars being spent for impoundments and structures will be of short duration if effective erosion control is not brought to millions of acres already in a sad state because of heavy overemphasis on a single use—grazing.

The extent to which the graziers can be trusted with custodianship of ranges on which the public depends for water, timber, and recreation is seen in their past accomplishments. The record is not a good one. In 1936, on request of the 74th Congress, the Forest Service submitted a comprehensive report on "The Western Range," based on many years of data gathering. It documented a situation already widely evident to all who had studied the matter:

"The major finding of this report—at once the most obvious and obscure—is range depletion so nearly universal under all conditions of climate, topography, and ownership that the exceptions serve only to prove the rule.

"The existing range area has been depleted no less than 52 percent from its virgin condition, using depletion in the sense of reduction in grazing capacity for domestic livestock. Practically this means that a range once capable of supporting 22.5 million animal units can now carry only 10.8 million.

"On nearly 55 percent of the entire range area, forage values have been reduced by more than half." As would be expected, by far the most extensive damage was on public property.

Our western public lands are needed for what they can best contribute to the nation. Well-managed (i.e. controlled) grazing is one such value. Use of a portion (about 65 million acres) of the national forests and much of the public domain for stock raising is proper, provided it be done harmoniously with those other more important national interests, water production, the building up of timber reserves, and wild land recreation. Each of these has a long-term essential value to all the people, whereas the additional beef, mutton, and wool these public areas will yield are of much less significance.

For all our uses the land itself is not enough. It needs to be upholstered with trees and grass. It must have clear streams, steady springs, and the flood protection of tens of thousands of beaver ponds and meadows—as it had in the days of Lewis and Clark.

We have noted that in the United States of America wildlife of all kinds belongs to the public. But we have found that on private land our use of the resource is abridged and our ownership largely theoretical. Somewhere, surely, this national asset should be wholly ours; and the logical place appears to be the land that belongs to all of us. This wildlife is our *public livestock,* and it needs space and a food supply. It includes not only deer and antelope, but Montana grizzlies, Minnesota wolves, California condors, and Arizona cougars. It also includes such lesser creatures as prairie dogs and marmots, ptarmigan and spruce hens, magpies and roadrunners—and chickadees, mountain bluebirds, whiskey-jacks, and hundreds of others. These are of interest and worth to millions of "impractical" taxpayers and citizens.

This is a puzzling concept to many people. But we probably could avoid needless troubles if it were well impressed on all those who crop a public resource. It seems logical to consider the salmon of the open ocean and the runs of our Alaskan and western rivers as public property. Yet those who take the harvest come to regard the capital stock as their own. There were those who demanded (and, for many years, got) a public bounty on every public eagle who ate a public (and probably dead) salmon. It made a welcome subsidy to a private hunter and conceivably (but improbably) it may have increased in minute degree the ease with which a private profit could be made.

This is not to disparage the public value of salmon—there is genuine cause for concern over the future of this resource. The damming of western rivers is cutting off valuable commercial runs from their upstream spawning areas. It appears that salmon are given recognition *after* the building of dams is underway; and if biologists, without benefit of resarch, cannot then say how the living resource is to be preserved, it's just one of those regrettable things. The term of usefulness of the dam will depend upon whether, or how soon, someone can get really effective watershed management into operation. The salmon, of course, are *the ancestors of all the salmon of this species the earth will ever have.* Their value must be calculated in terms of the crop for all time to come—in other words, it is incalculable.

There are some who feel in their bones that we will not need such fripperies as salmon anyway; that science will find a way to utilize the real but dilute fertility of the oceans to grow vast quantities of algae from which some ration adequate to sustain life can be derived. No doubt there are such possibilities, and valuable ones, but we hesitate to take this thinking to its logical conclusion.

Our inventory of public-land values emphasizes that there are other uses for grass than grazing and other uses for trees than timber, although this attitude represents indefensible, starry-eyed heresy to some people. Several years before Alaska statehood, representations were made to the Department of the Interior to remove the Kodiak bears from the island of that name. The Territorial House recommended a year-'round open season. If a few local residents had got their way, the world's greatest remaining carnivore would have disappeared from its native range to make it possible for cattle to crop *all* the forage of a rocky island. The cow has the advantage of a dollar value, whereas the bear is under the shadow of an economic bar sinister. For that matter, the Alaska Game Commission has determined that every bear killed by a sportsman in the territory brings in a minimum of $1,500; yet this is of minor moment compared with what it will be worth for all human generations yet to come to have even a few of these great brown bears alive and as wild as they have been since glacial times.

It seems hardly an extremist view that the deliberate extermination of another irreplaceable member of the world fauna would be an act of social vandalism. People who assume the burden of vigilance against such things seldom have anything solid to gain by it. They have, perhaps, a sense of moral responsibility and an abiding conviction that there are offenses against humanity for which ignorance should be no excuse.

LAST COMMUNION

The beginnings and background of the American people are closely involved with the out-of-doors, with forests, prairies, mountains, streams, and lakes. Our national heroes are conquerors of the wilderness—Daniel Boone, Kit Carson, and Buffalo Bill. The idyls of youth are those rustic adventures of Yan and Sam in the immortal Seton's "Two Little Savages." We hold in reverence a period when our country was awesomely big, green, and mysterious, when a man could travel for days and weeks and still be alone.

While our neighbors were few, we did just about as we liked, with no thought of spoiling the land. Sometimes damage was repaired while our backs were turned. Now we find that old customs will have to be changed. Habitable parts of the continent are nearly all inhabited and there are multiplying signs of congestion. The midden-piles of populous areas are suggestive of conditions when deer or hares become too plentiful and wear on the habitat begins to show.

Many people tend to judge our civilization by the number of bath-tubs, automobiles, and bottle-openers we can sell and use in a year. Karl E. Mundt, Senator from South Dakota, considered the extent to which we pollute our surroundings a proper judgment of social status. "Water pollution," he said, "is virtually the last important uncontrolled, unregulated, and unchecked pagan practice . . ." Actually, we can broaden that a bit; for pollution of the land is rapidly catching up. Any trail-end vista that can be reached by jeep will soon be dominated scenically by the keg-lined beer can. Every tenderfoot Boy Scout is taught to leave his camp-site "better than he found it," but country-wide they've been losing ground for thirty years.

A few score years ago, wilderness was a taken-for-granted part of life in America, and it was wild because men only seldom came that way. Then they came more often, and it was no longer wilderness. Roads, gas stations, summer camps, resorts, honky-tonks, motor boats, and airplanes changed its flavor and its quality.

Now we find that if we are to have wilderness, in various degrees of purity, we will have to make provision—quickly and with no half-measures. Then we will have to post a guard and insure a systematic vigilance; for in a populous country anything "undeveloped" is likely to be looked upon as going to waste.

Here we consider wilderness to be nearly any sample, approximate or otherwise, of the primitive. It includes parks where people go and see what they can from their cars, and it includes the more authentic wilderness where there are no roads or power lines and where travel is by pack horse or canoe.

The American public is awakening to the values in such reservations. Locally interest is growing in civic and garden clubs and in conservation organizations of all kinds. Positive and active programs for the preservation of natural areas are being pushed in many states, and this probably is the most important work in the field. Every locality should have samples of its virgin forest or grassland types for people to see and study. It's too late for many, but in others it still can be done.

National associations interested in wilderness have a growing roster of members—the National Parks Association, The Wilderness Society, Nature Conservancy, Izaak Walton League, American Forestry Association, American Nature Association, Sierra Club, and others feature wilderness in their principal objectives.

Locally we have found that, with space and a high standard of living, a well-peopled countryside can still be beautiful. We make no effort to justify the shrubs, lawns, and gardens around our homes. Likewise the natural areas that we are coming to insist upon are a part of our *national landscaping*. They represent our zoning regulations, by which we insure that a few corners will be kept green and orderly and pleasing to the eye.

Almost anyone will grant that we should preserve a few remnants of primitive America, and some of our best scenery has been set aside in the national parks and monuments. The 60 million people who (as of 1960) visit them annually attest that this type of use, which can continue in perpetuity, is more important to the nation than would be the benefits from harvesting the last few sticks of timber, drilling a few more oil wells, or flooding a valley to create one more power station. The claim is heard frequently that valuable resources, especially in timber and grass, are being allowed to waste away in uselessness in the parks. The truth is that these areas comprise just 65 one-hundredths of one percent of the land and water area of continental United States, and much of it is high and barren mountain land supporting but little vegetation.

If we need dollar values, an idea of what a park is worth is obtained from expenditures by visitors to Glacier in 1949. Tourists who came specifically to see the park spent approximately 15 million dollars. Capitalized at 4 percent, this would give this national reservation a tourist-attraction value of $375 million.

In the face of space and range difficulties we have attempted to use the parks as "living museums," in which the native fauna and flora can be preserved in sample communities as free from disturbance as possible and in something resembling the primitive condition. A release of the Nature Conservancy put this function in apt language when it stated that "We are obligated, as was Noah, to round up representatives of all living things, and see them safely through the flood—*the onrushing flood of civilization.*"

Most of our remaining samples of rare animal life are to be found in the parks, and they stand their best chance of surviving there. A few manatees and practically the entire population of American crocodiles are protected in Everglades Park. About a third of the grizzlies south of the Canadian border are in Yellowstone and Glacier. Outside Alaska, Isle Royale is the only national park with a few *resident* wolves. Incidentally, Minnesota is the only state with a reasonably "safe" breeding population of these great carnivores.

Other endangered species which parks and, in some cases, wildlife refuges and national forests are furnishing with a measure of needed protection are wolverine, fisher, marten, otter, lynx, cougar, kit fox, black-footed ferret, buffalo, bighorn, trumpeter swan, whooping crane, Florida crane, roseate spoonbill, California condor, and the Everglades and swallow-tailed kites. In 1960 there were 270 federal refuges comprising some 18 million acres, of which about 3.5 million acres were for waterfowl. Among the rare fauna these areas protect is a herd of original Texas longhorns which range on the Wichita Mountains Wildlife Refuge in Oklahoma.

The buffalo has offered a particular space difficulty. Ranges now available in the United States (except for Alaska, and leaving out Canada's Wood Buffalo Park) are inadequate. This species is one of our most valued relics of the past, and somewhere we need a stretch of country where a reasonable number of buffalo can "roam" as buffalo should. Shelford considered a million and a quarter acres to be about the minimum for plains animals, and Cahalane recommended a million acres in his plan for creation of a Great Plains National Monument.

Winter range for big-game herds has been an acute and widespread problem in the national parks. Large predators have been practically eliminated, and in the absence of hunting, hoofed animals have outgrown the capacity of areas available to them. A fundamental trouble has been that the parks were not planned as good, self-contained, ecological units. In fact we never completed the job of establishing them, and it is evident that further provisions to assure their future are much needed.

Specifically, there are more than half a million acres of privately owned land in the 23 million acres of parks and monuments. On these "in-holdings" there is no limit to forest cutting, mining, ranching, resorts, and other private developments that mar public values. Real-estate subdivisions represent the most pernicious kind of enterprise and the most costly to liquidate. There has long been widespread recognition that alien properties within the parks should be purchased, but for many years this need did not outweigh the political pressure that managed to have funds withheld and prevented the blocking out of public ownership. Real progress in this direction began in 1948, and in a 5-year period the Congress appropriated $975,-000 for the acquisition of in-holdings.

Scenic qualities are in some cases being impaired by grazing privileges dating from the time when parks were established, but these permits on public land are non-transferable, and the end of them can be foreseen. The difficulty will be removed in time, if recurring demands for more grazing as an "emergency" measure continue to be denied. It is evident that there are range components and scenic areas that, in the public interest, should be acquired and added to some parks and monuments. Parks also are needed in land types not now adequately represented—especially the great plains. Perhaps eventually it will be done.

There is timber in some of these areas that would make profitable cutting and would keep the mills of local communities running at a wide-open rate somewhat longer than will be the case otherwise. Strategically located individuals see good personal reasons for lopping off sections, for example, of Olympic Park and Katmai National Monument. We the people need to have an opinion on these cases and make it known.

The large carnivores have posed a difficult management problem. It is in the parks that they will need to be preserved, if anywhere. Yet where parks and monuments are small and surrounded by ranches, we cannot expect to harbor such wide-ranging species as the wolf and cougar.

In wilderness units that are large and isolated we can and should insist on keeping the carnivores. In addition to other values, their esthetic appeal probably is the highest of any of our wild creatures. Every schoolboy knows about the grizzlies of Yellowstone. In regard to the question of "controlling" predators and preserving game only, Cahalane observed:

"Sportsmen have their privileges, and no one wishes to take away that which is rightfully theirs. But consideration must also be given to the desires of the non-hunting public. Those persons who are interested in all animal life should have an equal opportunity to see wildlife in a natural setting and natural distribution. The sight of a gray wolf trotting across the tundra [McKinley Park] is far more rare than the sight of almost any hoofed mammal. To many persons, it is far more exciting. Those city dwellers who are fortunate enough to visit Alaska should also be afforded a chance to hear the eerie howl of the wolf—the most mournful sound in Nature."

For that matter, many sportsmen have a balanced view of such things. He who takes his young son into a truly "big" wilderness for the first time will inevitably be awakened in the middle of the night to the question in a tense undertone: "Hey, Pop—listen. Is that a wolf?" Probably it was only a distant loon, but at such a time what would a wolf be worth?

In certain kinds of wilderness the recreational function can have major consideration. This is best seen in the Quetico-Superior canoe country on the international boundary between Minnesota and Ontario. For a quarter of a century there was a running battle on behalf of this area by people who knew its possibilities.

Most of the big timber was gone, but the lakes—40 percent of it is water—were there. First, the roads were kept out that would have made it just another backwoods country. Then it was a power dam that threatened, but an international joint commission was prevailed upon to deny the petition, and the wilderness idea gained recognition in both countries. In 1926 the Forest Service set aside its first primitive area in the Superior National Forest along the boundary adjoining Canada's Quetico Provincial Park. Eight years later, Minnesota began to adopt policies which would bring the management of state lands within this area into harmony with the federal program.

It was a roadless canoe country, but then the bush pilots heard about it. Resorts dependent on air transport were set up on private lands in the interior. In the early forties, aircraft were taking the area over and opening up resort possibilities on more than 117 thousand acres of privately owned property. There was a real estate boom, and the wilderness was rapidly on its way out. Ely, Minnesota, had become the largest fresh-water seaplane base on the continent. "In addition to the twenty-five local planes which were operating with the regularity of suburban locals, there was a growing stream of traffic from the outside. Chicago, Duluth, Minneapolis, Cleveland and St. Louis advertised weekend fishing excursions into the hinterlands of the once wilderness areas of the Superior."

The planners of the wilderness did not take this lying down. The Izaak Walton League raised $100,000 to buy fourteen of the private sites. In 1948, Congress authorized an appropriation of half a million dollars for similar purchases and (through 1952) $350,000 actually was forthcoming. Then an executive order of the President declared an air-space reservation over the canoe country to take limited effect at the beginning of 1951 and full effect in January 1952. Agreements between the Canadian and United States Governments are not complete, and much private property remains; but the wilderness principle has been established, and the planes that could have negated its basic purpose have been eliminated.

Sigurd F. Olson, one of those who labored long for the Superior roadless area, states that there are 14 such reservations in the nation, only one of which is east of the Rockies.* Planes threaten the wilderness nature of all of them. They "use Forest Service airstrips, mountain meadows and lakes deep within the areas set aside primarily for packhorse travel. And when we think what will happen once the helicopter comes into its own, the problem becomes increasingly serious. . . . We must establish airspace reservations at once or soon all of them will be violated beyond any hope of restoration."

Even in areas where packhorse or canoe camping is a major motive, the wildlife attraction is not subordinate. No "natural area" is natural without its native flora and fauna. It is a part of the charm of such country that the traveler can expect its creatures to be truly wild and unmanaged—a sample of the primitive, just as it might have been a millennium before his time.

One of the reasons why we need to assume a "purist" attitude toward our samples of wilderness is that they have scientific value. Forests, ranges, watersheds, and wildlife lands must be handled with a knowledge of plant and animal succession. For many purposes, certain successional stages are far more productive than others. Undisturbed natural areas in various life zones will represent the climax, or they will be developing toward some other relatively stabilized condition. Whatever stages they represent at any particular time, this should be a complete plant-animal complex. If it is, then it can be used by the ecologist as a check or "control" with which he can compare land types in other stages of succession and in specialized uses.

The wildlife manager especially needs "complete" wilderness, since the elimination of certain species from the fauna (especially the predators) is so universal that he seldom has an opportunity to study freely functioning relationships. When he can make such studies, he frequently finds that Nature has provided a logical way out of some of his difficulties.

People who concern themselves with the nation's resource problems are backing the wilderness idea in increasing numbers. They see the essential services that undisturbed lands can render—preservation of unique scenery, vegetation types, and vanishing animal life; recreation in the out-of-doors; and educational and scientific uses. But the greatest appeal of wilderness probably is an elusive and esthetic one. Our

* The Forest Service has 77 wilderness-type areas of all sizes, but only 4 of these are east of the Rockies.

natural areas are the last opportunity Americans will have to view their country as it once was. They are a brief glimpse of history, a last communion with the primitive. In that alone they will be worth our efforts and whatever else they cost.

We have reviewed, inadequately, some of the wildlife issues in which you and I have a stake—and especially as they are affected by what happens on land that is our common property. If anything is clear, it is that we still are in the process of establishing a principle. This principle is that you and I must get some of the things we need by the long-term, extensive, *community* use of certain lands, and that this is justified if a city park is justified; it is defensible if a high standard of living is defensible. In line with our present discussion of natural areas, the principal was well stated by Anthony W. Smith, at that time representative on conservation of the C.I.O.:

"It should not be necessary for our park and wilderness people to fight forever with their backs to the wall to preserve these values, not only against commercial exploitation, but against otherwise progressive public development. Our over-all program should recognize the place of parks and wilderness in our scheme of things."

Here we are back to a main point in the last chapter—that the nation sorely needs a "scheme of things," that we should have national study of resource problems, a national plan, and effective national zoning that will indicate the sound economic function of specific lands and other assets. With the assumption of social responsibility by more people, perhaps stability can come even from the present economic free-for-all. But it's the hard way. It is a curious anachronism that in an age when physics, chemistry, and medicine are fields of almost incredible miracle-working, we seem to be mired down in an oaken-bough and rough-stone stage of culture as applied to social and economic affairs.

At best, this book can only begin the story of wildlife and its management as a public resource; that is all that space and knowledge permit. We have sketched a background of basic relationships in a wide field. Possibly a part of the background is faulty and will need shoring-up or replacement here and there. But for now it should serve as a framework on which more facts and details can be hung as they are acquired.

Such a treatment must necessarily be superficial in many places, but it seems timely and appropriate. The pros and cons of resource controversies are being featured in the public press—as they should be. What the average citizen has lacked is an orderly concept of the whole field to which he could relate isolated facts or claims. Our premise here has been that if we can equip him with such a concept—his own conservation philosophy—he will be able, like Agassiz, to take the facts into his own hands, look, and see for himself.

CHAPTER 19

The Pilgrim's Pride

FROM the facts and judgments in these chapters we might, perhaps, derive a conservation theorem of some sort. If it all reduces to any dependable theme, it probably is this: That there is a harmony in the natural world which makes the right thing easy and the wrong thing chaos; that the right thing is revealed in being right, not just for now and for us, but for the earth and all those who will inherit it; that there are natural principles, if we can discover them, to guide everything men may wish to do with land and water and the life they support.

The harmony results from trial and error over some two billion years—plus or minus a few million here or there. It has been an eternal weeding out of things that didn't fit. It is a good earth that God's chillun have come to dominate in their intelligence and their biological productivity.

We are sore beset to keep it good. The human culture is now considered to be a "geological force," and with good reason. But if we are at a stage where our actions are to decide the world's future, then surely we have also reached the level where we can be held accountable for the world's future. As the bathtub is an artifact of higher civilization, so also are the accumulating beer cans a sign of developing squalor.

As I have opined here and there, it is a fair question whether man the creature will overrun his environment and convert it into a biological slum. For the human race to continue to build its own numbers and to attenuate the means by which they are to live and enjoy existence is assuredly as immoral as it is improvident. In terms of Yankee respectability, it isn't even good business.

The conservation problem exists precisely in terms of those two dynamic quantities, the expanding population and the declining resource. The population must eventually level off, but will it be too high for comfort? Probably so. It is too bad we are so overawed by the sanctity of our own kind that we can't do a little tinkering with the birth rate—as we have with death rates. An understocked habitat is the basis of physical health and social welfare, whether we happen to be people, perch, or snowshoe hares.

There is ample evidence that a reasonably natural world is the only sanitary environment for a human being or any other animal. The nobility of man will be a vain and farcical idea if the earth is to be parceled out until every individual is competing with his equals for a meager share of pure air, clear water, green grass, and cool woodland. When we come to live by bread alone, we will have lost the something that makes us more than creatures.

What this country is like even fifty years from now will be decided by how successful we are in attaining a measure of social self-control. Americans don't like control. That's how they got here in the first place. But recently there are so many of them they are having to divide things; and that, too, was long beneath their dignity. Now they are discovering that there is a point where independence becomes irresponsibility and liberty becomes license. Even freedom of the personal kind must be abridged somewhat in order that others can enjoy it in equal measure.

Formerly resources belonged to everyone and therefore to no one. The new "conservation ethic" demands that they belong to everyone and therefore each of us.

Unfortunately, some of our biggest and most spectacular wildlife assets have been lost past all recovering. Some would ascribe this entirely to human avarice, and no doubt this has been involved. But a continent that supported perhaps a million and a half stone-age men must of necessity be different when it becomes the abiding place of some 200 million atomic-age citizens.

What we have now is largely a matter of chance; but what we are to have cannot be left to chance. It calls for understanding and design. The wildlife resource must be studied because we did not make the rules of the game and we are only beginning to know what the rules are. We tried our hunches and ideas—shots in the dark, and assembly-line methods. Sometimes they worked, but only sometimes, and certainly they were totally inadequate.

Of late, we are getting down more to the source of things. Nature, we have found, is a whimsical wench. But even her whimsy will be predictable—when we know enough. On mountain and forest, prairie and desert, stream and lake, we have seen her moods and her multiple character:

In spring we found her lush and lovely, a creature of bursting buds and cloying tendrils, fruitful beyond all imagining. Give her her way and she pours forth upon the earth a flood of new life that will shake down into every nook and cranny.

By fall she has matured and wearied of it all. Her spawn is everywhere, and she knows well enough she has overdone. Voluptuous jade, she'll have no more of the masses and callously slaughters her offspring.

Not quite all, for in winter we found her with snow in her hair, a solicitous old lady nursing the harried remnant of her last-spring ardor. The cruel and the innocent are one with her, and somehow she brings them through, then fades away for a reborning when the ice goes out.

Michigan's conservation philosopher, the late P. S. Lovejoy, was wont to speculate humorously on the life and times of those whose burden it was to "fetch the tablets off the mount" for the weal of their fellow men. Many such are putting together the story of the earth and of its life and workings; and what we are to do with it all depends upon them.

It is a labor of love, for none of them will be rich--except in knowing they helped do a job they thought was important and necessary. I have picked the minds and writings of many of these, without stint or hesitation. The portion of the story that is here is theirs. Some of it is good, but all is poor enough, and they'll have to keep working.

If precedent means anything, people will find in this book things that are not here. It is a collection of thoughts and facts—but also of interpretations that may cause some to regard it as a thesaurus of heresy. It has cited the overwhelming productivity of wild animals, under conditions that favor them. It has shown that a heavy toll by hunters and fishermen is not destruction; it may, in fact, be indispensible to continued production.

These chapters have drawn attention to the fallacies of preserving female deer from shooting and returning little fish to the water. They have impugned the efforts of the game farmer and the hatcheryman as regards the maintenance of public hunting and fishing. They have averred that the true faunistic villains are not the ravening flesh feeders, but rather the soft-eyed nibblers that blight the vegetation on which all creatures depend. Above all else, perhaps, we learned to respect the intricate organization of living things. When a life phenomenon appears simple, there is reason to suspect the explainers thereof.

I have assembled here what appears to be truth, but it seems to do violence to many of the preconceptions on which wildlife policies of the past were based. More than anything else it shows that our thinking must, periodically, be realigned. The best that can be done is to base present actions on present knowledge. And future methods will, we hope, be modified by future findings.

Like those animals which succeed in the wild, we must be resilient, adaptable, and forever searching outward in our environment for that which can benefit us.

Reference Notes

THIS book advances a philosophy of resource management that can be only as good as the evidence on which it is based. To permit the student and professional to judge interpretations for themselves, and to guide the reader to further information on subjects of interest, a selected bibliography has been appended. Some of these sources are quoted or referred to specifically, and others are cited in connection with statements which need more explanation or support than can be included here.

Notes and documentation are in a separate section for each chapter. Under these sections additional material can be found by page and line numbers referring to the body of the book. For ease in locating citations, PAGE NUMBERS appear in roman type at the left, LINE NUMBERS in **boldface**, and BIBLIOGRAPHICAL NUMBERS are in parentheses.

CHAPTER 1

4   The account of the "surround" is extrapolated from Catlin's observations. This is Catlin's spelling (Puncah) and his account. The old chief's pessimism was not completely borne out, for the Poncas lived to become citizens of the State of Oklahoma.

7   **15.** The buffalo sustained life wherever they ranged. In the winter of 1865-66, Alexander Toponce, a Montana freighter, was caught by a blizzard about 40 miles west of the junction of the Missouri and Yellowstone. For 15 days the party dared not all go to bed at once. It was so cold they had to bore through 8 inches of ice to drain a barrel of quartermaster whiskey labeled "110 proof." Horns of the cattle froze and burst off the pith. Both cattle and horses had to be destroyed.

Then buffalo began to drift in from the north. Those that could not crowd into the timbered bottom froze. In the following spring, carcasses were so thick it was possible to walk on them "for miles" without touching the ground.

Toponce had two mules that, true to their kind, survived the ordeal on a diet of buffalo meat and cottonwood bark. Said he: "We would take a quarter of buffalo meat and hang it up in a tree by means of a long pole and build a good fire under it and roast it as well as we could, and when it was done we would lay it on the ground before the mules. They would set one foot on the meat to hold it steady, and start in and tear off big chunks of hot meat and fat with their teeth and chew it like hay. The two mules would gnaw the meat clean to the bone on a quarter of buffalo."

In this wise he nursed the hardy animals through 2½ feet of snow for some 500 miles and arrived safely at Helena (464).

30 (431) **35** (128).

8 **17** (386, p. 73); **33** (167, p. 25).

9 **5.** A statement by DeVoto on the use of fat is of particular interest since this was of undoubted value in rounding out the buffalo ration. ". . . to the greases that stained the mountaineer's garments were added the marrow scooped from bones and the melted fat that was gulped by the pint. Kidney fat could be drunk without limit; one was more moderate with the tastier but oily belly fat, which might be automatically regurgitated if taken in quantity, although such a rejection interrupted no one's gourmandizing very long." (Reprinted by permission from *Across the Wide Missouri*, by Bernard DeVoto. Copyright 1947. Houghton Mifflin Company. 128, p. 42).

30. Significant also is Stansbury's observation on the attitude of the beneficiaries of this seemingly limitless beef-herd of the plains: "It is vain to remonstrate against this wholesale destruction. The hunter, this morning, rather plumed himself on his great moderation in only killing four, when it was wholly within his power to kill as many as he pleased; at the same time he knew that one would have amply supplied all our wants. Indeed, of the four killed, but three were butchered (that is, the choice parts only taken away), and we left the ground, having two pack-mules and all the riding-horses loaded down with meat, the fourth animal being wholly untouched; thus abandoning to beasts of prey enough of the richest and sweetest beef to supply a very respectable market for a week. All intercession in favour of the poor buffalo is looked upon by these old mountain-men with a strange mixture of wonder and contempt . . ." (431, p. 248); **35** (163).

10 **14** (132, p. 287); **25** (132, p. 274); **35** (132).
11 **25** (11).
12 **4**. A measure of the easy-going, boom-time spirit of this period is contained in an excerpt which Hornaday (241, p. 500) took from the Wichita, Kansas, *World* of February 9, 1889:

"In 1871 and 1872 the buffalo ranged within 10 miles of Wichita, and could be counted by the thousands. The town, then in its infancy, was the headquarters for a vast number of buffalo-hunters, who plied their occupation vigorously during the winter. The buffalo were killed principally for their hides, and daily wagon trains arrived in town loaded with them. Meat was very cheap in those days; fine, tender buffalo steak selling from 1 to 2 cents per pound . . . The business was quite profitable for a time, but a sudden drop in the price of hides brought them down as low as 25 and 50 cents each . . . It was a very common thing in those days for people living in Wichita to start out in the morning and return by evening with a wagon load of buffalo meat."

8. In a letter to Hornaday, Colonel Dodge gave the approximate proportions of this mass of buffalo:

"The great herd on the Arkansas through which I passed could not have averaged, *at rest*, over fifteen or twenty individuals to the acre, but was, from my observation, not less than 25 miles wide, and from reports of hunters and others it was about five days in passing a given point, or not less than 50 miles deep. From the top of Pawnee Rock I could see from 6 to 10 miles in almost every direction. This whole vast space was covered with buffalo, looking at a distance like one compact mass, the visual angle not permitting the ground to be seen. I have seen such a sight a great number of times, but never on so large a scale." He added that this was the last of the great herds." (241, p. 390).

17 (241, p. 391). The irresponsible waste was not universally approved, even in the West, as indicated by a statement from the *New Mexican*, a Santa Fe newspaper, which Representative McCormick of Arizona inserted in the *Congressional Record* in 1874:

"The buffalo slaughter, which has been going on the past few years on the plains, and which increases every year, is wantonly wicked and should be stopped by the most stringent enactments and most vigilant enforcement of the law. Killing these noble animals for their hides simply, or to gratify the pleasure of some Russian duke or English lord, is a species of vandalism which cannot too quickly be checked. United States surveying parties report that there are two thousand hunters on the plains killing these animals for their hides. One party of sixteen hunters report having killed twenty-eight thousand buffaloes during the past summer. It seems to us there is quite as much reason why the Government should protect the buffaloes as the Indians." (475).

    22 (241, p. 501).

13   **3** (11, p. 214).

    13 (181, p. 125). To make the story complete, a small band was found later in Texas and a total of 56 animals killed—the last four in 1889.

    15 (47, p. 128); **36** (181, p. 153).

14   **7** (241, p. 446); **27** (47, p. 175).

15   **2.** Representative Fort, of Illinois, explained the purpose of the measure:

    "The object of this bill is to prevent the early extermination of these noble herds from the plains. It is estimated that thousands of these harmless animals are annually slaughtered for their tongues alone; and that many thousands, perhaps hundreds of thousands, are killed every year in utter wantonness without any object whatever except to destroy them." (475).

16   **8** (475); **15** (47).

    32. He stated further: "Every military post in the Indian country is besieged by these starving people. The slop-barrels and dump-piles are carefully scrutinized, and stuff that a cur would disdain is carried off in triumph. The offal about the butcher shop is quarrelled over, and devoured raw and on the spot. The warm blood of the slaughtered beeves is sucked up by numerous mouths before it has had time to sink into the ground. Every horse that dies of disease or by accident, is at once converted into meat, and at Fort Reno, under the aegis of the Interior Department, and where hunger is supposed by people generally to be impossible, a dead horse or mule is no sooner dragged away from the vicinity of the post, than it is pounced upon, cut up, and carried off by the starved Indians. They ask no questions, and meat is meat, even though it was killed for farcy or glanders. Nothing is too disgustingly filthy to come amiss to the starving Indians." (132, p. 280).

17   **4** (8).

CHAPTER 2

20   **2** (103, 126).

    16 (296). Two other soils in Missouri have been compared for

production of such game and fur species as quail, rabbits, muskrat, opossum, skunk, mink, and coyote. Gerald and Cherokee are the two principal soil types of Jasper County. They are similar in many respects, the main difference being the higher fertility and agricultural productivity of Gerald. In terms of acres per animal, Gerald soil was found to support one bird or mammal per 16 acres. The less fertile Cherokee produced one animal per 41 acres (2).
36 (3, 4, 224, 225).

21   **5** (130). Investigations of the fox squirrel in Illinois showed a significant difference in litter size between rough, wooded areas, where soil fertility is low, and fertile prairie farmlands. A good supply of corn was considered to be one condition contributing to larger litters among farmland squirrels (50). A Missouri study gave a like result (103).
21 (177, p. 484).
36 (239). A detailed study of the feeding habits of the California ground squirrel was carried out at the Forest Service's San Joaquin Experimental Range. It was found that this animal selects out of its pastures those kinds of plants which are best nutritionally. The fed-upon herbage had a relatively high content of crude protein and essential minerals and correspondingly less fiber and cellulose (170).

22   **6** (60).

23   **2** (39, 393); **32** (447), **37** (426). During the late war, experiments were carried out in Scottish sea lochs to determine whether their production of food fish could be increased by the use of inorganic fertilizers.
Loch Craiglin, a shallow, enclosed loch of only 18 acres, was dammed at the narrow sea outlet and fertilized in 1942 and 1943 with some 1,200 pounds of sodium nitrate and 600 pounds of superphosphate. Plaice (a flatfish akin to the flounder) less than 9 centimeters in length were transferred to the fertilized water and grew an average of 12 centimeters (4¾ inches) in one year as compared with a 3- to 8-centimeter gain by similar fish in their natural waters.
Flounders less than a year old were similarly stocked and completed in 21 months a gain equal to 5 or 6 years of growth in other waters. The growth of these fish was 3 to 4 times faster by length and 16 to 19 times faster by weight than "normal." A stock of flounders in the 1- to 2-year class attained a normal 2-years' growth in about 6 months.
Another loch, of 160 acres and with the outlet open, was fertilized at the rate of about 300 pounds per acre. In spite of adverse

winds and tides, no great loss of fertilizer occurred. In this loch, Kyle Scotnish, plaice grew at 5 times the normal rate and flounders showed a 400 percent increase over that observed on normal grounds (372).

Yields of rough fish, principally carp, taken by commercial fishermen from Wisconsin lakes show a decided correlation with fertility from domestic sources. Three lakes which receive discharge waters from the Madison metropolitan sewage district showed yield figures far above those of comparable but unfertilized waters. Lake Waubesa, which receives the flow directly, produced 439 pounds of fish per surface acre. "The fertilization promotes tremendous growths of algae which require constant chemical treatment to render the lake shore habitable. In all probability the carp utilize the algae and other vegetable growth directly and they are thus able to exist in tremendous densities. The other two Madison lakes show degrees of this condition." (462).

24   **12** (423); **15** (157); **16** (335).

21. Commenting on the greater production in Illinois as compared with less fertile areas, D. H. Thompson of the Illinois Natural History Survey stated:

"In contrast to the 500 pounds of fish per acre found in most Illinois waters, the carrying capacities of waters in northern Wisconsin and northern Michigan . . . are less than one-tenth as large, 50 pounds per acre or less. Intermediate regions with more fertile soils than the northern woods show intermediate poundages." (456).

A survey of the fishes of Champaign County, Illinois, indicated that streams of a particularly fertile region were strikingly rich in aquatic life as compared with those of other parts of the state. In an area of about 50 square miles in the eastern part of the county, soils were derived from a drained marsh and were found to be high in organic matter and calcium. Streams of this area produced fish in abundance and with exceptional rates of growth and adult size. A tract drained by the Spoon River "yielded twice as many fishes to a given area and four to five times as many pounds of fish as the average for the county." (457). Two TVA lakes also furnished good information on the effects of watershed fertility (72).

22. Two lakes in northern Indiana were inventoried for two and three years respectively and the population of *legal-sized game fish* was found to vary between 113 and 232 pounds per acre (376).

25   **2** (22); **9** (486).
26   **32** (201).

CHAPTER 3

29 **4** (140).
30 **28** (85, 440, 441).
31 **13** (306); **22** (269, 348).
32 **10** (432).
    32. The myxoma virus is transmitted by blood-sucking insects, a fact not fully appreciated in early Australian experiments. But in 1950 the inoculation of rabbits on the Murray River flats coincided with a wet period, and the disease was spread rapidly by mosquitoes, resulting in local kills of 99 percent of the wild rabbits. In subsequent years, outbreaks occurred wherever favorable moisture conditions developed, but the proportion of rabbits killed was reduced. This trend resulted from a decline in virulence of the virus (a strain recovered in Brazil in 1911 and maintained in laboratory animals), and possibly from increased resistance in surviving rabbits. A more virulent strain of virus was introduced into France by the inoculation of two animals in June 1952. Within two years it had killed an estimated 90 percent of the rabbits in the country. The disease appeared in Great Britain in 1954 and has run a similar course. In that country the principal vectors are rabbit fleas (14, 458, 459).
33 **21** (438); **23** (154).
    32 (29). Work on Hungarian partridges (317, 502) and various species of grouse has told about the same story (56, p. 527, 65).
34 **6** (441).
    26. In addition to these seasonal trends, David Lack of Oxford University demonstrated that from the tropics northward many species of birds show an increase in average clutch size. He associated the greater production of eggs and young in the North with the longer period of daylight and the fact that parent birds have a longer workday in which to rustle food for their more numerous offspring (274). It is also true, however, that certain fish lay more eggs in the northern parts of their range, which seems to be an adaptation to the longer period (and hence greater hazards) required to bring a young fish to maturity (417).
    Lack's observation of multiple broods in the presence of increased food has been duplicated by a biologist in the Soviet Union who found that ". . . during years in which rodents appear in great quantities, owls and diurnal predatory birds lay eggs two or three times

in the course of the year, so that the last fledgelings leave the nest in the autumn or even winter." (174).

33. The increase in vigor exhibited by reduced populations in favorable habitats is not an attribute peculiar to wild birds and mammals. It has been equally evident among tribes of men since the beginning of recorded history.

In his book *Mainsprings of Civilization*, Huntington drew attention to the repeated pattern of conquest and progress that has taken place wherever nomadic peoples were so situated that they could leave their semi-arid grazing lands and invade agricultural regions inhabited by sedentary folk less gifted in the arts of aggression and leadership. Population reductions, which inevitably attended such adjustments, set the stage for an ensuing era of expansion, invention, and prosperity (249, p. 198).

35   **24** (398, vol. II, p. 918).

37   **12** (89, 355, 482). Man is the only inhabitant of the earth who, over short time periods, changes his cultural level—that is, his practices in using the resources on which he lives, his extractive technology. Elsewhere I have suggested that the relationship of any human population to its resource environment can be expressed by the conceptual equation:

$$\frac{\text{Resources X Culture}}{\text{Population}} = \text{Living Standard}$$

The totally dynamic nature of this relationship is evident in the fact that each quantity is a variable except "Resources," which includes space and all other raw assets of this finite world (9).

38   **3** (148); **29** (5).

39   **10** (6); **20** (295); **25** (345).

40   **2** (407); **9** (92); **29** (402); **35** (301).

41   **9.** One of the most clear-cut and meaningful studies of annual turnover in the bobwhite was made by Marsden and Baskett on a Missouri refuge. They found the winter-to-winter "disappearance rate" of birds from the study area to be 98.6, of which 82 percent represented annual mortality and 16.8 percent was due to movements. The life expectancy of a quail after the first of October was 8½ months, and the oldest bird of record was shot in its fifth year (312). **18** (276); **21** (263); **26** (12); **31** (95).

42   **14** (41); **20** (342); **27** (232); **36** (42).

43   **2** (443); **4** (272).

CHAPTER 4

45 **38** (74).

47 **2.** Essentially this is the same situation described by Hubbs and Eschmeyer in discussing the improvement of lakes for fish populations: ". . . an effort should be made to build up first the weakest element in the fish-producing environment, so as to provide for the maximum fish population which can be maintained by the other environmental conditions. When the least developed or most limiting factor has been built up and has increased the fish production, some other factor may then become under-developed in terms of the increased population. Thus an increase in spawning induced by adding spawning beds may render inadequate the shelter for young fish, even though sufficient cover had previously been available. The increased numbers of growing fish may then consume what previously was a surplus of natural food. In this way the balance would tend to be successively overthrown. Each attempt at restoring the balance should be continued to the practicable limit, which will depend on the intensity of fishing and on the economic values involved." (243).

25 (183); **37** (285).

48 **9** (165); **19** (501); **20** (5); **33** (168).

49 **20.** As evidence of the widespread recognition of this trait in birds, Margaret Morse Nice published a brief historical review of the subject in 1941, appending a bibliography of 387 titles (349). Yet this work by many investigators represents only a sketchy knowledge of territorialism in birds and other animals—an evidence of the complexity of such phenomena.

50 **5** (141); **27** (271). It is notable that in three years of intensive study on the bobwhite in south Texas, Lehmann (285) found that breeding densities over large areas did not exceed a pair per 7.8 acres, or approximately the same "saturation level" found by King in the ruffed grouse.

31 (285). Even sparsely distributed predatory species tend to show a relative uniformity in numbers on the same areas year after year, although where animals are few the percentage of variation usually will be greater than in more dense populations. At Faville Grove, a 2500-acre area studied by University of Wisconsin students, the numbers of resident horned owls from 1936 to 1944 were as follows:

2, 4, 4, 4, 3, 2, 4, 3, 4—average 3.3   (317)

For three years (1959-61) on Isle Royale, a range of 210 square miles, Mech found a wolf population of 21 or 22 animals. Although sexual activity was evident in the winter breeding season, there was no increase. The food supply appeared adequate, and the limitation on numbers probably was sociological in nature (322).

51 **34** (234).

52 **25** (387). Errington's summary of 15 years of quail studies on a 4,500-acre area at Prairie du Sac, Wisconsin, shows a similar picture of annual increase as correlated with breeding-season populations. For five years, in each of which the breeding stock was less than 100 birds, annual increase averaged 212 percent. Four years with breeding stocks between 100 and 200 birds showed increases averaging 128 percent and the increase for five years with more than 200 breeders was only 74 percent. The maximum fall population was reached in 1933 with 433 birds. That year the breeding population also had been maximum with 339 birds in spring. Obviously, this large number of breeders had been thwarted by the fact that about a bird per 10 acres was all this area could carry. The largest recorded spring population showed the smallest percent of increase to fall (150).

53 5. Actually there were fewer hens in 1937 than in 1936.
7 (209); **12** (333, 356).

54 **12** (137); **35** (456).

55 **13** (456).

56 **14** (447, 448); **23** (456); **27** (244, 497); **32** (34).

57 **19** (456); **33** (330); **36** (331).

58 **12** (456). R. W. Eschmeyer explained this food-chain difference in most vivid terms. A bass food chain is the long variety that must progress from plankton to insects to small fish to bass. Roughly it might take 5 lbs. x 5 lbs. x 5 lbs. of various stages, or 125 pounds of plankton, to make one pound of bass. On the other hand, 5 pounds of plankton might make one pound of carp. The case of the carp is like a sheep eating grass but the bass food chain is like a super-wolf, eating a wolf, which eats a sheep, which eats the grass.

59 **20** (272).

60 **13** (271).

CHAPTER 5

62 **9** (288); **30** (171).

63 **9** (54); **36** (15).

64 **19** (193).

37. During the late war farmers were encouraged to increase production, and every square foot of available land was put into crops. Exemplifying the trend, Iowa hay, pasture, and small grains decreased in acreage while corn and beans increased. Old fences were torn out and land was cultivated to the very edge of the field. There was more pasturage of woodlands. Quantitatively, the changes in that state from 1941 to 1946 were summarized as follows (164):

Row crops: Increased 2,600,000 acres.
Waste land: Decreased 132,000 acres.
Woodlands: Decreased 120,000 acres.
Crops not harvested or pastured: Decreased 387,000 acres.

65 22 (13). **26.** After a study of this type of forestry in New York, Edminster concluded that game productivity was reduced from 50 to 75 percent and that "coniferous plantings should be made in units never to exceed 600 feet in diameter and preferably not over 400 feet in diameter, these units to be separated by plantings of hardwoods, food-bearing shrubs and by open land in narrow concentric strips." (136).

66 7 (357).

69 2 (294); **12** (438, 439); **27** (258); **29.** (See also Grange, 203, p. 215).

70 32 (354).

71 23 (38).

72 10 (291, p. 128); **34** (492).

73 27 (370).

74 6 (180).

76 22 (48).
35. The fish management program which Langlois drew up for the State of Ohio embodies the principles mentioned here, involves sound practices in almost every kind of land use, and automatically includes a basis for the management of every bird and mammal that lives in fields and woodlands. It features control of habitat conditions and measures to speed up the harvest (hence turnover) of excess fish populations. (277).

77 2 (165).

CHAPTER 6

79 18 (287).

80 8 (450); **16** (78); **31** (83).

81 16 (451).

82   **9** (149, 192, 469); **30** (469).

83   **13.** In Oregon a somewhat similar situation was followed through to its logical end, but with a different outcome. The sage grouse inhabits semi-arid country, and it appeared that water developments would be of benefit to the species.

In 1937 a Federal Aid project was set up to develop springs in the portion of the State where the bird ranges. Easements were secured on blocks of land varying from one to 20 acres. The springs were cleaned, covered, fenced, and supplied with pipes leading to stock troughs. The overflow was then picked up and carried to the land under easement and spread for irrigation to form a protected meadow.

Following this work a comparative study was made of the game birds around 29 improved and 30 unimproved springs. The sage grouse actually were more plentiful around water without all the modern conveniences.

It was found that the thicker vegetation on the protected areas was a liability rather than an asset. For a long time sage grouse have lived in land of sparse grass and far horizons. They do not depend on cover for concealment and they like a full view in all directions. They took no stock in the human concept of "improvement."

The spring-site developments were not a complete loss. It was found that they had helped to extend the range of the pheasant and Hungarian partridge, even though they didn't function as originally intended (325).

84   **18** (434). It is disillusioning to learn what happened in the years following active support and promotion of this project. While in some cases farmers continued to use soil-building practices for which benefit payments were available, the wildlife management phases of the program were almost completely abandoned. Cover plantings were torn out or grazed and land use intensified. By 1958 quail had declined on both the West Ashland and New Salem areas.

85   **24** (7, 201); **34** (115, 117, 329).

Chapter 7

89   **28** (218); **34** (267, 399).

90   **12** (267).

91   **19** (5).

33 (276). Radical fluctuations in the bag of squirrels have also been recorded in the Soviet Union, where the harvest is taken commercially as a food crop. The variation may be from 30 to 1,500 or more per rifle per season. In a 10-year study in Gorki Province a direct correlation was found between populations of squirrels and the crop of spruce seeds (175).

92 **21** (425).
93 **21** (208); **32** (308).
94 **32** (206, 207).
95 **10** (5); **37** (384).
96 **11** (23); **19** (175).
97 **8** (399, Vol. I, p. 183). Seton related that the rabbits of the Mackenzie River Valley reached their peak of abundance in the winter of 1903-04 and that by 1907 they had died off so completely it seemed there was not one left in the country.

That winter the lynxes would enter any kind of trap that was baited. During a 7-month trip he encountered a dozen animals that were "mere walking skeletons—." "There were thousands of starving lynxes roaming the country, combing the woods for any last vestige of animal food. Every item of evidence helped to emphasize the dire story of the plague and of the famine that came after."

22 (145). The Bureau of Animal Population, at Oxford, has assumed a leading role in studies of cyclic species in the Arctic. Its Director, Charles Elton, made a painstaking analysis of fox fur returns from the Moravian Missions and Hudson's Bay Company posts along the Ungava and Labrador coasts. The records covered a period of more than a hundred years, the earliest being for 1830 (145).

33 (213, 405). These are well-known examples of animals having a 3-4 year rhythm of numbers in common with their rodent prey. In connection with his studies of cycles, a Finnish biologist, Siivonen, indicated that the same is true of the lynx in southwest Finland and the goshawk in Norway (411).

98 **6** (145, p. 442). It is of interest that in Greenland there are large regions where the arctic fox lives without benefit of lemmings or other cyclic rodents. In a more recent report Elton has cited references to show that in these areas there is no 4-year cycle among the foxes (146). After a thorough investigation of available records for West Greenland, F. W. Braestrup, of the Copenhagen Museum, could identify no regular pattern (45). E. C. Cross also found a complexity of trends and no regularity in the records of fox abundance in Ontario (107).

19 (144). A type of encephalitis appears to be particularly important in bringing about declines of the arctic fox. On Soviet fur farms there is a regular recurrence of encephalitis that breaks out into a serious epizoötic about every 3 years, (254) and fur farmers in Minnesota have had to contend with an apparently identical trouble. First-year cubs are chiefly affected and mortality is high. Between peaks the animals tend to acquire a temporary 2- to 3-year immunity that imparts a cyclic behavior to the action of the epizoötic virus (205).

How many cycles are we dealing with? Is there, perhaps, a disease-immunity variable that might help account for some of the unexplainable irregularities that occur? Someone needs to find out, **30** (102).

99   **5.** Personal communication from C. H. D. Clarke, Ontario Department of Lands and Forests.
    28 (10).

100   **32** (427).

101   **5** (391); **25** (56); **33** (202).

102   **16** (202, p. 91); **22** (55; 138, p. 316; 290, p. 137); **25** (147, 392); **29** (84).

104   **14** (12).

22. One of the earliest comprehensive investigations of a game bird was on the part of a committee appointed by the British Parliament to study the red grouse—a bird of the Scottish moors. In 1911 the committee filed a report that included a vast amount of material still valuable today in its biological implications and as a guide to management.

An item of interest here is the fairly regular recurrence of strongylosis, known as *grouse disease*. The affliction was caused by a fine, threadlike worm found in the intestinal caeca—blind pouches comparable to the human appendix.

These worms were found in 95 percent of all the birds examined. It was evident that even healthy grouse were carrying ". . . an inherent liability to disease which only requires certain specified conditions to develop and turn the hardiest of all game birds into a badly-feathered, rusty piner, scarcely able to fly, and ripe for death."

The conditions referred to were brought about in a dense population by contamination of the winter food supply and unfavorable weather during the nesting season (299).

Grouse disease was found in a regularly recurring sequence of events: After a year of heavy infection and mortality, there would be one or two years of recovery followed by two or three years of average production and then one or two seasons of maximum abundance. The die-off could then be expected.

The British grouse malady has similarities to the effects of *Leucocytozoön* in Canada. The operation of both may be dependent on population density, which is not inconsistent with the fact that both lightly stocked moors in Scotland and marginal grouse range in America are affected by the die-off. On the other hand, diseases, like predation, can be a secondary factor.

27 (68). By the mid-thirties Professor Rowan had established the fact that on the northern prairies the introduced Hungarian partridge had fallen into the cyclic pattern of our native grouse (384). On a basis of what happened in 1943 to 1950, it can hardly be doubted that the pheasant got into the "swing of things" also. However, in the case of this bird there was a suggestive association of the decline with weather trends. The drastic phase of the reduction appeared to be correlated with exceptionally high rainfall and low temperatures during the spring breeding period. This was reported at various locations from New York to Oregon (6, 268, 284, 318, 360).

36 (147).

105 **17** (479, 480).

107 **2** (456); **5.** There was ample evidence of abundance cycles varying in length, some of which were explainable and others that were not. In New Brunswick's Miramichi River most salmon spend three years in fresh water before going to sea. It is three years between big catches in the river and this appears to result from the fact that every third generation is a big one which takes over water and food supply to the detriment of young fish produced in the two years that follow. After third-year smolts have left the river, another big generation can survive.

Other similar interactions of different generations of fish appeared to account for cycles from 2 to 8 years in length in various rivers of the Maritime region. There also was evidence of a 48-year period between major peaks in numbers for the entire area (250).

32 (410). Weather changes are obviously involved in many of the major trends of animal numbers, and studies of climatic change are much needed in connection with animal cycles. As an outstanding example, Neil D. Richmond compiled 35 years of gray fox bounty records in Pennsylvania and found that "marked increases in the number of gray foxes were in years with January, February and

March wetter and warmer than average. And the lowest fox populations were in years when the same months were colder and drier than normal." He concluded that a natural control of gray foxes was correlated with the *frequency* of precipitation. Sequences of deviation since 1900 occurred at 10-year intervals "with the latter half of each decade wetter than the first half." Richmond's graph of precipitation frequency shows peaks that coincide remarkably with what are commonly considered to be low years of the northern game cycle (374).

108   25 (78, 79, 397).

36. Now that biologists are on the lookout for such information, it is likely that stress phenomena will be recognized in many unsuspected places. Leon Hornkohl, of the Forest Service, was on the Kaibab in 1926-27 at the time of the deer die-off. He informed me that many of the animals were found in a state of shock. They could be approached easily, roped, and led into camp. A more recent example of a drastic deer reduction, in the absence of evident malnutrition, has been reported for a population of introduced Japanese sika deer on James Island in Chesapeake Bay. These animals had an abundant and varied food supply and they built up to a density of one per acre. In January and February, 1958, 60 percent of the population (principally females and young) died. Autopsies indicated physical changes characteristic of the general adaptation (shock) syndrome. "It was concluded that physiological derangements resulting from high population density produced the observed effects." (80).

110   **17.** Johnson also cited the fact that H. Helm Clayton had made a study of atmospheric pressures at several points around the earth and "found, in 20-year intervals, six oscillations in pressure averaging about 3.32 years in length. At higher latitudes such as San Diego, U.S.A. and Santiago, Chile, a reversed pattern was evident. There appeared to be a heavy indrought of air into the tropics and a marked increase in rainfall in a cycle averaging 3.32 years in length." At Kualapuu, Johnson found high probability of a 3.35-year cycle in mean temperatures and indicated that "Clayton's 3.32-year cycle in pressures appears correlated with this 3.35-year periodicity in mean temperatures." (260). (Reprinted by permission from *Cycles in Weather and Solar Activity*, by Maxwell O. Johnson. Copyright 1950. Paradise of the Pacific Press, Honolulu.)

In these studies there were indications of numerous other periodisms, many of them much longer than any cited above. Climatic fluctuations of various kinds tend to overlap in seeming confusion, with mutually inhibiting or reinforcing effects that obscure one phenomenon and make an extreme of another. In the Pacific, solar radiation effects on the Japanese current showed up 3 to 4 years later in mean temperature records at Kualapuu, Hawaii. Variations in temperature were small but more constant and significant than differences in precipitation. An increase of 2 degrees F. in the temperature of the earth would be enough to affect the stability of polar ice sheets, and a reduction of 5 to 10 degrees C. probably would bring on an ice age. Hence it appears that minor regular departures of temperature might have important and equally regular effects on living things around the earth.

111 2. We could hardly quit the subject of population changes without recognizing a mathematical study by Cole in which he showed that in a purely random series of fluctuations the mean cycle length in years would be three. The 3-year peak would, in turn, be subject to the same kind of analysis and the mean period for high peaks would be three short cycles. It resembles very much the results obtained by Siivonen and others, and raises the question of how much of the apparent regularity in natural phenomena is due to mathematical expectation (88).

CHAPTER 8

116 **2** (51).

117 **16** (91); **33** (24); **35** (487).

118 4. Fish and Wildlife Service news release, July 20, 1961.

119 **7** (403); **22** (119).

120 5. See Day (120). **33** (300).

123 **11** (6).

125 **20** (200); **26** (442); **33** (209); **34** (408).

126 4. From available evidence, there is no certainty that this would not be a workable sex ratio. In captivity a single cock can adequately service 50 hens (474). Lauckhart observed that "Game technicians generally agree that cock pheasants virtually cannot be overhunted in suitable habitat if illegal kill is held to a minimum." (282).

     6 (473).

127 **35** (268, 269).

128 **12** (348); **20**. M. O. Steen summed up the case for and against hen shooting in discussing complaints of Dakota farmers:

"To meet these conditions the Dakota game departments find it necessary to allow the taking of hen pheasants. Other states have adopted this practice, usually without justification. For while it is true that the only effective method of reducing the annual crop is to shoot hens, it is equally true that the only justification for so doing is an urgent necessity for the reduction of the annual crop. . . . The limited number of crossing hens that are killed in a legitimate accident—while firing at a cock bird in the same rise—can well afford to be lost, and constitutes no justification for letting the bars down in a state that has need of all available breeding stock." (433).

129 **12.** Leopold pointed out that in Scotland where there are 213 red grouse per square mile, the annual harvest is 160 birds, or two thirds of the fall population. But in Wisconsin sand plains the unthrifty prairie chicken might run 16 to the square mile and there a kill of only one bird per section probably injures the breeding stock (289).

31 (3, 4).

130 **7** (226); **18** (271).

131 **11** (183).

24 (177). In Iowa, quail populations surviving the hunting period on 14 experimentally shot areas lost 10.3 percent of their number during a winter observation period. There were losses of 28.3 percent on four comparable, but unshot, check areas. The "exposed surplus" on the unshot areas suffered a higher predation rate than the populations from which a shooting kill had been removed (153).

37 (333).

132 **10** (209).

133 **11** (5). It was an appreciation of these relationships which prompted Thomas R. Evans to make this general statement in an article on predator losses:

"Harvest of the population surplus by hunting in the fall so the remaining winter population will fit securely into the capacity of the range to support and protect it through the winter *not only gives the hunter the most sport but also reduces winter losses."* (162).

29 (116); **34** (231); **36** (342).

CHAPTER 9

135 **13** (399); **18.** My figures are extrapolated from (476).

136 **2.** For this purpose a fawn is considered to be a "deer" at 4 to 5

months of age, after it has survived to its first fall season. Previous to the hunting season, the herd is at its annual maximum, and this figure is the convenient base for figuring losses and composition ratios. The common practice in the West of calculating everything as a percentage of the year-end (after hunting) herd is unwieldly and biologically unrealistic. My 40 percent annual turnover figure may be somewhat high for western mule deer, in which the percent of fawns breeding is lower than in the whitetail. However, much of the available statistical information is from poorly fed herds (See Robinette, 378). In referring to the Kaibab herd (1951-55) Swank observed, "It appears that an average productivity of 40 percent is not unusually high, but compares favorably with herds in other western states." (445).

13 (262).

137   8 (27).

138   12. Mast feeding may be of particular importance in the South. Goodrun and Reid indicated that "The woody browse of the long-leaf pine belt, and the south as a whole, undergoes a sharp drop in nutrient content in the winter. It is highest in the spring and is closely associated with succulence. The drop may be as much as 50 percent from spring to winter for some of the best forage. This points up the need for some form of fall and winter food high in nutritive content. Under natural conditions this is normally sup-plied by acorns and other kinds of mast." (197)

21 (253); 27 (315); 29 (369).

139   10 (259); 12 (236).

140   7 (264); 13 (219); 21 (253); 36 (400).

141   12 (108); 17 (319). In Pennsylvania, Bramble carried out studies of deer damage to conifer plantations as correlated with actual deer populations: "Where deer were in low populations (1 deer to 50 acres or more), the losses were relatively light on all species. How-ever, where deer were in medium concentrations (1 deer to 30-35 acres), damage went up to as high as 86.3 percent on preferred conifers such as pitch pine and hemlock. The damage to spruce [unpalatable to deer] under light or medium deer populations was slight. Where the deer were in high populations (1 deer to less than 30 acres), the damage was considerable on all species and ranged from a low of 2.4 percent in a planting of white spruce to 85.7 in a mixed plantation of pitch and Banks pine . . . One of the most important damages to conifers in recent years has been to Christmas tree plantations. While losses to trees that were

planted for purposes other than Christmas trees per thousand trees
planted amounted to an average of $29.67, loss per thousand
trees planted for Christmas trees amounted to $36.45. In many areas,
heavy populations of deer have made Christmas tree growing impractical and entire plantings have been destroyed."

In regard to forest-tree reproduction, studies indicated that "where
deer populations were light to moderate (approximately 1 deer to 75
acres) a maximum of 7 percent of the stems were browsed heavily
while 50 percent were browsed lightly. However, on areas containing
heavy populations of deer (approximately 1 deer to 30-35 acres or
less), heavy browsing occurred on 25 to 78 percent of the desirable
reproduction. This means that where deer were in heavy concentration it was practically impossible to practice good forestry and to
reproduce the present forest stands after cutting in desirable timber
species." (46)

34 (455).

142   **2** (279); **7** (366); **10** (109, p. 141); **30** (279).

143   **27** (76); **36** (77, 400).

144   **4** (259, p. 40); **20** (265); **28** (279). On the Edwards Plateau of
Texas, heavy grazing by livestock has so depleted the grasses that the
range has largely been taken over by woody vegetation. Shrub
growth has favored the deer, but browsing by sheep and goats is
direct competition for the food supply. Browse lines are apparent
and the deer are degraded. In some of the hill country, an average
hunting season buck dresses out at about 75 pounds. Some deer
were removed from this area to better range in the eastern part of
the state. They increased sufficiently in 5 years to permit a hunting
season, and it was found that they averaged 32 pounds heavier than
the parent stock (216, 217).

146   **10** (133); **27** (66).

147   **11** (395); **23** (259); **36** (123).

149   **7** (124); **15.** In the course of long continued deer studies in New
York, C. W. Severinghaus obtained unique information on 10½
square miles around his home at Delmar. With the help of neighbors and the local game protector, he made a record of every dead
deer over a 10½-year period. The talley included legal and illegal
kills and every other type of loss. In a total of 101 known losses, 34
were legal kills in hunting season—this included an either-sex
season in 1952. Automobiles and dogs accounted for 14, and there
were 53 illegal kills at all seasons of the year. Of course, this is a
new kind of information, but it helps to give perspective on the

situation in a well-settled region to know that more than half of the losses that could be accounted for were illegal kills.

Severinghaus also took advantage of an opportunity to assay the *hunting season* loss in another part of Albany County. The buck season ended on November 30, and he learned that a state gypsy-moth survey was to be made from November 25 to December 30. The crews worked at 100-foot intervals, and they agreed to record all dead deer found. The average legal buck kill in the area was slightly less than 1 per square mile, but the crews found 1.9 doe and fawn carcasses per square mile. Since some remains probably were missed, this is a minimum figure, and it indicates that at least two-thirds of the total hunting kill was illegal and wasted. It compares closely with the situation found in Wisconsin (Personal communication from C. W. Severinghaus).

27 (259); **29.** Taber and Dasmann found no such high illegal kill in their studies of blacktails in California. While there was a fairly high "accidental" shooting of illegal spike bucks, "the number of antlerless deer shot illegally during the season is, in our experience, extremely small." (449).

150 **21.** It will occur to some that in the Southeast deer have not in many areas outstripped their food supply. "Other checks" obviously are operating, and periodic die-offs from disease probably are an important key to the situation.
33 (189).

151 **20** (189); **36** (196). Table of deer kill statistics, *Pennsylvania Game News*, May 1961, p. 41.

152 **35** (238). The case of the Stanislaus herd also illustrates how commonly the numbers of deer are underestimated. When the slaughter started, it was believed that there were about 10,000 deer on the forest. However, from the summer of 1924 to March, 1926, the number of dead deer accounted for was 20,698. The actual kill undoubtedly was higher than this, being estimated up to some 40,000. Within 10 years after the reduction campaign, the herd had built back to its former numbers (298).

153 **1** (266); **18** (409); **28** (245). Utah began statewide either-sex hunting in 1951, and in 1953 the legislature delegated broad authority to the Board of Big Game Control. In the first 10 years of this program annual kills averaged more than 100,000 animals out of a state herd (pre-hunting) of around half a million. Utah is divided into 68 management units with regulations tailored to local conditions. In 1960 Reynolds summed up their progress:

". . . deer numbers have remained high but hunting records indicate that, at least, population increases have been arrested on a statewide basis. Some herds have begun to show the desired reduction in numbers [to achieve balance with the food supply], others have not. Before management plans can be drafted to perpetuate well-balanced herds more reductions must be made." (373).

154   **10** (270); **31.** This is the premise in all states. In regard to the California situation, Longhurst *et al.* had this to say: "We cannot overemphasize the fact, however, that range improvement is essentially wasted effort unless it is accompanied by herd control. Unregulated deer populations will destroy more range than any public agency can afford to create." (303).
36 (278).

155   **5.** A significant development in Michigan grew out of the appearance, in post-war years, of a new process for using poplar in paper manufacturing. By 1955 the American Box Board Company had their consultant working in the state's 400 square miles of heavily browsed, under-hunted club country. Contracts were negotiated for rotation cuttings under a written management plan which would improve deer range and produce pulp for the indefinite future. Under company guidance the clubs were adopting more liberal deer harvest regulations to protect their management program. It was a self-supporting plan that looked durable (489).
11 (28); **17.** One of the beneficial effects of burning in southern range is on food quality. Lay found that "Burning increased protein content as much as 42.8 percent and phosphoric acid [the "most critical nutrient"] content as much as 77.8 percent in the species involved, but most of the benefits disappeared within a year or two." He recommended controlled burning in spring or summer as often as would be in keeping with good forestry. (283).
21 (44, 449); **35** (67); **37** (373).

CHAPTER 10

159   **3** (158).
160   **6** (385).
161   **10** (37).
162   **4** (456); **14** (335); **31** (456).
37. "Natural mortality is a more important cause of death than fishing, for every species encountered. Estimates of its magnitude range from 32 to as high as 90 percent per year. Like the total mortality,

of which it is the principal component, natural mortality rate increases sharply with age among such species as pumpkinseeds, crappies, and bullheads. In general, predation is not an important cause of mortality among legal-sized fish in these lakes, so that the causes of natural mortality must be sought elsewhere; senility appears to be the most likely alternative cause." (376).

163   9 (375). Harvest figures from Illinois demonstrated that there, too, the ordinary license holder has an extremely small effect on the resource: "Our creel census data," said Thompson, "show that the catch of the average hook-and-line fisherman does not exceed five pounds per year, and it may be as low as two pounds. Incidentally, this yearly catch is also the hook-and-line yield per acre, since there are almost exactly as many licenses as there are acres of water in the state. In Illinois the fish fauna has been studied as long and as intensively as in any place in the Western Hemisphere, but there is no evidence that any species has become extinct or depleted as a result of hook-and-line fishing." (456).

23 (159).

164   3. This situation is well described in a report from Minnesota:

"It is conceded that angling pressure is not without its effects on fish life of northern lakes—especially the walleyes, northern pike, trout and bass. Under primeval conditions these lakes apparently contained considerable numbers of large predatory fishes which ruled the lake to the detriment of smaller forage fishes and their own young. It seems probable that as anglers removed these fishes, the forage and pan-fishes become more abundant and even over-populated in some lakes, so that the remaining game fishes have ample food supplies [and hence don't bite readily]. Fish numbers probably have increased and weights per acre seem to remain steady in spite of exploitation. This sequence is not true in richer southern lakes." (261).

35 (235).

166   9 (481); **25** (460).
168   6 (210); **21** (33); **26** (161).
169   **15** (320); **27** (456); **33** (481).
170   9 (118); **29** (81); **36** (110).
171   **10** (321).
172   2 (49); **34** (227).
173   **20** (227); **36** (228).

CHAPTER 11

177   8 (362); **17** (142, 362); **38** (176, 306).
178   **11** (491); **21** (344); **37** (222).
179   **21** (435); **31** (98).
180   **37** (90).
181   **10** (69); **18** (43); **22** (401); **35** (25, 143).
182   **20** (100); **30** (194).
183   **14** (471); **30** (113).
184   **7** (75); **10** (327); **17** (82).

26 (75). From Mono Lake southward, the eastern slope of the Sierra Nevada and most of the mountain lakes along the crest of the Sierra were originally without trout. "Much of the high altitude fishing in the Cascades and the Rocky Mountains is also the result of man's incurable habit of carrying trout to every remote stream and lake." (424).

The stocking of Kamloops trout in Lake Pend Oreille, Idaho, achieved not only the establishment of a new species but something new in the way of big fish. This lake has 150 miles of shoreline and depths to 2,500 feet. It also has an abundant food supply in sockeye salmon that run about three to the pound. The combination proved to be what was needed to permit the introduced trout to reach proportions almost unheard of in inland waters.

The first eggs of the Kamloops were received in Idaho in 1941. They were hatched and a portion of the resulting fish were placed in Pend Oreille. Just four years later a record fish of 32½ pounds was caught by an angler. This was bettered in 1947 by a 36-pound fish. It seems to take the big lake to grow such fish, as several other plantings in similar-appearing waters failed (413).

Paul Lake, British Columbia, had no fish life at all until it was stocked with Kamloops trout in 1909. In 1931 an evaluation of the fishing in the lake indicated that it was worth about $10,000 in terms of the additional tourist money it brought in for the people of the district (379).

35 (380).

185   **9** (419).

16. Curiously, shad seem to have found a niche in the community of Pacific Coast fishes not occupied by any other species. There it has been quite as successful as in its original home along the Atlantic seaboard, where it is distributed along an equal extent of coastline from the mouth of the St. Lawrence to Alabama. The species is growing in popularity as a sport fish, and in Washington and Oregon the Pacific branch of the family supports a commercial fishery that yielded more than 351,000 pounds in 1939. Thus far almost nothing has been said against transfer of the fish to those waters—an all-too-rare record.

31 (195); **38** (96).

186   **16** (286).

34. A realization of such possibilities was expressed in 1947 in the attitude of the Wisconsin Conservation Commission toward applications for permits to import cottontail rabbits and jackrabbits. The permits were refused on the basis that out-of-state rabbits might be a source of infection for tularemia and Rocky Mountain spotted fever, and that it was impossible by inspection to guarantee the "purity" of brought-in stock.

It was pointed out further that rabbits grown in Missouri very likely were best adapted to Missouri conditions, and those grown in Wisconsin or any other locality probably were best suited to that particular area. Thus, the mixture of outside blood into the local stock stood a good chance of adding weakness rather than strength.

Finally, it was indicated that this heavily grazed, hay-and-dairying country of Wisconsin would need to be improved if its capacity to support rabbits were increased, and that more stocking would not change this situation (19). In 1950 two eastern states stopped the importation of cottontails, in part for reasons of "public health."

187   **5** (316); **29** (362).

188   **8** (281); **10.** It is to be expected that a species which stays put like the quail should become in some measure regionally adapted and that nearly-related animals from outside would tend to be less well fitted than the natives to exist in a given local area. Migratory birds, whose broad range makes them more cosmopolitan, may not have such limitations in the same degree. There is a suggestion of this in the approaching fate of a native gray duck in New Zealand.

Some 600 species of foreign animals have been let loose to work out their future in that biologically outraged but still-beautiful land, and among them is the North American mallard. Unfortunately, it crosses readily with the gray duck. And still more unfortunately, the mallard characteristics appear to be dominant. It is only a matter of time until the New Zealand duck is completely absorbed by the newcomer and we will check one more species off the shrinking list of the world's game animals (96).

27 (472).

189   3 (297, 358); 12 (340); 20 (214).

190   9 (341).

191   6 (97, 496); 27 (96).

192   25 (497).

193   16 (359).

194   5 (359); 11 (20); 17 (35). The distribution and economic status of the nutria are reviewed in Periodical 1602 of the National Better Business Bureau, Inc., 1957, and in Wildlife Leaflet 389 of the U. S. Fish and Wildlife Service, 1957.

     23 (105); 32 (365); 38 (211).

195   26 (343).

196   13 (343); 26 (293).

CHAPTER 12

198   29 (304).

202   2 (199); 13 (188); 20 (59, p. 77).

203   6 (188); 29 (31).

204   26 (40).

205   15 (361).

206   25 (190); 28 (351); 30 (488); 32 (309); 38 (59).

207   2 (414).

     19 (305). See also the job done by California field men on the Sartain and McManus Ranches (166, 223).

     22. In Florida, on an experimental area near Welaka, pen-reared quail were released a few at a time with wild-trapped coveys. Many of them stayed in the coveys and showed a survival value equal to the wild stock (178). In California this did not work. Wild valley quail drove introduced birds out of the coveys (193).

     30 (273).

208   7. In 1945, a Michigan experiment was designed specifically to test this. Birds liberated in early August showed returns of 1.6 percent. Early September pheasants were recovered during the hunting season at the rate of 2 percent. Of late September cocks, 4.6 percent were shot, and of male pheasants liberated in October, one week before the opening, 9 out of every hundred paid off (134). Similar results appeared in a test in New Jersey and here it appeared that the most important factor was the number of weeks between releases and the hunting season rather than the age of the birds. Early releases tend to be younger than late ones, but somewhat surpris-

ingly, there was not much difference in survival at ages between 10 and 20 weeks (309). However in birds younger than 10 weeks, age seems to count. On the Sartain Ranch, California biologists made simultaneous plants of cocks 6, 8, and 10 weeks of age, and they got better survival in the older birds of these groups (166).

18 (26); **24** (454); **28** (470).

209 **7** (454).

10 (52, 367); **17.** An obvious means of improving returns from stocking is to hold cock pheasants at the game farm until fall and then release immediately before and during the hunting season. Summer-stocked game-farm pheasants on California's Sartain Ranch gave returns of 32, 35, and 33 percent for three years, respectively. But in each of the last two years (1948-49), the investigators turned out a group of birds just two days before the shooting started. These were taken by gunners at the rate of 81 and 84 percent, respectively. In 1949 a planting during the season returned 69 percent of the cocks to hunters. The fact that this in-season stocking was less productive than preseason plants shows that hunting pressure (which is highest on the first day) is definitely a factor in bringing about high recoveries (223).

35 (59, p. 80).

210 **3** (114); **14** (414). In publishing his policy on game stocking, North Dakota's Game and Fish Commissioner similarly indicated the economic shortcomings of such methods:

"It is interesting to note that one by one, states which a few short years ago were practicing stocking for the gun, are discontinuing this practice. It is not for this reason, however, that North Dakota has not and does not intend to follow this practice, but rather, because of the fact that its cost is prohibitive." (332).

211 **10** (185); **19** (21).

33 (187). In the thirties Ohio brought in as many as 100,000 rabbits per year, but the State abandoned this practice after examining the results. Stocked cottontails made no detectable difference in the number of animals available to hunters, and many of the displaced bunnies were found to be carrying ailments that did not augur well for their effect on native stock. When some of the shipped-in rabbits were held under controlled conditions for observation, 85 percent of them died within three months as against only 15 percent mortality in a group of Ohio rabbits (21).

212 **9** (125); **32** (52).

CHAPTER 13

215   **3** (461); **13** (215); **27** (310).

216   **22** (64); **38** (421).

217   **7** (490); **19** (93); **27** (184).

218   **5** (444); **16** (237); **25** (490); **33** (347).

219   **30** (93).

35. Results on some work of this kind in California were reported by Smith and Needham. In upper Angora Lake, near Lake Tahoe, they stocked 5-inch eastern brook trout and got returns to the angler of 25.6 percent. "In one year 77 per cent of the fish caught were marked fish. Fishermen report similar high returns from an intensive stocking program with rainbows by the California Division of Fish and Game in June Lake, Convict Lake and other accessible waters which can be stocked with large quantities of fair sized fish." (424).

We have previously taken note of the work with introduced Kamloops trout in Paul Lake, British Columbia. There conditions for natural spawning were found to be poor after dry seasons, and stocking with 200,000 fry per year was started in 1931. By this means the catch was raised from 3,000 fish in 1932 to 10,000 in 1938. In this case a recovery rate of only 5 percent in terms of fry stocked was quite satisfactory and enabled the lake to produce 10 pounds of trout per acre. Such production, of course, depended on efficient removal of the large fish by anglers (334).

220   **6** (335).

221   **14** (139).

222   **5.** Statistics on farm ponds and stocking are from a Fish and Wildlife Service news release dated April 15, 1956.

223   **6** (335); **20.** Of the marked fish recovered, more than three-fourths had been caught by the end of the fourth week of fishing. Hatchery trout made up 23 percent of the total catch (422).

26 (420).

224   **5** (494). The relatively good showing of these fall-planted rainbows is somewhat exceptional, but a similar result was obtained on Pennsylvania's Spring Creek. This project was planned to check plantings of brooks, browns, and rainbows made in October and the following April. Slightly more than half the hatchery fish were recovered, and the fall plants made nearly as good a showing as those in spring.

However, the fall fish did not "go wild"; they were more easily taken than the April fish (468).

16 (182); **36** (229).

225   5 (490); **24** (461); **35** (71).
226   7 (406); **22** (346); **26** (160); **28** (495); **30** (421).
227   18 (346); **38** (215).
229   8 (95).

CHAPTER 14

230   **11** (131).
233   **20** (382).
235   **5** (135); **14** (371); **35** (500).
236   **6** (36); **11** (371); **23** (500).
237   **2** (63); **27** (499).
238   **18** (337).
240   **11** (70); **15** (53); **30** (418); **33** (53).
241   **6** (328); **18** (99); **31** (430). Observations over three years failed to give any evidence of predation by golden eagles, even though these birds nested near the lambing grounds. "The known losses during 1940 were two yearlings killed by coyotes and one ewe killed by a mountain lion. These were on the winter range. There were, no doubt, other losses, but none of the coyote scats examined on the summer range, and very few of those from the winter range contained bighorn sheep hair. Examinations showed that rodents formed the main diet of the coyotes in the area."

About a third of this herd stayed year-long in the high country, near or above timberline. The remainder migrated to lower winter ranges, where domestic stock was present (430).

242   **7** (53, 246); **28** (338).
245   **9** (101).
246   **37** (5).
247   **11.** How easy it is to go astray on superficial observations is exemplified by a situation in Iowa described by Hendrickson:

"In an epizoötic of tularemia, whole counties may be almost depopulated of cottontails. The large hawks, often numerous then, arouse sportsmen who do not readily become aware of the hawks feeding largely on rabbit carrion on the highways and animals dead with tularemia in such periods of abundance. Foxes half-bury so many rabbits then that almost every hunter sees them and condemns the fox without realizing that the prey were disease victims.

In other counties, areas of a few sections to several townships show-ing a great deal of tularemia may be interspersed between areas of relatively little disease incidence. And even an occasional entire county quite free of tularemia is sandwiched between others heavily diseased. Such strange interspersion adds to the perplexity of cotton-tail hunters and raises much skepticism until all the facts on pre-dation and disease are considered. Other diseases and parasites such as the wart-disease, eye-disease, liver fluke, and the flesh-fly may de-crease rabbits on areas of varying extent and not be detected as causa-tive agents of decimation except by very detailed observation in the field." (233).

248   **2** (239); **16** (152).
249   **1** (169); **7** (112); **33** (3, 363).
250   **2** (394).
      21 (151, 155); **30** (230).
251   **14** (257).
253   **19** (323). The part that large predatory fish play in aquatic com-munities has a direct bearing on our luck with a casting rod next summer. It has been brought out elsewhere that a definitely lim-ited weight of fish can be supported by a given body of water, the usual limitation being food supply as governed by fertility.

With this in mind, consider the conditions necessary to produce *big fish*. If waters are heavily populated, the individual fish must necessarily be small. "There are bodies of water in which predation pressure is inadequate to keep the numbers of game or pan fish low enough so that they will be of attractive size to anglers. More predators might alleviate such a situation and provide the best fish-ing conditions possible for the existing conditions of the food for the preferred species." (275).

33 (399). The large herds of buffalo that formerly grazed the plains were invariably flanked by expectant bands of wolves which seemed to live for the most part on the turnover of aged animals or those subject to some misfortune. George Frederick Ruxton, a young man in his twenties, surely observed with impartial eyes when he de-scribed this scene during his western wanderings in the eighteen-forties:

"Dense masses of buffalo still continued to darken the plains, and numerous bands of wolves hovered around the outskirts of the vast herds, singling out the sick and wounded animals, and preying upon such calves as the rifles and arrows of the hunters had bereaved of their mothers. The white wolf is the invariable attendant upon the buffalo; and when one of these persevering animals is seen, it is certain sign that buffalo are not far distant." (386). Even with unlimited prey before them, the wolves evidently did not achieve sufficient abundance to have any real effect on the buffalo.

254   9 (127). This is not, by any means, a unique situation. In 1943 a Utah biologist pointed out that in Zion National Park "Deer and predators both have received near total protection for some 20 years. It is during these same 20 years that we have seen our deer problems grow in Utah. The National Park Service has been faced with a rather serious deer problem as a result of deer numbers and available range for the last 8 or 10 years. Thus, deer have continued to increase regardless of a near natural coyote-deer relationship. A like condition exists in Glacier National Park. A predator-deer relationship study in this park indicated that . . . 'The small percentage of the losses attributable to predators in comparison to the large percentage due to other causes definitely places the predator problem in a secondary status. The overcrowding of the winter range of the white tailed deer, resulting in an inferior and decreased forage supply, presents a problem of primary importance.' These conditions again are reported where a near natural predator-prey relationship exists." (368).

24 (500); 31 (275).

255   17 (242); 30 (275).
256   2 (58); 20 (1); 36 (364); 37 (131).
259   4 (172); 11 (191).

CHAPTER 15

26. Sometimes it is evident that a certain predator may be of importance to a prey species but nothing can be done about it. At the Delta Waterfowl Research Station in Manitoba it was found that of duck nests within habitats of the Franklin ground squirrel, 19 percent were broken up by the rodents. Crows destroyed 21 percent. If one of the predators could be eliminated, it is possible that a part of the "slack" might be taken up by the other, but this is a situation where elimination of the squirrels would be worth trying if a practical method were known.

Studies indicated, however, that squirrel control would be too expensive and too harmful to desirable animals. Fortunately, when ground squirrel numbers get sufficiently high, outbreaks of disease reduce them and give the ducks a respite. It is possible that control operations that would prevent population peaks might inhibit such effective natural reduction and actually increase the average yearly damage (429).

32 (377). On the subject of ducks, it might be in order to mention that there are many warm-water lakes in the United States where high populations of snapping turtles are a serious limitation to the rearing of young ducks. This seems to be equally true of concentrations of waterfowl and areas where only a few are present. There is, however, no good evaluation of the total effect of the snapper in limiting duck populations. Other underwater enemies play a part in certain areas. In the region of the Saskatchewan River delta, predation by northern pike destroys nearly 7 percent of the average annual production of young (428). Superficially that might appear to be fairly heavy pike pressure on the ducklings, yet a loss of this caliber is not likely to mean much by the time the birds have been screened by other factors and start south.

260   **19** (138). The summary results were: "From all the data on hand, we must conclude that intensive predator control of any type, while it may be markedly effective in reducing nesting losses, will not produce a higher shootable fall population of grouse during years of high abundance. During years of low grouse numbers, the evidence shows that predator control may increase appreciably the fall grouse population. But even under these conditions, with the grouse population increasing anyway, the justification for deliberate predator control is very doubtful." (Reprinted by permission from *The Ruffed Grouse,* by Frank C. Edminster. Copyright 1947. The Macmillan Company.)

33 (240).

261   **15** (179, p. 197).

262   **18.** In the Lake Superior country of northern Michigan and Wisconsin the wolf is down to a few dozen animals which may have ceased to breed. Probably this can be ascribed to the general disappearance of large areas of wilderness. Wisconsin cut off the wolf bounty in 1957, and Michigan dropped payments for wolves in March, 1960. It may have been too late to help this disappearing species.

265   **26** (302, 350). Apropos of another well-known range pest, work in British Columbia led to the conclusion that "Judicious management of cattle within selected grazing limits is the keynote of success in grasshopper control on the range." (466).

32. In fact, they suggested that such a campaign would distract attention from the real "cause of most difficulties encountered in the arid country—namely, too many livestock for the actual carrying capacity of the range." (485).

35 (350).

266 3 (383); **5.** As it turned out, the San Carlos area offered an opportunity to study comparative losses of calves among purebred Herefords on grassland in generally good condition and among grade cattle on badly overgrazed range. This furnished an important key to the role of coyotes.

Records kept for four years during which coyotes were plentiful on the Hereford range showed that 1,864 calves were born and 59 were lost to all causes. Six losses were attributable to coyotes. One was due to an infected bite, one was an abandoned calf, and 3 were from rabies presumed to have been carried by a coyote. All losses caused by coyotes totalled .3 of 1 percent. In 1945-46 coyotes were scarce as a result of intensive control, but calf losses did not diminish among the purebred cattle.

The grade cattle range was in an advanced state of overgrazing. As a result of malnutrition, the animals were in poor condition, and natural mortality left many carcasses to be fed upon by coyotes. Numerous calves were born weak or were suffering from a wide variety of ailments. A high loss resulted from disease, and coyotes frequently killed helpless or weakened calves. It was impossible to determine what percent of the loss was due entirely to coyotes, but it was evident that ". . . the basic cause of large losses appears to be past and present abuse of the range." (339).

267 **6.** Where the mountain lion is plentiful enough to support a few professional hunters, the animals probably can be killed as cheaply under a bounty as by paid government agents. As another example, it appeared that the bounty on the slow-breeding bald eagle, which was paid in Alaska for 35 years, considerably thinned the ranks of our national emblem in that area. Alaskan eagles finally came under legal protection in 1952. The golden eagle is still unprotected by federal law and subject to heavy hunting in parts of the West.

12 (127); **30** (106). In the early twenties, when Michigan's bounty system was under scrutiny, a communication was received from the State Auditor of Minnesota detailing experience with a wolf bounty. From 1919 to 1922 that state had paid out $238,066 for wolf abatement. The opinion was offered that:

"Personally I do not believe that this bounty is a benefit to the State and no doubt fraud is practiced, as the State has been paying bounty on wolves for twenty-five years and instead of the number growing less they seem to be increasing." (315). Wyoming, too, paid out half a million dollars in a 25-year period (1895-1919) for this kind of wolf control without solving the problem (252).

268 **18** (396); **26** (17).

269 **2** (173); **6** (221); **16** (220).

270 **38** (326).

271 **5.** A Michigan news release in 1957 summed up the state's outlay for bounties—which seemed destined to go on forever in spite of the opposition of the state sportsmen's federation, the Michigan United Conservation Clubs:

Since the first Michigan bounty law was passed in 1838, payments had aggregated more than $3,278,000, of which over $2,000,000 had been expended in the last 23 years. Coyotes alone had cost in excess of a million dollars since 1934, and foxes had cost a similar amount since the new payment program began in 1947. "The fox bounty is the most costly in Michigan's history," said Raymond D. Schofield, state predator specialist, "with as much as $142,000 being spent in one year. Meanwhile, foxes are at least as abundant today as they were in 1947."

24 (326).

272 **22** (186); **27** (415).

31. While Pennsylvania's weasel bounty has been ineffective in reducing the year-to-year numbers of this small predator, there is good evidence that the irruption of foxes which took place after 1935 was correlated with a drastic decline of weasels. Bounty records show a marked inverse relationship between the numbers of foxes and weasels, a trend evident in records for individual counties. Latham concluded that "it appears logical to assume that where foxes are numerous in Pennsylvania they are capable of reducing and controlling the resident weasel population." (280). This suggests that the weasel, a specialized carnivore in its own right, cannot function as a prey animal and maintain its numbers.

273 **35** (256).

274 **10** (256).

275 **23** (212); **32** (122). Debevec found that the annual bill for bounties in these 31 states aggregated more than $2,000,000, "Although . . . professional conservationists and game biologists are almost 100 per cent in agreement that it is a pure waste of money as far as attaining its objective: the control of predators."

276 **4** (186).

CHAPTER 16

279 **22** (252).

280 **7** (463).

281 **23.** My point is made without citing this reference specifically.

282 **5.** Congress started this program (under pressure from agricultural interests) with an annual appropriation of $2,400,000, and it was launched in 1957 by the Plant Pest Control Division of the Department of Agriculture. Field operations were preceded by little, if any, research on the methods to be used—principally aerial applications of granular dieldrin and heptachlor at the rate of 2 pounds per acre. There was no official liaison between the Department of Agriculture and the Fish and Wildlife Service until after operations were well under way and heavy wildlife losses had occurred in some areas. There was widespread reaction to the shot-in-the-dark approach to this problem, and one result was the establishment in the Fish and Wildlife Service of a substantial program for field evaluations of the more lethal products of the pesticide industry.
17 (106); **34** (483).

36. The studies of F. J. Trembley on lakes of the Pocono Mountain region of Pennsylvania showed with particular clarity how long-continued, unquestioned predator control was exactly the wrong approach to the poor-fishing problem. Failure to investigate scientifically resulted in wasted time and money and actually permitted the "remedy" to aggravate the situation (467).

283 **11** (204); **25** (268).

284 **2** (412); **14** (437); **29** (158).

285 **7** (251).

287 **13.** These figures are from a report, "Federal aid in fish and wildlife restoration, 1960," prepared in the Bureau of Sport Fisheries and Wildlife and published jointly by the Wildlife Management Institute and Sport Fishing Institute. This report is an example of the unnumbered useful services rendered by these privately financed conservation organizations.

288 **2.** In 1960 a mimeographed release of the National Wildlife Federation entitled "Compensation in the fields of fish and wildlife management" stated that "The average state wildlife agency administrator draws up to $11,329 . . . and may direct the work of 300 people and an annual budget of $3,000,000 for activities. What would be the pay of the head of a firm or factory with that payroll and output? $25,000? $35,000?" Compilations based on a survey of

the states indicated that junior wildlife and fishery biologists averaged approximately from $4,500 to $5,500. The Sport Fishing Institute BULLETIN for October 1957 gave $4,943 as the national average for 292 fishery biologists employed on state fish restoration projects supported by federal-aid funds.

289 **10** (292).
291 **5** (18); **27** (324).
292 **18** (18).

Chapter 17

296 **20** (241).
297 **11** (248).
300 **6** (436).
302 **6** (314).
303 **4** (180); **18** (452).
304 **27** (111).
306 **28** (389); **33** (307, 311).
307 **7.** At the meeting of the International Association of Game, Fish and Conservation Commissioners in 1957, the subject of agricultural subsidies in relation to drainage was brought up to date by Albert M. Day, former Director of the Fish and Wildlife Service (120). He pointed out that, although marsh restoration was one of the practices provided for in the soil bank act, it was largely being ignored—33 states had no such projects at all. Despite the lip-service given to wildlife in federal policies, county boards are in almost complete control of local action programs, and drainage continues to be a featured practice. The Conservation Year Book for 1956 indicated that when county boards of supervisors request the services of SCS technicians, the agreement "includes a promise that government technicians will be removed from a district on 60 days notice from the board of supervisors. This provision protects soil conservation districts from bureaucratic control." Day remarked that "It is difficult to see how a farmer-managed, farmer-voted, farmer-controlled local county committee could have any greater hold on federal civil service employees responsible for federal policies and federal programs than this device."

CHAPTER 18

310 **28** (465).
312 **33** (198).
315 **30** (388).
316 **32** (73).
317 **10** (493); **37** (255).
318 **31** (16).
319 **29** (129).
320 **4** (493).
321 **36** (388).
322 **33** (313).
323 **9** (446); **17** (388). That Saunderson's suggestion was reasonable is borne out by economic studies of outdoor recreation over the past quarter-century. As early as 1933 (depression days), 2,542 deer hunters on Utah's Fishlake National Forest spent $90,622 on equipment, transportation, and supplies (313). The Conoco Travel Bureau calculated that tourists brought $46,818,000 into Wyoming alone in 1939, and Colorado evaluated the 1946 tourist business at $150 million (255). The National Survey of Fishing and Hunting by the Fish and Wildlife Service in 1955 showed that approximately $2.9 billion was being spent annually by the public on this type of recreation—a figure that increased by a billion dollars in 5 years (57, 476). Clawson's studies for Resources for the Future indicated that recreational visits to the National Wildlife Refuges increased by 2½ times from 1951 to 1956. The same period saw an increase of 48 percent in visits to the National Park system and 75 percent on National Forests (86, 87). The total for each of these two types of public area exceeded 60 million visits in 1960. To meet this burgeoning challenge of public use, two "crash" programs, "Mission 66" of the Park Service and "Operation Outdoors" of the Forest Service were established for the development of more and better facilities. It is high time for such action: Clawson foresees a 10-fold growth in the demand for outdoor recreation by the year 2,000, a need that all available lands are likely to fall far short of satisfying.

26 (204); **31.** As an historic example, George Frederick Ruxton referred repeatedly to the wintering of big game, Indians, and mountain men in the "Bayou Salade" (South Park), Colorado, which had all the favorable characteristics of winter range for man and beast (386).

324 **26** (498).
325 **10** (388).
326 **2** (478).
328 **26** (336).
331 **8** (61, 404).
332 **28** (62).
333 **24** (352).
334 **7** (353).
335 **19** (416).

Bibliography

THE number appearing opposite each entry is keyed to one or more similarly numbered citations given in parentheses in the section on REFERENCE NOTES beginning on page 341.

1. Adams, Charles C. 1930. Rational predatory animal control. *Jour. Mamm.*, 11(4):353-362.
2. Albrecht, William A. 1946. The soil as the basis of wildlife management. 8th Midw. Wildl. Conf. (mimeo), 8 pp.
3. Allen, Durward L. 1938. Ecological studies on the vertebrate fauna of a 500-acre farm in Kalamazoo County, Michigan. *Ecol. Mon.*, 8:347-436.
4. ———— 1939. Michigan cottontails in winter. *Jour. Wildl. Mgt.*, 3 (4):307-322.
5. ———— 1943. Michigan fox squirrel management. Michigan Dept. Cons., Game Div. *Publ. 100*, 404 pp.
6. ———— 1947. Hunting as a limitation to Michigan pheasant populations. *Jour. Wildl. Mgt.*, 11(3):232-243.
7. ———— 1949. The farmer and wildlife. Wildl. Mgt. Institute, 84 pp.
8. ———— 1958. Too green the grass. *Jour. Soil and Water Cons.*, 13(3):113-116.
9. ———— 1959. Resources, people, and space: a critique of the 24th North American Wildlife Conference. 24th N. Amer. Wildl. Conf. *Trans.*, 531-538.
10. Allen, Durward L. and Warren W. Shapton. 1942. An ecological study of winter dens, with special reference to the eastern skunk. *Ecol.*, 23(1):59-68.
11. Allen, J. A. 1876. The American bisons, living and extinct. Geol. Survey Kentucky, *Mem. 1* (part 2), 246 pp.
12. Ammann, George A. 1947. Results of the 1945 and 1946 fall grouse surveys. Michigan Dept. Cons., Game Div. *Info. Circ. 42* (mimeo), 11 pp.
13. ———— 1957. *The prairie grouse of Michigan*. Michigan Dept. Cons., Game Div., 200 pp.

14. Andrewes, C. H., H. V. Thompson and W. Mansi. 1959. Myxomatosis: present position and future prospects in Great Britain. *Nature,* 184:1179-1180.

15. Anon. 1914. Frank Forester foresaw game destruction. A forecast written 60 years ago, worth reading today. *Forest and Stream,* 82:83-84, 90.

16. ———— 1926. Impossible demands of stockmen. *Amer. Game,* 15 (1):10.

17. ———— 1946. The fox and the bounty question. *Iowa Conservationist,* 5(3):17, 20.

18. ———— 1947. The case for research. *Michigan Cons.,* 16(5):2, 11.

19. ———— 1948. The rabbit hazard. *Wisconsin Cons. Bull.,* 13(1):7.

20. Ashbrook, Frank G. 1948. Nutrias grow in United States. *Jour. Wildl. Mgt.,* 12(1):87-95.

21. Atzenhoefer, Daniel R. 1951. Is it profitable to stock imported rabbits? *Ohio Cons. Bull.,* 15(2):10-11.

22. Avila, Enrique. 1948. New horizons in the Peruvian guano industry. Inter-Amer. Conf. Renewable Natural Resources *Proc.,* 331-340.

23. Bailey, Robert A. 1946. Reading rabbit population cycles from pines. *Wisconsin Cons. Bull.,* 11(7):14-17.

24. Banko, Winston E. 1960. U. S. Fish and Wildl. Service, *N. Amer. Fauna* 63, 214 pp.

25. Barker, Elliott S. 1948. Antelope comeback. *Field and Stream,* 53 (4):26-27, 121-123.

26. Barnes, William B. 1947. Is artificial propagation the answer? *Outdoor Indiana,* 14(2):8-10.

27. Bartlett, Ilo H. 1938. Whitetails, presenting Michigan's deer problem. Michigan Dept. Cons., Game Div., 64 pp.

28. ———— 1960. Where we stand after eight years. *Michigan Cons.,* 39(6):7-9.

29. Baskett, Thomas S. 1947. Nesting and production of the ring-necked pheasant in north-central Iowa. *Ecol. Mon.,* 17:1-30.

30. Baskett, Thomas S. and Roy E. Tomlinson. 1959. Bobwhites and benefit payments. 24th N. Amer. Wildl. Conf. *Trans.,* 289-302.

31. Baumgartner, F. M. 1944. Dispersal and survival of game farm bobwhite quail in northcentral Oklahoma. *Jour. Wildl. Mgt.* 8(2):112-118.

32. ———— 1944. Bobwhite quail populations on hunted vs. protected areas. *Jour. Wildl. Mgt.,* 8(3):259-260.

33. Beckman, William C. 1940. Increased growth rate of the rock bass,

Ambloplites rupestris (Rafinesque), following reduction in the density of the population. Amer. Fish. Soc. *Trans.*, 70:143-148.

34. ——— 1948. Changes in growth rates of fishes following reduction in population densities by winterkill. Amer. Fish. Soc. *Trans.*, 78:82-90.

35. Bednarik, Karl E. 1958. Nutria in the United States with management recommendations for Ohio. Ohio Dept. Nat. Resources, Div. Wildl., *Game Mgt. Publ. 165*, 22 pp.

36. Bell, H. S. 1928. The land of too many deer. *Nature Mag.*, 11: 299-303.

37. Bennett, George W. 1945. Overfishing in a small artificial lake. Illinois Natural Hist. Survey *Bull.*, 23(3):373-406.

38. Bennett, Logan J. 1938. *The blue-winged teal; its ecology and management.* Collegiate Press, Ames, Iowa, 144 pp.

39. Bennitt, Rudolf. 1939. Some agricultural characteristics of the Missouri prairie chicken range. 4th N. Amer. Wildl. Conf. *Trans.*, 491-500.

40. ——— 1946. Report on a three-year quail stocking experiment. *Missouri Conservationist*, 7(6):10-11.

41. Bennitt, Rudolf and Werner O. Nagel. 1937. A survey of the resident game and furbearers of Missouri. *Univ. Missouri Studies*, 12(2):3-215.

42. Benson, Dirck and Stacy B. Robeson. 1960. Winter feeding of pheasants. *New York State Conservationist*, 14(4):28-29.

43. Bever, Wendell. 1955. Rocky mountain goats trapped and transplanted. *South Dakota Cons. Digest*, 22(10):3-4, 10, 15.

44. Biswell, H. H. 1961. Manipulation of chamise brush for deer range improvement. *California Fish and Game*, 47(2):125-144.

45. Braestrup, F. W. 1941. A study on the arctic fox in Greenland. *Medd. Grønland*, 131(4):1-101.

46. Bramble, William C. 1958. Forester looks at Pennsylvania's deer herd. *Federation News*, 10(123):8-9.

47. Branch, E. Douglas. 1929. *The hunting of the buffalo.* D. Appleton & Co., New York, 240 pp.

48. Brown, Carl B. 1944. The control of reservoir silting. U. S. Dept. Agr. *Misc. Publ. 521*, 166 pp.

49. Brown, J. Hammond. 1949. Missouri finds a solution to the farm pond problem. *Outdoors Unlimited* (mimeo), June, 1 p.

50. Brown, Louis G. and Lee E. Yeager. 1945. Fox squirrels and gray squirrels in Illinois. Illinois Natural Hist. Survey *Bull.*, 23(5): 449-536.

51. Browning, Meshach. 1942. *Forty-four years of the life of a hunter* Winston-Salem, N. C., 400 pp.

52. Buechner, Helmut K. 1950. An evaluation of restocking with pen-reared bobwhite. *Jour. Wildl. Mgt.,* 14(4):363-377.

53. ——— 1960. The bighorn sheep in the United States, its past, present, and future. *Wildl. Mon. 4,* 174 pp.

54. Buell, Jesse H. 1949. Trees living together. U. S. Dept. Agr. *Yearbook,* 103-108.

55. Bump, Gardiner. 1940. Some characteristics of the periodic fluctuations in abundance of ruffed grouse. 4th N. Amer. Wildl. Conf. *Trans.,* 478-484.

56. Bump, Gardiner, Robert W. Darrow, Frank C. Edminster and Walter F. Crissey. 1947. *The ruffed grouse.* New York State Cons. Dept., 915 pp.

57. Bureau of Sport Fisheries and Wildlife. 1961. 1960 National survey of fishing and hunting. *Circ. 120,* 73 pp.

58. Burr, J. G. 1948. King of American cats. *Texas Game & Fish,* 6(4): 6, 17-18.

59. Buss, Irven O. 1946. Wisconsin pheasant populations. Wisconsin Cons. Dept. *Publ. 326,* A-46:1-184.

60. Butterfield, Robert T. 1949. Testing methods of increasing squirrel populations in Ohio. Ohio Div. Cons. & Natural Resources, PR Proj. 17-R, Final Rept. Unpub., 23 pp.

61. Cahalane, Victor H. 1940. A proposed Great Plains National Monument. *Sci. Monthly,* 51:125-139.

62. ——— 1946. Shall we save the larger carnivores? *Living Wilderness,* 11(17):17-21.

63. ——— 1948. Predators and people. *Nat. Parks Mag.,* 22(95):5-12.

64. Carbine, William F. 1939. Observations on the spawning habits of centrarchid fishes in Deep Lake, Oakland County, Michigan. 4th N. Amer. Wildl. Conf. *Trans.,* 275-287.

65. Carhart, Arthur H. 1942. A look at the record. Western Assoc. State Game & Fish Comm., 22nd Ann. Conf. *Proc.,* 77-81.

66. ——— 1943. Fallacies in winter feeding of deer. 8th N. Amer. Wildl. Conf. *Trans.,* 333-337.

67. Carroll, Theron D. 1960. Antlerless deer harvest (The first three years). Texas Game & Fish Comm. *Bull. 37,* 26 pp.

68. Cartwright, B. W. 1944. The "crash" decline in sharp-tailed grouse and Hungarian partridge in western Canada and the role of the predator. 9th N. Amer. Wildl. Conf. *Trans.,* 324-330.

69. Casebeer, Robert L., Merle J. Rognrud and Stewart M. Brandborg.

1950. Rocky Mountain goats in Montana. Montana Fish & Game Comm., Wildl. Rest. Div. *Bull.* 5 (mimeo), 107 pp.

70. Catlin, George. 1845. *Illustrations of the manners, customs, and condition of the North American Indians.* Henry G. Bohn, London, 2 vols.

71. Chamberlain, T. K. and W. W. Huber. 1947. Ten years of trout stream management on the Pisgah. *Wisconsin Cons. Bull.,* 12(12):8-12.

72. Chance, Charles J. 1950. Fish catch in Bedford and Tullahoma Lakes, Tennessee, with special reference to soil productivity. *Tennessee Acad. Sci. Jour.,* 25(2):157-168.

73. Chapline, W. R. 1933. Forest ranges (in *A National Plan for American Forestry*). 73rd Cong., 1st Sess., Sen. Doc. 12, 1:527-554.

74. Chapline, W. R. and C. K. Cooperrider. 1941. Climate and grazing. U. S. Dept. Agr. *Yearbook,* 459-476.

75. Chapman, Wilbert McLeod. 1942. Alien fishes in the waters of the Pacific Northwest. *California Fish and Game,* 28(1):9-15.

76. Cheatum, E. L. 1947. Whitetail fertility. *New York State Conservationist,* 1(5):18, 32.

77. Cheatum, E. L. and C. W. Severinghaus. 1950. Variations in the fertility of white-tailed deer related to range conditions. 15th N. Amer. Wildl. Conf. *Trans.,* 170-188.

78. Christian, John J. 1950. The adreno-pituitary system and population cycles in mammals. *Jour. Mamm.,* 31(3):247-259.

79. ——— 1958. The roles of endocrine and behavioral factors in the growth of mammalian populations. Naval Med. Research Inst., *Lec. and Rev. Ser.,* 58-1, 473-496.

80. Christian, John J., Vagn Flyger and David E. Davis. 1960. Factors in the mass mortality of a herd of Sika deer, *Cervus nippon. Chesapeake Sci.,* 1(2):79-95.

81. Churchill, Warren. 1957. Conclusions from a ten-year creel census on a lake with no angling restrictions. *Jour. Wildl. Mgt.,* 21(2): 182-188.

82. Clark, G. H. 1942. Economic appraisal of introduced fishes in the waters of California. *California Fish and Game,* 28(1):16 21.

83. Clark, O. H. 1945. Stream improvements in Michigan. Amer. Fish. Soc. *Trans.,* 75:270-280.

84. Clarke, C. H. D. 1936. Fluctuations in numbers of ruffed grouse, *Bonasa umbellus* (Linn.), with special reference to Ontario. *Univ. Toronto Studies, Biol. Ser.,* 41:4-118.

85. ——— 1947. Pelee Island pheasant shoot. *Sylva,* 3(4):45-55.

384 *Our Wildlife Legacy*

86. Clawson, Marion. 1958. Statistics on outdoor recreation. Resources for the Future, Washington, D. C., 165 pp.

87. ———— 1959. The crisis in outdoor recreation. *Amer. Forests,* 65:31, 40-41.

88. Cole, LaMont C. 1951. Population cycles and random oscillations. *Jour. Wildl. Mgt.,* 15(3): 233-252.

89. Cook, Robert C. 1951. *Human fertility: the modern dilemma.* William Sloane Associates, New York, 380 pp.

90. Cooney, Robert F. 1946. Trapping and transplanting mountain goats. Western Assoc. State Game & Fish Comm. 26th Ann. Conf. *Proc.,* 106-109.

91. ———— 1947. Grizzly bear notes. Western Assoc. State Game & Fish Comm., 27th Ann. Conf. *Proc.,* 122-126.

92. Cooper, Edwin L. 1959. Trout stocking as an aid to fish management. Pennsylvania State Univ., Agr. Expt. Sta. *Bull. 663,* 21 pp.

93. Cooper, Gerald P. 1948. Fish stocking policies in Michigan. 13th N. Amer. Wildl. Conf. *Trans.,* 187-193.

94. Costley, R. J. 1938. Stream improvement in the Intermountain forest region. *Univ. Idaho Bull.,* 33(22):94-98.

95. Cottam, Clarence. 1948. Does stocking pay? New York State Cons. Council, Ann. Meet. (mimeo), 2 pp.

96. ———— 1949. The effects of uncontrolled introductions of plants and animals. Internat. Tech. Conf. Prot. Nature, *Proc. & Pap.,* 408-413.

97. ———— 1949. A New Zealand appraisal. *Wood Thrush,* 5(2):47-54.

98. Cottam, Clarence and Jack A. Stanford. 1958. Coturnix quail in America. Internat. Assoc. Game, Fish & Cons. Comm., 48th Ann. Conf. *Proc.,* 111-119.

99. Couey, Faye M. 1950. Rocky Mountain bighorn sheep of Montana. Montana Fish & Game Comm., Wildl. Rest. Div. *Bull. 2* (mimeo), 90 pp.

100. Coughlin, Louis E. 1943. Wild turkeys on Laramie Peak. *Wyoming Wild Life,* 8(10):1-6.

101. Cowan, Ian McT. 1947. The timber wolf in the Rocky Mountain National Parks of Canada. *Canadian Jour. Research,* 25:139-174.

102. ———— 1949. Rabies as a possible population control of arctic Canidae. *Jour. Mamm.,* 30(4):396-398.

103. Crawford, Bill T. 1950. Some specific relationships between soils and wildlife. *Jour. Wildl. Mgt.,* 14(2):115-123.

104. Criddle, Norman. 1930. Some natural factors governing the fluctuations of grouse in Manitoba. *Canadian Field Nat.*, 44:77-80.

105. Crocker, Richard S. 1942. Introduction of exotic animals. *California Fish and Game*, 28(1):62-64.

106. Cross, E. C. 1937. Wolf! wolf! *Rod and Gun in Canada*, 38(8): 18-19, 32-33.

107. —— 1940. Periodic fluctuations in numbers of the red fox in Ontario. *Jour. Mamm.*, 21(3):294-306.

108. Dahlberg, Burton L. 1950. The Wisconsin deer problem and the 1949 hunting season. *Wisconsin Cons. Bull.*, 15(4):3-7.

109. Dahlberg, Burton L. and Ralph C. Guettinger. 1956. The whitetailed deer in Wisconsin. Wisconsin Cons. Dept., Game Mgt. Div., *Tech. Bull. 14*, 282 pp.

110. Dambach, Charles A. 1954. Why we have liberalized fishing. *Ohio Cons. Bull.*, 18(4):4-5.

111. Darling, Jay N. 1945. Poverty or conservation, your national problem. *Iowa Conservationist*, 4(3):113-115, 119.

112. Darrow, R. W. 1947. Predation. *New York State Conservationist*, 2(2):8-9.

113. Davidson, Frederick A. and Samuel J. Hutchinson. 1938. The geographic distribution and environmental limitations of the Pacific salmon (Genus *Oncorhynchus*). U. S. Bur. Fish. *Bull.*, 26: 667-692.

114. Davidson, Joe B. 1948. Pheasant hunting in Illinois on a put and take basis. 10th Midw. Wildl. Conf. (mimeo), 4 pp.

115. Davis, R. K. 1958. Farm pond management. Ohio State Univ., Agr. Exten. Serv., *Exten. Bull. 374*, 24 pp.

116. Davison, Verne E. 1949. *Bobwhites on the rise*. Chas. Scribner's Sons. New York, 150 pp.

117. —— 1955. Managing farm fishponds for bass and bluegills. U. S. Dept. Agr., *Farmer's Bull. 2094*, 18 pp.

118. Day, Albert M. 1943. Wartime uses of wildlife products. 8th N. Amer. Wildl. Conf. *Trans.*, 45-54.

119. —— 1946. The problem of increased hunting pressure on waterfowl. 11th N. Amer. Wildl. Conf. *Trans.*, 55-61.

120. —— 1957. Drainage in relation to soil bank program. Internat. Assoc. Game, Fish and Cons. Comm., 47th Ann. Conv. *Proc.*, 102-107.

121. —— 1959. North American Waterfowl. Stackpole, Harrisburg, Pennsylvania, 363 pp.

122. Debevec, Robert M. 1959. The bounty bonanza. *Sports Afield,* 142 (1):20-21, 89-91.

123. DeBoer, Stanley G. 1957. Waste in the woods. *Wisconsin Cons. Bull.,* 22(10):1-6.

124. —— 1958. Less waste in the woods. *Wisconsin Cons. Bull.,* 23 (10):13-17.

125. Dell, Joseph. 1950. Value of stocking imported cottontails. N. E. Fish & Wildl. Conf. *Proc.* (mimeo), 8 pp.

126. Denney, Arthur H. 1944. Wildlife relationships to soil types. 9th N. Amer. Wildl. Conf. *Trans.,* 316-323.

127. De Vos, Antoon. 1949. The value of the timber wolf bounty systems to northern Ontario. *Sylva,* 5(1):15-23.

128. DeVoto, Bernard. 1947. *Across the wide Missouri.* Houghton Mifflin, Boston, 483 pp.

129. —— 1948. Sacred cows and public lands. *Harper's Mag.,* 197 (1178):44-55.

130. DeWitt, James B., Ralph B. Nestler and James V. Derby, Jr. 1949. Calcium and phosphorus requirements of breeding bobwhite quail. *Jour. Nutrition,* 39(4):567-577.

131. Dobie, J. Frank. 1949. *The voice of the coyote.* Little, Brown & Co., Boston, 386 pp.

132. Dodge, Richard I. 1882. *Our wild Indians: Thirty-three years' personal experience among the Red Men of the Great West.* Worthington & Co., Hartford, Conn., 650 pp.

133. Doman, E. R. and D. I. Rasmussen. 1944. Supplemental winter feeding of mule deer in northern Utah. *Jour. Wildl. Mgt.,* 8(4): 317-338.

134. Douglass, Donald W. 1946. Results of releasing game farm pheasants. 8th Midw. Wildl. Conf. (mimeo), 3 pp.

135. Dutton, C. E. 1882. The physical geology of the Grand Canyon district. U. S. Geol. Survey, 2nd Ann. Rept., 49-166.

136. Edminster, Frank C. 1935. The effect of reforestation on game. 21st Amer. Game Conf. *Trans.,* 313-318.

137. —— 1938. Productivity of the ruffed grouse in New York. 3rd N. Amer. Wildl. Conf. *Trans.,* 825-833.

138. —— 1947. *The ruffed grouse.* The Macmillan Co., New York, 385 pp.

139. —— 1948. Farm fish ponds in the Northeast. Northeastern Game Conf. *Proc.* (processed), 49-52.

140. Einarsen, Arthur S. 1942. Specific results from ring-necked pheasant

studies in the Pacific Northwest. 7th N. Amer. Wildl. Conf. *Trans.,* 130-146.

141. —— 1945. Some factors affecting ring-necked pheasant population density. *Murrelet,* 26(1):2-9; Part II, 26(3):39-44.

142. —— 1945. The pheasant in the Pacific Northwest (in *The ring-necked pheasant,* edited by W. L. McAtee). Amer. Wildl. Inst., 254-274.

143. —— 1948. *The pronghorn antelope.* Wildl. Mgt. Inst., 238 pp.

144. Elton, Charles. 1931. Epidemics among sledge dogs in the Canadian Arctic and their relation to disease in the arctic fox. *Canadian Jour. Research,* 5:673-692.

145. —— 1942. *Voles, mice and lemmings.* The Clarendon Press, Oxford, 496 pp.

146. —— 1949. Movements of arctic fox populations in the region of Baffin Bay and Smith Sound. *Polar Record 37,* 38:296-305.

147. Elton, Charles and Mary Nicholson. 1942. The ten-year cycle in numbers of the lynx in Canada. *Jour. An. Ecol.,* 11(2):215-244.

148. Emlen, John T. 1940. Sex and age ratios in survival of the California quail. *Jour. Wildl. Mgt.,* 4(1):92-99.

149. Emlen, John T. and Ben Glading. 1945. Increasing valley quail in California. Univ. California Agr. Expt. Sta. *Bull. 695,* 56 pp.

150. Errington, Paul L. 1945. Some contributions of a fifteen-year local study of the northern bobwhite to a knowledge of population phenomena. *Ecol. Mon.,* 15:1-34.

151. —— 1945. The pheasant in the northern prairie states (in *The ring-necked pheasant,* edited by W. L. McAtee). Wildl. Mgt. Inst., 190-202.

152. —— 1946. Predation and vertebrate populations. *Quart. Rev. Biol.,* 21:144-177, 221-245.

153. Errington, Paul L. and F. N. Hamerstrom, Jr. 1935. Bob-white winter survival on experimentally shot and unshot areas. Iowa State College *Jour. Sci.,* 9(4):625-639.

154. —— 1937. The evaluation of nesting losses and juvenile mortality of the ring-necked pheasant. *Jour. Wildl. Mgt.,* 1(1-2):3-20.

155. Errington, Paul L., Frances Hamerstrom and F. N. Hamerstrom, Jr. 1940. The great horned owl and its prey in north-central United States. Iowa State College Agr. Expt. Sta., *Research Bull.* 277: 759-850.

156. Eschmeyer, R. W. 1936. Essential considerations for fish management in lakes. 1st N. Amer. Wildl. Conf. *Proc.,* 332-339.

157. —— 1939. Analysis of the complete fish population from Howe

Lake, Crawford County, Michigan. Michigan Acad. Sci. *Pap. 24* (Part II): 117-137.

158. —— 1945. The Norris Lake fishing experiment. Tennessee Dept. Cons., Div. Game & Fish *Bull.*, 31 pp.

159. —— 1946. Have we overregulated our sport fishery? Intern. Assoc. Game, Fish & Cons. Comm., 36th Ann. Conv. (mimeo), 11 pp.

160. —— 1949. Recent advances in fresh-water fishery management. 14th N. Amer. Wildl. Conf. *Trans.*, 207-224.

161. —— 1950. Too many panfish. *Maryland Conservationist*, 27(4): 12-13, 29.

162. Evans, Thomas R. 1948. What about those predators? *Cons. Volunteer*, 11(64):16-21.

163. Ewers, John C. 1955. The horse in Blackfoot Indian culture. Smithsonian Inst., Bur. Amer. Ethnol. *Bull. 159*, 374 pp.

164. Faber, Lester F. 1947. Farm crops temper pheasant production. *Iowa Conservationist*, 6(7):145, 147, 152.

165. Fearnow, Theodore C. 1948. Stream improvement. Northeastern Game Conf. *Proc.* (processed), 61-64.

166. Ferrel, Carol M., Harold Harper and Jack Hiehle. 1949. A progress report on pheasant hunting season studies for the years 1946, 1947 and 1948. *California Fish and Game*, 35(4):301-322.

167. Ferris, W. A. 1940. *Life in the Rocky Mountains (A diary of wanderings on the sources of the Rivers Missouri, Columbia, and Colorado from February, 1830, to November, 1835).* The Old West Publ. Co., Denver, 365 pp.

168. Figge, Harry. 1946. Scaled quail management in Colorado. Western Assoc. State Game & Fish Comm., 26th Ann. Conf. *Proc.*, 161-167.

169. Fitch, Henry S. 1948. A study of coyote relationships on cattle range. *Jour. Wildl. Mgt.*, 12(1):73-78.

170. —— 1948. Ecology of the California ground squirrel on grazing lands. *Amer. Midl. Nat.*, 39:513-596.

171. Flint, Richard F. 1957. Moving picture of the last ice age. *Nat. Hist.*, 65(4):188-189.

172. Foerster, R. E. and W. E. Ricker. 1941. The effect of reduction of predacious fish on survival of young sockeye salmon at Cultus Lake. Fish. Res. Bd. Canada, *Jour.*, 5(4):315-336.

173. Foote, Leonard E. 1944. A history of wild game in Vermont. Vermont Fish and Game Serv. *Bull.*, 51 pp.

174. Formozov, A. N. 1934. Birds of prey and rodents. *Zool. Zh.*, 13(4): 664-700.

175. ———— 1942. Study of fluctuations in the numbers of exploited animals and the organization of "yield forecasts" in game management in the U.S.S.R. between 1917 and 1942. *Zool. Zh.*, 21:251-258.

176. Forsythe, E. S. 1942. Our stocking experience in the province of Saskatchewan. 7th N. Amer. Wildl. Conf. *Trans.*, 152-161.

177. Friedman, M. H. and W. A. Turner. 1939. Nutrition and reproduction. U. S. Dept. Agr. *Yearbook*, 482-491.

178. Frye, O. Earle, Jr. 1942. The comparative survival of wild and pen-reared bob-white in the field. 7th N. Amer. Wildl. Conf. *Trans.*, 168-175.

179. Gabrielson, Ira N. 1943. *Wildlife conservation.* The Macmillan Co., New York, 250 pp.

180. ———— 1948. What is wrong with wildlife administration? *Sports Afield*, 120(1):40-41, 98-100.

181. Garretson, Martin S. 1938. *The American bison.* New York Zool. Soc., 254 pp.

182. Gee, Merle A. 1942. Success of planting legal-sized trout in the Southwest. 7th N. Amer. Wildl. Conf. *Trans.*, 238-244.

183. Gehrkin, George A. 1948. Factors influencing the winter survival of the bobwhite on the Virginia Polytechnic Institute college farms, Montgomery County, Virginia. Virginia Polyt. Inst., Dept. Biol., Unpub. Thesis, 95 pp.

184. Gerking, Shelby D. 1949. Characteristics of stream fish populations. *Invest. Indiana Lakes and Streams*, 3(7):283-309.

185. Gerstell, Richard. 1935. Pennsylvania's experiments in the propagation of cottontail rabbits. *Maryland Conservationist*, 12 (Summer Issue):17-18.

186. ———— 1937. The Pennsylvania bounty system. Pennsylvania Board Game Comm., *Research Bull. 1*, 28 pp.

187. ———— 1937. Management of the cottontail rabbit in Pennsylvania. *Pennsylvania Game News*, 7(12):6-7, 27, 30; 8(1):15-19.

188. ———— 1938. An analysis of the reported returns obtained from the release of 30,000 artificially propagated ringneck pheasants and bob-white. 3rd N. Amer. Wildl. Conf. *Trans.*, 724-729.

189. ———— 1938. The Pennsylvania deer problem in 1938. *Pennsylvania Game News*, 9(5):12-13, 31; 9(6):10-11, 27, 32; 9(7):6-7, 29.

190. Ginn, William E. 1947. Band returns from Indiana club-reared pheasants. *Jour. Wildl. Mgt.*, 11(3):226-231.

191. Glading, Ben. 1938. Studies on the nesting cycle of the California

valley quail in 1937. *California Fish and Game,* 24(4):318-340.

192. —— 1943. A self-filling quail watering device. *California Fish and Game,* 29 (3):157-164.

193. —— 1946. The role of the game farm in upland game bird management. Western Assoc. State Game & Fish Comm., 26th Ann. Conf. Proc. (mimeo), 114-119.

194. Glazener, W. C. 1946. Technique in restoring the wild turkey. Western Assoc. State Game & Fish Comm., 26th Ann. Conf. Proc., 131-132.

195. Godby, M. H. 1927. The acclimatization of fish in Canterbury (in *Natural History of Canterbury*). Philosoph. Inst. Canterbury, Christchurch, N. Z., 226-240.

196. Golden, M. J. 1960. A review of deer harvests in Pennsylvania and predictions for the future. *Pennsylvania Game News,* 31(5): 32-33.

197. Goodrum, Phil D. and Vincent H. Reid. 1958. Deer browsing in the longleaf pine belt. Soc. Amer. Foresters Proc., 139-143.

198. Gordon, Seth. 1950. What about the future of hunting and fishing in North America? Internat. Assoc. Game, Fish & Cons. Comm., 40th Ann. Conv. (mimeo), 18 pp.

199. Gould, Ernest W. (no date). A study of the pheasant in New Hampshire during the spring and early summer. New Hampshire Fish and Game Dept. (mimeo), 10 pp.

200. Gower, W. Carl. 1942. Pheasants and pheasant hunters go together. *Michigan Cons.,* 11(8):9.

201. Graham, Edward H. 1947. *The land and wildlife.* Oxford Univ. Press, New York, 232 pp.

202. Grange, Wallace B. 1948. *Wisconsin grouse problems.* Wisconsin Cons. Dept. Publ. 328, 318 pp.

203. —— 1949. *The way to game abundance.* Chas. Scribner's Sons, New York, 365 pp.

204. Granger, C. M. 1933. The national forests (in *A National Plan for American Forestry*). 73rd Cong., 1st Sess., Sen. Doc. 12, 1:565-605.

205. Green, R. G. 1931. Epizoötic encephalitis of foxes. II. General consideration of fur-range epizoötics. *Amer. Jour. Hygiene,* 13: 201-223.

206. Green, R. G. and C. A. Evans. 1940. Studies on a population cycle of snowshoe hares on the Lake Alexander area. I. Gross annual

censuses, 1932-1939. II. Mortality according to age groups and seasons. III. Effect of reproduction and mortality of young hares on the cycle. *Jour. Wildl. Mgt.*, 4(2):220-238; 4(3):267-278; 4(4):347-358.

207. Green, R. G., C. L. Larson and J. F. Bell. 1939. Shock disease as the cause of the periodic decimation of the snowshoe hare. *Amer. Jour. Hygiene*, 30:83-102.

208. Green, R. G. and J. E. Shillinger. 1934. Wild-life cycles and what they mean to the grouse supply. 20th Amer. Game Conf. *Trans.*, 182-185.

209. Green, William E. 1948. The development of experimental management areas for the ring-necked pheasant, *Phasianus colchicus torquatus* Gmelin, in northern Iowa. Iowa State Col., Unpub. Thesis, 168 pp.

210. Greene, C. W. 1942. New York State's fish yield and suggestions for increasing fresh-water yields in wartime. 7th N. Amer. Wildl. Conf. *Trans.*, 417-423.

211. Grim, John S. 1950. The carp. *New York State Conservationist*, 5(1):10-12.

212. Griswold, Gordon. 1943. Subsidizing coyote fur production. *Nat. Wool Grower*, 33(11):17-18.

213. Gross, Alfred O. 1931. Snowy owl migration—1930-1931. *Auk*, 48(4):502-511.

214. Hadwen, Seymour and Lawrence J. Palmer. 1922. Reindeer in Alaska. U. S. Dept. Agr. *Bull. 1089*, 74 pp.

215. Hagen, William and Joseph P. O'Connor. 1959. Public fish culture in the United States, 1958. U. S. Fish & Wildl. Serv. *Circ. 58*, 44 pp.

216. Hahn, Henry C., Jr. 1945. The white-tailed deer in the Edwards Plateau region of Texas. Texas Game, Fish & Oyster Comm., 52 pp.

217. —— 1947. They die young. *Texas Game and Fish*, 5(11):5, 25-26.

218. Hahn, W. L. 1909. The mammals of Indiana. Indiana Dept. Geol. & Nat. Res., 33rd *Ann. Rept.*, 417-654.

219. Hall, John M. 1953. Game-livestock relationship studies in Arizona. Western Assoc. State Game & Fish Comm., 32nd Ann. Conf. *Proc.*, 86-89.

220. Hamilton, W. J., Jr. 1946. The bounty system doesn't work. *Animal Kingdom*, 49(4):130-138.

221. —— 1947. The bounty system. *New York State Conservationist*, 2(1):4-5.

222. Harper, Harold T., Beverly H. Harry and William D. Bailey. 1958. The chukar partridge in California. *California Fish and Game,* 44(1):5-50.

223. Hart, Chester M., Ben Glading and Harold T. Harper. 1956. The pheasant in California (in *Pheasants in North America,* edited by Durward L. Allen). Stackpole Co. and Wildl. Mgt. Inst., 90-158.

224. Haugen, A. O. 1942. Life history studies of the cottontail rabbit in southwestern Michigan. *Amer. Midl. Nat.,* 28:204-244.

225. ——— 1942. Home range of the cottontail rabbit. *Ecol.,* 23:354-367.

226. ——— 1943. Management studies of the cottontail rabbit in southwestern Michigan. *Jour. Wildl. Mgt.,* 7(1):102-119.

227. Hazzard, Albert S. 1943. Fish trout for fun—not for food. *Michigan Cons.,* 12(10):4-5.

228. Hazzard, Albert S. and K. F. Fukano. 1948. Special regulation trout ponds. *Michigan Cons.,* 17(5):6-7, 14.

229. Hazzard, Albert S. and David S. Shetter. 1938. Results from experimental plantings of legal-sized brook trout (*Salvelinus fontinalis*) and rainbow trout (*Salmo irideus*). Amer. Fish. Soc. *Trans.,* 68:196-210.

230. Hellyer, David. 1948. Is the bounty system a national farce? *Nature Mag.,* 41(9):482-484.

231. Hendrickson, George O. 1942. Ecology and management of the bobwhite. *Iowa Conservationist,* 1(9):7.

232. ——— 1943. Mearns cottontail investigations in Iowa. *The Ames Forester,* 21:59-74.

233. ——— 1947. Cottontail management in Iowa. 12th N. Amer. Wildl. Conf. *Trans.,* 473-479.

234. Hensley, Max M. and James B. Cope. 1951. Further data on removal and repopulation of the breeding birds in a spruce-fir forest community. *Auk,* 68(4):483-493.

235. Higgins, Elmer. 1941. The control of overfishing. *Fishing Gazette,* 58(3):15, 25; 58(4):24; 58(5):48.

236. Hill, Ralph R. 1956. Forage, food habits, and range management of the mule deer (in *The deer of North America,* edited by Walter P. Taylor). Stackpole Co. and Wildl. Mgt. Inst., 393-482.

237. Holloway, Ancil D. and Thomas K. Chamberlain. 1942. Trout management and stocking results in the national forests of the southern Appalachians. 7th N. Amer. Wildl. Conf. *Trans.,* 245-249.

238. Holmes, Lawrie. 1949. Ways of deer and laws of men. Bar Harbor Times Publ. Co., Bar Harbor, Maine, 11 pp.

239. Honess, R. F. 1941. The factors determining abundance of Rocky Mountain bighorn sheep in northwest Wyoming. *Pittman-Robertson Quart.,* 1(1):94-96.

240. Horn, E. E. 1941. Some coyote-wildlife relationships. 6th N. Amer. Wildl. Conf. *Trans.,* 283-287.

241. Hornaday, William T. 1889. The extermination of the American bison. U. S. Nat. Mus., *Ann. Rept. 1887,* 367-548.

242. Hubbs, Carl L. 1936. Fish management: looking forward. Amer. Fish. Soc. *Trans.,* 66:51-55.

243. Hubbs, Carl L. and R. W. Eschmeyer. 1938. The improvement of lakes for fishing. Michigan Inst. Fish. Research *Bull.* 2, 233 pp.

244. Hulsey, Andrew H. 1958. A proposal for the management of reservoirs for fisheries. Southeastern Assoc. Game & Fish Comm., 12th Ann. Conf. *Proc.,* 132-142.

245. Hunter, Gilbert N. 1952. Application of practical big-game management techniques. 17th N. Amer. Wildl. Conf. *Trans.,* 437-446.

246. Hunter, Gilbert N. and Richard E. Pillmore. 1954. Hunting as a technique in studying lungworm infestations in bighorn sheep. 19th N. Amer. Wildl. Conf. *Trans.,* 117-131.

247. Hunter, Gilbert N., Theodor R. Swen and George W. Jones. 1946. The trapping and transplanting of Rocky Mountain bighorn sheep in Colorado. 11th N. Amer. Wildl. Conf. *Trans.,* 364-371.

248. Hunting, J. Carlton. 1926. Notes on the Hungarian partridge. *Amer. Game,* 15(1):12-14, 20.

249. Huntington, Ellsworth. 1945. *Mainsprings of civilization.* John Wiley & Sons, New York, 660 pp.

250. Huntsman, A. G. 1931. The maritime salmon of Canada. Biol. Bd. Canada *Bull.* 21, 99 pp.

251. ——— 1945. Freshets and fish. Amer. Fish. Soc. *Trans.,* 75:257-266.

252. Huskins, C. Leonard. 1951. Science, cytology, and society. *Amer. Scientist,* 39(4):688-699, 716.

253. Interstate Deer Herd Committee. 1954. The Devils Garden deer herd. *California Fish and Game,* 37(3):233-272.

254. Isakov, Yu. A. 1945. On the periodic immunity of foxes to encephalitis. Soc. Nat. Moscou, Sec. Biol. *Bull.* 50:72-79.

255. Izaak Walton League of America. 1947. Our public lands, their administration and use. *Bull.,* 62 pp.

256. Jacobsen, W. C. 1945. The bounty system and predator control. *California Fish and Game,* 31(2):53-63.

257. Janson, Reuel. 1948. Grouse cycles. *South Dakota Cons. Digest,* 15(5):10, 13, 16.
258. Jenkins, Ben C. 1946. What about controlled burning? *Michigan Cons.,* 15(4):12-14.
259. Jenkins, David H. and Ilo H. Bartlett. 1959. *Michigan Whitetails.* Michigan Dept. Cons., Game Div., 80 pp.
260. Johnson, Maxwell O. 1950. *Cycles in weather and solar activity.* Paradise of the Pacific Press, Honolulu, 224 pp.
261. Johnson, Raymond E. 1948. The problem of "poor" fishing. *Wisconsin Cons. Bull.,* 13(8):7-8.
262. Jones, Fred L. 1959. Deer management. *Outdoor California,* 20(10): 1-3, 23.
263. Jones, R. L. and R. E. Trippensee. 1948. Sex ratios and age classes of ruffed grouse in Massachusetts as indicated by wing and tail samples. Northeastern Game. Conf. *Proc.* (processed), 19-29.
264. Julander, Odell. 1953. Deer and livestock competition in Utah. Western Assoc. State Game & Fish Comm., 32nd Ann. Conf. *Proc.,* 79-85.
265. Julander, Odell, W. Leslie Robinette and Dale A. Jones. 1961. Relation of summer range conditions to mule deer herd productivity. *Jour. Wildl. Mgt.,* 25(1):54-60.
266. Keane, Charles. 1927. The outbreak of foot and mouth disease among deer in the Stanislaus National Forest. California Dept. Agr. *Monthly Bull.* 16:213-226.
267. Kennicott, Robert. 1856. Quadrupeds of Illinois injurious and beneficial to the farmer. 34th Cong., 3rd Sess., Ex. Doc. 65, Rept. Comm. Patents 1856, 52-110.
268. Kimball, James W. 1948. Pheasant population characteristics and trends in the Dakotas. 13th N. Amer. Wildl. Conf. *Trans.,* 291-314.
269. Kimball, James W., Edward L. Kozicky and Bernard A. Nelson. 1956. Pheasants of the plains and prairies (in *Pheasants in North America,* edited by Durward L. Allen). Stackpole Co. and Wildl. Mgt. Inst., 204-263.
270. Kimball, Thomas L. 1956. Manipulating hunting pressures in Colorado to provide an adequate deer harvest. Western Assoc. State Game & Fish Comm., 36th Ann. Conf. *Proc.,* 124-126.
271. King, Ralph T. 1937. Ruffed grouse management. *Jour. Forestry,* 35:523-532.
272. Kittams, Walter H. 1949. Remarks on northern Yellowstone big

game range. Absaroka Cons. Comm. Meet., *Sec. Rept.* (mimeo), 46 pp.

273. Kozlik, Frank M. 1949. The 1948 hunters' check on Potter's Marsh. *Wisconsin Cons. Bull.*, 14(3):16-18.

274. Lack, David. 1947. The significance of clutch-size. *Ibis*, 1947:302-352.

275. Lagler, Karl F. 1941. Predatory animals and game fish. *Amer. Wildl.*, 30(2):87-90.

276. Lampio, Teppo. 1948. Luontaiset edellytykset maamme oravata-louden perustana (Squirrel economy in Finland based on natural prerequisites). *Suomen Riista*, 2:97-147.

277. Langlois, Thomas H. (no date). Ohio's fish program. Ohio Div. Cons. & Nat. Res. *Bull.*, 40 pp.

278. Latham, Roger M. 1943. Our deer—past, present, and future. *Pennsylvania Game News*, 14(9):4-5, 26-27.

279. —— 1950. Pennsylvania's deer problem. *Pennsylvania Game News, Spec. Issue 1*, 40 pp.

280. —— 1952. The fox as a factor in the control of weasel populations. *Jour. Wildl. Mgt.*, 16(4):516-517.

281. Latham, Roger M. and C. R. Studholme. 1947. The bobwhite quail in Pennsylvania. *Pennsylvania Game News, Spec. Issue 4*, 95 pp.

282. Lauckhart, J. Burton. 1946. Habitat areas and their relation to pheasant management. Western Assoc. State Game & Fish Comm., 26th Ann. Conf. *Proc.*, 120-123.

283. Lay, Daniel W. 1957. Browse quality and the effects of prescribed burning in southern pine forests. *Jour. Forestry*, 55(5):342-347.

284. Leedy, D. L. and E. H. Dustman. 1948. Pheasant population characteristics during years of high and low productivity. 10th Midw. Wildl. Conf. (mimeo), 4 pp.

285. Lehmann, Valgene W. 1953. Bobwhite population fluctuations and vitamin A. 18th N. Amer. Wildl. Conf. *Trans.*, 199-246.

286. Leonard, J. W. 1939. The Montana grayling in Michigan. *Michigan Cons.*, 8(9):8.

287. —— 1948. Importance of fish food insects in trout management. *Michigan Cons.*, 17(1):8-9.

288. Leopold, Aldo. 1929. Report of the Committee on American Wild Life Policy. 16th Amer. Game Conf. *Trans.*, 196-210.

289. —— 1931. Game restoration by co-operation on Wisconsin farms. *Wisconsin Agriculturist and Farmer* (Apr. 18), 5, 16.

290. —— 1931. *Game survey of the North Central States.* Madison, Wisconsin, 299 pp.

291. —— 1933. *Game management.* (Reprint 1947). Chas. Scribner's Sons, New York, 481 pp.

292. —— 1937. The research program. 2nd N. Amer. Wildl. Conf. *Trans.,* 104-107.

293. —— 1938. Chukaremia. *Outdoor America,* 3(3):3.

294. Leopold, Aldo and John N. Ball. 1931. British and American grouse management. *Amer. Game,* 20(5):70, 78-79.

295. Leopold, Aldo, Theodore M. Sperry, William S. Feeney and John A. Catenhusen. 1943. Population turnover on a Wisconsin pheasant refuge. *Jour. Wildl. Mgt.,* 7(4):383-394.

296. Leopold, A. Starker and Paul D. Dalke. 1943. The 1942 status of wild turkeys in Missouri. *Jour. Forestry,* 41:428-435.

297. Leopold, A. Starker and F. Fraser Darling. 1953. *Wildlife in Alaska, an ecological reconnaissance.* Ronald Press, 140 pp.

298. Leopold, A. Starker, Thane Riney, Randal McCain and Lloyd Tevis, Jr. 1951. The jawbone deer herd. California Div. Fish & Game, *Game Bull. 4,* 139 pp.

299. Leslie, A. S. and A. E. Shipley. 1912. *The grouse in health and disease.* Smith, Elder & Co., London, 472 pp.

300. Lincoln, Frederick C. 1947. Keeping up with the waterfowl. U. S. Dept. Interior, Fish & Wildl. Service, *Wildl. Leaf. 294,* 10 pp.

301. Linduska, Joseph P. 1947. Longevity of some Michigan farm game mammals. *Jour. Mamm.,* 28(2):126-129.

302. Linsdale, Jean M. 1946. *The California ground squirrel: a record of observations made on the Hastings Natural History Reservation.* Univ. California Press, 475 pp.

303. Longhurst, William M., A. Starker Leopold and Raymond F. Dasmann. 1952. A survey of California deer herds. California Dept. Fish & Game, *Game Bull. 6,* 136 pp.

304. Lovejoy, P. S. 1935. Natural as against artificial propagation. 21st Amer. Game Conf. *Trans.,* 74-83.

305. Low, Jessop B. 1948. A summary of the restocking of pheasant habitat in Utah with farm-reared birds. Utah Coop. Wildl. Research Unit, *Spec. Rept.* (mimeo), 43 pp.

306. Lowe, William. 1942. Propriety and results of game stocking in the Dakotas. 7th N. Amer. Wildl. Conf. *Trans.,* 162-168.

307. Lynch, R. G. 1956. Ditches, dust and ducks [reprint of articles from *The Milwaukee Journal*]. Nat. Wildl. Fed.

308. MacLulich, Duncan A. 1937. Fluctuations in the numbers of the

varying hare (*Lepus americanus*). *Univ. Toronto Studies, Biol. Ser. 43*, 136 pp.

309. MacNamara, L. G. and E. L. Kozicky. 1949. Band returns from male ring-necked pheasants in New Jersey. *Jour. Wildl. Mgt.*, 13(3):286-294.

310. Madsen, M. J. 1942. Objectives of fisheries management in Utah. Western Assoc. State Game & Fish Comm., 22nd Ann. Conf. *Proc.*, 41-43.

311. Mann, Grady E. 1960. Water for waterfowl, soil and—man. *Cons. Volunteer*, 23(133): 26-31.

312. Marsden, Halsey M. and Thomas S. Baskett. 1958. Annual mortality in a banded bobwhite population. *Jour. Wildl. Mgt.*, 22(4): 414-419.

313. Marshall, Robert. 1933. The forest for recreation (in *A national plan for American forestry*). 73rd Cong. 1st Sess., Sen. Doc. 12, 1:463-487.

314. Martin, Glenn L. 1947. Sportsmen flunk conservation. *Iowa Conservationist*, 6(10):169, 174.

315. Mass, Fred H. 1938. The deer situation in northern Idaho. *Univ. Idaho Bull.*, 33(22):30-34.

316. Mathey, W. J., D. E. Stover and J. R. Beach. 1950. Asiatic Newcastle disease. *California Agr.*, 4(9): 7, 15.

317. McCabe, Robert A. and Arthur S. Hawkins. 1946. The Hungarian partridge of Wisconsin. *Amer. Midl. Nat.*, 36(1):1-75.

318. McCabe, Robert A., Ralph A. MacMullan and Eugene H. Dustman. 1956. Ringneck pheasants in the Great Lakes region (in *Pheasants in North America*, edited by Durward L. Allen). Stackpole Co. and Wildl. Mgt. Inst., 264-356.

319. McCullough, James M. 1952. Deer—or timber? *Pennsylvania Game News*, 23(6):30, 35.

320. McCutchin, Thayre. 1949. Balancing an unbalanced lake. *Wisconsin Cons. Bull.*, 14(11):3-5.

321. McReynolds, H. E. 1958. Liberalized fishing questionnaire. Indiana Dept. Cons., Div. Fish & Game (mimeo).

322. Mech, L. David. 1962. Ecology of the timber wolf (*Canis lupus*) in Isle Royale National Park. Purdue Univ., Ph.D. Thesis.

323. Meehean, O. Lloyd. 1941. Fish populations of five Florida lakes. Amer. Fish. Soc. *Trans.*, 71:184-194.

324. Mees, C. E. K. and John A. Leermakers. 1950. *The organization of industrial scientific research*. McGraw-Hill, New York, 383 pp.

325. Meyers, A. V. 1946. History of sage grouse habitat development in

Oregon. Western Assoc. State Game & Fish Comm., 26th Ann. Conf. *Proc.*, 147-149.

326. Michigan Department of Conservation. 1922. *Biennial report.* Cons. Comm., Lansing, Michigan, 358 pp.

327. Miller, Robert R. and J. R. Alcorn. 1943. The introduced fishes of Nevada, with a history of their introduction. Amer. Fish. Soc. *Trans.*, 73:173-193.

328. Mills, Harlow B. 1937. A preliminary study of the bighorn of Yellowstone National Park. *Jour. Mamm.*, 18(2):205-212.

329. Missouri Conservation Commission. 1957. Ponds for fish and wildlife production. Missouri Cons. Comm. *Bull.*, 32 pp.

330. Moen, Tom. 1947. Why rough fish removal? *Iowa Conservationist*, 6(8):153, 156-157.

331. ———— 1953. Food habits of the carp in northwest Iowa lakes. Iowa Acad. Sci. *Proc.*, 60:665-686.

332. Morgan, H. R. 1951. Game stocking. *North Dakota Outdoors*, 8(9): 2, 8.

333. Mosby, Henry S. and Walter S. Overton. 1950. Fluctuations in the quail population on the Virginia Polytechnic Institute farms. 15th N. Amer. Wildl. Conf. *Trans.*, 347-355.

334. Mottley, C. McC. 1939. The production of rainbow trout at Paul Lake, British Columbia. Amer. Fish. Soc. *Trans.*, 69:187-191.

335. Moyle, John B. 1948. Two centuries of fish propagation. *Cons. Volunteer*, 11(65):19-24.

336. Mundt, Karl E. 1948. Pollution a measure of civilization. *Wisconsin Cons. Bull.*, 8(1):14-15.

337. Murie, Adolph. 1940. Ecology of the coyote in the Yellowstone. U. S. Dept. Int., *Nat. Parks Fauna 4*, 206 pp.

338. ———— 1944. The wolves of Mount McKinley. U. S. Dept. Int., *Nat. Parks Fauna 5*, 238 pp.

339. ———— 1951. Coyote food habits on a southwestern cattle range. *Jour. Mamm.*, 32(3):291-295.

340. Murie, Olaus J. 1935. Alaska-Yukon caribou. U. S. Dept. Agr., *N. Amer. Fauna 54*, 93 pp.

341. ———— 1950. Planning for Alaska's big game. 1st Alaskan Sci. Conf. *Proc.*, 104-107.

342. Murray, Robert W. 1948. Wintering bobwhite in Boone County, Missouri. *Jour. Wildl. Mgt.*, 12(1):37-45.

343. Myers, George S. 1947. Foreign introductions of North American fishes. *Prog. Fish-Culturist*, 9(4):177-180.

344. Nagel, Werner O. 1945. Adaptability of the chukar partridge to Missouri conditions. *Jour. Wildl. Mgt.*, 9(3):207-216.

345. Naumov, N. P. 1934. Determining the age of the squirrel (*Sciurus vulgaris* L.). Moscow State Univ., *Sci. Rept.* 2:275-290.

346. Needham, Paul R. 1959. Counterfeit catchables. *Outdoor America*, 24(5):5-7.

347. Needham, Paul R. and D. W. Slater. 1944. Survival of hatchery-reared brown and rainbow trout as affected by wild trout populations. *Jour. Wildl. Mgt.*, 8(1):22-36.

348. Nelson, Bernard A. 1946. Population characteristics of South Dakota pheasants. 8th Midw. Wildl. Conf. (mimeo), 3 pp.

349. Nice, Margaret M. 1941. The role of territory in bird life. *Amer. Midl. Nat.*, 26(3):441-487.

350. Norris, J. J. 1950. Effect of rodents, rabbits, and cattle on two vegetation types in semidesert range land. New Mexico Agr. Expt. Sta. *Bull. 353*, 23 pp.

351. Olds, Hayden W. 1940. Ohio pheasant banding results 1930-1939. Ohio Div. Cons. & Nat. Res. *Bull. 191*, 44 pp.

352. Olson, Sig. 1948. Wings over the wilderness. *Amer. Forests*, 54(6): 252-254, 279, 282-283.

353. ———— 1949. Airspace reservations over wilderness. *Sports Afield*, 121(1):58, 106-107.

354. Osborn, Ben and Philip F. Allan. 1949. Vegetation of an abandoned prairie-dog town in tall grass prairie. *Ecol.*, 30(3):322-332.

355. Osborn, Fairfield. 1948. *Our plundered planet.* Little, Brown & Co., Boston, 217 pp.

356. Overton, Walter S. 1950. Factors influencing the bob-white quail population on the Virginia Polytechnic Institute farms, Montmorency County, Va. Virginia Polytechnic Inst., Master's Thesis (mimeo), 100 pp.

357. Oxtra, Andrew T. 1930. Plant and animal life (in *Ponsfordian*, compiled by Benno Watrin). Press of the Park Rapids (Minnesota) Enterprise, 55 pp.

358. Palmer, Lawrence J. and Charles H. Rouse. 1945. Study of the Alaska tundra with reference to its reactions to reindeer and other grazing. U. S. Dept. Interior, Fish & Wildl. Serv., *Research Rept. 10*, 48 pp.

359. Palmer, T. S. 1898. The danger of introducing noxious animals and birds. U. S. Dept. Agr. *Yearbook*, 87-110.

360. Perry, Robert F. 1946. An appraisal of pheasant abundance in New York State during 1945 and some of the factors responsible

for the recent decline. 11th N. Amer. Wild. Conf. *Trans.*, 141-152.

361. Phelps, Chester F. 1948. Some results of quail restocking experiments in Virginia and neighboring states. *Virginia Wildl.*, 9(4): 16-18, 25.

362. Phillips, John C. 1928. Wild birds introduced or transplanted in North America. U. S. Dept. Agr., *Tech. Bull. 61,* 64 pp.

363. Pirnie, Miles D. 1949. A test of hunting as cottontail control. Michigan Agr. Expt. Sta. *Quart. Bull.*, 31(3):304-308.

364. Poirot, E. M. 1946. A farmer looks at wildlife management. 8th Midw. Wildl. Conf. (mimeo), 3 pp.

365. Potter, Robert E. 1948. Minnesota carp. *Cons. Volunteer,* 11(66): 10-14.

366. Powell, Stephen E. 1949. Crop protection through a new deer repellent spray. 14th N. Amer. Wildl. Conf. *Trans.*, 567-575.

367. Pushee, George F., Jr. 1948. A survey of pheasant stocking in the United States. Massachusetts Dept. Cons. (mimeo), 10 pp.

368. Randle, Allan C. 1943. Relationship of predatory control and big-game problem areas. 8th N. Amer. Wildl. Conf. *Trans.*, 329-333.

369. Rasmussen, D. I. 1939. Mule deer range and population studies in Utah. 4th N. Amer. Wildl. Conf. *Trans.*, 236-243.

370. —— 1940. Beaver-trout relationship in the Rocky Mountain region. 5th N. Amer. Wildl. Conf. *Trans.*, 256-263.

371. —— 1941. Biotic communities of Kaibab Plateau, Arizona. *Ecol. Mon.*, 3:229-275.

372. Raymont, J. E. G. 1947. A fish farming experiment in Scottish sea lochs. *Jour. Marine Research,* 6(3):219-227.

373. Reynolds, Temple A. Jr. (no date). The mule deer, its history, life history and management in Utah. Utah Dept. Fish & Game, *Info. Bull.* 60-4, 32 pp.

374. Richmond, Neil D. 1952. Fluctuations in gray fox populations in Pennsylvania and their relationship to precipitation. *Jour. Wildl. Mgt.*, 16(2):198-206.

375. Ricker, William E. 1944. Were our lakes overfished? *Outdoor Indiana,* 11(8):2,16.

376. —— 1945. Abundance, exploitation and mortality of the fishes in two lakes. *Invest. Indiana Lakes & Streams,* 2:345-448.

377. Riter, W. E. 1941. Predator control and wildlife management. 6th N. Amer. Wildl. Conf. *Trans.*, 294-299.

378. Robinette, W. Leslie. 1956. Productivity—the annual crop of mule

deer (in *The deer of North America,* edited by Walter P. Taylor). Stackpole Co. and Wildl. Mgt. Inst., 413-429.

379. Rodd, J. A. 1936. Fish management, Paul Lake, British Columbia. 1st N. Amer. Wildl. Conf. *Trans.,* 324-326.

380. Rodman, O. H. P. 1944. *Striped bass, where, when and how to catch them.* A. S. Barnes & Co., New York, 96 pp.

381. Roe, Frank Gilbert. 1951. *The North American buffalo.* Univ. Toronto Press, 957 pp.

382. Roosevelt, Theodore. 1913. A cougar hunt on the rim of the Grand Canyon. *The Outlook,* 105(5):259-266.

383. Rosko, Leo. 1948. Losses of sheep from predatory animals on summer ranges in Iron County, Utah. Utah Coop. Wildl. Research Unit, *Spec. Rept.,* 16 pp.

384. Rowan, William. (no date). The ten-year cycle. Univ. Alberta Dept. Exten., 12 pp.

385. Russell, E. S. 1942. *The overfishing problem.* Cambridge Univ. Press, 130 pp.

386. Ruxton, George Frederick. 1849. *Life in the Far West.* Harper & Bros., New York, 235 pp.

387. Sanders, Earl. 1943. Development of a bob-white management area in Southern Iowa. Iowa Agr. Expt. Sta. *Research Bull.* 317:699-726.

388. Saunderson, Mont H. 1950. *Western land and water use.* Univ. Oklahoma Press, 217 pp.

389. Schoenfeld, Clay. 1949. Good-by potholes. *Field and Stream,* 53 (12):35-37, 150-153.

390. Schorger, A. W. 1944. The prairie chicken and sharp-tailed grouse in early Wisconsin. Wisconsin Acad. Sci. *Trans.,* 35:1-59.

391. —— 1944. The quail in early Wisconsin. Wisconsin Acad. Sci. *Trans.,* 36:77-103.

392. —— 1945. The ruffed grouse in early Wisconsin. Wisconsin Acad. Sci. *Trans.,* 37:35-90.

393. Schwartz, Charles W. 1945. The ecology of the prairie chicken in Missouri. *Univ. Missouri Studies,* 20(1):3-99.

394. Scott, Thomas G. 1947. Comparative analysis of red fox feeding trends on two central Iowa areas. Iowa Agr. Expt. Sta. *Research Bull.* 353:425-487.

395. Scott, W. E. 1948. Administrator's dilemma—sportsmen's burden. *Michigan Cons.,* 17(11):6-7, 12-13.

396. Seagers, Clayton B. 1944. The fox in New York. New York State Cons. Dept. *Bull.,* 85 pp.

397. Selye, H. 1946. The general adaptation syndrome and the diseases of adaptation. *Jour. Clin. Endocrin.*, 6:117-230.

398. Seton, Ernest Thompson. 1909. *Life-histories of northern animals.* Chas. Scribner's Sons, New York, 2 vols.

399. ——— 1929. *Lives of game animals.* Doubleday, Garden City, New York, 4 vols.

400. Severinghaus, C. W. 1950. Deer of either sex season needed to perpetuate good deer harvests. *New York Game and Fish News* (June-July), 4 pp.

401. Shaw, A. C. 1941. The European wild hog in America. 5th N. Amer. Wildl. Conf. *Trans.*, 436-441.

402. Shaw, Samuel P. 1951. The effect of insufficient harvests on an island deer herd. N. E. Wildl. Conf. (mimeo), 6 pp.

403. Shaw, Samuel P. and C. Gordon Fredine. 1956. Wetlands of the United States, their extent and their value to waterfowl and other wildlife. U. S. Dept. Int., Fish & Wildl. Serv. *Circ.* 39, 67 pp.

404. Shelford, Victor E. 1939. The large mammals of the Great Plains. *Science,* 90(2347):591-592.

405. ——— 1945. The relation of snowy owl migration to the abundance of the collared lemming. *Auk,* 62:592-596.

406. Shetter, David S. 1944. Further results from spring and fall plantings of legal-sized, hatchery-reared trout in streams and lakes of Michigan. Amer. Fish. Soc. *Trans.*, 74:35-58.

407. Shetter, David S. and Justin W. Leonard. 1942. A population study of a limited area in a Michigan trout stream, September, 1940. Amer. Fish. Soc. *Trans.*, 72:35-51.

408. Shick, Charles. 1947. Sex ratio—egg fertility relationships in the ring-necked pheasant. *Jour. Wildl. Mgt.*, 11(4):302-306.

409. Siegler, Hilbert R. 1951. Has the lack of a buck law harmed New Hampshire's deer herd? 16th N. Amer. Wildl. Conf. *Trans.*, 472-491.

410. Siivonen, Lauri. 1948. Structure of short-cyclic fluctuations in numbers of mammals and birds in the northern parts of the northern hemisphere. Finnish Found. Game Pres., *Game-Research Pap. 1*, 166 pp.

411. ——— 1950. Some observations on the short-term fluctuations in numbers of mammals and birds in the sphere of the northernmost Atlantic. Finnish Found. Game Pres., *Game Research Pap. 4*, 31 pp.

412. Simon, James R. 1938. The organization of the Wyoming fisher-

ies program. Western Assoc. State Game & Fish Comm., 18th Ann. Conf. *Proc.*, 22-25.

413. Simpson, James C. 1947. Idaho's game fish policy. Western Assoc. State Game & Fish Comm., 27th Ann. Conf. *Proc.*, 140-142.

414. Skiff, J. V. 1948. Is there a place for stocking in game management? 13th N. Amer. Wildl. Conf. *Trans.*, 215-227.

415. Slaybaugh, Nelson E. 1948. Conservation costs! *Pennsylvania Game News*, 19(9):5-9.

416. Smith, Anthony W. 1949. Policies and objectives of regional development. Nat. Emergency Conf. on Resources (mimeo), 11 pp.

417. Smith, Charles G. 1941. Egg production of walleyed pike and sauger. *Prog. Fish-Culturist*, 54:32-34.

418. Smith, Dwight R. 1954. The bighorn sheep in Idaho, its status, life history, and management. Idaho Dept. Fish & Game, *Wildl. Bull. 1*, 154 pp.

419. Smith, Hugh M. 1896. A review of the history and results of the attempts to acclimatize fish and other water animals in the Pacific States. U. S. Fish Comm. *Bull.* 15:379-472.

420. Smith, Lloyd L., Jr. 1940. The results of planting brook trout of legal length in the Salmon Trout River, Northern Michigan. Amer. Fish. Soc. *Trans.*, 70:249-259.

421. ———— 1948. Effectiveness of modern fish management practices: planting. Internat. Assoc. Game Fish & Cons. Comm., 38th Ann. Conv., 42-48.

422. Smith, Lloyd L., Jr. and Beatrice S. Smith. 1943. Survival of seven- to ten-inch planted trout in two Minnesota streams. Amer. Fish. Soc. *Trans.*, 73:108-116.

423. Smith, M. W. 1945. Preliminary observations upon the fertilization of Crecy Lake, New Brunswick. Amer. Fish. Soc. *Trans.*, 75:165-174.

424. Smith, Osgood R. and Paul R. Needham. 1942. Problems arising from the transplantation of trout in California. *California Fish and Game*, 28(1):22-27.

425. Smith, R. H. and E. L. Cheatum. 1944. Role of ticks in decline of an insular cottontail population. *Jour. Wildl. Mgt.*, 8(4):311-317.

426. Snieszko, Stanislas F. 1941. Pond fish farming in Poland (in *Symposium on Hydrobiology*). Univ. Wisconsin Press, 227-240.

427. Snyder, L. L. 1935. A study of the sharp-tailed grouse. *Univ. Toronto Studies*, 40:3-66.

428. Solman, Victor E. F. 1945. The ecological relations of pike, *Esox lucius* L., and waterfowl. *Ecol.*, 26(2):157-170.

429. Sowls, Lyle K. 1948. The Franklin ground squirrel, *Citellus franklini* (Sabine), and its relationship to nesting ducks. *Jour. Mamm.*, 29(2):113-137.

430. Spencer, Clifford C. 1943. Notes on the life history of Rocky Mountain bighorn sheep in the Tarryall Mountains of Colorado. *Jour. Mamm.*, 24(1):1-11.

431. Stansbury, Howard. 1852. *Exploration and survey of the valley of the Great Salt Lake of Utah, including a reconnaissance of a new route through the Rocky Mountains.* Lippincott, Grambo & Co., Philadelphia, 487 pp.

432. Stead, David G. 1935. *The rabbit in Australia.* Sydney, 108 pp.

433. Steen, M. O. 1942. Too many game birds. *North Dakota Outdoors*, 5(5):14-15.

434. ———— 1950. Road to restoration. 15th N. Amer. Wildl. Conf. *Trans.*, 356-362.

435. ———— 1955. Report of the committee on the introduction of exotic animals. Internat. Assoc. Game, Fish and Cons. Comm., 45th Ann. Conv., 78-81.

436. Stephens, E. Sydney. 1946. Where are we and what time is it? 11th N. Amer. Wildl. Conf. *Trans.*, 21-27.

437. Stiles, Bruce F. 1945. Brief analysis of Iowa game and fish policy. *Iowa Conservationist*, 4(10):169, 173-174.

438. Stoddard, Herbert L. 1931. *The bobwhite quail. Its habits, preservation and increase.* Charles Scribner's Sons, New York, 559 pp.

439. ———— 1939. The use of controlled fire in southeastern quail management. Coop. Quail Study Ass'n., 21 pp.

440. Stokes, Allen W. 1954. Population studies of the ring-necked pheasants on Pelee Island, Ontario. Ontario Dept. Lands & Forests, Tech. Bull., *Wildl. Ser. 4*, 154 pp.

441. ———— 1956. Pelee Island pheasants (in *Pheasants in North America*, edited by Durward L. Allen). Stackpole Co. and Wildl. Mgt. Inst., 357-386.

442. Stokes, Allen W. 1955. Patterns of pheasant harvest in Utah. Utah Acad. Sci. *Proc.*, 32:51-58.

443. Stuewer, Frederick W. 1943. Reproduction of raccoons in Michigan. *Jour. Wildl. Mgt.,* 7(1):60-73.
444. Surber, Eugene W. 1940. Lost: 10,839 fingerling trout! An appraisal of planting fingerling trout in St. Mary River, Virginia. *Prog. Fish-Culturist,* 49:1-13.
445. Swank, Wendell G. 1958. The mule deer in Arizona chaparral. Arizona Game & Fish Dept., *Wildl. Bull.* 3, 109 pp.
446. Swift, Lloyd W. 1950. Report of the Forest Service wildlife management work for the year 1949. 81st Cong., 2nd Sess., Hearings on Wildl. Cons. Activ. of Fed. Govt., 97-125.
447. Swingle, II. S. and E. V. Smith. 1938. Fertilizers for increasing the natural food for fish in ponds. Amer. Fish. Soc. *Trans.,* 68:126-135.
448. ———— 1939. Increasing fish production in ponds. 4th N. Amer. Wildl. Conf. *Trans.,* 332-338.
449. Taber, Richard D. and Raymond F. Dasmann. 1958. The blacktailed deer of the chaparral. California Dept. Fish & Game, *Game Bull.* 8, 163 pp.
450. Tarzwell, Clarence M. 1936. Experimental evidence on the value of trout stream improvement in Michigan. Amer. Fish. Soc. *Trans.,* 66:177-187.
451. ———— 1938. An evaluation of the methods and results of stream improvement in the Southwest. 3rd N. Amer. Wildl. Conf. *Trans.,* 339-364.
452. Taylor, Carl C. 1951. Conservation: A social and moral problem. *Jour. Soil and Water Cons.,* 6(1):7-9, 14.
453. Taylor, Walter P., Charles T. Vorhies and P. B. Lister. 1935. The relation of jack rabbits to grazing in southern Arizona. *Jour. Forestry,* 33:490-498.
454. Texas Game, Fish and Oyster Commission. 1942. The propriety of attempting to restore bobwhite quail in Texas by raising the quail in pens for release in the wild. (mimeo), 14 pp.
455. Thomas, D. Woods and Jerome K. Pasto. 1956. Costs and benefits of the deer herd. Pennsylvania State Univ., Agr. Expt. Sta. *Bull. 610,* 33 pp.
456. Thompson, D. H. 1941. The fish production of inland streams and lakes (in *Symposium on Hydrobiology*). Univ. Wisconsin Press, 206-217.
457. Thompson, D. H. and Francis D. Hunt. 1930. The fishes of Champaign County. Illinois Natural Hist. Survey *Bull.,* 19(1):5-101.

458. Thompson, Harry V. 1956. Myxomatosis: a survey. *Agriculture*, 63:51-57.

459. ——— 1958. Rabbit control in Australia and New Zealand. *Agriculture*, 65:388-392, 440-444.

460. Thorpe, Lyle M. 1942. Application of fishery survey data to heavily fished lakes. 7th N. Amer. Wildl. Conf. *Trans.*, 436-442.

461. ——— 1948. Some observations on stocking. N. E. Game Conf. *Proc.* (processed), 69-71.

462. Threinen, C. W. 1949. An analysis and appraisal of the rough fish problem of Wisconsin. 11th Midw. Wildl. Conf. (mimeo), 19 pp.

463. Titus, Harold. 1936. Confessions of an ex-commissioner. *Amer. Wildl.*, 25(6):87, 94-95.

464. Toponce, Alexander. 1923. *Reminiscences of Alexander Toponce, pioneer, 1839-1923*. Ogden, Utah, 243 pp.

465. Toynbee, Arnold J. 1947. *A study of history* (abridgement of vols. I-VI by D. C. Somervell). Oxford Univ. Press, New York, 617 pp.

466. Treherne, R. C. and E. R. Bucknell. 1924. Grasshoppers of British Columbia. Dominion of Canada, Dept. Agr. *Bull.* 39, 47 pp.

467. Trembley, F. J. 1948. The effect of predation on the fish population of Pocono Mountain lakes. Pennsylvania Acad. Sci. *Proc.*, 22:44-49.

468. Trembley, Gordon L. 1943. Results from plantings of tagged trout in Spring Creek, Pennsylvania. Amer. Fish. Soc. *Trans.*, 73:158-172.

469. True, Gordon H., Jr. and Ben Glading. 1946. Catchment and other devices for supplying water for wildlife in California. Western Assoc. State Game & Fish Comm., 26th Ann. Conf. *Proc.*, 156-160.

470. Tubbs, Farley F. 1946. Pen-reared birds don't help sport. *Michigan Cons.*, 15(3):10-11.

471. Turcek, Frantisek J. 1949. The Slovakian mouflon, *Ovis musimon* Schreber. *Kniznica "Pol'ovnickeho Obzoru" Svazok C.*, 4:5-45.

472. ——— 1951. Effect of introductions on two game populations in Czechoslovakia. *Jour. Wildl. Mgt.*, 15(1):113-114.

473. Twining, Howard. 1946. Pheasant management problems. Western Assoc. State Game & Fish Comm., 26th Ann. Conf. *Proc.*, 110-113.

474. Twining, Howard, Henry A. Hjersman and Wallace Macgregor.

1948. Fertility of eggs of the ring-necked pheasant. *California Fish and Game*, 34(4):216.

475. United States Congress. 1874. Proceedings and debates ("Protection of buffalo," 2105-2109). 43rd Cong., First Sess., *Cong. Record*, 2(3):2001-3008.

476. United States Fish and Wildlife Service. 1956. National survey of fishing and hunting, 1955. *Circ.* 44, 50 pp.

477. ———— 1960. Big game inventory for 1959. *Wildl. Leafl.* 425, 4 pp.

478. United States Forest Service. 1936. *The western range*. 74th Cong., Sen. Doc. 199, 620 pp.

479. Van Oosten, John. 1936. The dispersal of smelt, *Osmerus mordax* (Mitchell), in the Great Lakes region. Amer. Fish. Soc. *Trans.*, 66:160-171.

480. ———— 1944. Mortality of smelt, *Osmerus mordax* (Mitchell), in Lakes Huron and Michigan during the fall and winter of 1942-43. Amer. Fish. Soc. *Trans.*, 74:310-337.

481. Viosca, Percy, Jr. 1942. Untrapped [sic, Untapped] fishery resources of Louisiana. 7th N. Amer. Wildl. Conf. *Trans.*, 423-425.

482. Vogt, William. 1948. *Road to survival*. William Sloane Associates, New York, 335 pp.

483. Vorhies, Charles T. 1937. Inter-relationships of range animals. 2nd N. Amer. Wildl. Conf. *Trans.*, 288-294.

484. Vorhies, Charles T. and Walter P. Taylor. 1933. The life histories and ecology of jack rabbits *Lepus alleni* and *Lepus californicus* ssp. in relation to grazing in Arizona. Univ. Ariz. Agr. Expt. Sta. *Tech. Bull.* 49:467-587.

485. ———— 1940. Life history and ecology of the white-throated wood rat, *Neotoma albigula albigula* Hartley, in relation to grazing in Arizona. Univ. Arizona Agr. Expt. Sta., *Tech. Bull.* 86:455-529.

486. Walford, Lionel A. 1946. Correlation between fluctuations in abundance of the Pacific sardine (*Sardinops caerulea*) and salinity of the sea water. Sears Found., *Jour. Marine Research*, 6(1):48-53.

487. Walkinshaw, Lawrence H. 1949. The sandhill crane. Cranbrook Inst. Sci. *Bull.* 29, 202 pp.

488. Wandell, Willet N. 1945. Results of the 1943 and 1944 pheasant banding studies. Massachusetts Dept. Cons. *Research Bull.* 4, 22 pp.

489. Westell, Casey E., Jr. 1956. Industry, deer and club country. *Michigan Cons.*, 25(6):12-15.

490. Westerman, Fred A. and Albert S. Hazzard. 1945. For better fishing! Michigan Dept. Cons., Fish and Fisheries Div., 14 pp.

491. Westerskov, Kaj. 1948. Management practices for the European partridge in Ohio and Denmark and remarks on general decline factors. 10th Midw. Wildl. Conf. (mimeo), 4 pp.

492. Wheeler, Robert J., Jr. 1948. *The wild turkey in Alabama.* Alabama Dept. Cons., Game Fish and Seafoods Div., 92 pp.

493. Wildlife Management Institute, *et al.* 1947. Our western public lands. 16 pp.

494. Williamson, Lyman O. and Edward Schneberger. 1942. The results of planting legal-sized trout in the Deerskin River, Vilas County, Wisconsin. Amer. Fish. Soc. *Trans.*, 72:92-96.

495. Williamson, Richard F. 1947. From egg to trout brook. *Pennsylvania Angler*, 16(2):2, 11-13.

496. Wodziki, K. A. 1950. Introduced mammals of New Zealand. Dept. Sci. and Indust., *Research Bull. 98*, 255 pp.

497. Wood, Roy K. 1951. The significance of managed water levels in developing the fisheries of large impoundments. Tennessee Acad. Sci. *Proc.*, 26(3):214-235.

498. Woodward, Hugh B. 1947. The sportsman's place in future fish and game management. Western Assoc. State Game & Fish Comm., 27th Ann. Conf. *Proc.*, 17-25.

499. Wright, George M., Joseph S. Dixon and Ben H. Thompson. 1933. A preliminary survey of faunal relations in national parks. U. S. Dept. Int., *Nat. Parks Fauna 1*, 157 pp.

500. Wright, George M. and Ben H. Thompson. 1935. Wildlife management in the National Parks. U. S. Dept. Int., *Nat. Parks Fauna 2*, 142 pp.

501. Yeatter, Ralph E. 1950. Effects of different preincubation temperatures on the hatchability of pheasant eggs. *Science*, 112 (2914):529-530.

502. Yocom, Charles F. 1943. The Hungarian partridge, *Perdix perdix* Linn., in the Palouse Region, Washington. *Ecol. Mon.*, 13: 167-202.

Index

control, biological (*contd*):
 rabbit, 32, 191
 of range rodents and predators,
  259, 265, 282
 of small animals by predators,
  248
Cooper, Edwin L., 40
Cooperative Wildlife Research
  Units, 286
Costley, R. J., 80
Cottam, Clarence, 41, 228
coturnix quail, 179
cougar, 233, 235, 254, 255, 256,
  264, 373
Cowan, Ian McT., 98, 245
coyote, 235, 267
 control, 264
 mortality, 238
 predation on game, 260
 predation on stock, 247, 265,
  373
crocodiles, 330
crops, fish, 157-174
 game, 115-134, 157, 234
Cross, E. C., 267, 282, 353
cycles, 88-111, 283, 352-357
 in Arctic, 98, 353
 cosmic influences, 109, 356
 grouse, 101-104
 rodent, 97-98, 264, 265, 353
 snowshoe hare, 93-97, 353
 See also populations, predators.

damage, by wildlife, 89, 140, 264-
  265, 311, 323, 359
Dambach, Charles A., 170
Darling, Jay N., 304
Davison, Verne E., 133
Day, Albert M., 376
De Boer, Stanley G., 147
deer, 135-156, 234-235
 annual increase and turnover,
  135, 143, 144, 359
 buck laws, 137
 condition relative to range, 144-
  145
 damage, 140-142, 359

deer (*contd*):
 feeding, artificial, 145-147
 food relationships, 138-140,
  144, 150, 359
 and forestry, 140-141, 359
 history, 135-137
 hunting, 136, 151-153, 155
 illegal kill, 147-149, 360, 361
 Kaibab, 234, 356
 key, 117
 livestock relationships, 139, 360
 losses, 139, 149, 360, 361
 management, 154, 362
 migrations, 138
 numbers and kill, 135, 136,
  139, 140, 148-149, 151-
  153, 361
 predators, 137, 142, 149, 235
 production relative to range,
  135, 136, 139, 143
 range, 136, 138-139, 143, 150,
  362
 regulations, 136, 137, 141,
  148, 150, 151-154
 starvation, 139, 149, 155
 yarding, 138
Delano, Columbus, 14
Dell, Joseph, 212
Delta Waterfowl Research Station,
  371
Denny, Judge O. N., 177
density factors, 93, 95-99, 108-109,
  263
 See also disease.
De Vos, Antoon, 267
DeVoto, Bernard, 7, 9, 319, 342
diminishing returns, in hunting,
  124, 163
 in predation losses, 251
Dingell-Johnson Act, 286
disease, characteristic, in carnivores,
  98-99, 263, 353
 in fish, 105, 168
 in fox, 98, 353
 grouse, 103, 356
 hoof and mouth, 152

fox squirrel, effects of hunting, 132
    food, 91, 345
    habitat, 90
    mortality, 91, 246
    population mechanics, 90

Gabrielson, Ira N., 74, 302, 304
gallinaceous guzzler, 82
game. *See* crops, hunting, wildlife.
game birds, egg losses, 33-34, 260, 371
    foreign, 176-179, 196
    mortality, 34, 251, 371
game farms, 205, 208, 213
    See also game stocking.
game management, ideas, 199
    See also wildlife management.
Game Research Institute, Finland, 107
game stocking, 198-213, 365-367
    costs, 205, 208-209, 211-212
    pheasant, 201, 202, 206-207
      survival relative to range, 202
    policy, 212, 367
    popular ideas on, 199
    on public shooting areas, 209-210
    quail, 203-205, 208-209, 212
    rabbit, 210-212, 365, 367
    wild vs. propagated birds, 202-205
Gee, Merle A., 81
Gerstell, Richard, 150, 211, 272, 276
Glading, Ben, 82
goats, Asiatic, 188
    See also mountain goat.
Golden, M. J., 151
Gordon, Seth, 312
Grange, Wallace, 101
Grant, Ulysses S., 16
grasslands, 6-17, 316
    adjustment of fauna and flora, 6, 16-17, 70, 264, 372, 373
    as buffalo habitat, 6-7

grasslands (*contd*):
    fertility, 6, 16
    overgrazing, 325
grayling, 186
grazing, 140, 265, 315-325, 326, 373
    regulation on public lands, 316, 319
Green, Fred J., 177
Green, Robert G., 94
Green, Seth, 184
Greene, C. W., 167
grouse, cycles, 101-104
    red, 354, 358
    sage, 352
    sharptail, 65, 100
    territorialism, 50
    See also ruffed grouse.
guano birds, 25

habitat, and animal numbers, 44, 109, 150, 328
    changes, 37, 63, 64, 136
    characteristics. *See* carrying capacity, edge, interspersion.
    destruction, 64, 118, 137, 150
    as a factor in predation, 243, 248, 250, 266, 373
    improvement, 61, 71, 78, 83, 199, 263, 349, 352
    niches, 176, 180, 186
    See also range.
Hamerstrom, Frances and F. N. Hamerstrom, Jr., 250
hares, 93-97, 253, 353
    See also cycles, rabbits.
harvest. *See* fishing, hunting.
hatcheries, fish, 85, 166, 215
    quail, 208
hawks and owls, protection of, 261
Hazzard, Albert S., 172, 224
hedges, 85
Hendrickson, George O., 133, 369
history, wildlife, 62-66
Hornaday, William T., 12, 296, 343
Hornkohl, Leon, 356
horse, in culture of Indian, 6, 9